EARTHWALK

Earth-walk

Philip Slater

ANCHOR PRESS/DOUBLEDAY
Garden City, New York
1974

ISBN: 0-385-03277-3
Library of Congress Catalog Card Number 73–83671

To Jackie

Contents

PREFACE   1

*The Extensions of Man or Say Hello to the Nice
    Fist*   9

Social Metastasis or Spreading the Word   37

The Ugly Swan or Curbing the Prophet Motive   69

*Because She's There or Social Climbing Begins at
    Home*   105

*Designing the Lead Balloon or The Descent to the
    Future*   137

Watermelon Seeds and the Ways of Change   161

The Broken Circuit   185

EPILOGUE   211

NOTES   213

INDEX   221

Preface

With the mania for classification that taints our cultural heritage, critics tend to dismiss all radical analyses of modern society as pessimistic or optimistic, according to whether or not the virulent diseases diagnosed are accompanied by spontaneous regenerative processes. This leaves the field clear for "practical," "balanced" analyses which argue that nothing is fundamentally wrong with modern society—that its ills can be cured with enough will power, education, liberal values, and a half-dozen proposals for legislative reform.

I have a personal investment in this issue since I have been dismissed into both wastebaskets: called dour for suggesting that our society's difficulties lie at its very root—in its most treasured values, assumptions, and thought patterns—and cannot simply be pruned away; and called a Pollyanna for suggesting that solutions already exist and do not need to be invented or legislated, but only fostered.

Some people will react to the opening chapters of this book as an invitation to despair, but for me real hope begins with the recognition and identification of dilemmas. I see no purpose in refusing to consider the possibility that our society is founded on pathological premises, or that our species itself may not be viable. To evade these possibilities is to rob ourselves of the opportunity to examine the problem in its fullness.

To argue that Western civilization at some point took a wrong turning is not to say that we can retrace our steps. It is simply a recognition that we cannot construct a humane society out of the dominant trends of our present one. A patient in psychotherapy does not literally return to childhood to unlearn the self-destructive pattern he evolved in growing up, although he may engage in much regressive experimentation in order to undo that negative learning. What is essential is that he be able to relinquish his attachment to his pathway—be able to say to himself, "I have wasted X years of my life in a painful and useless pursuit; this is sad, but I now have an opportunity to try another approach."

This is hard for people to do. There is a strong temptation either to rationalize our wrong turnings as a necessary part of our development ("it taught me discipline"), or to deny that we participated fully in them ("that was before I became enlightened"). Giving up these two evasions leads initially to despair, but as Alexander Lowen points out, despair is the only cure for illusion. Without despair we cannot transfer our allegiance to reality—it is a kind of mourning period for our fantasies. Some people do not survive this despair, but no major change within a person can occur without it.

People get trapped in despair when their despair is incomplete —when some thread of illusory hope is still retained. When artificial lights are turned off in a windowed room at night, it takes a little time to become aware that the darkness is not total, and the longer we are bedazzled by the after-image of that artificial light, the longer it takes to perceive the subtle textures of natural light and shadow—to realize that we can, in fact, see.

One of our most familiar illusions, for example, is the idea of progress: the past was barbarous, the present an improvement, the future will be glorious. Gangrene on the body politic is just a stage we are going through and will respond to social antibiotics. Ecological deterioration is a matter of getting the bugs out of technological development. So long as we imagine things are getting better we will never re-examine basic assumptions. The core fallacy of the idea of progress is the notion that it is possible to optimize everything at once. This is a cherished liberal illusion in America, and its collapse leads naturally to apocalyptic visions. Once we realize, however, that the idea of progress is not merely a dream unfulfilled but an inherent absurdity, then its opposite also becomes absurd. It was silly for people to keep saying, as the technocrats do, "*this* autumn will not lead to winter but to something unimaginably wonderful"; but it is just as silly to think winter will not be followed by spring.

Culture, like personality, is merely a pattern, an arrangement of universal but dissonant elements. In a given time and place one arrangement may be more convenient than another, but every culture makes selections maximizing the fulfillment of some human needs and neglecting others. Nothing can be utterly eliminated. Social change is merely a rearrangement of elements, the expression of a preference for one kind of inconsistency over another. Once we relinquish the fantasy that it is possible to combine all good things in one cultural package we are in a position to realize that the cures for our worst social ailments are already present.

Despair is incomplete (and therefore chronic and suicidal) when we still believe in the *possibility* of an illusion such as progress and imagine only that we have failed to achieve it. This is the worst of both worlds—to be committed to an enterprise without the hope of success. Once we recognize that the illusion *itself* is absurd we can invest our energies in the possible. Who would not like to believe, for example, in the possibility of a society that would maximize personal autonomy and relatedness at the same time? But there is no way to guarantee that one man's need to be alone will never coincide with his neighbor's need to be with him. Every society tends to protect one need more than the other in a given situation. Accepting the fact that this issue must always be negotiated between people—that privacy and community are antithetical needs and cannot simultaneously be maximized—leads to full and complete despair, the despair of disillusionment. But it also enables us to notice and build upon our own fulfilling experiences.

A Note on Language

This book discusses certain aspects of a gigantic symbolic conglomerate: usually designated as "Western civilization" when considered as a long event, "industrial society" when discussed as a much shorter event, or "post-industrial society" when discussed as a very short event. The geographical boundaries of the conglomerate are extremely fuzzy even when the temporal boundaries are more clearly specified. Some of what I will have to say applies to Western industrialized countries, some to all urban centers around the globe, some to all of the notable civilizations of history, some merely to the United States. Most of the time, however, I will use the terms "our society" or "our culture" to designate the conglomerate, allowing context to locate it in time and space. For I am describing processes, not entities, and the processes are found throughout the conglomerate, although more sharply concentrated in some areas than others.

A second terminological awkwardness centers around the terms "man" and "mankind," when used to denote humanity. While sensitive to the issues of sexism involved in such usage, I feel it would be equally unjust to talk about "womankind" or "humanity" when referring to the follies of patriarchal history. I have attempted, therefore—I hope successfully—to use the term "human" when referring to events in a humane potential condition, while reserving the term "man" for events in the male-dominated past. To refer to technology as an "extension of woman" would seem to me to miss the very important point that women have not generally displayed the same need to monumentalize themselves all over the environment.

To tell the truth ineptly is to lie. Most arguments about the truth or falseness of concepts, furthermore, are really disagreements as to their importance. Truth is relative to time, place, and person, and an absurd emphasis may be necessary today to make tomorrow's truth available. Thus to talk of disease, as I have done throughout this book, is not, in the long run, a useful way to think about social processes, any more than it is useful in thinking about psychological or physiological processes. It often creates the illusion that there are processes that are simply bad and can be dispensed with—a notion that contributes much to the awkwardness and destructiveness of Western ways. This defect to me seemed outweighed by the value of the parallels that could be drawn, but it is a mode of thinking that I hope will be outgrown as soon as possible.

Many contemporary authors are struggling with some of the same issues I attempt to confront in this book. Those that seem to pluck the strongest chords of recognition in me are Gregory Bateson, Norman Brown, David Bakan, and William Thompson, but there are obviously many others. In the case of Bateson there is a specific debt to acknowledge, since his presence, along with Warren Brodey, at a conference in which I also participated, was an important precipitant of this book.

Parable 1

Once there was a man who lost his legs and was blinded
in an accident. To compensate for his losses, he developed
great strength and agility in his hands and arms, and
great acuity in hearing. He composed magnificent music and
performed amazing feats. Others were so impressed
with his achievements that they had themselves blinded
and their legs amputated.

THE EXTENSIONS OF MAN
or
SAY HELLO TO
THE NICE FIST

*[People] have to make themselves
predictable, because otherwise the
machines get angry and kill them.*

Gregory Bateson

It looks better out there.

R. J. Gatling

Discussions of technology usually point out that tools and machines are extensions of the human organism: the hammer an extension of the fist, the wheel an extension of the foot, the computer an extension of the brain, and so on. Through these extensions, it is said, humanity gains control over its environment. It is true that there are certain unpleasant side effects. People must be more cautious, they say—plan ahead a bit more. Technology must be controlled: A greater part of technology must be devoted to the problems created by technology, and so on.

If this were a psychological problem instead of a social one, the therapist to whom it was brought might tactfully suggest that the difficulty lay in the way the "patient" defined it. Therapists are not usually hopeful that an obsessional patient will achieve serenity by devoting additional hours each day to ordering his thoughts, or that a paranoid patient will achieve security by taking additional precautions against his pursuers, or that a heroin addict will vanquish his dependence on the drug by taking a particularly large dose. The circularity of all our thinking about technology suggests that we are in some way recreating the problem in our efforts to solve it.

To exercise control over the environment limits its freedom to influence us. We act on it in such a way as to make its influence a product, in part, of our own efforts—that is, we help create the stimulus to which we respond. Control means that we put a bit of us in the environment and then treat it as if it were a wholly independent stimulus.

Control thus dulls and deadens our experience. The more we control our environment the less possible it is to experience novelty, however avidly we seek it and seek to coerce it. For novelty and freshness cannot be coerced—cannot be commissioned or scheduled, like a happening. They are dependent for their very existence on our having no control over them. To pursue them is to destroy them.

The attempt to control and master the environment thus automatically pollutes it, for it decreases that aspect of the environment that renews, refreshes, surprises, and delights us. The purpose of control is to generate predictability, but predictability is boring as well as secure, fatiguing as well as comforting. Each act of mastery replaces a bit of the environment with a mirror, and a house of mirrors is satisfying only to very sick people.

If this were the only form of pollution resulting from our attempts to master the environment, we could probably live with it, and liberal efforts to solve the technology problem with more technology might be endorsed, albeit without much enthusiasm. But the problem is more serious than this.

I observed that control means putting a bit of ourselves in the environment. But which bit? Something good or something bad? Something known or something unknown? Of what is our man-made environment composed? From what parts of ourselves do these choices come?

Norman Brown summarizes psychological thought on this question, and it is not reassuring.

"The self . . . is maintained by constantly absorbing good parts . . . from the outside world and expelling bad parts from the inner world."

If this is true, then pollution is not merely an accident—a function of carelessness or old-fashioned industrialism. Pollution is an inescapable part of humanity's relationship with the environment —*our very identity rests upon psychic pollution,* just as our physical integrity rests upon expelling organic wastes.

But the environment can absorb a man's organic wastes, and even turn them to good use; and as to his psychic pollution, what difference do fantasies make? Let him project his evil-heartedness wherever he likes—what does it matter?

The danger arises when a man's psychic excretions are given material form—when his projections appear as physical objects. We cannot ignore his fantasies of superpotency when they are represented by overpowered automobiles that claim a thousand lives a week; his paranoid fears when they are expressed in bugging devices and security data banks; his hatreds when they appear in the form of a nuclear arsenal capable of eliminating vertebrate life on our planet.

Our psychic excretions, in other words, show an annoying tendency to become part of our real environment, so that we are forced to consume our own psychic wastes in physical form. Instead of being recycled, as they are in emotional exchanges between people—thus keeping the level of psychic poison relatively constant—their materialization leads to increasing poison accumulation. People have known for centuries that any place inhabited in large numbers by humans is not healthy.

Recycling requires an acceptance of the mortality of individual structures, and the technological impulse—that is, the tendency to give material rather than interpersonal form to psychic impulses —is strongly influenced by the need to deny human mortality.

A science-fiction film some years ago dramatized the problem of psychic waste materialization in the following way: Space explorers discovered a planet that had once boasted a civilization of the highest order, the inhabitants of which had found a way to materialize thoughts directly. The explorers could not understand why this civilization had vanished utterly, until gigantic monsters began to appear. They then realized that the planet's inhabitants had neglected to consider that unconscious wishes and fantasies would materialize along with their consciously purposed thoughts, and had been destroyed by this lack of perspicacity.

This drama is a parable for our time. Our own reality differs from the space fantasy primarily in that (1) thought materialization takes a longer time, and (2) there is no separation between conscious and unconscious products. Every technological advance contains within itself a monster, for each one expresses in one form or another man's monstrous narcissism as well as the simple desires of which it appears superficially to be an expression.

Consider the notion of "finger-tip control" or "push-button control" and the way it appeals to fantasies of infantile narcissistic omnipotence: I am the world, it is my body. The infant cries, the breast arrives, the world smiles. This is finger-tip control. Press a button and all wants are met. But how is it that fantasies (and the reality) of finger-tip control seem to lead to the fantasy (and the reality?) of "pressing *the* button"? Why does the dream of narcissistic omnipotence always lead to that of universal destruction? Why is it that the push-button satisfaction of needs does not evoke bliss?

To understand this process we must first remember that the fantasy of infantile omnipotence is delusional. Personal mastery over the environment plays almost no part in gratification at the beginning. The infant is helpless, and its needs are met not because it is omnipotent but because, and only insofar as, someone loves it. Pleasurable gratification is centrally associated with *not having to satisfy one's own needs*—with what Grace Stuart calls "leisure from self-concern." Primitive societies understand this very well, and devote great amounts of energy to reciprocal gift giving, a practice that Western anthropologists and sociologists usually interpret as promoting all sorts of social and economic side effects. But while these by-products are important and interesting, they are not needed to account for the existence of the practice. We would not think of attributing our preference for sexual relations over masturbation to the fact that the former promotes community solidarity by creating a network of social bonds. We merely say that it is more pleasurable, and the same holds for reciprocal gift giving.

Our own culture seems to have lost track of this point and is fully committed to the narcissistic delusion that pleasure can be obtained through mastery. But being able to command pleasure or love has a built-in self-contradiction. The desire lying at the root of the compulsive striving for mastery is that someone will love me without my having to do anything to bring it about, that I shall receive gifts without having to ask, and that pleasure will come to me that I did not expect or seek. The more control one has over the process—the more one can command these bounties —the less gratifying they automatically become. Control and pleasure cannot coexist, for they destroy each other. The quest for security debases the currency of whatever it seeks to ensure.

A vicious circle is now set in motion. Since the more we can control the production of pleasure the less pleasurable it becomes, pleasure is made scarce by our efforts. The more scarce it is, the more we seek to control it—to ensure it—which, in turn, diminishes the gratification value of the pleasure-source, and so on. The decadent tyrant is a familiar symbol of the advanced stages of this process: "Your wish is my command" is all he hears, yet he is bored and dissatisfied. He wants his wishes satisfied because someone spontaneously *wants* to satisfy them, but there is no way to command this. The tyrant also wants someone to love him for himself, but he dares not risk this and mistrusts any love he does receive. "I would give my kingdom for one true friend," he says, but never does. He seeks more and more exotic pleasures, but they always end by boring him. He requires constant diversion, but it takes increasingly sadistic forms as he tries to test the love of those who seek to satisfy him. He sleeps poorly, and experiences a need to act out destructive fantasies, to risk death and loss.

This is how push-button control leads to fantasies of pushing the nuclear button. The unloving, ungiving, unsatisfying world must be destroyed, along with the worthless, unlovable self. The ceaseless quest, the unbearable tension must be brought to an end. It is the ultimate command, seeking the ultimate satisfaction. It is also the ultimate challenge to the world, containing as it does the secret hope that an even more powerful but loving being will finally come to the rescue at the last minute and gratify the wish to be relieved of the responsibility of self-nurturance.

Humans are the only malevolent animals. They kill for sport and have impulses that cannot be extinguished. Their extensions create an environment that is correspondingly malevolent and unmanageable. Historians have long observed that war is the prime progenitor of technological development. From the materialization of a need to coerce, what else can come but discord and destruction? And when war, cold or hot, is not available to stimulate technological growth, competitive greed seems to be the major spur. Technology, in other words, is an extension of the scarcity-oriented, security-minded, control-oriented side of man's nature, expressed vis-à-vis a world perceived as unloving, ungiving, and unsatisfying.

It is absurd, therefore, to talk of using technology for good or evil, just as it is absurd to talk of using a bomb constructively. The impulse that goes into designing, building, and dropping a bomb is inherently destructive, and the technological impulse by the same token is inherently suspicious, coercive, and life hating.

This has been the theme of science-fiction and monster films for decades, and while it is easy to disdain the simple-minded science-is-dangerous message of such films, perhaps we should not too abruptly dismiss a warning repeated so often, even from so humble a source.

The typical film of this type features a scientist who discovers a secret that confers a special power of some kind. The scientist is usually extremely vain and ambitious. Through his discovery he either creates a monster, becomes one himself, or in some other way lets loose a terrible force on the land, by which he is ultimately destroyed, along with many others. The rather stupid but good-natured folk who oppose him survive the calamity, and the malevolent force is by some (usually rather unconvincing) means destroyed. The last scene often shows the discovery itself being destroyed—the laboratory exploding in flames, the notebook consigned to the living-room grate.

Perhaps through this crude formula we are trying to tell ourselves something. For men in pursuit of personal fame and glory *have* created monsters that are destroying us. The formula film is simply a dramatization of the past century.

Scientists, inventors, engineers (as well as many other prominent persons who fortunately have a less concrete impact—

writers, artists, musicians, and so on) are rather too frequently people who have failed to draw love and admiration from those around them by their intrinsic qualities and have, therefore, turned to the non-human environment in an attempt to extract these responses through their personal accomplishments. When we talk about the extensions of man, then, we should recognize that what is being extended into the environment is not joy and the fullness of life, but jealousy, bitterness, frustration, and revenge. It is very little wonder that when we look at the man-made world around us it contains so much that is ugly and life hating, and forces us to flee to some relatively untouched bit of countryside.

Our mastery of the world has proceeded to the point where the parts of ourselves that we have extruded into it keep backing up and flooding the personality with its own rejected components. This also happens in the interpersonal sphere, where we again have more control over our environment than is beneficial for us. In small, stable communities you can pick your closest friends, but not your total social environment—it is given. Everyone knows everyone and must interact with everyone to some extent. This guarantees a certain balance of interpersonal styles and expressive patterns. Everyone is obliged to have a balanced interpersonal diet as it were.

But urban and suburban Americans do not live in communities, they live in networks. A network is an address book—a list of people who may have little in common besides oneself. Each network has only one reference point that defines it. No two people have the same precise network. This means that everyone controls her own social milieu, and if she likes can subsist entirely on interpersonal candy bars. The persons in her network do not all know each other, so she is never forced to integrate the disparate sides of herself but can compartmentalize them in disconnected relationships. This is one reason why people so often experience anxiety upon entering encounter groups—the exposure of compartmentalized aspects of themselves to different people at the same time makes them feel their whole personality is on the line. On the other hand, this anxiety is accompanied by feelings of excitement, risk, and vitality.

The network system forecloses the possibility of novelty—one tends simply to repeat the same experience in successive encounters. One may have different types of friends but is never forced to experience new combinations of types, while many types are selectively excluded altogether. No true community (one in which everyone interacts with everyone else) is entirely balanced, of course—there are always gaps and limitations. But a true community *maximizes* the utilization of whatever human resources exist in it—that is to say, all possible combinations tend to be realized in the communication system—while networks *minimize* such utilization, since it is limited by each individual's capacity to absorb unsettling stimuli (new combinations).

A true community is like an ecological system where one species' waste is another species' sustenance, like the oxygen-carbon dioxide exchange between plants and animals. What one extrudes, another seeks. The full range of human emotionality and behavior can thus be realized in some form or another. In a network, however, we create closed circuits in which we continually re-encounter what we have dumped. As Ross Speck has shown, intervening in a network in such a way as to make it more like a true community tends to have profound reverberating impacts on the individuals involved. It also produces a general group effect—a heightening of feelings of aliveness, emotional availability, and compassion. This heightening is like the effect of breathing fresh air after a long period indoors inhaling one's own exhalations.

People in our society are indoctrinated from birth with the notion that personal choice is an unqualified boon to humankind —that all our ills derive from the persistence of obstacles to its fullest realization. Yet rats, faced with the choice between a healthy diet and saccharine will select the latter and starve to death, and the frantic buying activity that Americans exhibit is perhaps the same phenomenon.

Choice tends to be liberating and exciting when it is dualistic —when one can either accept what appears to be one's fate or reject it. This is the situation facing those who first leave a stable community. But the life-space of most middle-class Westerners —in which any number of possibilities can, in fact, be realized —is considerably less joyous. If all options are equally pleasurable and there are more than two choices, then on a purely mathematical basis more would be lost than gained with each decision. Nor is this merely mathematical frivolity: Kiyo Morimoto of the Harvard Bureau of Study Counsel writes poignantly of the sense of depression and loss that seems to accompany choices made by students for whom almost anything is possible.

There is probably no arena in which free personal choice is more universally valued than that of marital selection, and certainly much misery and horror resulted from the imposition of cultural norms and parental wishes on reluctant brides and bridegrooms. At the same time it would be difficult to maintain that free choice has brought any substantial increase in marital bliss throughout the land. What was lost when people began to choose their own mates was serendipity. When the choice was made on purely practical, social, or economic grounds there was an even chance that one might marry a person whose personality and interpersonal style would necessitate a restructuring of one's own neurotic patterns. The compulsive tendency people now have to reproduce their childhood experiences in their marriages is jarred in such a system by the reality of the other person. While I would never advocate a return to the older system, we should be alert to its advantages as well as its more familiar drawbacks.

Much of our current pathology is based on an unfortunate human tendency to seek autarchy. If the species turns out to be a flop, it will probably owe its demise to this urge. By autarchy I mean self-sufficiency—the ultimate high tariff system in which nothing goes in and nothing goes out. But lack of exchange is death—living systems are in constant physical interchange with their environments. What makes humans seek quiescence so avidly?

Humanity achieved its present dominance through prolonging infantile dependency. The human infant is the most helpless cub on earth, assaulted from within and without by stimuli over which it has no control. But every thrust has its counterthrust, and when the species took this terrible risk it simultaneously developed a fierce longing for security and self-sufficiency. We may feel most alive and thrilled when we allow ourselves to re-create our early vulnerability, but few humans can tolerate it for any length of time.

Yet security is death just as surely as life is vulnerability. Never to risk terrible hurt and suffering is not to be alive. "Life is problems," decides the hero of Chayefsky's film, *Middle of the Night,* in opting for a troublesome but lively future, and Norman Brown argues that "to be is to be vulnerable." Security mechanisms mimic death and bring one closer to it. Life is gaining all and losing all; security is gaining nothing and losing nothing. Insurance is death on the installment plan.

Autarchy emphasizes not only security, but also the importance of individual boundaries—of identity. And this identity is also a dead thing—only individuated organisms are mortal. Human individuality begins with mausoleums—pharaohs and rajahs invented it. Life is merging and flux and movement: That which has no identity lives forever. To announce oneself is to announce one's death.

Individuality began with kings because they were the first to be set apart and seduced into the fantasy of autarchy. Kings, and authoritarian systems generally, arose only when small organic social units collided, were disrupted or uprooted by involuntary migration, or fell victim to hypertrophy as a result of prosperity, and had somehow to be welded together in oversized units. The loss of a sense of a total and manageable relatedness to the personal and physical environment generated both dependent longings and the quest for autarchy, the first of which was directed toward, and the second projected upon, the king.

But consciousness of self with its illusion of self-sufficiency engendered in kings the fear of death. When men lose awareness of their connectedness they are afraid to die. They wish to live a long time and to immortalize themselves through children or monuments ("Great king, live forever!"). This need to extend oneself in a linear way into the environment is called narcissism and is no longer the exclusive province of kings. It constitutes the single greatest threat to our species. The result of men's fear that dying is ultimate loneliness is an increased likelihood that all humanity will die together.

The West lives amidst the advanced stages of the disease. Millionaires try to add to their wealth, or seek to have their names put on piles of stone. A few people even want their corpses frozen so they can be revived when the cure for their illness is found (the first act of any vital society would be to pull the plug on these refrigerated mummies). Yet all this extraordinary behavior is regarded as perfect sanity by most Americans. Western culture is a kind of Maginot Line of the mind.

Now it may be objected that this gloomy picture rests upon a limited and biased notion of technology—that what I have described reflects merely the mechanical *weltanschauung* of the early industrial revolution, ignoring the more holistic and sophisticated vision of the electronic or cybernetic revolution. Yet if the technological impulse is fueled by the kinds of needs I have described, the role played by technology in human affairs will remain the same, regardless of how sophisticated that technology becomes in its imitation of life. In the original *Frankenstein,* the tormented doctor tries to undo the mischief caused by his first creation by making a second, but at the last minute—realizing that generating a whole race of monsters is a dubious solution to the problems created by a single one—destroys his new Eve. Unfortunately, no technocrat since has shown the same intelligence, possibly because *Frankenstein* was written by a woman.

To make my point clearer, I would like to look ahead to the *third* technological revolution—that which will soon be ushered in by our ability to manipulate genetic codes. Before many decades have passed most existing technology will have been rendered obsolete by the ability to program living matter. Who will bother with anything as clumsy and rigid as a machine when living monsters with specialized adaptations can be created to do the same tasks? Once the genetic code is completely mastered we can create living beings of inordinate strength, or fantastic intelligence, or huge or tiny size, or abundant nurturance, or docility, or sensuality. Hands, eyes, and ears can be modified in a hundred ways for a hundred tasks—the horse's hoof is just a big fingernail, after all. Not only will these monsters be more flexible and adaptable than machines, but also more interesting—sexier, if you will—because they fit more closely our fantasies of power. Also they will reduce, in the short run, the pollution of the environment, since they will be biodegradable and will require only biodegradable energy fuel. The ancient metaphor that opposes greenness and metal will no longer be relevant to ecological issues if, indeed, it ever was.

Science-fiction writers have been playing with the idea of such "androids" for years. Usually they are portrayed rather unimaginatively as a sort of servant class created on a rigid human model and carrying out routine domestic tasks—as if there would be any point in bothering with the whole idea unless one created an infinite variety of new species. In some stories there is a revolt, in which the androids take over and destroy their makers, following the example of their mechanical and electronic predecessors.

My point is that even this genetic form does not and cannot avoid the basic dilemma of technology—*that it facilitates the replacement of real (bilaterally determined) relationships with fantasied (unilaterally determined) ones.* Indeed, the problem is actually heightened, since the difference between a truly separate being and a being programmed by oneself will become more difficult to ascertain. In this new era everyone can be a Pygmalion, constructing lovers, friends, parents, protectors, sex objects, slaves, disciples, and twins. Indeed, bilateral reproduction may disappear altogether when people are faced with the tempting process of reconstituting themselves in an exact genetic likeness. An individual, as Wiener points out, is fundamentally a message, and being able to transmit this message over time is even more likely to titillate immortality freaks than the refrigeration of corpses. Androids, just like machines, can outdistance their creators, conquer, and reinfluence them. But they cannot transcend the vanity and fatuity of their makers without destroying them, since their existence is in itself an expression of the human false-self system. One of the most hopeful possibilities for the human species has been its inability to control the genetic process, thus allowing for an occasional curative dose of serendipity. The loss of that degree of freedom will probably sound the death knell for humanity—whether for good or evil I cannot say.

Alvin Toffler anticipates that people will soon be able to "fill the world with twins of themselves," create human beings with gills for living under water, increase the life span indefinitely, and keep alive disembodied brains: "The human body will come to be seen as modular." While he permits himself an uncharacteristic twinge of discomfort over these developments, the assumptions on which they are based are not questioned. First, technology and the demands of engineering are the master, human beings the servant. For Toffler, who represents a kind of Neville Chamberlain in humanity's relation to technology, the human body is simply an object to be manipulated for mechanical ends. If a gibbon is better adapted to space travel than a human, we will construct humans built like gibbons. If tails are useful, we will graft tails onto people. If legs are superfluous, we will chop them off. One can hardly object to these brutalities since they differ only in degree from the callousness with which humans ordinarily treat their bodies. Whatever is "needed"—that is, whatever someone's arbitrary blueprint calls for—humanity will adapt itself. The feelings aroused by these forced adaptations are of secondary importance, to be dumped on the towering slag heaps of accumulated human misery that encircle every technological enterprise.

Second, power is the only legitimate human motive. One of the most common words in Toffler's book, besides "will" (referring to the inevitable "progress" of science and technology) and "must" (referring to the required human adaptation to this juggernaut), is "able." Human beings will be *able* to live at the bottom of the sea, *able* to miniaturize themselves, *able* to create other humans in the laboratory, *able* to construct machines to make everyday decisions for them. To live at the bottom of the sea, under the ground, on the surface of the moon, or in a space capsule is undoubtedly a great accomplishment—like being able to fart "Annie Laurie" through a keyhole—but one wonders why anyone would bother to do it except to show off. When we look at these "ables" more closely, moreover, a lot of them turn out to be "musts" as well. Because we are "able" to keep more people alive some of us "must" live at the bottom of the sea, some in Antarctica, some on Mars. And if we seek to discover why we should want to be "able" to keep embryos living *ex utero*, we find that it is a matter of economy: The weight of full-grown humans in a space capsule bound for Mars would require more fuel! Thus, to the absurdity of having one's existence determined by some government bureau's arbitrary decision to colonize Mars, would be added the absurdity of having the *form* of that existence determined by the agency's desire to stay within its budget. Leaders of alien civilizations in space fantasies often have motives that seem hilariously trivial, but the joke is on us since those fantasies are simply projections of our own culture. It is in *our* culture that people's lives are threatened or destroyed because some unknown person is consumed with dispassionate scientific curiosity, or mechanically carrying out some bureaucratic procedure, or obeying an order whose premises have been forgotten.

Third, the body is viewed, in accordance with Western medical thinking, as a machine rather than an organism. This machine has replaceable parts which are thoroughly understood, but the whole is of little interest and comparatively unknown. The problem-solving part is most highly valued and the fantasy of separating it from the rest is extremely popular. The conviction of many schizophrenics that the brain could function better if only the annoying body in which it is embedded could be lopped off, is now shared, not surprisingly, by scientists. "Better" means that it could pursue its own logic without distracting feedback from the real world. Since the troubles that currently surround us are largely a product of such disembodied thought, however, perhaps this assumption, too, needs to be re-examined.

When man invented the machine, for which there is no external model in nature, he invented it in his own image. The machine does not come from nowhere—it mirrors man's mechanical head. The human is the only animal programmed to ignore the very feedback that it is simultaneously programmed to utilize, which is why only a human can make an animal, or another human, neurotic or crazy. As Weston La Barre points out, reality alone cannot make an animal neurotic—it takes the mechanical application of some twisted symbolic system to wreck an animal's responsivity. This is perhaps why autistic children are usually the offspring of intellectuals. Psychopathology is an inherent by-product of the ability to generate symbols, which is always presented, in renditions of the comedy of evolution, as humanity's unique strength. But attached to this strength is a fatal flaw, built into the species at the start—a capacity to disregard significant feedback in favor of inner symbolic circuitry.

Freud once commented on the widespread fear of automata, and in the same context suggested that uncanny (*unheimlich*) sensations were activated by familiar (*heimlich*) but repressed visions. Putting these two ideas together I would argue that what is *heimlich* and *unheimlich* about automata is that they reflect a quality repulsively and uniquely human. Our fear of robot-like creatures that move in mechanical disregard of external consequences is a fear of the human head. The heroine in a horror film pleads for mercy but the monster is oblivious. "It is in-human," she shrieks, but she is wrong. Humanity is the only species that disregards its own surrender signals. Human beings are "freed" from the instinctual necessity of inhibiting aggression when a cospecific yields. A machine is free from everything but its program. A blind man is free from the blinding sun, a deaf man from the deafening thunder. Much of the time when we talk of freedom we mean freedom from messages—the ability to pay attention only to interior conceptual patterns. This schizoid freedom—the capacity to operate solely in response to internal logic, to ignore feedback—is what makes mass killing possible. Hiroshima, Dresden, Auschwitz, Vietnam—all rest on this liberation—this ability to proceed according to a set of systematic principles, mechanically, bureaucratically, rigorously.

But horror is not the only reaction to automaton behavior. Henri Bergson pointed out long ago that "mechanical inelasticity," or the presentation of "something mechanical encrusted upon the living" was an important source of humor, and inspirational narratives of a patriotic or religious nature also draw heavily on the capacity to ignore feedback. Following an internal script regardless of external information is comic, horrifying, or heroic, depending on how the culture defines the situation. The mechanical monster that frightens us, the clown who sits on a non-existent chair, and the thin red line of soldiers marching bravely to their death merely represent different attitudes toward the same phenomenon.

In the past the tendency to ignore feedback, both from the gut and from the external world, was called "courage" and highly valued. Courage has always been carefully distinguished from mere valor or recklessness—to be courageous you had to be able to recognize your mortal peril and at the same time disregard both the danger and your life-preserving instincts. There is no such thing as a courageous animal: if it does not run when in danger, it is either because (a) it is trapped, or (b) it is more angry than afraid. When fear outstrips anger it will run if it can.

A machinelike response in the face of danger had no real value until men began to make war on each other—it was of no use either in hunting or in surviving other predators. The most mechanical peoples won over those less so, so that a profound cultural selection took place. Evolution is full of such mistakes.

If this process is not reversible, our species will destroy the planet—hopefully before it has an opportunity to excrete any colonists. When human beings were freed from dependence upon instinct for communication, they were also freed from having to communicate about their instincts at all, or having to respond to such communications. This means simply that we who share space on the same little planet must try to get our needs met in the face of our "freedom" to misrepresent those needs to each other and our "ability" to disregard the needs of others, whether misrepresented or not.

Many of the most treasured virtues of the past several thousand years no longer have survival value. From an ecological viewpoint virtues such as courage and perseverance are simply bad habits. We should consider the possibility of giving medals for cowardice, for a coward is responsive to the environment and to the bodily needs of at least one human being. The virtue of being able to complete a task might also be examined with more suspicion. What is distractibility but responsiveness and sensitivity pejoratively defined? From the viewpoint of a horse with blinders, horses without blinders are distractible. Western culture looks at its "undeveloped" (i.e., no blinders) contemporaries in the same way, disdaining their slight tendency to be distracted by the relationship of a single innovation to everything else in their lives. To be distractible is to be aware of the indissoluble interconnectedness of living matter—clearly no way to get things done.

To exemplify this issue, let me quote from a letter written by a Moroccan graduate student:

". . . Every single little act becomes a very complicated interaction. I live in the old Arab city where there are not many phones. I need a phone to contact the people I am to interview and who happen to be the bourgeois modernized élite who will be choked if I drop by as we traditionally do. I went to the public phone which is not an automatic one. I gave my list of numbers to the operator who happens to have known me since ages. He wanted to know why I want to call all these people. I explained briefly that I was doing a sort of sociological survey. He wanted more details. I told him that it will take us about an hour, and that by then the post office will have to close. He took it as an insult and asked me to wait until he called me. I did. He called me to say that the numbers were either busy or not answering, and that in any case I should not try to monopolize a public phone by calling so many people. I then told him I was sorry

I was so worried about the time, and that I was ready to tell him what I was doing. I did. He wanted to know how can 10 or 20 people, very special and particular, be representative of hundreds and thousands, who only have some things in common with them. So I proceeded to explain 'la théorie de la probabilité.' He then disagreed and rejected the theory as being junk. I told him that it was his right to reject it, that that was the normal destiny of a theory—some accept it and some reject it. He did not like my attitude and said that I was avoiding discussing the matter with him, because I think in my head that he is not worth discussing with because he did not have my chance to carry on his studies and ended up doing a stupid job, etc. I tried to convince him of the opposite. It took me two more sessions and three days to get to use the phone.

"The famous 'anesthésie' which bothered me so much in Cambridge is in fact what allows you to be efficient there, and its absence leaves you completely immersed in an environment you can't control because you are so emotionally involved and at such a passionate level."

A traditional culture is full of distractions. One cannot deal impersonally with the environment, or follow out an internal program in the mechanical, linear way we are used to doing in the West. One is caught in an intricate web of ties that pull one back and demand an examination of how every new act interrelates with everything else. Relationships are primary, taking precedence over the pursuit of knowledge or personal achievement.

The ecological problems we face today are not possible so long as this kind of thinking persists; the absorption in interrelationships prevents one from even contemplating the kind of mechanical response that leads to ecological imbalances. One is not allowed to postpone (indefinitely) dealing with the "social" or "human" consequences of some narcissistic pursuit. Until the foundations of a traditional society have been shattered, the development of such grotesqueries as nuclear weapons and sociological surveys are out of the question, even if the technical knowledge were available. Their value, *weighed against everything else in the society,* would have to be established *prior* to embarking on the enterprise, rather than being asserted by a public relations department after it was a *fait accompli,* as is the practice in our own society. Americans delight in the ease with which they can get things done, but we owe it all to the simple device of having abolished every social mechanism for weighing actions in advance. This is done largely through absolutistic slogans like free enterprise, scientific freedom, freedom of choice, and so on. These slogans have been marketed so successfully that most civilized peoples, confronted daily with the disastrous consequences of the removal of social balancing mechanisms, feel that the price is worth paying.

Virtues such as courage, perseverance, and personal achievement are fundamentally disconnectors. They rip the individual or group out of the social and ecological fabric in which they are embedded and set them on autonomous linear courses, looking neither right nor left. If you remove part of the forebrain of a fish, it loses its schooling response, and presumably, if enough other parts were removed as well, it would ignore its environment altogether and swim right around the world, following a course as true as that of a human navigator. As things are, it must be admitted, fish never get anywhere. Nature, in her primitiveness, has arranged that all they ever do is hover uselessly, like butterflies, around their food supply, their breeding grounds, and each other.

All of the disconnector virtues—courage, perseverance, rectitude, chastity, ambition, honor, dutifulness, self-discipline, temperance, purity, self-reliance, impartiality, incorruptibility, dependability, conscientiousness, sobriety, asceticism, spirituality —are ecologically unsound. All express the same arrogant assumption about the importance of the single individual in society and the importance of humanity in the universe. To imagine that it matters (except to those in immediate contact with him) whether or not a man is righteous, holy, or self-actualized is the height of pomposity.

The opposite qualities—cowardice, distractibility, sensuality, inability to complete tasks or resist temptations, partiality, dependency, inconsistency, corruptibility, and so on—are humble virtues. They express humanity's embeddedness in a larger organic system—a system that has its own laws and justice. As such they ultimately have higher survival value than the disciplines since they serve to reconnect the individual with his or her environment. This is not to say that the arrogant virtues should be extirpated from the human repertory. We need only recognize the *price* of the disconnector virtues.

Anglo-Saxons, for example, have always aimed a good bit of mockery, tinged with envy, at the *"mañana* mentality" of Latin proletarians. In most cases, however, saying *"mañana"* is simply a matter of putting first things first—of being unwilling to sacrifice joy and good relationships in the service of the get-rich-quick schemes of industrial hustlers. As we discover increasingly that much of what the poor Latin has been unable to get done would have been better left undone in our own society, we begin to develop more respect for his priority system.

Yet few peoples have been able to hold out against the assault of Western ideology. Seduced by the promise of a little affluence and a longer life, they have deserted in droves. Is this not an indication of the superiority of our achievement-oriented culture? Our own ancestors presumably lived in some kind of stable, present-oriented culture and apparently were dissatisfied with it. Since there is no going back, in any case, and since most peoples seem to have rejected it when they had a choice, what is the point of these invidious comparisons?

There is enormous variety among cultures that are present-oriented or traditional or "primitive," so let me state what I am lumping together in making comparisons with the industrial West. I call a "simple community" one in which people live in a small village or band; are rarely exposed in a lifetime to a place lying outside their village, hunting territory, or nomadic circuit; will gain few new relationships in a lifetime except through births, and lose few except through deaths; live largely in the present; and feel themselves to be an organic and undetachable part of their immediate social and natural environment. Half the population of the world still lives under conditions that approximate this type in many respects, but their numbers are decreasing with great rapidity.

I do not wish to hold up the simple community as a utopia. People raised in an industrial society are unfitted for life under such conditions and would be miserable if they tried. Furthermore, the simple community has one enormous weakness—it is highly vulnerable to conquest. Nor should we be so naïve as to posit some sort of primeval bliss in the simple community. Even among those uncontaminated by Western contact, many are plagued by oppressive social mores, and if the joys of such living appear to be far more intense, so are the miseries. Life, furthermore, although emotionally richer, is also shorter. Westerners would also find it dull, if only because of their own blunted senses and flattened emotionality—necessary for life under conditions of urban chaos.

I dwell on the simple community only because the relation between what we lost when we gave it up and our present crisis is so poorly understood. Our cultural history tends to be presented either as an uninterrupted ascension into paradise (not quite yet achieved, but just around the corner) or as a brave venturing forth from comfortable dependency to lonely but admirable freedom. Occasionally someone suggests, with bleak nostalgia, that the entire enterprise was an unmitigated disaster—like Napoleon's invasion of Russia or the Vietnam War—but they are usually dismissed as nervous Nellies.

My purpose is not to condemn Western culture or idealize the past. I want only to correct the balance a little. The vituperation that writers like Toffler heap upon those who reflect with any affection upon the past betrays a stubborn unwillingness to make the radical changes necessary to extricate ourselves from our present difficulties. If we take the position that every move Western humanity has made thus far was necessary and desirable we are unlikely to come up with any new thinking on the matter.

Let me return, then, to the simple community and the reasons for its rejection. First of all, it is incorrect to say that such communities have always chosen "progress" when given a choice. Our own country contains many Amerindian tribes who have clung desperately, against absurd odds, to their own way of life, and others may be found in every part of the world. Again and again individuals in "primitive" societies have made lucid and articulate comparisons between their own and Western culture, showing a clear understanding of the latter and what they found wanting in it. Indeed, their criticisms are substantially the same as those made by Westerners themselves.

Furthermore, what is glossed over as "choosing" Western culture often turns out to be more a matter of having it jammed down one's throat. Decimated by armed slaughter and Western diseases, flooded with Western artifacts, and with their own institutions overthrown by violence, it has become a matter of adopting Western ways or having no coherent culture at all. In South Vietnam we have created a whole nation of displaced persons, many of whom will undoubtedly "choose" Western patterns.

But even in the case of those who have freely chosen Western culture, we need to look at what it is they are choosing. What impresses non-Western peoples most about our culture is its power. Guns, bombs, bulldozers, helicopters—all express the power of the colonialist. There is no question of Western culture providing more pleasure, more wisdom, better relationships between people or with the environment—only power. Few people would argue seriously that a volcano is better than a flower, but humans have always been more inclined to worship volcanoes than flowers. When someone comes and repeatedly hits you with a club, you respect and envy his club and his power to get away with that hitting, and try to emulate it, if for no other reason than self-protection.

Co-operative assumptions always give way to competitive ones when one powerful body begins to play by its own competitive rules. This is all it takes to destroy trust and give rise to a competitive system. The history of the West is simply the progressive dissemination of this infection: A dominant society brutalizes a simple one, which ultimately overwhelms its oppressor and becomes itself an oppressor.

To say that Western peoples became dissatisfied with primitive life and moved beyond it is therefore misleading. It would be more accurate to say that cultural selection has populated the world with dissatified people—people incapable of enjoying the world around them as it is. This is hardly surprising—dissatisfied people make better fighters. But it is ultimately destructive to life on the planet to have an ecological whole dominated by those who are so alienated from it as to have lost the capacity to perceive it. If we are not content with our planet, we should perhaps commit suicide and leave it to those who are. But in any case the conditions that gave competitiveness survival value have long since evaporated, as many observers have pointed out, and we are looking now to the losers to see how the ultimate victory may be gained.

The difference between the two modes of thinking is nicely exemplified in the area of health. It has taken more than a century for Western medicine to rediscover what witch doctors and shamans have known all along: (1) that a disease occurs in a whole organism, not, as in a machine, in one defective part; and (2) that every organism is organically related to others, and to the total environment, and hence any "cure" that does not take account of these relationships is likely to be ephemeral. What we stigmatize as magic is scientific inasmuch as it teaches the wholeness and interconnectedness of living forms. Scientific medicine, on the other hand, is irrational in that it treats the organism as if it were a machine, disconnected from its surroundings and internally disconnectable. As Bateson observes, medicine is a science "whose structure is essentially that of a bag of tricks," with "extraordinarily little knowledge" of the body as a "systematically cybernetically organized self-corrective system. Its internal interdependencies are minimally understood."

Doctors are fond of saying things like "your body needs fuel, just like your car," or more ambiguously, "your body is the only machine that improves with use." The technique of the Western doctor is essentially that of the plumber or mechanic—to locate the problem in a specific site and then deal with that part as if it were independently malfunctioning—consider the fascination with transplants, for example. Once the problem is localized the automobile model is again employed in "fixing" it. The faulty part is removed or replaced, or its functioning improved through the use of chemicals. The patient's capacity to verbalize her distress is given the same weight as a mechanic would give to remarks coming over a car radio. The answer to "I hurt" is a series of tests. The doctor listens to the motor, checks the pressure in the tires. While the witch doctor responds to the patient's own message and to his or her life situation and relationships, the Western doctor responds to his own equipment. Doctors frequently will ignore a confusing complaint from a patient in favor of treating a "disease" (revealed by tests) of which the patient is unaware and from which he or she does not suffer. This fragmented and invasive approach to the organism threatens the individual's psychic boundaries and hence generates anxiety, which produces more symptoms to be treated in the same fragmented way, so that the physician is constantly trying to cure the effects of his own bad medicine.

Western medicine exemplifies strikingly our alienation from

the body—viewing it as a machine that doesn't belong to us, and which we are willing to ply with poisons at a moment's notice in order to chastise those parts not "working" in a way that allows *us* to work. Even when someone comes along to point out our neglect of the body, it is usually to say that "it" will work better if "its" needs are catered to: "relaxing will give you renewed energy for work," or "paying attention to your natural body rhythms will make you more efficient." Nothing could provide a more chilling example of schizoid detachment from the body than such phrases, yet they appear daily in the media. It has been suggested, for example, that pills will soon be developed to cure jet lag—a beautiful example of our willingness to brutalize the body in the service of technology, and one that typifies the manner in which technology "solves" the problems it creates. A human need is sacrificed to further some instrumental task. But since a scorned body tends to take its own revenge, a problem is created for the task-minded: days off from tasks will be required to adjust the body to the shock. To save more time (since this is why we have jets in the first place) a pill is designed to obviate the necessity of such adjustment. The side effects of such a pill may well require another pill to offset it—for such chain reactions are the bread-and-butter of pharmacology in America, where a large proportion of all disease is drug-produced. This may hasten the emergence of cold-turkey health retreats where people will go for a period of time to unravel the multiple interactive effects of all the pills they take, under cautious medical supervision. And so another industry will have been spawned by the classic American technique of proliferating disharmony. The striking increase in cancer in the United States is hardly surprising: A disintegral medicine is merely reflected in a disease of bodily disunion.

But aside from these peripheral follies, hasn't Western medicine generally been a success? Is it fair to put the Western physician down in comparison with the witch doctor, when, in fact, he has achieved far more with his supposedly inadequate theory than the witch doctor has?

No one could deny that the Western doctor has "achieved" more—that, after all, is what Western civilization is all about. Whether he has cured more people of what troubles them is far more doubtful—it depends, as usual, on which criterion we use.

Western medicine always uses that of longevity—a revealing choice given the role of immortality yearnings in forming the technological impulse—and there is no question of the extraordinary power of Western doctors to keep people alive, even against their will and the welfare of the species.

But if we use the criterion of healthiness per capita, the much-touted triumph of Western medicine begins to look like a pyrrhic victory. What we appear to have bought is a longer life but a more sickly one. Doctors who have had an opportunity to examine "primitive" peoples living under stable but rigorous conditions, protected from Western contact, and not grossly malnourished, have been impressed with their healthiness by contrast with Westerners. This good health, it is true, owes more to the absence of change, stress, and urban confusion than it does to the occasional ministrations of the witch doctor, whose principal contribution may be his adherence to Hippocrates' cardinal rule—so consistently and grossly flouted by those who are taught it. René Dubos emphasizes the importance of unchanging conditions for health, and cites, as does Toffler, the overwhelming evidence that environmental change tends to foster disease.

But it would be foolish to rest this argument on a few unspoiled Edens. For every one of these islands of health there is an equally "primitive" tribe debilitated by poor nutrition and parasitic infestation. Western medicine could make it on the healthiness criterion if it could show that Western populations were by and large free of disease a majority of the time.

Unfortunately, this is not the case. Recent efforts to assess the health of the population at large have suggested that almost everyone is diseased at least to the point of "requiring" medical attention. This might be dismissed as an effort to whomp up more business for doctors, but other studies have found that in a 24–36 hour period, from 50 per cent to 80 per cent of the entire population takes at least one medical drug. Whether or not the United States is a sick society, it certainly *thinks* it is. With all the brilliant medical achievements of the past two hundred years, it appears that the average person on an average day feels, if anything, a little worse than before.

But the "advances" of medicine were only secondarily motivated by a desire to increase health. Their primary motive, as in the case of other technological and scientific achievements, was to gain and display power. Western physicians have always been more enthusiastic about conquering the body than curing it. The old joke about the operation being a success although the patient died still expresses the fundamental disparity between the goals of the patient and those of her supposed healer, but it seems a little off center today, since the major non-pecuniary goal of the profession seems to be to display its godlike power over death. Consider the fanatical zeal with which moribund patients are kept alive with tubes, wires, and chemicals. For whom is this heroic effort made? For the patient, who is unconscious? Had she been asked (and of course she never is—her body belongs to the institution, it would seem), she would probably have expressed a desire to leave this inhuman environment and die at home among her loved ones. For the relatives, who are going into bankruptcy to pay for this magnificent achievement, and are unable either to mourn or to carry on their lives? Hardly. It is for the doctor himself and his profession. He has "done all he could" (note the narrow assumption on which that phrase is based—his role is to keep a body alive, not to minister to the health of the living, which might require letting the dead die), and the medical priesthood has celebrated its famous victory dance over death for a time.

Boosters of technological progress have always emphasized the joys of mastery. Yet it is interesting that the word "accomplishment" means to fill up, to complete. But what is lacking? No one on earth seems to feel as incomplete as the Western man. Has he made a hole in himself just to fill it up? Could there be any relationship between his stubborn insistence on perceiving the world as a series of disconnected parts and his inability to feel whole? And could the frantic and ceaseless energy output of Western man, as well as the bewildering proliferation of information, artifacts, and enterprises, all come from trying desperately to create the missing whole by the futile procedure of adding more disconnected parts?

These questions must be postponed for now. For the present I want merely to point out that the inability to perceive wholes usually goes by the name "rationalism," for some reason. The strategy is a simple one. If you operate with quantitative criteria, as rationalists always do, then it is more important to be right about details than about totalities, since there are far more parts than there are wholes. Now science, medicine, and technology have shown a masterful accuracy about countless details and a trained incapacity to grasp a total organic system—an incapacity they have passed on to all of us, however much we may struggle against it. This adds up, quantitatively, to a pretty good record, and is the basis of all of our arrogance in relation to primitive magicians and medicine men, who tend to be correct about totalities and absurd about many details, and thus do far worse on a purely quantitative basis.

But even granting all of the above, the argument is often made (usually with ill-concealed pride) that "technology cannot be stopped." If this means that legislation "forbidding" technological innovation is unlikely to be passed, or if passed, enforced, I would agree. I can't think of anything more absurd, offhand, except perhaps the notion, shared by Toffler and most observers, that technological growth will just continue in the same linear, accelerative path it has followed thus far. Both notions share a misconception about how social change occurs, a question I would like to postpone until a later chapter. Technological growth will sag drastically when the motivational pathology that drives it dries up, and there are signs that this has already begun to happen. On the other hand, if it does not happen soon, the current impetus of technology is sufficient to destroy the planet in thirty years, and this also has begun to happen. Which will happen first is a matter of guesswork, but the drying up of the technological impulse depends in part upon the diffusion of uncharacteristic thought patterns, a largely spontaneous phenomenon of which this book is a slightly self-conscious example.

Parable 2

A girl from Berkeley told a story about People's Park.
When people were fixing up the park some of them took shovels
and just started digging a hole. They had not really talked
about why they were digging the hole, but every day they
continued. Other people would also stop and dig for a while,
and the hole got deeper and deeper. They did not recognize
any kind of leadership. At first they thought they should make
a fountain, but the hole was getting too big for a fountain.
So then they thought a wading pool for kids would be the
thing, but the hole was getting too big for a wading pool.
Then they thought a swimming pool would be nice, but that
would be dangerous without lifeguards or a fence around it. But
they kept digging anyway.

One day a guy came up, picked up a shovel and started
shoveling dirt back into the hole. "Hey, what do you think
you're doing?" someone shoveling the dirt out shouted angrily.

"You feel like shoveling dirt out of the hole, I feel like
shoveling dirt into the hole. I'm doing my own thing, just like
you."

(Glenda Cimino, from *Venceremos Brigade*)

SOCIAL METASTASIS

or

SPREADING THE WORD

> *If we would have pure knowledge of anything we must be quit of the body.*
> **Plato**

> *Apart from the body, life is an illusion.*
> **Alexander Lowen**

> *Freedom's just another word for nothing left to lose.*
> **Kristofferson and Foster**

Dirt has been defined as matter in the wrong place. Similarly, a poison can be defined as a substance ingested in too great a quantity over too short a time.

We are just beginning to awaken from a kind of madness, under the influence of which it was believed that growth was a magic quality not subject to this definition. No amount was considered harmful, no speed too great. The importance of balance and harmony, which peoples around the globe had hitherto recognized with reverence and wonder, was forgotten during these centuries of delirium. Western man instead worshipped imbalance and hypertrophy. "Maximal" and "optimal" became interchangeable terms. Growth was regarded as an unmixed blessing to such a degree that the term was even applied to improvements in personal character. To "change and grow" became an imperative of the American leisure class, raising the specter of a race of psychic behemoths.

In the organic world hypertrophy is pathology. Growth is regarded as healthy only when the rate of change is in the long run decelerative—an accelerative rate of growth is usually deemed malignant. A human child, for example, grows more in the first year of life than in any other. If it grew at a higher rate each year the monstrosity would collapse from gravitational stress before it reached school age. Yet the growth of technological change and its correlates: science, knowledge, the production of material artifacts, legislation, population, and so on, is viewed as healthy even when constant or accelerative.

The kind of growth Western culture has experienced over the past three hundred years would be considered a sign of gross malfunction in any other context. Healthy growth is paced differently—it does not absorb or destroy everything living around it. It is cancerous cells that grow and reproduce rapidly in total disregard of their connection with surrounding cells. From this viewpoint technology would have to be regarded as a cancer on human culture, Western culture a cancer on the human species, and the human species as a cancer on terrestrial life—a cancer that may in the end be treated by radiation and radical surgery at the same time.

Let us hope another cure can be found. The problem has at least been diagnosed in the report of the Club of Rome called *The Limits to Growth,* in which it was finally recognized that the only conceivable outcome of the present philosophy of constant economic growth is ecological catastrophe. Our task here is to understand the origin of the growth delusion, how it took hold of us so violently, how it ramifies through our thought processes, and how to eradicate it.

We are used to hearing pathological growth figures cited with pride and awe, only recently tinged with alarm: that scientific knowledge doubles every ten years, that half of all the energy consumed in the last two millennia has been consumed in the last century, that the tempo of human evolution is 100,000 times as rapid as that of prehuman evolution, that the earth's urban population will double in eleven years, that a civilized teen-ager is surrounded by twice as many newly manufactured goods as she was as an infant, that 90 per cent of all the scientists who ever lived are now alive, and so on. But *why* are humans consuming all that energy, for example? What is the motive behind such frenzied activity? When animals become this restless we assume they are under some kind of stress.

In these three chapters I will try to trace some of the factors responsible for this pathological growth. At times my remarks may seem to imply that the species was doomed from the very start. Yet for hundreds of thousands of years humans were only potentially destructive. One might say that the disease was present, but only in the same sense that harmful bacteria are always present in the body. René Dubos observes that "the severity of a microbial or toxic disease is determined as much by the intensity of the body response as it is by the characteristics of the microbe or toxin involved." Similarly, David Bakan, following Selye and Freud, sees the organism as in more danger from its adaptive reactions than from external agencies.

We are in the acute phase of a virulent disease, and while it is of some value to trace its ultimate sources, it is more important to look at how it got out of hand. Our species has always been vulnerable to the disease. Yet only a portion of humankind fell victim to it, while others are still resisting it, although with rapidly decreasing success. The vulnerability is depressing, but the existence of healthy tissue is encouraging. We need to understand both our intrinsic vulnerability to the disease and the nature of the forces that facilitate or resist it in its acute form.

I find I make frequent use of the cancer metaphor in discussing our society. It is difficult to see the recent technological explosion, with its extraordinary proliferative irrelevance, as anything but a neoplasm. But the analogue is deeper than that: "It has been demonstrated that when normal tissues are grown on a glass surface, the cells stop growing when they touch each other. But cancer cells similarly grown on a glass surface continue to grow, unimpeded by cellular contact." (Bakan) Studies of cancer cells seem to suggest that some kind of mutually limiting communication present between normal cells is weak or absent between cancer cells. It is as if cancer cells had been heavily indoctrinated with the ideology of individualism and personal achievement.

Imagine a mass of cancerous tissue, the cells of which enjoyed consciousness. Would they not be full of self-congratulatory sentiments at their independence, their more advanced level of development, their rapid rate of growth? Would they not sneer at their more primitive cousins who were bound into a static and unfree existence, with limited aspirations, subject to heavy group constraint, and obviously "going nowhere"? Would they not rejoice in their control over their own destiny, and cheer the conversion of more and more normal cells as convincing proof of the validity of their own way of life? Would they not, in fact, feel increasingly triumphant right up to the moment the organism on which they fed expired?

Yet it would be a mistake to imagine that our tendency to embrace our disease ever more fervently is merely a matter of arrogance. There is a spiral effect that comes from the fact that our disease is continually being externalized. The more we create a diseased environment the more frantic we become in our efforts to escape it. And each motion in the service of escape carries us farther and farther from the state of health to which we are so desperately seeking to return. Toffler, for example, sees more clearly than anyone the devastating impact of our frantic change pattern, yet demands that we increase our adaptability to change, thus insuring that change will further accelerate. He wants to "free" human beings from those spontaneous reactions that tend to slow down or interfere with the rate of change. He wants us, in other words, to adapt to a bad environment.

Now adaptation to a bad environment not only provides positive feedback for that environment, but also reduces one's ability to respond to a good one. The small child left for weeks in a hospital remains in a psychically healthy state just so long as it continues to cry bitterly for its parents. Psychic damage begins from the moment it settles down to a peaceful indifference, making what pleased hospital personnel call a "good adjustment." The consequences of prolonged adaptation to that impersonal and somewhat inhuman environment are an emotional shallowness, an inability to form lasting attachments, and chronic depressiveness. Similarly, recent studies of schizophrenia show that the patient's illness can be considered a reasonable adaptation to a grossly malfunctioning family communication system. In fact it would not be far from the mark to say that all disease—psychological, physiological, societal—is adaptation to a bad environment. If this is true, then the difficulty in recovering health when a disease is externalized becomes clear. The environment cannot improve since the disease is continually fed back into it. Further adaptation yields further disease which worsens the environment, necessitating a more exaggerated adaptation, and so on. The most obvious examples of this process would include such fatuities as adapting to overpopulation by learning to live under the sea, or adapting to the surplus of cars by building more roads.

But there are other examples that I personally find more painful. The search for social justice over the past century has rested in large part on principles of consistency, objectivity, equality, fairness, and so on. In the fight against oppression and exploitation a major weapon has been to expose the fact that two individuals from different backgrounds are not treated the same before the law, or that they have unequal opportunities, or that they receive different responses for the same behavior. Another is to demonstrate that a value embraced in the abstract is notably flouted in some specific instance.

Our society is riddled with oppression, and not to utilize these weapons would be a crime of omission against humanity. Yet we need to recognize the degree to which objectivity is a symptom of our cultural disease, and consistency the mechanism of its metastasis. The assumption that progress is achieved by trading the brutalities of a personal slaveowner for those of an impersonal one needs to be examined.

In the simple community, objectivity as we understand it scarcely exists. Almost all acts, decisions, and rewards are based on particular relationships and positions within the community. There is inequality, there is inequity, even a modest degree of exploitation. There is certainly scapegoating and personal misery. Still, everyone is recognized as having some sort of value, and some sort of meaningful connection with everyone else. No one dies unnoticed or unmourned. When, with increasing size, this form breaks down and authoritarianism takes its place, we begin to encounter exploitation and brutality on a scale and in a form familiar to us. Here for the first time rewards and decisions tend to be based on a kind of crude principle: the closer to the center of power, the more rewards. The distribution of rewards can now be predicted by an outsider without knowing the entire network of relationships and customs in the community. And as power becomes more centralized and less hedged with legitimacies, anyone can achieve material success simply by managing to please the tyrant. Social mobility begins with autocracy.

But with further increases in size and complexity, authoritarianism itself breaks down. The personal limitations of despots give rise to demands for objective, mechanized systems for distributing rewards. People begin to feel that personal relationships should play no part in arriving at political or economic decisions. Power increasingly lies in impersonal mechanisms, although those who reside at the center of the machinery are paid off so handsomely in counterfeit rewards for the stress they endure that they imagine themselves to be the masters of it—a fantasy endorsed by those at the periphery.

As the system becomes more and more objective and depersonalized, any remaining tendency toward corruption or exploitation becomes grossly magnified; and as the web of personal relatedness becomes further shattered by the emphasis on universal and objective criteria, the consequences of exploitation become more vicious. The possibility of appeal through personal channels is lost and whole categories of individuals can simply be forgotten. The unimportant individual in a simple community has rights, merely by virtue of his being a relative and neighbor of everyone in the system, that his counterpart in a society like ours can never achieve. In the most corruption-free bureaucratized society the individual can appeal only to a series of abstract principles which may not apply to her and which ignore her personal condition. Exploitation and oppression tend to assume a form that is massive and impersonal. The system is unwieldy and has high inertia: Anything moving is hard to stop and vice versa. In a personalized system, on the other hand, while there is much movement, nothing can go too far in any direction without corrective forces coming into play.

We respond to this unwieldiness by adapting to the principles on which it is based, accepting and trying to expand them. But striving for more consistency and fairness exaggerates the unwieldiness and inertia of the system still further. In a simple community everyone is treated differently because her position in it is unique. Since in most of the business of everyday life we *have* no relationship with those with whom we deal, we seek ways to be more fair, to make sure that everyone is treated alike, to apply abstract criteria that ignore particularities. The brutalities of judges, doctors, and administrators in our society derive less from their failure to apply equitable principles than from their total ignorance of the people affected by their decisions.

Organic networks are full of inconsistency. They arrive at some sort of balance through spontaneous blundering toward multiple accommodation. The application of abstract principle destroys this balance irrevocably, and the efforts to re-establish that balance on a mathematical basis are a little like trying to balance a ball on the point of a sword by firing bullets at it whenever it starts to lean. The demand for consistency treats the disease by seeking to extend it to the entire organism.

Since I feel somewhat uneasy about putting this argument into the hands of conservatives, I want to add a word of clarification. No significant radical social movement in America today derives its validity and meaning from these principles, although all radical movements use them as political arguments. While such movements begin with the rhetoric of equality, fairness, and consistency, they tend to shift—in response to radicalization and continual social analysis—to a conviction of the particularized superiority of their own constituents. Women, blacks, Indians, and third-world nations still lay considerable stress on equality, but their more militant representatives have come to recognize that the dominant Western white-male society needs them a great deal more than they need it, independent of all issues of fairness and justice. The dominant forces in society tend not to perceive this distinction, since it is far more comfortable to assume that someone merely wants a share of your pie than to acknowledge yourself a prisoner in a diseased and moribund system.

Linearity and Principle

Much of what I have said seems to cast a suspicious eye on the use of abstract concepts and principles in human affairs— even though I have not hesitated to employ my own. Now since the first (usually the only) three skills taught to intellectuals are

(a) how to classify an argument without listening to it, (b) how to find internal contradictions in it, and (c) how to turn it against its author, it is clear that I have strayed into troubled waters.

Perhaps I need to stress that I am not interested in eliminating any human qualities but only in assessing their cost. Had anyone fully understood, at the time, the social cost we would have to pay for the privilege of riding around in a machine on rubber wheels, the automobile might not have been marketed. Or it might simply have been approached very differently. Even qualities like individualism that have become poisonous through exaggeration are in some more minute proportion indispensable. My wish is not to expunge, but to rebalance and reintegrate. But the reader must not expect this desire to be clothed in the garb of serenity in a world where the very idea of harmony only arouses impatience and irritability.

Harmony lacks a sense of movement, and this produces a caged feeling in people under severe stress. Western civilization is a man running with increasing speed through an air-sealed tunnel in search of additional oxygen. You can quite reasonably tell him he will survive longer if he slows down, but he is not likely to do it. Without detracting in any way from the importance of McLuhan's contribution, it must be said that linearity in human culture is more than a stylistic orientation derived from sensory ratios. The sense of unimpeded motion in linearity expresses a desperate need for headlong flight that a mosaic pattern completely frustrates.

Straight lines are something of a rarity in nature—the sight of one usually suggests a civilized human presence. And when humans have departed or allowed nature to reassert herself the straight lines are rounded out. The beauty of fallen snow is that it restores to even the most rectilinear city an appearance of organicity. A flight of steps becomes a rippled sand dune shaped by a set of forces that are in some kind of playful balance with one another, rather than by a single ruthless and domineering concept. The sense of some frantic and insatiable human need—always suggested by the straight line—is muted and softened.

Perhaps there are no straight lines in nature—our most certain candidates keep turning out to be curved in the long run. Perhaps the straight line is merely a human figment—a fantasy of utter independence and irresistibility. Ultimately everything reveals itself to be interconnected and subject to external influence, but the dearest wish of the thoroughly indoctrinated individualist is that he might pursue a life devoid of negative feedback—that he would be "right on" eternally, never deflected from his rigid and purely self-perpetuating course.

In brief, the existence of linearity betrays the absence of negative (that is, corrective) feedback, and the inability to receive negative feedback is ultimately calamitous. Nothing, for example, has contributed more than the myth of pure science to the grotesqueness of its applications. If the concept of pathology has any utility at all, linearity is pathological.

The problem remaining for this chapter is to examine the form and nature of that pathology at its most elementary level. We cannot begin all over again, nor will anything be gained by trusting to a spontaneity that no longer exists in an organic system that is severely damaged. But it may be useful to understand how we got here—to assess the soft spots in the psychosocial equipment of the species. Every human virtue contains an evil, and we need to understand the price paid for the qualities we hold dear and deem essential.

The Schizoid Mammal

In *The Divided Self* Ronald Laing describes schizoid techniques for obtaining security in a psychically dangerous environment. Although intended as a psychological description it might also serve as a metaphor for the evolution of Western culture. As such, it points up a serious flaw in the species and suggests the hazards of cultural as compared with biological evolution. Of most acute relevance is the schizoid quest for autarchy, which reproduces with some precision the changing relation between the individual and her environment produced by the technological revolution.

The schizoid process begins by detaching a piece of oneself from connectedness with the environment. This piece, which is regarded as the inner or "real" self, is thus disengaged, unresponsive to feedback, unembodied. It observes everything that happens to the rest of the organism (from sexual gratification to beatings) with dispassionate detachment. All transactions with the environment are unreal, since the "real" self is not involved. Yet because nothing real is coming into the self nothing real can go out of it, and hence it experiences even itself as increasingly unreal, dead, and meaningless. The search for safety through detachment proves ultimately unsafe, for as the self becomes progressively emptied of life it becomes more vulnerable to engulfment by others, who are real, and to implosion from real external stimuli. The sense of freedom and autonomy that this autarchy provides is illusory, since it is exercised in a vacuum, and that which is free is continually diminished and made lifeless. The sense of identity requires the existence of another by whom one is known, and in relation to whom one's existence finds expression. Gregory Bateson once remarked on the folly of trying to delimit something by cutting the pathways that are the definitions of its being.

What Laing describes is a defensive posture available to the entire species. The schizoid defense becomes possible with the emergence of the capacity to generate, manipulate, and relate symbols. Once that ability exists it is possible for the organism to withdraw from the complex network of mutual feedback in which it is embedded and respond to its inner circuitry alone. Nature and the body no longer rule the organism.

This is one way to interpret the Garden of Eden myth. Originally, the harmony of the planet was maintained by a balancing of forces in which all species participated unwittingly, each organism ruled by its efforts to avoid discomfort or seek pleasure. Humanity alone opted out of the system, forswearing pleasure and uncertainty in order to be "free."

In the biblical story the first symptom of the disturbance is a sudden loss of comfort with the body—a tendency to feel detached from it and be ashamed of it. "The [schizoid] individual's being is cleft in two, producing a disembodied self and a body that is a thing that the self looks at, regarding it at times as though it were just another thing in the world." (Laing) When Adam and Eve cease to be *in* their bodies they cease to be capable of living in Paradise and are driven out. Having taken the schizoid route, they must now toil endlessly to approximate the equilibrium they have forsaken.

The source of the fall is vanity: "You will be like God, knowing good and evil," and the illusion that a man can "rise above" his body has led to history's most impressive atrocities. The source of the illusion is the peculiar petulance many humans exhibit when confronted with the fact that all specific organic structures are temporary—indeed, more or less irrelevant. They cling to the notion of personal continuation the way a pedant does to a concept or a bureaucrat to a procedure. It is as if a particular configuration in a game of Cat's Cradle, say a passably executed Jacob's Ladder, wished to preserve itself eternally in stone—that *particular* child, that *particular* string, and that *particular* mediocre representative of the form. The child knows she can do it again, probably better. The technique, after all, like the genetic message, transcends the moment. But the particular trial exists only in that time, and must be content with the fact that it will *always* exist in that moment—that it is located in time, that it has a place. But humans have difficulty accepting that limitation, and in their frantic efforts to spread themselves over a larger temporal area they have often ended by scarcely existing at all. Like the man who wants to be everywhere at once and ends by being nowhere, the man who seeks immortality ends by not being present in his own time. Yet no matter how much people rejoice in the changing seasons, in the sunset and sunrise, and in birth—the passing of their own configuration is distressful.

The desire to borrow more time is the sign of an unlived life. The man who most wants a party to last longer is the one who has spent the evening not approaching a girl he is attracted to, out of fear of rejection. Furthermore, this sense of temporal scarcity, like all such scarcity, is contagious. The man who invades posterity's time dilutes the lives of his descendants, and leads them also to seek immortality, just as the horde that invades another's country motivates those invaded to invade others.

The connection between narcissism and the longing for immortality explains why the serpent and Eve receive all the blame in the Eden myth. Early humans envied the serpent because it sloughed its skin and hence was imagined to be immortal. And men have always envied women because they can visibly reproduce themselves. Eve is, in fact, punished for this: childbearing is made painful. But the myth is really about Adam's fall: The idea that he was tempted by Eve is merely the oppressor's way of saying that he became envious of her. "Temptation" is to Adam what "provocation" is to a big country that wants to attack a little one. As C. S. Lewis remarks, "We think the lamb gentle because its wool is soft to our hands: men call a woman voluptuous when she arouses voluptuous feelings in them." Since men are in poorer touch with their feelings than women, they tend to blame women whenever their own feelings get out of hand. But it is men who have most enthusiastically opted for disembodiment and the quest for spiritual immortality.

But I realize that I am presuming upon a sympathy the reader may not feel. Wasn't the "Fall" in fact a great victory, in which humanity was freed from dependence on impulse? Hasn't it brought us all the benefits we now enjoy and allowed us to control our own destiny, unlike other species whose spontaneity has permitted us to extinguish them?

It is certainly true that the withdrawal into inner circuitry has had a certain survival value in the short run, and I would advise anyone concerned with longevity against seeking a return to the paradisiacal condition so long as there are any beings like us in the immediate neighborhood. As to the relative advantages of a short flavorful life and a long unfeeling one, we must all weigh this for ourselves. And as to the benefits of civilization, they are unquestionably, each and every one, a product of man's schizoid proclivities, as are all the cruelties of civilized life. There is absolutely no way to keep the goodies and toss away the evils —it's a package deal and we will make no headway whatsoever so long as we try to evade this fact. You cannot hang a Rembrandt on a palm tree. People talk, for example, of the Peloponnesian War or World War I as putting an end to the Golden Ages that preceded them—ages in which arts and sciences flourished with particular abandon. This is nonsense, for in both cases the wars were as true an expression of the age as any work of art, and indeed, great art and major wars proceed from the same grandiose impulse. There is no way to retain great art without the narcissism that makes war inevitable. If we wish to moderate the conditions that give rise to war, we must settle for a more modest level of individualistic achievement in other spheres.

But it is the issues of freedom from impulse and control of one's own destiny that need most clarification. No word has ever done heavier labor in the service of mystification than "freedom" (in America one of the most popular euphemisms for rejecting a lover is, "I'm going to set you free"). No one who has become alienated from his body is in control of his destiny, however much he may be able to throw his dissociated weight around in the external environment. To whatever degree we take refuge in inner circuitry and break communication with bodily and outer circuitry, the freedom we achieve is illusory and temporary, as in the term "free fall" in sky diving.

For a living organism there is no such thing as full autonomy. There is only variability in the pathways through which its parasitical dependency can be exercised. A fish is not autonomous in relation to water at the moment it is gasping its life out in the bottom of a boat. Nor is an astronaut in relation to the atmosphere or the earth when he is shut up in a metal ball a hundred thousand miles out, sucking oxygen and responding to messages from someone he cannot see, while relying on the construction skills of men he may not have known. Whether one is aware of being controlled by bodily needs and impulses, by one's own cultural norms and values, by neurotic aspirations, or by some set of ideological vanities from some other culture makes very little difference. Our existence is in fact defined by all of these things—only the proportions change, and that much less than we like to imagine. Without air we die, without love we turn nasty, without feedback we go crazy. We are born with energy, matter, and information going in and out of us, and we continue in this way until we die. Too great a deviation from the normal degree of inflow and outflow is disturbing to our sense of our own boundaries, which means that *too little influence, stimulation, control, or whatever, from outside is just as likely to be experienced as an invasion of our being as too much, even though we have been trained not to perceive it.* The notion that people begin as separate individuals, who then march out and connect themselves with others, is one of the most dazzling bits of self-mystification in the history of the species. Through this mystification we make ourselves vulnerable to manipulation by essentially mechanical forces: technological systems, bureaucratic regulations, ideological consistencies. The paranoid who imagines himself to be controlled electronically is in better shape than most of us—he at least has some sense of where his self-mystification has led him.

Weston La Barre summarizes humanity's much-touted freedom from instinct by pointing out that a man, through his dependence on learning, "meets reality very largely via the not disinterested individuals that make up his immediate family and society. He adjusts perforce to their mistakes . . . not to nature itself . . . as a man he will be whatever outlandish domesticate his parents unconsciously prefer or unwittingly shape." Freedom from instinct, then, means a transfer of dependence from something that cannot make you psychotic to something that can. Freedom from instinct is the freedom to have reality falsified for you. Freedom from instinct is the beginning of psychic pollution. As La Barre says, man is unique among animals in "his practiced ability to know things that are not so."

This is, of course, a one-sided view. If you can imagine what is not, you can behave in such a way as to bring it about, instead of merely searching aimlessly until a stimulus fits your yearning. The price paid is that while you are imagining, you are not experiencing what is—which may be even nicer. And by the time the imagined blessing is brought into being you may have lost the capacity to experience *it*, and will already be imagining some other non-existing state.

Now a pimple is a long way from a terminal cancer, just as smoking dope or chewing gum is a long way from shooting heroin. The first time a man killed something that he didn't eat and that wasn't trying to eat him, a channel was opened that made Hiroshima possible, but it certainly didn't make it inevitable. By the same token, the capacity to create and manipulate symbols, while it opens the door to a schizoid process, doesn't make it universal and mandatory. When men take to the sea they create for the first time the possibility that they will drown. But when an epidemic of drownings occurs we begin to look for other reasons, like faulty boats. It is enough to suggest at this point that the capacity to symbolize contains a danger, like boating, and requires safeguards that have as yet been insufficiently stressed.

Another channel is opened with the emergence of culture. If humanity is a schizoid animal, culture is a schizoid approach to evolution. As La Barre observes, schizophrenics are only exaggeratedly human individuals, since "qualitatively there is no discernible difference in content between a culture and a psychosis." The only difference is quantitative—if many people share a symbol-system it is a culture, if only one does, it is a psychosis. Both are independent of reality and both provide specious solutions to security problems, but as La Barre points out, a culture has the advantage that if many people believe a lie, its power to allay anxiety is immensely heightened thereby. Furthermore, if a whole group of people are behaving as if some social fiction were true, it tends to acquire a degree of reality—one which at the very least will help prevent the truth from emerging in that setting. Children, for example, can be warped in a great variety of ways, and if some breed is believed to be superior or inferior or lazy or aggressive or brittle or stupid or tempestuous, they will tend, in fact, to exaggerate those traits. A paranoid person is likely sooner or later to get himself persecuted, hence confirming his view of reality, but with a culture likelihood approaches inevitability. Sociology, economics, and political science are to a large extent studies of the materialization of schizoid process.

Culture, then, frees humanity still further from reality, for as La Barre points out, there is no natural selection among ideas and beliefs; millions can believe the same falsehood for thousands of years. This is not in itself harmful—many delusions are after all innocuous. But there is danger in the shift away from being deeply in touch with the external environment and one's own bodily sensations. Once lost, that tactile immediacy, that groundedness in experience, can never be entirely recaptured. A connection is broken, a balance wheel lost, and the system becomes capable of exponential growth, of robot-like movement, of running amok.

Yet clearly this doesn't happen immediately. All cultures, even very simple ones, seduce their adherents into commitment to outlandish and absurdly inconvenient beliefs and practices, but not all of these take people far out of contact with their bodies and their natural environment. Some of those beliefs and practices that seem most irrational to Westerners are in fact expressions of that sense of closeness. Several further steps are necessary before the danger becomes acute.

Giving a name to an experience detaches us a little from the experience itself, as many people have pointed out. Combining those names into some sort of conceptual system detaches us a good bit further, since we begin to seek our sense of coherence from the conceptual system rather than from reality itself and our embeddedness in it. But as long as the system is merely a kind of rough contour map that reflects the relative emotional or practical significance of various features in the environment, its capacity to pull us out of the world and into inner circuitry is limited. It is when we begin to manipulate that system as an end in itself—rationalizing it, ordering it, applying principles of logic and consistency to it—that the void begins to yawn beneath us. At this point it has become an inner world capable of detaching us from our tactile world. This is not to say that such a system may not be an excellent guide for grasping certain aspects of the real world and manipulating it in specific directions. But we are no longer *in* it—we think of ourselves as *outside* (usually *above*) the world looking at it. Furthermore, *since we have detached ourselves from the rest of the totality, totality is the one thing we cannot see.* As Bateson observes, "consciousness is, almost of necessity, blinded to the systemic nature of the man himself. Purposive consciousness pulls out, from the total mind, sequences which do not have the loop structure which is characteristic of the whole systemic structure." *It is "objectivity," in other words, that prevents us from seeing the totality of which we are a part.*

Mechanistic knowledge of the physiology of the body, for example, is an excellent device for blunting awareness of one's own bodily responses and their relation to environmental stimuli. Treating the body as an object takes one *out* of the body and hence out of the environment. This enables someone in an anxiety-laden setting to take a pill instead of yelling or running out of the room, but this in turn increases the possibility that whatever is amiss in that room will not be corrected, thus requiring further anesthesia. Our society is built up of millions of such small choices, and this necessitates an enormous amount of anesthesia for its participants.

What I am saying is that abstract concepts facilitate self-objectification, which in turn tends to deprive our man-made environment of the negative feedback necessary to prevent it from behaving inhumanly. An architect who treats his own bodily needs and emotional responses as an annoying impediment to rapid completion of his task is unlikely to design a building that is pleasurable to live in, and the same may be said of planners, executives, technologists, teachers, parents, and so on. We cannot live without conceptual systems, but we must be alive to the dangers to which they expose us.

The capacity of conceptual systems to suck us into their own machinery and detach us from our organic connections is a familiar topic for humor, pathos, and satire: the army officer who treats his son "just like any other soldier," the rule-bound bureaucrat, the ideologue whose belief system deprives him of simple pleasures. Perhaps the most classic example is our tendency to lose contact with our own emotional needs in the face of economic logic—as in the phrase, "it's so cheap you can't afford not to buy it." It is the power of such purely economic considerations to overwhelm the imagination that lends truth to the notion that "money can't buy happiness." In principle, money can buy happiness or anything else—if it doesn't, it is because people don't use it that way. The kind of commitment necessary to accumulate money often seduces people into responding to economic rather than emotional yardsticks—"It's overpriced," instead of, "I want it that much," or "It's a giveaway," instead of, "I don't want it in my life." People abandon homes to which they have devoted decades of love and energy because they are "too expensive to keep up," and spend years in deep depression or even die in response to the loss of familiar and loved surroundings. The reasoning behind such an act is that money will thereby become available for many more reasonably priced goods and services which are not nourishing to the soul, however enjoyable or even necessary they may seem to be. This is called being "sensible" about money, i.e., accepting external criteria of value—using money primarily to buy more money. The opposite tendency, using money primarily to buy happiness or satisfy deep internal needs is usually called being "capricious," "inconsistent," or "irrational" about money.

Mechanical Responsivity

Although organic responsivity is lost through the evolution of formal structures and logical principles, the capacity of human beings to respond to influence is not. The illusions of individualism blind us to the fact that a single human being is born as a *part* of an interaction system—he is not and cannot ever be a complete and self-sufficient entity. Part of the genetic message of a human being is a complex pattern of receptivity to influence, especially from other humans. The individual is like a template requiring some external message to complete it. It is programmed to imitate and accommodate, however much we may detest these words. When organic responsivity is deadened, the readiness to react to external messages still remains. In the absence of the original channel others will be used. Authoritarian submission is one such channel, with symbolic authorities (traffic lights, signs, written instructions) being increasingly substituted for personal ones as the anesthesia progresses. Another channel is ideology: that is, a general instruction which has been internalized and from which specific rules for behavior and attitude can be logically deduced.

The problem with these impersonal channels of conformity— which I have grouped under the term mechanical responsivity —is that they lack fine tuning. Logical systems tend to be a bit simple. A substantial proportion of bureaucratic rule making, for example, consists of efforts to prevent a single unfortunate event from recurring by the crude device of eliminating some category to which it belongs. A public scandal or threatened lawsuit will almost guarantee the promulgation of new regulations (each of which erodes the vitality of the organization) to ensure against an event whose probability of recurring is infinitesimal. If a scandal occurs in a particular room, that room will be declared off limits henceforward; if it occurs after hours, doors will be locked and time checks instituted. If an embezzler uses green ink, green ink will be banned. Security is sedulously pursued by the futile device of using bigger and bigger conceptual nets to catch smaller and smaller particularized fish. No one in the history of the world has ever succeeded in finding a general formula that would ensure happiness or avoid evil in any given context, but the search goes on, so great is the desire for freedom from the ambiguity of daily living.

But there is a more serious problem with the rule of law as compared with more personal and informal modes of social control. The objectification of morality makes it possible for an individual to feel moral or assuage guilt by conforming to a set of abstract rules even in the process of committing all sorts of viciousness. For there is no behavior so cruel or outlandish that it cannot be justified in terms of some perfectly reasonable principle, just as there is no place on the globe so "out of the way" that it cannot be reached by flying in a straight line in some direction.

Unfortunately, the kind of social control that exists in simple communities cannot be reproduced on a large scale, while a return to complete localization would simply start the whole historical process all over again. Even the simplest communities have some abstract rules, so we know the seeds are already there. We are stuck with size and we are stuck with abstract principles. But we need to be more clearly aware of the dangers they pose —humans have a horrible weakness for making virtues out of ugly necessities, thereby allowing them to become more ghoulish in their impact than need be.

The ideology of individualism exemplifies this weakness. No one could have done more than the popular social critics of the 1950s (Fromm, Riesman, Whyte, et al.) to convince people of the virtues of disconnectedness and smooth the path of mechanical responsivity. By raising the specter of immersion in group life —of losing one's narcissistic consciousness—they frightened and shamed people into an ever more frantic pursuit of autonomy and self-sufficiency. Thus disconnected, more and more of the population became available for attachment to the impersonal machinery of modern life. Americans can be so easily manipulated by advertising *because* they are individualistic. Ripped out of their social fabric their social responses are constantly seeking a missing stimulus to which they can attach themselves. A flock of ducklings deprived of their mother became "imprinted" on Konrad Lorenz whom they then followed about. Humans deprived of community can become, in a sense, "imprinted" on rules, machines, ideologies, and bureaucratic structures. The anticonformity critics, therefore, helped create precisely what they were attacking. By heaping scorn on social responses fundamental to humankind, they helped further the process of disconnection in the society, thus making the population ever more vulnerable to authoritarian and impersonal manipulation. For the forms in which conformity and authoritarianism appear in modern society are a *product* of the ideology of freedom and individualism—desperate and shamefaced efforts to fill the hole left by the every-man-should-strive-to-be-a-lonely-genius-head-and-shoulders-above-the-worthless-gregarious-dependent-masses guilt trip. The illusion that the individual is an independent

entity threatens the *internal* integrity of the organism, which is rooted in interdependence. The individual is an arrangement of ways of relating. Without any object for these relational responses, she must either hallucinate or crumble, just as a victim of sensory deprivation must. (The hermit, for example, relates to fantasy objects—parent figures, gods, the entire community, or whatever, sometimes disguised as parts of the self.) Detachment, in other words, is as likely to produce internal disintegration as overinvolvement.

This tendency to see the individual organism as an entity rather than a process, a terminal rather than a conduit, has led to some odd cultural norms, such as the high value placed on the capacity to be alone—the psychic equivalent of the ability to hold one's breath, or go without sleep, or twist oneself into a pretzel, or otherwise torture an alienated body in the service of vanity. To praise the ability of a social animal to trash its biological equipment is a little like saying that the most virtuous bird is the one that can tunnel through the earth. Fritz Perls, the father of Gestalt therapy, maintained that "to grow up means to be alone," which he apparently did not recognize as a violation of his view that therapy should not consist in bringing about adjustment to a sick society. Yet this is precisely what Gestalt therapy does most effectively. In a society founded on unstable, fragmentary, transient, competitive, and unco-ordinated relationships the Gestalt approach is a survival kit, although it also contributes to and fosters the *status quo*. There is something a little eerie about the sight of 200 million people slavishly adhering in the same unhappy way to a norm of personal independence and uniqueness.

Our era has been inundated with literary, cinematic, and video fantasies of overintegrated societies. In our present condition they seem a little comic, like the fantasies of an overcontrolled man that his rage, if it ever broke through, would be homicidal or world destroying. There is a grain of truth in such fantasies; namely, that control exaggerates the longing it suppresses. But there is also a grain of deceit in that the fantasy of exaggerated strength can encourage continued suppression of a perfectly ordinary impulse. In our bogey-books about overintegrated societies (*1984, Brave New World, We, Fahrenheit 451*) that impulse is the longing to abandon one's isolated autonomy and become a

part of something. Marcia Millman shows how underneath the surface horror of these fantasies lies a hidden conviction that happiness lies in loss of self. The societies are portrayed in such grotesque forms (all of them are sociological anomalies, containing many traits that could only arise in an individualistic society) in order to frighten us out of realizing that need even in the mildest form.

Drama and Detachment

Drama has also contributed to this process, serving both as a substitute for, and a vehicle for the erosion of, community life. Drama as we know it begins when community street life ends—when a person cannot assume that she will run into the people she wants to see in the normal course of a day.

The most powerful source of drama is the family—the great tragedies are mostly family affairs. In a simple community when a family crisis occurs people run into the street and the community gathers around to mediate, nourish, and absorb. As a community becomes larger and less integrated the capacity of the family to generate drama does not change, but it can no longer be shared. The community becomes privatized, the family isolated, the streets empty. It is at this point that drama in the form familiar to us begins to emerge—as if people had to have some place to go with their collective responsivity. Into the hole left when the family retires inside the dwelling a dramatic scene is poured, enacted by performers.

We can see this transition most clearly in Greek tragedies, which are generally set in the street outside the family home. Indeed, the killings and mutilations usually take place *inside* the home, offstage, and then are reported to the chorus, just as if they, and the audience, were villagers gathered in the street. Athens, in the period when Greek drama was at its peak, had witnessed a rapid urbanization, with shrinking and isolation of the family unit, not unlike what we have experienced during the past century.

Occasionally performers have tried to ply their trade in communities that have not lost their social responsivity, with unfortunate results. The simple people forget the artificiality of the setting and are prone to enter the action. A villain risks his life in such a setting. We smile condescendingly at this behavior, but it is this responsivity and sense of interconnectedness that make such communities nourishing social environments. It is not that the people are childish or stupid, only that their social impulses are still working in an intense and automatic way, whereas ours have atrophied. Supposedly we have substituted rational and judicious behavior for this responsivity, but how poorly it works can be seen at a glance. Referral agencies, mental hospitals, prisons, and nursing homes are a few of the tardy, impersonal, inhumane, and generally rather dilapidated mechanisms we have evolved to replace this naïve responsivity.

The drama—live, on film, or on video—is one of the ways we deaden this response. We are conditioned very early to look on passively while people are being beaten and killed, or suffering in every conceivable way. The success of the drama in anesthetizing our social impulses is apparent on any city street corner. The theater helps train us in non-responsiveness so that the formal institutions that depend for their existence on our social narcosis can survive.

It is the theater itself that has begun to develop an antidote to this condition, not without considerable resistance from its case-hardened audiences. Environmental theater seems almost to pinpoint this issue—not only in its efforts to engage the audience in action, but in its impulse to return to the street.

Freedom and Will

The more closely we examine the search for freedom, the more suspiciously it looks like a search for interpersonal security—for a predictable, no-risk human environment. What the freedom addict seeks is control and order through the blocking of constraining or disturbing feedback. Freedom means maximizing the extent to which one controls one's own input, which is another way of saying that I am most "free" when the form and content of what I encounter as stimulus is myself. Freedom is thus inherently illusory since one cannot in fact alter the interdependence of living matter—indeed of all energy—one can only alter one's perception of it. This, as David Bakan observes, is the paradox of mastery: "In order to master, the ego rules things out of existence. Yet it is often what is ruled out that arises and asserts itself, so there is no mastery precisely where mastery was sought." Freedom, in short, is what Kitty Genovese enjoyed: the freedom to be leisurely stabbed to death in a New York street for an hour without some small-town busybody poking his nose in her private affairs.

The capacity to symbolize is often described as having freed humanity from the instinctual prison in which all other animals are forever pent. This freedom is a freedom of the mind—the freedom that allows a man to starve amid plenty and glut himself on dreams—the freedom manifest in the term "freeway." The mechanism that enabled humanity to leap beyond all other species in the evolution fairy tale ("thus man evolved from the hominids and lived happily ever after") is the same that Laing describes as the root of the schizoid process. It is the capacity to ignore information coming from the body or the environment in favor of conceptual circuitry. But he who frees himself in this way from a friend is chained to his own need, loss, and pain, while he who frees himself in this way from an enemy is bound to uncertainty, fear, and paranoia.

I have suggested that the human capacity to create and manipulate symbols opened the door to pathology, and that this was heightened by the evolution of culture and the ability to organize symbols into hierarchies of abstraction. Thus far we seem to be dealing with irreversible and perhaps essential attainments. Given these dangers it seems vital for the survival of the species that it foster an avid commitment to maintaining awareness of organic interconnectedness, since it is forever in acute peril of losing this awareness. Grounding the individual in the here-and-now—in concrete, immediate reality—is the antidote to schizoid collapse, and the same holds at the cultural level. Given our unavoidable susceptibility to schizoid responses, we need to guard against gratuitous encouragements. The mind-body dualism that has dominated Western thought (and much Eastern thought as well) is clearly one of these; few ideas provide a more fertile context for schizoid development than the notion that the spirit is independent of the flesh. Another, even more potent, is the emergence of cultural patterns that encourage the hypertrophy of will.

As Alexander Lowen points out, will is an emergency mechanism. Under ordinary conditions the controlling principle of an organism is pleasure. Bodily pleasure not only integrates the organism itself but maintains harmony in the organism-environment system. Behavior that is based on pleasure, Lowen observes, seems co-ordinated and effortless, whereas behavior based on will tends to be jerky, rigid, and mechanical. The schizoid individual, whose entire life tends to be governed by will, not only inhibits impulses, but in order to achieve this inhibition shuts off the information channels along which they normally travel, so that he has difficulty knowing what he wants and tends to base all his behavior on principles. "Normally, one eats when one is hungry, but in the schizoid state one has lunch because it is twelve o'clock. . . . The schizoid individual engages in sports . . . to improve his control over his body and not for the pleasure of the activity or the movement."

As an emergency mechanism will power is useful as a biological short cut when all other means have failed. Normal desires for pleasure and safety are circumvented so that the unnatural can be accomplished. We might view this mechanism as a way of bringing the organism back into synchrony with its environment when it has for some reason fallen out. Persistent use of will, however, takes one *out* of synchrony and tends to encourage its further use in an increasingly self-defeating effort to re-establish synchrony. This use of will power in normal, routine activities is diagnostic of a schizoid condition: "When the will becomes the primary mechanism of action, displacing the normal motivating force of pleasure, the individual is functioning in a schizoid manner." (Lowen) Since in our society this tendency is the rule rather than the exception, it becomes reasonable to speak of it as a schizoid society.

The futile effort to achieve synchrony is to some extent responsible for our efforts to "live by the clock." Unfortunately, we are out of phase with the rest of the ecological system—not because we are too slow, but because we are too fast, which is why efforts to "catch up" are self-defeating.

Living by the clock is, for all its absurdity, a genuine effort to maintain connectedness. What it overlooks is that connectedness between organisms and between organism and environment already exists. This is a characteristic schizoid maneuver: to lose awareness of a real connection and attempt desperately to construct a conceptual one to replace it. Thus mechanical clocks take the place of biological clocks. Thus the schizoid character cannot understand how his body can keep working all by itself, without his willing it. And thus the politician believes that no social change will occur without legislation.

Freud once said that civilization is a process of exchanging joy for security, and Lowen seems to be making the same point when he contrasts the primitive sense of unity with the linear cause-effect thinking of Western peoples. The latter view provides security against the vicissitudes of experience, Lowen argues, but at the expense of a feeling of harmony with nature and body. But cultural patterns that exaggerate will and ego controls go far beyond the effects of citification in creating the kinds of problems we now face.

Lowen sees the evolution of the human ego as following the typical course of the heroic leader brought in to protect the people, who then usurps power and becomes a tyrant. He points out that while the alleged function of the ego is to *test* reality, in actuality it is largely engaged in *dictating* reality. "The ego creates the discontinuities which it then attempts to bridge with knowledge and words." Life becomes an exercise in power, control, and self-deception instead of a pleasurable interplay of interdependent organisms. While ideally the ego is held in check—bodily sensation balancing ego imagery, feelings balancing ideas, pleasure needs balancing power needs, and so on—these checks and balances collapse in a "culture which values knowledge above feeling, power above pleasure, and the mind above the body."

The evolution of culture parallels this process. Among lower animals culture is limited to a small amount of acquired and transmitted knowledge about poisons, and so on, and some patterning of learned relationships. At this level culture merely mediates between the organism and reality in a useful way. But at the human level, culture, like the ego, assumes the function of defining and dictating reality so that delusions can be widely shared.

Culture also tends to reinforce the tyrannical proclivities of the ego through surplus negative feedback. Nature responds to exploratory behavior in a neutral manner: correct motions yield success, incorrect ones yield failure. Failure, in other words, is its own punishment. The exploring individual is not subjected to any additional punishment for her incorrect behavior.

Cultures, however, are not so kind. An individual who makes a cultural blunder, a social error, is shamed, humiliated, frightened, or made to feel guilty. The reason for this is obvious: since cultural knowledge has no intrinsic validity it cannot rest on intrinsic reward and punishment. Cultural laws are arbitrary and must, therefore, be reinforced by surplus negative feedback to ensure learning. No one needs to be ridiculed or humiliated in order to learn the futility of trying to start a fire with wet leaves or use a piece of loose shale as a tool. Such errors are self-punishing through failure—an error in etiquette is not.

The effect of punishing an individual for making an error is obviously to discourage exploratory behavior and to reward conceptualization. Conceptualization is a kind of security mechanism —a device for anticipating outcomes and reducing risks. This, in turn, facilitates the emergence of the kind of automatically self-validating conceptual systems of which Lowen speaks.

Technological Culture

Still another threshold is crossed when the schizoid processes described above are combined with an ability to give concrete form to one's conceptual imagery—permitting, in Laing's terms, the organization of a false-self system around a material reality. The development of an unembodied inner self is greatly facilitated by the presence of an externally embodied false self.

There is much confusion about this issue in contemporary thought. The United States, for example, is described as a "materialistic" culture, apparently because it is deluged with material artifacts. Yet there has probably never been a people with less emotion invested in specific material possessions. Americans as a rule are Platonists when it comes to possessions—it is the *idea* or *form* of a house, car, chair, or bowl to which they are attached rather than the specific object. One has only to observe the care, devotion, and human meaning invested in some possessions by people in less "developed" societies to realize just how shallow our supposed materialism really is. In part, of course, this is simply a matter of numbers. The maternal instinct in animals is an inverse function of litter size, and, similarly, one cannot be as intensely involved with a hundred objects as with two or three. Equally important, however, is our utilitarian orientation to objects, and their replaceability. Mass production is based upon, and in turn encourages, a conceptual attitude toward objects. It is more difficult to particularize and love a house, shirt, or car that is virtually identical with many others and will be abandoned for a replacement before long. The value we attach to possessions tends to be based on quantitative criteria (money, status) which reduce all differences to a single standard. This in turn facilitates an attitude in which objects have no independent reality but are merely manifestations of our own conceptual processes.

The self, says Laing, "seeks by being unembodied to transcend the world and hence to be safe. But a self is liable to develop which feels it is outside all experience and activity. It becomes a vacuum. Everything is there, outside; nothing is here, inside." But what if the only part of the external world in which the self participates consists of embodied fantasy images? Will not the same vacuum occur? Since one is continually breathing one's own exhaust the same impoverishment must result, although, since the person appears to be fully engaged with his environment, the illusion of normality can be somewhat more easily maintained.

Laing says that in the schizoid condition, "the self can relate itself with immediacy to an object which is an object of its own imagination or memory but not to a real person." This provides an illusory sense of freedom, since one cannot be hurt by an image; but of course one cannot be gratified either. "The self's relationship to the other is always at one remove." But insofar as technology has provided us with highly tangible images that predefine most of our relationships we are all living in the schizoid condition, since it is virtually impossible to experience an adult relationship that has not been previewed and rehearsed in the media. The media mediate our interpersonal encounters. Furthermore, what communications technology does symbolically, other technologies do in actuality. Laing points out that in the non-schizoid person only a certain number of his or her actions are mechanical. But Western culture has progressively expanded this mechanical domain to the point where average citizens of a technological society can feel, in schizoid fashion, that they are being lived *by* their mechanical actions rather than the reverse. They eat, sleep, awaken, work, and stop work when mechanical contrivances tell them it is time to do so. They even eat laxative foods to keep their eliminative processes "on schedule." And should all this become so painful to them that they seek psychiatric assistance, they will find that even their therapeutic encounters are occasioned, not by the intensity of their distress, nor by their readiness to confront their problems and work, but according to a mechanically preset schedule.

Technological culture, in other words, helps generate a false-self system even in the absence of individual pathology. The same search for security and freedom that motivates the schizoid character in Laing's analysis has produced in modern culture the same kind of personal autarchy, the same internal atrophy, the same robot-like behavior, the same feelings of inner deadness, falseness, and unreality. There is the same longing for intimacy, experience, stimulation, life, and the same fear that any genuine feelingful encounter would implode the personality. David Bakan observes that "much of the contemporary hunger for meaningfulness is based on the monotonousness of what the ego will allow and the deep but unacknowledged fear of what is not acknowledged."

This ambivalent urge to make contact with reality is reflected in the attempts of the media to borrow reality from dramatic events. Laing's description of one of his patients could be applied with very little strain to network television: "If anyone said anything to her which she classified as 'real,' she would say to herself, 'I'll think that'; and she would keep repeating the word or phrase over and over again to herself in the hope that some of the realness of the expression would rub off on her."

The failure of all these devices is as visible in the rigidification and disintegration of our own society as it is in the frankly psychotic individual. "The tragic irony is that even finally no anxiety is avoided"—for technology has created worse dangers than those it has removed. "In the escape from the risk of being killed, [the self] becomes dead"—our society sees threat as coming from without, yet is in danger of being destroyed by its own defensive system. In a technological society everyone "is related primarily to objects of [their] own fantasies."

If the dynamic that Laing describes can be applied to technological culture, we may expect the following developments:

(1) The technological system will become more extensive and autonomous;

(2) Those enmeshed in it will be "charged with hatred in [their] envy of the rich, vivid, abundant life which is always elsewhere; always there, never here";

(3) Since, however, this life is too frightening to be grasped, and the longing for it too acute to be denied, they will attempt "to destroy the world by reducing it to dust and ashes, without assimilating it";

(4) Reality will be courted by sadistic and masochistic means —proving one's reality by the distressful effects one is able to produce in others (I bomb, therefore I am) or by subjecting oneself to pain and terrifying risks.

In the individual this process culminates in a psychotic explosion, which Laing sees as a revolution in the mind—the dissolution of a decayed structure into the ocean of boundless possibility. Sometimes a new, richer, and more flexible structure emerges from the plunge; sometimes the individual drowns. So, too, Western culture may undergo chaos, confusion, and cataclysm before a new and viable system emerges, if, indeed, it emerges at all.

Only those fascinated with *Gotterdammerung* fantasies would actively seek such an outcome, which might well reduce Spaceship Earth to a wandering cinder. While there is still time to change, it seems absurd not to try. And if it turns out we must die as a species, we will at least have a better idea why.

We know that by detaching ourselves from the rest of the organic system of which we are a part and retreating within our technologically-insulated schizoid security turret we have "beaten" nature, much the way our teeth defeat us when they bite our tongue. Whether a species could ever evolve with a knowledge of *things* (as opposed to an understanding of *relationships*) equal to ours without following the same course is uncertain. In any case this line of "progress" has reached a dead end—the most sophisticated thinkers in all fields are busy trying to mimic the relational thought processes of primitive peoples. We must simply accept the proneness to schizoid ideation that is part of the human condition and try to isolate those patterns that engender the kind of full-blown pathological eruption in which we now live.

We can look back on our own childhood or youth and say, "I was sick in such-and-such a year and almost died." But a social illness may span many lifetimes, even in its acute phase, and hence cannot be distinguished from normality by those who live in it, for it is all they know. This makes our task more difficult, but also more necessary, lest we adapt still further to the pathology in which we find ourselves.

Parable 3

A man went crazy and started running down the street,
claiming that people were pursuing him, trying to kill him.
The bystanders were mightily impressed by his energy and
speed. "How is it you are able to run so fast?" they asked.
"I am running for my life, you fools!" he gasped. His terror
spread panic among the bystanders and all began
to run. More and more people joined the swelling group
of runners, half in admiration, half in fear, until it had become
an enormous crowd that ultimately poured over a cliff
into the sea.

THE UGLY SWAN
or
CURBING THE PROPHET MOTIVE

Exterminate the sage, discard the wise,
And the people will benefit a hundredfold;
Exterminate benevolence, discard rectitude,
And the people will again be filial;
Exterminate ingenuity, discard profit,
And there will be no more thieves and bandits.

Lao Tzu

It is only those who are not working in the
fields who have time to wonder about
grain. It is they, too, who have no right to
do so, for they have not tasted it, nor
are they working towards the production
of flour for the people.

Idries Shah

There is a cybernetic law that states that the more probable a message is, the less information it provides. The information contained in a message, for example, decreases with its repetition. This creates a curious dilemma for any group: the longer its members are together, the less they have to say to each other—at least about the group's own relational structure. Since the circuitry of the group is known to everyone, the information value of what is being communicated is going downhill all the time. The more effectively a group communicates about itself and its constituents, the more quickly it will stagnate in the absence of inputs from outside.

Even *with* outside inputs information will tend to decrease, since the structure itself acts as a filter for screening out jarring information which it interprets as noise. Only stimuli that affect the group's circuitry are at issue here—those that affect relationships within the group.

Those participants most central to the group—those most invested in the structure (most "influential," therefore)—must protect it from such disturbing stimuli. They are like sense organs for the group—letting in what will help preserve it, but keeping out (for our senses keep out far more than they let in) anything that challenges its circuitry. If they fail to do this, the group will lose its integrity. If they succeed, it may stagnate or become oppressive.

A system, in other words, needs occasionally to achieve a perception of the universe, including itself, through eyes other than its own, since its sense organs are designed to exclude most information from awareness. The only way to achieve this is to extrude a bit of circuitry which will evolve a perceptual apparatus different from the parent circuit and hence inhale a different vision. But at this point the parent circuit can no longer "understand" the extruded segment except with reference to residual similarities between the segment's present and original circuitries. In other words, the more information the segment acquires the less able the parent circuit will be to absorb it. The process must therefore be repeated. A prophet is extruded into the desert, obtains a vision, and returns. He is then either rejected or his vision absorbed and a new circuitry evolved in the parent system. A new prophet is extruded, and so on. Clumsily the parent system hunches along, like an inchworm, on the information provided by its extruded members—toward an ever-receding and unattainable goal of total, perfect, and conscious circuitry.

What the prophet sees in his vision is of trivial significance—it is *how* he sees that is important. He is not merely a scout exploring unknown territory, he is the territory—not the experimenter but the experiment. What he innovates is his own internal structure. Most of these innovations, like most mutations, turn out to be pointless and grotesque: The prophet returns from the wilderness with seven toes on each foot and a ring in his nose, proclaiming that life is a waterfall. He is scorned and discarded, for prophets are highly expendable.

The path to joy leads
through despair.

List Of Cans For Sister Marcia
Moleskin
Bandaid
Spice
6 oz. Juice cans
Ringless soup cans
Charcoal starter
Talcum
Tea
Ham cans
Meat cans(treet,spam etc.
Flat oval sardine cans
Religious statues.

But occasionally the prophet actually evolves an inner circuitry that would confer a boon on the parent circuit if it were reintegrated with it. At this point a dilemma arises: How can a system absorb an external modification which came into being through a procedure premised on the system's inability to tolerate such a modification? It is a little like the socially ambitious parents who send their child to an elitist school so that the child will evolve a life-style uncorrupted by their own crudities. They want the child to be "better" than they are, but when the child returns they are dismayed and say, "Who are you? I can't relate to you. How can you snub your own parents who gave you everything?" Parent and child will be able to maintain a close bond only to the degree that the child's attempted metamorphosis was unsuccessful.

In the case of the social climber, the problem can be handled to some extent by compartmentalization: The child can maintain two identities, one for the parents and one for the rest of the world. So long as the two worlds never come into contact, everyone will be spared embarrassment and conflict. But in that case the parents will be unable to share in the child's life, and their own system will remain uninfluenced.

Or imagine that an organism needs, for survival, to alter the composition of its bloodstream. Since it is not possible to do this within the context of its own programming, it extrudes a small quantity of blood, which, freed from the constraints of the total organism, manages, with the aid of external influences, to achieve the desired change. The moment the changed blood is reintroduced, however, the entire organism will be mobilized to destroy the intruder utterly.

At the cultural level this dilemma is solved by an interesting mechanism. The extruded circuit is attacked and often destroyed, while its message—the *form* of its newly evolved circuitry—is absorbed and incorporated. In this way, the parent system is able to preserve intact its boundary-maintaining and sensory-screening apparatus while it alters its internal circuitry. This is why the first step in the acceptance of a totally alien idea is to attack it, to show all the reasons why it is wrong, illogical, inappropriate— that is, in conflict with existing circuitry. If the attack is at all intelligent, in the sense that the idea is accurately shown to be non-derivable from accepted premises, then the idea has in fact become part of the culture, albeit an unabsorbed part. All that remains is to simplify the circuitry of the culture by modifying its premises—that is, by developing a higher synthesis that embraces the new idea (this is usually called co-optation). The circuitry of the idea itself has already been taken in, although with a minus sign attached to each node that connects to the old circuitry.

This is why the "truth squad" approach to propaganda is so self-defeating. To attack an idea tellingly is to understand it and internalize it. An irrelevant and stupid attack is effective as long as it can be sustained, but is vulnerable to counterattack, thus provoking the attacker to a more telling follow-up. The only way to resist an alien idea is to ignore it.

Weston La Barre suggests that psychotics are potential culture heroes who have not been successful in communicating with their peers. Successful communication, however, is no guarantee against incarceration or destruction. A prophet is simply a tool of the larger system and what happens to his personal being is of no importance. Success and failure are terms that only have meaning in relation to the message he carries. He may survive the attack on him and be honored in his own time, if not in his own country. What is honored, however, is (like what is attacked) his status as carrier of the message, not his own personality. The visible personality of the prophet, even in the absence of public relations specialists, is an artificial construct—a creation of the recipients of the message in co-operation with the prophet himself in the fulfillment of his role. This is why all public figures and famous personages seem so much alike. Furthermore, the half-dozen character types available for adoption by the famous are, although stereotypical, powerful in their impact upon the inner person when reinforced by constant interaction with others. It is extremely difficult to protect the private inner person from complete absorption by the stereotypic public personality. Those who succeed are able to do so only by rigorously avoiding interaction with strangers—that is, with those who know them as prophets. They must instead surround themselves with people who "knew them when"—that is, as persons rather than message carriers. Even this is difficult, for they are likely to find themselves playing out the role of shy, modest, and still-humble prophet—even in the privacy of their own homes. And while friends and relatives may be able to reinforce the private person by behaving as if the public one did not exist, this will require the prophet to renounce the needs for respect and esteem that led him to accept induction into the prophet role in the first place. Most prophets are strangers, seeking either in a strange land, or by returning with a visibly transformed personality, to achieve the respect they were denied in the first place by their community. Their need for respect not only makes them vulnerable to induction but also makes them susceptible to the belief that the new circuitry they evolved while in the state of extrusion was a conscious and deliberate act of personal creation on their part.

This individualistic delusion arises in part from the circumstances surrounding the prophet's extrusion and in part from those associated with his return. The prophet always returns as a stranger. Often his return is indirect, in the sense that he goes to another country. If his message is accepted there, it will later reach, by diffusion or conquest, the circuit from which he was extruded. "A prophet is not without honour, save in his own country . . ." That is to say, the parent circuit is often the last to know that its effort to transcend itself has been successful.

Should the prophet return directly to the parent system he must be conspicuously changed. Otherwise his former associates will recognize and relate to him in the old way ("It's just old Henry being silly"). His first task as message carrier is to convince everyone that something significant has happened to him—that he is not the same person. It is easy to see, then, why the prophet has such a hard time retaining any sense of personal integrity and continuity apart from his role as message carrier. His existence as a person is so fragile, so dependent upon the response of those around him, that he is sorely tempted to comfort himself with the delusion that he is self-made.

Most of the narcissism of the prophet, however, comes from the conditions surrounding his extrusion. If the extruded segment is to be in a position to evolve new circuitry, it must be cut off in some way from the parent circuit and assigned a degree of autonomy and independence. This is facilitated if the prophet is poorly connected in the first place, as is usually the case. The prophet is expected, at the time of his extrusion, to withdraw his emotional investment from all his relationships and invest it instead in the map of that circuitry that he carries within himself. Gestaltists refer to this process as "taking back one's projections."

Freud once said that the individual ego was merely a precipitate of past relationships; the Gestaltists argue the reverse—that an individual's relationships are merely a stage on which her internal conflicts are acted out. The parent circuitry, when it extrudes a prophet, adopts the Gestalt viewpoint. The prophet is expected to dissolve as many complementarities as possible and rediscover all that variety within. This is not outlandish, for the potentiality for all human traits is within everyone. Every human being knows all the roles that exist in any human drama and can play them, once her revulsion is overcome. In this respect the Gestaltists are utterly correct.

The prophet, then, is forced to cease and desist from allowing other persons to play out aspects of himself. He must develop autonomy, totipotentiality, self-sufficiency—and will inevitably do so to some extent merely by virtue of his extrusion. This creates a strong likelihood that new patterns will evolve—just as a colony that must survive on its own without help from the mother country is likely to evolve a somewhat variant culture.

An unfortunate result of all this is that the prophet comes to imagine that his extrusion was his own doing, and that the new circuitry evolved during his isolation (exile, vigil, peak experience, or whatever) was a personal achievement instead of an almost inevitable result of the situation in which he was placed. This is a natural hazard of the process. The prophet is, after all, a throwaway. Most are flops. From such a miserable condition one must take what comforts are available, and these are unavoidably narcissistic and delusional.

This was harmless enough so long as each extruded segment remained in temporal and spatial isolation. A serious problem emerged, however, when humans began to record their history, thus allowing a culture of prophets to emerge. Not only did this teach future extruded segments how to behave (a useful feature on the whole), but it also made available to them the comforting fantasy that they were not expendable castoffs, but chosen heroes. Once this vision of the prophet became widely broadcast, what was originally a mere analgesic became a way of life, and people began actually to seek out the once-shunned role.

What we see around us now is a social system whose highest priority is given over to the manufacture of mutations. This is essentially what the concept of individualism is all about—the elevation of the peripheral instance to a position of centrality. For the past two centuries Western culture has been moving rapidly toward a system in which every single individual would be socialized to be a heroic castoff—a prophet-mutation for a core system which would thereby have ceased to exist. Like the mechanism of will, discussed in the last chapter, this everyone-a-mutation pattern is an emergency function run amok. It is one thing for a system to throw off a few oddments from time to time as a hedge against the unexpected—a recognition that the circuitry it has evolved, while viable and elegant, is limited and vulnerable to changing conditions. It is quite different for a system to treat the unexpected as an inevitable commonplace and throw off its entire circuitry fragment by fragment. This is a self-perpetuating disease, since the system that continually fragments and expends itself can scarcely claim a workable core. The more castoffs it extrudes the more prophets it can reasonably claim to need, until it reaches total dissolution.

Heroizing the castoff role in our society has reached a point close to this. It is no longer merely the deviant who is socialized to disregard his connectedness with others. Even the ordinary pillars of the community are trained to think for themselves in every conceivable sense of that phrase. If it were only a matter of our being afflicted with thousands of third-rate artists of various kinds, each imagining himself to be the founder of a new creative dynasty, we could survive the influx. The civilized world has never lacked for pomposity. But the spread of the heroic mutation principle has also helped to give us the kind of scientists and physicians we have.

Americans are trained from infancy for mutationhood. They are taught to ignore their connectedness with others and to imagine that whatever successes or failures they experience in life are a function of their own dissociated agency. They are taught to destroy continuity, to adapt mechanically and slavishly to change, and to regard relationships as having no meaning apart from the achievement of instrumental goals. This has produced certain gains: There has never been a people or species better equipped to survive and adjust to some cataclysmic change in the environment. On the other hand, there is a certain futility in living one's entire life around anticipated disaster. It tempts one to produce a disaster just to give the whole thing meaning. Furthermore, readiness for change tends to create change, and our preparedness has led us into a condition in which as a people we are under chronic severe stress from perpetual novelty, as Toffler has shown. Our capacity to deal with this distress, meanwhile, is sapped by our ideology, which tells us that change is necessary and good. A politician who stood up and argued that change of any kind (backward or forward) was usually pernicious would achieve a reputational ranking in our society somewhat below Adolf Hitler. Finally, since changes occur at different rates and since they occur at such a speed that one process is not completed before another begins, the experience of equilibration and integration is now virtually unknown. The proliferation of disharmony is self-generating.

As a result of their socialization, Americans as a group are addicted to the romantic image of the lonely castoff hero who forges his (it is largely a male image) own destiny and changes the parent circuit by his own unique efforts. Children are indoctrinated with this idea early in life by means of fairy tales in which the rejected youth triumphs over the rejecting group; their later childhood years are filled with biographies, both real and fictional, of lonely or scorned adults who achieve pre-eminence through creative achievements. All of these tales indoctrinate the child with the notion that these "successes" were attributable *solely* to individual art and *in spite of* the group in which the individual was embedded. The fact that in reality the individual can achieve nothing without a social context is lost to vision amid the glories of egoistic triumph.

The fantasy of individualistic detachment leads many people to confuse living in organic relation to others with being imprisoned in some sort of authoritarian system. If one begins with the illusion of autonomy all forms of connectedness seem alike, and equally oppressive. Western culture has for two centuries been engaged in a very gradual shift, institution by institution, and with many relapses, from authoritarian to "democratic" modes of organization. This shift has been a pervasive image in Western minds for so long that it is very difficult for us to view social change in ways uncolored by that process. Yet it is, after all, only a brief episode in human cultural history, and must be placed in context. The implication that authoritarianism is an ancient or primeval form of social organization is quite simply false. Authoritarianism as a social form has not even completed the process of diffusing itself throughout the world, even while it is being supplanted in the most urbanized parts of Western society. Western peoples, particularly Americans, have been caught up in the democratization drama for so long that they tend to view the entire past as one long homogeneous era of authoritarianism. Toffler, for example, talks about life in simple communities as "tightly regimented" and restrictive. But this "imprisonment of the past" that seems to dismay him so greatly is not characteristic of the simple community but of the authoritarian forms that overwhelmed, absorbed, and superseded it. The bulk of human history has been taken up with *increasing* individual powerlessness in human societies rather than decreasing it. This is not to say that the more recent push toward democratization (confused and ambivalent as it is) is in any way a return to an ancient form. Mass democracy and the simple community both bear more resemblance to authoritarianism than they do to each other.

The organic social form of the simple community gives way to authoritarianism with increasing size and complexity. The simple community is not centralized and communication is both intense and evenly distributed. (Leaders, after all, are only necessary when a group is too large or too new to act organically.) Much of the collective behavior of the community appears to the outsider as spontaneous, unplanned, almost organismic—as if communication were extrasensory. In fact it is simply automatic —things are "understood," and collective needs are experienced with the intensity that we experience personal ones.

The delicate multiple attunement of such a community cannot altogether survive fusion with an alien tribe. The wars of small tribes usually involve a lot of scuffling, very little killing, and few territorial changes. But when, with large-scale disruptions and movements of peoples, groups engage in conquest and absorption of other groups, we begin to find (a) centralization of power and communication, and (b) hierarchy. That is to say, there comes into being a chief or king, and nobles and commoners.

William Stephens discusses this transition in a cross-cultural analysis of family patterns, finding the most authoritarian forms at an intermediate level of cultural sophistication, with "democratic" patterns at both extremes. He calls the authoritarian form a *kingdom,* defined as having a centralized organ of political control with coercive armed power, a single hereditary ruler, at least two social classes, and economic exploitation. By contrast the *tribe* (equivalent to the simple community) has no centralized power, no chiefs or nobles, no exploitation, no cities, no civilization. Stephens suggests that the authoritarian formula was invented to enable conquering groups to maintain control of a subjugated people and its territory. He finds that son-to-father deference and wife-to-husband deference is low in tribes, high in kingdoms, and low again when the kingdom evolves into a democratic state, and he argues that these authoritarian family forms are simply a by-product of the authoritarian state.

Authoritarianism, however, is an awkward and rigid social form. In times of rapid change it tends either to ossify and shatter or to dissolve into democratic forms that have more flexibility. This is in no way a return to simplicity or to greater organicity. On the contrary, democratization usually carries further the process of disconnection that authoritarianism began—the conversion of organic units into masses of unrelated atoms.

These three stages are in fact an illustration of the prophet dynamic—the idea that change occurs in living systems by the extrusion of particles that are reingested when they have evolved new circuitry. The movement from the simple community to mass democracy is neither a straight line nor a mere oscillation. It is a pulsating movement in which change is brought about by an initial concentration and a subsequent diffusion. Relatively innocuous microorganisms, isolated in a biological warfare laboratory, can be mutated into virulent strains that will, when reintroduced into human organisms, spread rapidly and destroy them. In such a case the microorganism—originally a comfortable parasite—is the prophet, the laboratory the desert, the message death. In the case of the transition from simple community to mass democracy, the prophet is the chief or king, the desert is authoritarianism, and the messages are linearity, individuation, and inhibition.

The simple community is not held together by principle. This is not to say that categories do not exist: Kinship categories are probably of great importance, even allowing for the inherent bias of Western ethnographers trained to assume that all people relate to one another in terms of the categories to which they belong. But kinship categories are bounded and static—they do not lead very far in the direction of more abstract generalization. While they do tend to blunt organicity to some extent, they also form a barrier against the emergence of other kinds of mechanistic order.

In any case, the individual holds a fixed position in the community, one which alters only gradually and very predictably through the life cycle. She is defined by her relationships—if we attempted to examine her in isolation, tabulating individual attributes on IBM cards, we would learn very little about her that would predict her behavior. She is a *part* of something to a much greater extent than a Westerner, for whom such a tabulation would tell us a great deal.

With the centralization of power this begins to change. Initially, power is fixed and hereditary, but the more power the king or chief holds the more dynamic the power variable tends to become. Initially viewed as a representation of powerful environmental forces, kings are hedged about with constraints and restrictions. But over time, by virtue of the power concentrated in them, their individual preferences, whims, and needs weaken and erode the fixed and hereditary limitations. As Henry V says, "Nice customs courtesy to great kings." Modernism begins with despotism.

Kings, then, are the first individualists. They are encouraged, as their power increases, to develop narcissistic and noninterdependent attitudes. They are the prophets of individualism. The people, cut adrift from their social moorings by the collision of alien cultures and increasing size and complexity, have formed an unstated contract with the ruler: He will create an order, they will accord him deference; he will gratify their dependency needs, they will gratify his narcissism. In the simple community both of these needs are almost automatically gratified: Everyone has a place, is embedded in nourishing relationships, perceives order and meaning, and is relatively unselfconscious. Interdependency *exists*, so dependency is highly muted. Narcissism is almost irrelevant since no one views herself as an isolated entity, but only as part of a whole. Authoritarianism restores to the uprooted a facsimile of wholeness and belonging. Dependency needs are now gratified while narcissistic needs remain irrelevant. But for the king this is less true. He is made aware of his separateness and uniqueness, and hence must be flattered and petted to compensate him for his isolation.

This is a gradual process. The court of the ruler is a laboratory or desert in which individualism may take centuries to evolve. When it does the stage is set for the next development—the diffusion of individualism to the masses. This is the process we call democratization. It is often accompanied by an attack on the prophet (king) according to the mechanism described earlier. The king is dethroned, but his narcissism is devoured and absorbed by all the people. The contented social indifference of a Nicholas and Alexandra becomes the cozy callousness of the entire middle class. This is the process that Freud's myth of the primal horde attempted to portray.

The process is the same for linearity. The king, isolated in the laboratory of centralized power, learns to pursue a concept in an unbounded "logical" fashion—to ignore feedback. This, too, is internalized by the masses during the democratization or diffusion phase. Technological culture is simply the internalization of tyranny by the masses. Relationships *within* such a society take on the same chaotic, competitive form that previously characterized relations *between* warring kingdoms.

Finally, authoritarianism is the first step in the development of internalized inhibition of impulse and feeling—the capacity to postpone gratification in the service of narcissistic goals. Stephens observes that kingdoms have more sharply segregated sex roles, and suggests that they are generally more inhibited and restrained than tribes. He cites Rattray Taylor's discussion of the "patrist" syndrome: sexual restrictions, derogation of women, political authoritarianism, fear of spontaneity and pleasure, and so on. Other studies confirm this association between authoritarianism, patriarchy, and sexual repressiveness, when simple communities are compared with kingdoms, although it is not at all clear that sexual constraints diminish immediately in response to democratization. In any case, the inhibition that takes place in kingdoms is external and coercive. The king may be forced by his responsibilities and position to become a specialist in inhibition and gratification postponement (a "bad" ruler is one who fails too conspicuously to do this—he is usually replaced, at least

de facto, by someone who can—a prime minister or usurper).
But the individual citizen is not expected to restrain her *own*
impulses in the absence of outside pressure.

We have for two centuries or so been in the second phase
of this process, in which the mass attacks the prophet and devours
his message. The mass throws off the force and inhibits itself.
The entire population begins to exhibit an ethic of control,
achievement, and inhibition. Max Weber describes how the kind
of asceticism originally consigned to monastic specialists (another
group of prophets) was later diffused through the population during the Reformation, and the diffusion of achievement motivation
seems to have taken the same form.

One can also see this process at work in the diffusion of earnest-
ness and pomposity. Kings and queens used to play children's
games when at leisure. During the nineteenth century this disappeared altogether. By now, as a result of Little Leagues, educational toys, and other forms of adult invasion of the world of
children, the children themselves can scarcely play games. I have
often been struck by the relative inability of college students (in
comparison with their elders) to respond to the invitation to engage in pretending or ritualized play of any kind.

Two points need to be made about this dynamic before leaving the topic of authoritarianism. First, I want to underline the
fact that all three of these trends—individualism, linearity, and
inhibition—are only partially present under authoritarianism. The
most important characteristic of authoritarianism is its compartmentalism. One mode of behavior operates in the court, another
in the villages. This is another way of saying that in a stable
authoritarian system the simple community remains largely intact
all around the edges of the society. Generalizations about the
social forms of kingdoms tend in actuality to be about the court
and the noble class. The culture of the commoners often remains
essentially unchanged. From the point of view of the masses the
court really *is* an extruded segment—one that may impinge dis-
astrously upon individuals from time to time but does not immediately affect their culture. True, unbearable taxation, passing
armies, or widespread conscription may eventually erode or completely obliterate the organicity of villages, leading to dislocation,
wandering, banditry, and urbanization, but by and large the dis-

appearance of the simple community occurs with democratization—with the diffusion of the prophet-king's message.

The second point has to do with our tendency to confuse the organic connectedness of the simple community with the coerciveness of authoritarianism. We have so little experience of prolonged and stable group life that we tend to imagine any intensification of relationship as if it involved being fettered and manipulated. But there is a difference between being a leaf on a tree and a pawn on a chessboard. Being a non-autonomous part of a whole in no way requires being subject to an alien individual's conscious will. Authoritarianism arises when the whole no longer functions spontaneously and intuitively as a unit. Despots and edicts emerge as substitutes, *faute de mieux*. In an organic group no will is necessary to cement the group. But that degree of collective attunement requires long periods of stable relatedness unimpinged upon by outside forces—it is a delicate balance that could not exist in our own society. Hence we have difficulty in conceiving of any intense collectivity not dominated by some form of conscious will—a despot or oligarchy.

But the major flaw in this perception is that it looks at relatedness unilaterally. Americans see "freedom" as the absence of being influenced or controlled, *but it is also the loss of influence and control over others.* The condition that Toffler slanders as "regimented" is simply one in which people are highly responsive to one another. One is more subject to the demands of others (an American nightmare) but one can also count on others being there to meet one's own demands. Individualism is a shell game that distracts us from the rigors of mutuality—from the fact that in a society in which I am powerless to affect you, you are also powerless to affect me. The powerlessness endemic in modern society is produced by the simple device of disconnecting us.

One reason Americans are so prone to fall for this shell game is that they tend to place value on themselves only as *actors,* not as *responders* or *feelers.* (I suspect this is less true of women than of men, wherein lies some hope for the future.) If I only attach importance to what I and others *do,* and not what we *feel,* then close relationships will seem dangerous, since they will seem to impede my action, while their potential for satisfying my needs and desires is less salient in my consciousness.

Specialization and the Household Prophets

The division of labor in society is based upon the odd assumption that the efficiency of the part is more important than the efficiency of the whole. The history of human culture has included an increasingly vigorous commitment to this point of view, despite the considerable cost in human pleasure. Toffler, for example, touts the advantages of "modular" or segmented relationships, to which each individual commits only a fragment of her personal involvement. He points out, quite correctly, that "freedom" and fragmentation go together and chastises modern social critics for not recognizing this. Since freedom, like motherhood and apple pie, is an unquestioned good in American society, he feels he has disposed of the issue. But partial involvement means partial fulfillment: A person who is never more than fragmentarily in the here-and-now is only minimally alive.

Activities that are shared on an undifferentiated basis (everyone doing the same thing together) are more enjoyable but take longer than tasks that are parceled out on a differentiated basis. The time that is saved is meaningful only if the activity is unpleasant, but insofar as it is done collectively it usually is not. Furthermore the efficiency gained by each person acquiring skill at his or her differentiated task is often dissipated through the ravages of boredom, and usually lost in any case through the problems of co-ordinating the differentiated tasks. In our modern sophistication we are supposed to know this—to know that communication and co-ordination are far more important than mere mechanical exactitude in some functioning part. We are also supposed to know that compartmentalization is destructive of the integrity of the person, who cannot be altogether squeezed into some limited function. Yet these apparently obvious truths have had very little impact on the progressive "modularization" of social organization in the West.

Why is this so? How did competence at part tasks come to be valued more highly than co-ordination and integration of the whole? The notion that anything beyond short-range and narrow-gauge efficiency can be achieved in this way is a patent absurdity. Are we then to assume that humanity is simply idiotic?

And what of nature itself? Are we to assume that the blind forces that produced plant and animal organisms are also misguided? Such an assumption—that nature could systematically and consistently err—would throw all knowledge into chaos, and while the possibility is not to be utterly excluded, it would be frivolous to embrace it without exhausting less horrendous alternatives.

One obvious difficulty is that we are using integration as the ultimate criterion, thus implying that an integrated organism is absolutely more viable than one that is not. But we saw at the beginning of this chapter that integration contains its own dilemmas. The division of labor is useful not because (as some social theorists have implied) it leads to integration but precisely because it does not. The communicational difficulties it creates provide opportunity for change and movement.

The usual metaphor for specialization of function is the finely-articulated machine in which everything goes "like clockwork," but this is misleading. The value of the division of labor is that it introduces a bit of chaos into the system. A part that has a specialized function has achieved an autonomy of meaning. This is usually obscured by the fact that physical autonomy is thereby lost. Physical autonomy depends on uniformity: If an organism composed of identical parts is broken up, the parts can survive because they are self-sufficient—each contains some of everything that was present in the whole. If, however, the organism is composed of differentiated parts, they will perish apart from the whole—this is what is meant by interdependence.

In what sense, then, does a differentiated part possess autonomy? I have called it an autonomy of meaning, and by this I intend something rather simple and obvious. Two identical parts, when separated, are independent of each other, but they experience the world (that is, it impinges upon them) in the same way. Two differentiated parts, while dependent upon each other for survival, have an entirely different experience of their environment. The hand does not encounter the world in the way the eye does. The receptors and categories of the one are not available to the other.

This issue is usually passed over by noting that the hand and eye can exist only in conjunction with the total organism, and that their differentiated information is co-ordinated at a higher level. What is overlooked is the fact that such higher level co-ordination is possible only by proceeding to a higher level of abstraction. That is to say, only that information is available to the brain which is translatable from one system to the other. *This means that the eye (or the hand) "knows" much that the brain cannot know because its language is too abstract.* The brain has a kind of international *lingua franca* which does not deign to concern itself with the trivialities of local dialects.

Now, as we have seen, an identical segment can change only if it is isolated from the whole and placed in an altered environment. A specialized segment, on the other hand, can change *without* separation from the whole. Its internal "language" creates slippage, disorder, a lack of full articulation with the total system, and the possibility of independent evolution within itself. The increasing chaotic quality of the system yields increasing flexibility. The system must work harder to maintain its integrity under these conditions, and this will take the form of attempting to extend the range of its abstract language system, or to restrict the independent movement of the subsystems.

Our conceptualization of the prophet dynamic must therefore be elaborated into three different forms. The first and simplest is that already described: A homogeneous system detaches an undifferentiated segment of itself; in an altered environment the segment evolves a new structure, and if this is of value to the parent system, it reincorporates the modified segment and thereby has its own structure modified.

The second form involves a differentiated system. Here a specialized segment is extruded, and the altered environment is unnecessary since the segment is already different from the totality. To survive, however, the specialized segment must complete itself—must evolve ways of meeting needs originally met by other specialized segments. If it should succeed in becoming whole, it will only partly resemble the parent system, since the articulation of the various segments will necessarily differ according to the special circumstances of its own history, its original specialization, the nature of its private language, the conditions of its self-generalization.

The third form is the division of labor itself, even when extrusion and reincorporation do not occur. Every segment of a differentiated system is in effect a prophet, but the desert is inside—a product of its linguistic diversity. In the division of labor each segment stands with its head in the void and its feet firmly planted in the parent system. The latter occasionally allows the kind of meta-information that would revise its circuiting to penetrate it, but this is rare. By and large, change is forced on the parent system by its efforts to maintain integrity in the face of the chaos generated by the evolution of its specialized components.

The division of labor, then, is a kind of compromise formation in which everyone is a prophet but the prophets are kept at home. In the undifferentiated system adaptive flexibility is sacrificed to integrity. That is to say, adaptation is made problematic while integrity is taken for granted. With the division of labor the reverse obtains: Adaptation is taken for granted and integrity becomes problematic.

It would be pleasant to say that what we are experiencing today is merely a state in which the division of labor has become highly elaborated at the expense of integrity, and that it is beginning to correct itself. But the problem is more complicated than this. In our system everyone is a prophet, but the prophets are not kept at home. That is to say, it is not merely the prophet *function* that has been generalized but also the prophet *mentality*. The division of labor minimizes the physical autonomy of prophets while maximizing their number. In our system number, physical autonomy and meaning autonomy are *all* maximized. It is as if, in the diffusion or democratization phase of the prophet dynamic, not only the message was incorporated but the process itself. What was sought was not the new circuitry evolved by each prophet, but his special status.

The Patriarchal Revolution

This state of affairs owes much to what might be called the patriarchal revolution: the emergence of a complex cultural system, exerting controlling power over a society, from the day-to-day operation of which women are largely excluded.

There are those who actually argue that the present (decaying) system of male dominance over women is "natural." Since it certainly is not universal among individuals, nor among human societies, nor among other species, such an assertion is patently ridiculous. One can find examples of almost anything in nature, and anyone who tries to bolster his position by pointing to the way baboons manage relations between the sexes must be prepared to listen to discussions of the praying mantis and black widow spider or, at the very least, the less sexist gibbon.

The fact is, there *is* no natural relation. Across individual couples, societies, and species a great variety of arrangements can be found, all of which have benefits and costs, and all of which fit comfortably into some larger pattern of functions. If I talk about a patriarchal revolution, then, this is not meant to imply that patriarchy as I have defined it is "unnatural"—only that it is, in the history of the species, a relatively recent phenomenon.

I also want to avoid any implication that the condition prior to this revolution was some sort of matriarchy. All social forms become fragile as they become extreme, and all exaggerated patriarchies have been plagued by a pervasive terror of feminine power. Through such eyes the relative sexual equality of a neighboring or conquered tribe tends to take on sinister overtones. The most educated guess we can make is that the typical primeval condition was one of rough equality. While some extremely "primitive" tribes today exclude women from much of the ritual life, real discrepancies in power require a rather high subsistence level. Finally, the term "revolution" is a bit misleading, implying a rapid transition of some kind. The revolving in this case was extremely gradual, occurring over a period of many centuries.

Patriarchy, which appears throughout the world in many forms, was a cultural invention of some importance, with obvious benefits and even more obvious drawbacks. Giving power to a group of specialists means that some needed traits will be heightened while others will atrophy.

The development of a high degree of specialization requires a certain amount of leisure. H. R. Hays points out that in very simple societies women show a great deal of creative energy, but that as soon as a society reaches the point where some function, such as pottery, can be given over to specialists, it is taken over by men. In other words, it is not that women in such societies are uncreative, but rather that they do not have the leisure to specialize. Men have taken over one field after another from women as soon as it became clear that status and prestige could be derived from superior specialized performance. We can see this in our own society, in which men have become chefs and obstetricians. Even without the time and energy and fame-hunger to make a full-time specialty of it, it is quite possible that the best cooks and potters in history were all women who died unknown and unrecognized outside of their families and neighbors. It is also quite possible that none of them felt any need for recognition from people with whom they had no personal connection, however much they may have felt disadvantaged and oppressed in their role as women. By and large it has been men who have felt driven to push any sort of skill into a specialized occupation from which glory could be extracted.

The patriarchal revolution did not "cause" specialization, but was a by-product of it. In the preservation of the species men play a less elemental role than women, and such peripherality tends to be a great advantage in social evolution. As has been suggested elsewhere it is the uncommitted who are in the best position to take advantage of changing conditions or cultural innovations. Being less tied to essential maintenance functions, men in some primitive societies had the leisure and uninvolvement to specialize, to invent, to create further leisure for themselves. The dominance that emerged in the patriarchal revolution was based on unimportance.

Indeed, women are now beginning to achieve power for the very same reason. Just as men became dominant because they were less committed to (and important in) the ongoing everyday functions of primitive life, so women today are less committed to and important in the mechanized culture that men have created. It is women who are in the best position to take up the reins in the more pleasure-prone, aesthetically absorbed, and love-oriented culture that lies ahead. Men may be ideologues of our future culture, but as a group they are too imbued with work and machismo ethics to enjoy anything very thoroughly. Furthermore, those that have attempted to make a career out of hedonism have divorced themselves from any kind of maintenance function and become parasitic. It is women who have best retained the primeval sense of balance, and who are best capable of combining an orientation toward love and pleasure with the optimal performance of necessary maintenance functions.

The particular form of specialization that men adopted is of interest because it reproduces the universal contract between those of differing social status. In relation to women, men have taken the stance assumed by the warrior-aristocrat toward the peasant: "If you will feed me, I will protect you." Before long, of course, every protection contract becomes a protection racket: "Give me what I want and I will protect you against me."

But it is with the results of the patriarchal revolution that we are primarily concerned here. If men were the prophets, what was the message? Men have evolved many bits of new circuitry, most notably the warrior ethos and industrial civilization. In both cases they achieved their innovations by the schizoid device of deadening themselves to their own feelings and substituting the emergency will mechanism for spontaneous bodily responsivity. The cultural contribution of male specialists was the detachment of libido from emotional relationships and bodily pleasure, and the investment of this libido in narcissistic pursuits, achievements, work, power, glory.

No social invention, unfortunately, is without its costs, despite our progress mythology. This male commitment to narcissistic pursuits was purchased at the price of a lowered capacity to tolerate pleasurable stimulation. Pleasure for males became increasingly a matter of tension release: loving, touching, caressing, all became heavily subordinated to an exaggerated emphasis on orgasm. By making a heavy investment in ego pursuits men became sensually crippled relative to women. Rather than attempting to redress this inferiority, however, or accepting it as an unfortunate price paid for their cultural ambitions, they have sought to cripple women as well. Their sexual inferiority was disturbing, not merely because of the reduction in their pleasure capacity, but because of the narcissistic wound formed by *any* sensed inferiority. The history of sexual mores has been one long series of ingenious efforts to reduce women to a condition in which this wound would not be experienced. From enforced chastity to the inculcation of bizarre beliefs about their own bodies to criticism of their inability to abbreviate their pleasure as much as men do, women have been led a most unmerry chase in the service of assuaging this self-inflicted wound to male vanity.

Changes in sexual mores are primarily changes in what is considered acceptable for *women* to do—variations in sexual restrictions on males are relatively miniscule. Sexual rules are by and large made by men and enforced on women, even though women have frequently shared in the enforcing, with the self-destructive enthusiasm characteristic of oppressed groups. But women often become mothers, and whatever cultural poisons they are forced to endure are passed on to their male offspring with talionic precision. The cultural impact of sexual restrictions, therefore, is multiple and cyclical.

But leaving aside these costs, there are others directly attached to the benefits themselves. The cultural innovations derived from male specialization in ego-aggrandizement and bleached-out rationalism exhibit the limitations of that specialization. Only a male-dominated culture, for example, could have invented the jackhammer, with its brutal assault on the senses, in order to save time digging a hole in the ground—an invention only needed in the first place because other males decreed that the earth should be covered with macadam and concrete, depriving the feet of texture, the world of life and color, and the air of oxygen. Men are fond of saying that women have emasculated the modern male, but this is mere projection. If modern man is emasculated, he managed it quite by himself through his own emotional self-castration and the resultant profusion of grotesque machines and mammoth organizations that have constantly diminished him while feeding his narcissistic dreams.

Male specialization in the exercise of will is facilitated by their freedom from the experience of childbirth. Bateson suggests that the alcoholic, when sober, suffers from the delusion that he is master of his fate, a psychic malady that is cured the moment he takes his first drink. Women are less vulnerable to such ecological innocence, since a woman who has experienced childbirth knows what it is like to have one's own body completely taken over by an internal force over which conscious will has no control. It is therefore of great importance that in the advanced stages of our cultural degradation men attempted to gain willful control over the childbirth process, seeing that it took place in impersonal and unemotional male-dominated environments, that the mothers were rendered insensible during the process so that the male obstetrician could "deliver" the baby—thus acting out a ritual pretense of conscious masculine will—and that the baby was instantly deprived of the kind of warm human tactile contact that would help it evolve into a sensitive, sensual, and responsive human being.

Furthermore, from the middle of the eighteenth century through World War II, male doctors and educators leveled a consistent attack on maternal behavior, appointing themselves rationalistic experts in a field that had been a feminine preserve for millions of years. The thrust of this attack was that touching, affection, warmth, cuddling, nursing, body contact, reassurance, protection, soothing, and the spontaneous exercise of bodily functions were all pernicious and should be suppressed as much as possible. A type of maternal behavior that had previously been the prerogative, *faute de mieux*, of the destitute, the indifferent, the sadistic, and the psychotic, was now enjoined on the entire population—even on the wealthy, affectionate, healthy, and well-disposed.

The culmination of this attack came toward the end of the last century, when doctors attempted to eliminate the use of the cradle and, indeed, to persuade mothers that holding or rocking a baby to sleep was "vicious" and "habit forming." For the sheltering, enclosed, and moving cradle was substituted the open, stationary, prisonlike crib. A decade or two later the behaviorists moved in to insist that any show of love or physical contact made the child too dependent. Infants were to be fed by the mechanical clock rather than by their own biological ones, and were generally regarded as little machines to be wound up properly and otherwise left alone. Maternal impulses to love and care for them were to be squelched manfully.

Civilized Western infants are still treated in a highly impersonal manner relative to those elsewhere in the world—born in hospitals, separated from their mothers at birth, given minimal body contact in their early years, weaned early, isolated a great deal, and so on. Fronted by the glamour of Western medicine, furthermore, these barbarities are rapidly being diffused to other cultures.

The future of all this is highly confusing. The schizoid circuitry of the male prophets is every day being diffused more and more widely. Women in Western societies are increasingly caught up in it, and for most men it simply represents normality. But at the same time a new process has begun, as *women* have become prophets evolving (at times) an antithetical system. These two streams are in utter collision at present, forming a cultural whirlpool from which almost any social phenomenon might conceivably emerge.

The Duckling Delusion

The exaggerated spirit of competitiveness spawned by the patriarchal revolution, and the increasing domination of childbirth and child rearing processes by males, has played some part in the evolution of a major mythical theme in our society—that of the ugly duckling. In this myth (Rudolph the Red-nosed Reindeer is one of dozens of examples) an individual, shunned by his fellows by virtue of some defect, demonstrates that the defect is actually a virtue and proves that his alienation from others is due to superiority rather than inferiority.

The function of the myth of the ugly duckling is to hide an ugly reality. The reality is that ugly ducklings usually turn out to be ugly ducks. Even the rare misplaced swan is likely to be pretty ugly on the inside by the time he finds his proper milieu. Mutation is a tragedy for the individuals concerned no matter how the issue turns out for the species. *The Ugly Duckling* is a mutation fairy tale that attempts to hide this tragedy.

The myth also serves to justify past crimes committed in the name of individualism. No one amasses a grossly disproportionate share of wealth or power as a reward for intrinsic virtues. All great fortunes were initially stolen from the people, directly or indirectly. One important function of the police—subsidiary to their primary role of maintaining order and predictability—is to prevent any of the people from stealing it back. The reason radicals are a greater threat to law and order than ordinary criminals is that they wish to steal it back collectively rather than individualistically (the way it was stolen in the first place). Criminal theft does not threaten the structure of our system—it is a technical *faux pas,* a faulty and risk-laden method utilized by those who lack the knowledge and skills to steal without risk.

Once a man has stolen his fortune he must find some way of keeping it. Sometimes naked power suffices, but ultimately, in a stable society, his act must be ratified in some way. In the past this has usually taken some time—at least a generation. The rule is that anyone who inherits a stolen fortune is entitled to it, and after it has been peacefully transmitted from parent to child for a few generations the family that has succeeded in hoarding their ill-gotten gains is regarded as a superior breed of persons. Some of the money is expended on educational, cultural, and status-linked accouterments which serve to nourish this impression, but by and large the mere fact of having been able to retain the money is proof enough. To view social inequality as anything other than deserved would threaten the very foundation of social order, and people are quite reasonably willing to put up with almost anything rather than have their everyday world plunged into chaos, unpredictability, and confused violence.

This mode of ratification, however, is paced too slowly for modern society. Today we more often utilize the myth of personal achievement—the notion that one individual can stand so far above others that he or she *merits* receiving far more rewards. We pay lip service to the notion that any success is a collective effort (Academy Award presentations abound in this sort of thing), but no one really wants to believe such statements even though they are true.

The duckling myth plays an important role in buttressing the individualistic justification of social inequality. In it an individual overcomes the low opinion and expectations of his group and proves in the end to be their superior. Furthermore, he does this without any help from them—indeed, over their scornful resistance. In ancient hero myths the hero received many magical gifts, blessings, or useful information from those around him. In the legends of Perseus and Jason, for example, the hero is merely a representative of powerful forces; like the private eye or secret agent of many adventure stories and films, his only special virtue seems to be an ability to expose himself to danger and be in the right place at the right time. In the scorned-outcast genre, however, the hero is presented as utterly isolated and autonomous. That for which he is scorned turns out to be a saving virtue—a valued mutation, such as Rudolph's nose.

This theme is not restricted to fairy tales, however. It also dominates the simplified biographies of "great" men that are designed for children. Whether inventors, artists, or robber barons, they tend to be shown as "self-made." They are usually poor, educated with difficulty or not at all, rejected by their peers, and surrounded with obstacles. Whatever education they receive is portrayed as useless—everything derives from the skills they develop alone, in their study or workshop, whither they have withdrawn from the insensitivity of the clods that surround them. One always wonders, in stories of this genre, why the hero is so anxious to coerce the love of such despicable persons, but one should not look for reasonableness where wounded narcissism is at issue. In *The Ugly Duckling* itself, the hero finds himself a superior group to which he truly belongs, but the more typical outcome is that the group who rejected the hero now sings his praises.

The special message of these stories is that a defect can be made into a virtue through the exercise of will, and that love can be forcibly extracted from others through successful individualistic achievement. The worthlessness of any love founded on impersonal fame ("spread some of that on me, please") is slyly concealed in these little pep talks—much as the difficulties inherent in intense and exclusive dyadic relationships are masked in the phrase "they lived happily ever after."

This vision of life, wherein the most warped shall ultimately be worshipped by those who initially scorn them, is imbibed by middle-class Americans with their jarred baby foods. It contributes not a little to the monotony of American culture, which mass-produces goods and services for those who fancy themselves to be the "saving remnant." But this bit of self-deception is harmless enough. The real impact of the duckling delusion lies in the way it detaches individual consciousness from its human, bodily, and environmental contexts so that it becomes autarchic and mechanical. The individual's intrinsic connectedness with others is denied—the only dimension of relation that is recognized or valued is superiority-inferiority. The winner of the competition—*any* competition will do—is portrayed as having all needs met, even those that were sacrificed to the achievement of superiority. Mechanical responsivity in the Western World owes much to the duckling myth.

Jonathan Livingston Strangelove

Nothing could demonstrate more dramatically the vitality of the duckling myth in American society than the extraordinary popularity of the best-selling book, *Jonathan Livingston Seagull*—a kind of Christian Science Dawn Patrol rendering of the Rudolph story. Even humanists, radicals, and counterculture freaks were entranced by the story—a puerile tale that glorifies overweening narcissism, compulsive striving, and schizoid alienation from the body. *Jonathan Livingston Seagull* epitomizes the American dream. It reveals the same victory-at-any-price mentality described so poignantly by Gary Shaw in connection with college football, and satirized so brilliantly by Philip Roth in connection with the President of the United States.

The hero of the story is a sort of avian Charles Atlas or self-made entrepreneur—his whole life given over to ambition, mastery, and "self-betterment." While the other gulls are simply grooving on life, he is absorbed in the seagull equivalent of practicing body-building exercises in front of a mirror, or studying the intricacies of the stock market. His control needs are uncontrollable, and he is the helpless servant of his need for mastery. As a result—like the old captains of industry—he is both admired by the masses and viewed as a menace to the community.

This he very shortly proves to be. In his frantic pursuit of speed and glory he almost kills some of his fellow gulls and is therefore banished by the elders of his tribe, who have failed to appreciate that he is a superior being. The book is in fact full of elitism. Jonathan is guiltless for breaking a self-made promise, since "such promises are only for the gulls that accept the ordinary" whereas Jonathan is "a one-in-a-million bird." When he achieves a higher state there is a long discussion as to the desirability of returning to the flock to teach the benighted savages he left behind, before he finally decides that one or two might be worthy to receive the white man's message.

The callous indifference to the lives of those deemed inferior ("The Gull of Fortune smiled upon him this once, and no one was killed") is reminiscent of American pilots in Vietnam: since Jonathan is a superior being, the welfare of the plodding masses (read "gooks" or "niggers") is beneath notice. The difference is merely one of scale, and the scale itself (a B-52 raid, for example) comes from precisely the mastery-power neurosis that Jonathan epitomizes. If you want to know how we got to Vietnam read *Jonathan Livingston Seagull*.

Also of interest is the basis for this superiority. Jonathan wastes no time in idle concern for the near death of his friends, for he has achieved a new speed record: *"two hundred fourteen miles per hour!* It was a breakthrough, the greatest single moment in the history of the Flock" (his italics). Later, furthermore, he flies "the first aerobatics of any seagull on earth," and feels that thereby he has found a "reason to life." It would be difficult to find a better illustration of the deep inner emptiness of Americans, who so often seem incapable of finding joy in living, but must fill up their days with frantic striving after mastery—either inner or outer. Even when he reaches a kind of heaven, as he shortly does, it turns out to be simply another gym, where the Superbirds spend "hour after hour every day practicing flight, testing advanced aeronautics." Speed, power, and striving are all that this new world has to offer, but he is pleased with it for he has a new body. I am reminded of a magazine ad that began, "Don't Be Caught in Last Year's Body If You Want To Be a This-Year Girl!" Jonathan has traded in his old model for a new one, and his response sounds so much like an automobile commercial that we realize at once why the book was so popular: "With half the effort, he thought, I'll get twice the speed, twice the performance of my best days on Earth!" Ultimately, he pushes this alienation from the body one step further, and becomes "not bone and feather but a perfect idea of freedom and flight, limited by nothing at all."

Other themes we would expect to find are all here: the yearning for immortality (Jonathan is a Methuselah among gulls and he and his disciples ultimately transcend death altogether), the demand for linearity, for total absence of feedback ("Heaven is being perfect," "perfection doesn't have limits," "In heaven . . . there should be no limits," and "whatever stands against that freedom must be set aside, be it ritual or superstition or limitation in any form"), and a view of the body as merely the servant of the will (when Jonathan encounters a gull with a broken wing he comes on like a coach in a Pat O'Brien football movie—telling him he can fly if he wants to, which, this being a narcissistic fantasy, he of course does). All of these express the same impatience with the realities of interdependence and corporeality —an impatience that betrays a deep sense of helplessness and impotence. The organism that cannot cope with limitation is one that is incapable of nourishing itself. It is as if the burden of having to deal with the reality of another person would cause the ego to collapse altogether. The demand for infinite space springs from terror at the prospect of having to confront another, or meet her needs. It is the infant at the breast who cannot tolerate limitation—this is the closest that humans ever come to being without limits.

The rest of the story follows the duckling pattern closely. The outcast finds a group of superior beings to which he truly belongs ("Here were gulls who thought as he thought"), thus proving that his banishment was a result of the elders' inferiority, not his. As is probably obvious by now, there is a heavy undercurrent of racism in the duckling myth, and *Jonathan Livingston Seagull* is no exception. The compulsive need to establish one's superiority, which is what the story is all about, requires the definition of some group of beings as constitutionally inferior.

Finally, as if this weren't enough, Jonathan must return to his original, inferior flock, and show off his superior attainments to the amazed crowd—his enormous speed, his transcendance of death. He and his disciples live happily forever after, thus ending the most recent contribution to the culture of prophets, ecological illiteracy, and the Emotional Plague.

The Well-meant Disaster

The sources of the duckling myth's pre-eminence in modern society are complex. It might have something to do with the frequency with which academics and other high-achievers started as teacher's pets—resented and scorned by their peers. In the United States it may result from having a population of migrants: in animal societies, and generally among humans, it is the losers who are forced to migrate—the United States is thus a nation composed of losers who made it rich in exile. But perhaps the most important factor in popularizing the duckling myth has been the success of Western medicine in keeping alive children who would otherwise die from lack of love and care. Their fantasies and destructiveness have become the myth of our age.

It may seem cruel to engage in speculations of this kind, but should this hypothesis prove correct there are solutions available to us more humane than letting the unloved die. We might find ways of giving them love, for example, instead of merely feeding medical narcissism. And in the meantime we are breeding, every day, more misery, pain, and hatred.

There is by now ample evidence, from both human and animal studies, that inadequate loving and too little tactile contact in infancy lowers the organism's resistance to infection, slows down recuperative powers, and produces chronic depression. In the nineteenth century half of all children born died in the first year. As late as the second decade of the twentieth century, moreover, the death rate for children under one year in *institutions* was 100 per cent. Now, while Western medicine has not succeeded altogether in eliminating this effect, it prides itself on having kept alive large numbers of children who would have died without medical intervention. For this many loving parents have been grateful. We have, of course, no way of knowing which of these children would have rallied without such assistance, nor which parents may have generously extended gratitude to doctors that might more appropriately have been directed toward themselves for having fostered a strong, healthy, and well-beloved child and for tending her lovingly when she was under stress. What we do know is that statistically the medical claim is just: many who would have perished did not.

Eugenics enthusiasts have long pointed out that while this was good for the individual (although the high suicide rate in medically sophisticated countries throws even this assertion in doubt), it was bad for the species. Their arguments tend to be dismissed as callous and elitist, as indeed they often are—full of a rather archaic Darwinian concern about the necessity of "eliminating the weak and unfit" before they reproduce.

But this is not the real issue. Our species will not soon disappear through weakness and genetic dilution, but it may rapidly vanish through its homicidal proclivities, its mad race to destroy its own environment, its burgeoning mechanical malevolence. It is not a genetic flaw that is spreading like an epidemic among us, but a cultural one. Keeping the unloved alive has loosed an infectious emotional disease—the origin, perhaps, of what Wilhelm Reich called the Emotional Plague.

Love is contagious. So is its lack. Those who are truly loved are recognizable by their lovingness, generosity, beauty, strength, health, responsivity, and joyousness. The unloved can be recognized by their misery, malevolence, ugliness, rigidity, and spite. The unloved cannot love, and hence spread the disease to their children. Since unloved children are highly susceptible to infection and sickness, the great epidemics of history tended periodically to purge the species of its potentially most destructive members. This is not to say that only the unloved died—Nature is statistical and careless of individuals. But one must assume that the unloved died in disproportionate numbers. Plagues like the Black Death selected out the most-loved individuals to procreate and raise children—a selection, in other words, that was cultural as much as genetic. Any purificatory effects were probably offset by the horrendous social dislocations involved—Nature's brutalities thus prove to be as inefficient as those of humans. At best, a kind of balance was maintained.

Western medicine, however, has managed to keep alive vast numbers of the unloved to wreak havoc and spread misery through the world. For Nature's callous slovenliness is now substituted Man's perfectionistic perversity.

Love cannot be faked. Yet in our culture it is assumed that all parents will love their children. If there are several children in a family most parents pretend to love all equally, even though the children themselves and outside observers have little trouble deciphering their preferences. Some parents are perfunctory in their love, some are guilty, overprotective, or smothering. The kind of love that really nourishes is not as common as we like to imagine. In task-oriented America, parents often assume that if they behave according to certain precepts laid down by child rearing experts, they will turn out a desirable product, but no technique has ever been a successful counterfeit for love to a child, who needs it to survive.

Western thought is highly combative. It tends to view all conflict as a war of extinction rather than a source of balance. It is only our mad individualism, for example, that makes us see species as competitive because they prey on each other. *Natural selection does not operate to give one species victory over another but to preserve balance.* A species evolves to a point (ever shifting) where a healthy adult can evade its predators but others cannot. Should it become so "successful" that *all* its members could evade all predators it would endanger its food supply, and thus be in as much trouble as if it fell short of this point. The predator is the population czar for the species it preys upon. The lion protects the food supply of the antelope. Birds protect the food supply of caterpillars, who, in turn, prevent plants from exhausting the soil. Predator and prey are in a symbiotic relationship with one another. Each is as important to the other *as a species* as if they were in some sort of friendship-dependency. The individual, however, is completely trivial in all this, which, given our cultural indoctrination, is rather upsetting to us.

Humans lack predators, and have had to rely more on disease to perform this vital function for them. To our species, therefore, the germs that kill us are as valuable as the billions of benign ones that inhabit our bodies and perform various useful functions.

Animal predators prey not only on the weak and ailing, but also on the young. It is primarily the unprotected young that get caught, just as it is more often the unprotected human children who are borne off by predatory microbes. But failure to protect can come from inability as well as indifference. The poor and ill-fed have always died in disproportionate numbers, whether loved or not. Thus the effect of Western medicine has been primarily one of providing an artificial protection to the privileged unloved, a particularly unfortunate combination.

I have suggested that the patriarchal revolution, along with the duckling delusion and the medical tinkering that helped give rise to it, contributed to the creation of a prophet-minded culture —a culture dominated by the outsider mentality. These observations should not be viewed as justification for some kind of repressiveness. All groups need both to maintain structures and occasionally to alter them, to limit the (infinite) number of alternatives available at any moment and yet keep open possibilities that are not normally envisioned. These needs are inherently contradictory—there has never been and never will be a permanent solution. No living organism can survive without predictability, nor without flexibility. No group can survive without cohesion, nor without permeability. The continual renegotiation of these dilemmas is the foundation of social life.

Every viable organic entity must include an ordered base and an element of chaotic instability. These depend upon each other for their existence. There can be no swindlers if there is no trust. Yet trust would have no meaning without swindlers. To attempt the extermination of all swindling would be a gross error, as humanity has dimly recognized throughout most of history. On the other hand, to create an entire economy predicated on swindling, as we have done, is equally dangerous. One tries merely to keep the ratio low enough to permit predictability and high enough to prevent the population from lapsing into idiocy.

But how can we damp down the prophet conflagration without becoming even more repressive than we are? How can we maintain flexibility and restore connectedness at the same time? And does not the connectedness we have lost require a kind of blind adherence that is forever closed to those who have the sight given by self-consciousness? Can organicity coexist with awareness?

We imagine that we are more aware than our primitive forebears, but we are also *less* aware. We are painfully aware of our separateness, but utterly blind to our connectedness. We usually conceive of this blindness as a kind of liberation. The Horatio Alger version of Western history tells how an ignorant, dependent nobody freed himself from medieval embeddedness and became a free and powerful modern being, master of his own fate. The tale is a bit tarnished now and stands on the threshold of high camp, but perhaps it still needs to be pointed out seriously that another way of looking at the last seven centuries is in terms of humanity's increasing myopia about its relation to the rest of the world. We need, in other words, to become not less aware, but more aware. *Self-consciousness is not awareness, it is merely grasping one aspect of reality at the expense of another.* The "great" scientist, entrepreneur, artist, or writer imagines he or she is responding simply to individual goals. So, perhaps, does the hen who lays eggs by artificial light.

Parable 4

A man was hammering a nail and hit his thumb by mistake. The pain was so excruciating that he shouted and leaped about. The people nearby were full of admiration: "How beautifully he sings and dances," they said.

BECAUSE SHE'S THERE
or
SOCIAL CLIMBING
BEGINS AT HOME

> *He who loves his body more than dominion over the empire can be given the custody of the empire.*
>
> **Lao Tzu**

> *Chorus: Why has the queen gone, Oedipus, in wild grief rushing from us? . . .*
> *Oedipus: Perhaps she is ashamed of my low birth . . .*
>
> **Sophocles**

It is customary to blame the isolated-nuclear-family system for many of America's social ills, despite the fact that it does exactly what it is supposed to do: socialize children to live in an individualistic society. To change it would be to change everything, and yet it is changing. Most of us will not live to see this transfiguration proceed any great distance, but if such things can be said to have a beginning, it has begun. I am speaking here, by the way, of real social change, not merely changes in intellectual fashion, such as are annually announced by academics and news commentators. Real social change is like geological change, while media-defined social change—the kind that makes one feel, in 1974, that 1968 belonged to a different era—is like the loose dirt daily blown about by the afternoon wind, subsiding in a slightly different place.

In the last chapter I tried to trace some of the more recent sources of Western social pathology, such as the culture of prophets and the duckling delusion. The transmission belt for these phenomena, as for most social processes, is the family. For while the family by no means transmits all of our culture from one generation to the next, it does transmit what is most elemental: the way feelings and close relationships are dealt with. Television, school, and other institutions may talk of these things and teach the child how to conceptualize them, but this is only as important as words like "balance," "wheel," "handlebar," and "falling off" are to someone trying to learn to ride a bicycle. Parents don't teach the culture, they *are* the culture. No matter what they do or how many child rearing manuals they read, they will transmit in spite of themselves the accepted cultural mode of mangling feelings and distorting relationships. This is not to say parents are helpless—only that they cannot disguise what they are, and that this is the only thing a child pays close attention to. The parents' insistence that a child *not* pay attention to this is what makes children schizophrenic.

The nuclear family is a social system with two castes—male and female—and two classes—adult and child. In the class system there is an avenue of social mobility, which is called growing up. In American families, the lower-class term for the higher class is, in fact, "grown-up," although the higher class itself uses the label "adult."

The adult class has certain privileges and powers. As in all class systems—since the family is the model for all class systems —the basic contract is one involving responsibility and the obligation to protect, in return for power, narcissistic rewards, and a disproportionate share of scarce resources. But, as I observed earlier, all such contracts are in part a protection racket: "If you do as I say I will protect you against my own wrath." It always seems like a terrible bargain, and yet is often accepted with pleasure by the oppressed, so repugnant is the burden of responsibility. If it were not for the extreme intensity of human dependency needs, political oppression would be a rare event.

What is unique to this prototypical class system is that social mobility is so complete. Almost every child who lives long enough becomes an adult. Furthermore, this mobility is not only expected but carefully prepared for: Each child is carefully indoctrinated into the behavior appropriate to her eventual initiation into the higher class.

This does not mean that other class systems have deviated in any essential way from the model. The adult class is constantly losing members, and any social class faced with the same problem of diminution behaves in exactly the same way—replenishing itself with energetic (if crude) new blood from the lower classes. Any ruling class that fails to do this is doomed.

Class behavior is learned in the nuclear family. By this I mean not only the specific behavior appropriate to one's social class, but also the underlying concept of social division, the whole minuet of interclass behavior, the fundamental contract between classes, and what it feels like to live in each one. This learning is not intellectual, but emotional and experiential. It is like learning to play baseball by simply being asked to play every position in turn. By the time the child reaches school she knows all about how class systems work, and while she may be naïve about the particular social class system of her own society and how she fits into it, the essential structure of all such systems is bred into her very bones by her family experiences.

One learns, for example, that those in the lower class are expected to be deferential to those above, and that when the highers boss them around they are not expected to be insulted or humiliated. The use of different terms of address (first name vs. Mr. and Mrs.) between members of different classes is also derived from the family, in which children are usually called by first names and parents by titles (such as "Mom" and "Dad") which call attention to their parental function. Control and allocation of resources is largely reserved to the higher class, which is then expected to protect and ensure some minimum provision for the child-serf class.

Class distinctions within the family tend gradually to decline over time, and each child ultimately graduates into the higher class (i.e., becomes adult). There is considerable variation in the timing of these changes ("You'll always be my baby" vs. "You're old enough to support yourself now"), but the rule holds. In this miniature two-class society proper social mobility behavior is learned by virtually every member of the lower class. All children know how to be social climbers, although they are seldom able to use this knowledge in the far less receptive outside world. Every child is expected to become an adult, but serfs are not expected to become nobles, and workers are not expected to become managers. There is a place for each child in the adult world, but most members of the lower social orders already have the only place they are likely to have—they are expected to "know their place." There is no vacuum for them to fill. Ordinarily, then, each individual is socially mobile within the family but not outside. Yet there are some individuals who use their mobility knowledge very aggressively outside the family, without any particular societal encouragement or demand for new blood. What motivates these people who do not "know their place"?

Family patterns vary a good deal from one society to another, and most of the prerogatives usually reserved to the parent are permitted the child in some society or other. There is one adult prerogative, however, that is clutched with particular intensity in virtually every society: the monopoly on sexual intercourse within the nuclear family. The family class system, in other words, is maintained by the incest taboo—the most fiercely endorsed taboo of our species. By the same token, since the nuclear family molds our social responses, it is highly unlikely that such a thing as a classless society could ever exist so long as there is an incest taboo.

Yet there are societies—small and simple, to be sure—in which social class as we know it does not exist. Stratification is by age only, so that it does not merely mimic the class system within the family but is a direct extension of it. The only superior beings are the elders, and everyone who lives eventually becomes one (in the absence of Western medicine anyone who lives to an advanced age is likely to be a rather superior specimen, psychically, physically—in wisdom as well as in status). This system thus retains the benign feature of the family itself, already mentioned: Everyone who lives out her life participates in both classes. Even more important, movement into the higher class does not necessitate separation from one's friends, all of whom are engaged in the same movement at roughly the same time.

Social class mobility, on the other hand, enables just a few individuals to make this transition alone, at the cost of rupturing most of their relationships. This is a sharp departure from the family model—as if the mobile individual were saying, "I alone am capable of achieving the status of adult."

Now some social tension arises in societies with fixed social strata—tension between the sense of movement *within* the nuclear family and the lack of movement outside it. This tension generates a variety of interesting beliefs—the notion of reincarnation and the idea of heaven, for example. Christian teachings exhibit the tension most strongly: "The last [poor] shall be first and the first [rich] shall be last," which is congruent with: "The children become adults, the adults grow old and die." If we take this as a kind of baseline for mobility strivings, then it becomes apparent that what the mobile individualist is seeking, from a familial perspective, is to become adult *ahead of his time*. Leaving his peers behind he wants to leap into adult status *contemporaneously* with his parents. In a word, he seeks to violate (but by no means to rescind—no radical he) the incest taboo. The prototypical social climber is Oedipus.

The myth of Oedipus itself reveals the importance of time. Oedipus is "out of sync" with his family, his period, his environment. Once it is discovered when, where, and to whom he belongs, he is like a wraith—no one knows what to do with him or how to relate to him. Much is always made of the duality of his family relationships (mother-and-wife, sister-and-daughter, brother-and-son); that is, he occupies not only his own family roles but *simultaneously* those of his father, whom he has killed in a fury of injured narcissism. Oedipus is a man who has o'erleaped his proper time and thereby disrupted the flow of life; hence the plague that afflicts Thebes.

This leads us to the deeper meaning of the riddle put to him by the Sphinx: "What is that which has one voice and yet becomes four-footed and two-footed and three-footed?" By answering "Man," Oedipus wins his kingdom and his mother's bed, and is doomed to a lifetime of misery and horror (so much for success and living happily ever after). It is rather surprising that Oedipus' luckless predecessors had never heard the Sphinx's riddle, since it is found in some form or another in almost every part of the globe. An African version has it: "four legs in the morning, two at midday, and three in the evening," which keeps the proper time perspective. The Sphinx, however, slurs the temporal aspect and talks of "one voice," which is misleading, since the voice of an infant, a young adult, and an old man are hardly identical. Oedipus, however, *does* speak with one voice from two different stages of life.

This sense of temporal confusion appears in Sophocles' drama. It seems odd that the plague sent to Thebes as a consequence of Oedipus' crimes should appear only after he has been married to his mother long enough to have fully grown sons. In all these years, furthermore, Oedipus has learned nothing of his predecessor on the throne—seems hardly even to have heard of Laius or his murder. When Oedipus asks why the murder had never been investigated by the Thebans, he is told that the neglect was caused by their troubles with the Sphinx, who, however, died shortly after the murder. All the action of the drama seems predicated on the obviously false assumption that Oedipus is newly arrived in Thebes, newly married, and newly king. The time is out of joint, as it has to be for a man to be simultaneously son and husband.

This out-of-jointness is expressed in the plague visited on Thebes. Because Oedipus has gone out of sync with his environment he has polluted it. Plants are blighted, animals will not reproduce, women are barren. This should hold meaning for us for we are once again out of sync with our environment and the result is again a blight—albeit a more subtle one—which has left no living thing unaffected.

The impulse toward social mobility—that is, the individualistic migration from one class to a higher one—does not occur in the absence of powerful oedipal strivings. This is not to reduce a social phenomenon to a psychic one—one might just as easily view the oedipal situation as a mere subdivision of social-class dynamics. Both represent the violation of temporal and spatial harmony through the exercise of will. I suggested earlier that will was a concentration of energy necessary to bring an individual or part back into synchrony with the whole, or to force it *out* of synchrony with the whole. Individualistic social mobility and oedipal striving exemplify this process.

Before examining the mechanism through which this occurs I would like to say a little about oedipal culture. We use the term "oedipal" to describe adult responses governed by the childhood infatuation with the parent of the opposite sex. Now, according to Freud, time does not exist in the unconscious. Early images of a loving face, of exchanged tendernesses, of blissful feelings, of youthful and idealized parents—are preserved unchanged, uninfluenced by the reality of subsequent and less-pleasant images of family interaction. They form the raw material of romanticism in adult life. The overwhelming importance of the face in romantic ideation—as opposed to personality traits or bodily charms —suggests that some of these images may go back to infancy, when the face dominates the child's stimulus field.

This is not to say that all aspects of being in love are oedipal. Tenderness and sexual pleasure are powerful and reality-based components in their own right. It is the mystical, spiritualized, idealized feelings, the sense of enthrallment and destiny, that reveal the presence of incestuous undertones. Those who feel that sex without romanticism is meaningless are saying that sex must have an incestuous tinge to be enjoyable.

Romantic love also reveals its oedipal nature by its efforts to transcend consensual time. Romantic fantasies are either heavily nostalgic or seek escape into a different temporal realm. One popular form of nostalgia in early American films, for example, was the reappearance theme: The loved one is seen *not for the first time*. Often the lovers had been together at some earlier point but were parted, so their reunion is highly dramatic, particularly if some obstacle is present. *Casablanca* is the classic oedipal film of this type. Sometimes the loved one has only been experienced symbolically—in a photograph or painting (this occurs also in *The Arabian Nights*). In *Laura*, another forties classic, a detective becomes attached to a painting of the woman whose supposed murder he is investigating. When she later turns up he falls in love with her. The title song for the movie, a typical oedipal ballad, contains the lines: "She gave your very first kiss to you—but she's only a dream."

The theme of the familiar stranger, the meeting that is not the first meeting, reflects the fact that a stranger sometimes taps into a buried oedipal fantasy channel, allowing old longings to burst forth, often taking the individual quite by surprise. The *déja vu* so often associated with romantic love is in reality a *déja senti* experience, and its attached fantasy—the idea of "soulmates" —has an infantile origin. In the world of adult reality no two psyches fit together perfectly—human complexity being what it is—but the *feeling* of complete oneness with another person is given to almost everyone at moments during the first year of life, when one's needs are anticipated by the mothering one.

Some romantic fantasies seek, not the past, but a time out of time altogether. They express a yearning to be ripped out of the organic context in which each living thing has a temporal-spatial place of its own—child as child, adult as adult—and to find a new, mystical space-time in which generations fuse and those never-to-be-united finally *are* united. *A Portrait of Jenny, Peter Ibbetson*, the novels of E. R. Eddison, Nabokov, C. S. Lewis, and countless poems and science-fiction stories exemplify this theme. The escape from organic time into oedipal time is simply a more creative and willful form of nostalgia.

The fantasy of the time machine also expresses the wish to escape the boundaries of the life span. For some people, to become aware of the multiplicity of times and places is to experience one's own time and place as a prison. The joyousness that can only come from being completely present in one time and place is lost. The attention wanders, like that of a man at a party who imagines that the room holds somewhere a partner more interesting than the one with whom he is engaged, and ends by relating fully to no one. This wish, then, is the ego's wish not to die, the wish to build itself a monument—to smear itself all over the temporal-spatial landscape, like some proliferating science-fiction monster, for which, indeed, the human ego, with its infinite capacity for symbolic self-engorgement, is always the model.

While it would be ridiculous to speak of oedipal strivings as the "cause" of this hypertrophy of the ego, they provide important leverage in dislocating human beings from embeddedness in the real world. Earlier I used the term "oedipal culture," for just as there is a culture of children's games and jokes passed on from older to younger, virtually independent of adult society, and just as there are separate male and female cultures passed down within each sex, so, also, there is an oedipal culture passed down through the generations from mother to son-who-becomes-father, who in turn passes it to daughter-who-becomes-mother, and so on. It is a culture of nostalgia and dreams, of unrealizable yearnings, utterly detached from the everyday realities of family life, and this gossamer quality, far from signifying fragility, is what gives it its immortality and invulnerability.

Consider once again the socially mobile individual. Toffler points out that those who are most skillful at breaking off relationships are rewarded with success in our society. He cites studies showing that successful executives are unusually gifted at dissolving their early family ties, dissociating themselves from friendships that would be career liabilities, leaving the physical environment in which they grew up, sloughing off lower-status clubs, relatives, and acquaintances. Executives are even advised on techniques for withdrawing gracefully from these inconvenient ties.

At first glance this may seem like a contradiction: The upwardly mobile individual is gifted at sloughing family ties, yet his mobility is rooted in oedipal strivings. The contradiction is only apparent. The "successful" individual's ability to slough family ties is possible precisely because in that secret fantasy world he has never left home and never will. Once again, it is precisely the detachment and insulation of the oedipal culture from the realities of everyday life in the family that give it its peculiar invulnerability. The real mother can easily be left behind because the fantasy ideal is carried inside. It is the possession of that untarnished internal image that enables Peer Gynt to be a complete troll in his daily existence.

The role played by the father is also important in generating the oedipal impulse. Social mobility by definition requires that the son surpass the father (in a more subtle way this is true of all high achievement) and that the mother transfer from husband to son her status aspirations and security needs. (The women's movement demands that she transfer them to herself.) David McClelland, in his studies of achievement motivation, found that high achievers have mothers who are dominant and demanding, but not restrictive. Their fathers, on the other hand, tend to play an insignificant role in the family. He cites a study by Abegglen of business leaders who rose from lower-class status: Most of their fathers were frequently away from home, or ill, or absent altogether. McClelland suggests that wars and seafaring increase the achievement level of societies by removing fathers from the home.

Successful men, then, are brought up by mothers who make certain they reject and transcend their fathers. The son in such a family is encouraged to break out of his temporal setting and become a being who belongs to no place and no time. He has hitched his wagon to a star and ceases to pay emotional heed to the here-and-now. He is out of synchrony with his environment, living only for achievements that will make him worthy of a maternal ideal that can only be possessed in some beyond-space outside of time. A rather bizarre notion when one considers it coldly, yet such individuals, whose lives are sacrificed to an almost hallucinatory vision, are accounted the most sane and superior beings in our society (except, perhaps, by those closest to them).

The family dynamic of the socially mobile male is captured in the tale of Jack and the Beanstalk. A boy lives alone with his mother. They are poor, and he is doing a most inadequate job of trying to fill the gap created by the absence of an adult male. He is not overly bright and trades the family cow, virtually their only food source, to a stranger for a handful of worthless beans. The mother, in rage and despair, flings the beans out the window, cursing the fate that gave her such a naïve and incompetent booby for a son. At this point reality is left behind and we are plunged into the world of magic, for if we can believe a sharp-dealing stranger who says his beans are enchanted, we can believe anything. The beanstalk fantasy is like a daydream concocted to salve the boy's wounded feelings. It is his manhood that his mother has treated with such contempt, and with an "I'll show her," up springs a gigantic beanstalk reaching to the sky. The boy climbs the stalk, steals wealth and potency from the fearsome giant (with the help of the giant's wife, naturally—what can a little boy do without Mother's support, and what can he *not* do *with* it?), escapes, cuts the giant down to size, and lives alone with his mother happily ever after.

In essence, this is a story of successful social mobility according to the McClelland pattern. The father is both absent and (in his giant form) completely rejected by the son. The mother is exclusively absorbed with the son, and makes stern demands on him for independent and responsible behavior. The son devotes his entire being to meeting these needs of his mother.

Priorities of Pleasure

Beneath all voluntary postponement of gratification—all voluntary inhibition, suppression of feeling, commitment to a task—lies a kind of arrogance. Setting oneself above one's own bodily responses is an act of snobbery, of satanic pride. (Pride might even be defined as self-induced scarcity.) Pleasure-loving peoples are modest and unassuming by and large ("feeling good was good enough for me"). They are less given to rank-ordering people and things. Social climbing and spiritual climbing (which are merely two different expressions of the same impulse) hold no interest for them. What is it that creates such interest?

Alexander Lowen offers an answer: "An organism's natural striving for pleasure is normally suspended in only two situations: in the interest of survival *and for the sake of a greater pleasure.*" Since survival is not really at issue here, the second of Lowen's two situations seems the more interesting. It suggests that invidiousness, ambition, vanity, arrogance, endurance, jealousy, striving, spirituality, competitiveness, avarice, intellectuality, envy (all the qualities that make our country strong) spring from the perception that one pleasure is greater than another. Once pleasures are ranked, in other words, we have left pleasure behind.

Yet surely there is some ranking of pleasure within every organism. All organisms sense that some objects promise a greater quantity of pleasure than others, and are drawn to those that promise most. But what can we say of the capacity of many humans to relinquish an available pleasure for one that is not even remotely present? This ability is not automatically available to members of the species—it is merely a potentiality that can be activated by early experiences. The folklore of preindustrial peoples, for example, is full of moralizing tales in which a golden opportunity was lost because the hero or heroine responded to the seductions of a lesser but more proximate pleasure.

In non-stress situations, pleasure is an organizing principle. The pleasure centers of the brain determine which messages coming into the brain are to be given priority. Now, one way people establish gratification hierarchies is through the relative importance of the various other persons in their lives—whether they are roughly equal or highly unequal in their pleasure-giving potential. If we imagine all the "others" in a person's life arranged in rank order on a pleasure-giving continuum, the resulting gradient would be very flat for some individuals and very steep for others. For the flat-gradient individual, one person is about as likely to give pleasure as another. For the steep-gradient individual, on the other hand, one or two persons will hold a much higher pleasure potential than all others. Their loss will be severely felt and difficult to replace. Flat-gradient individuals tend to be impulsive and unable to postpone gratification, while steep-gradient people are planners, schemers, inhibitors.

A child who has many caretakers, many sources of love and nurturance, will tend to respond to each in terms of the gratification they actually provide. The child whose life is dominated by a single nurturer, on the other hand, must cope with a deficiency of options. The one source is so important that its loss would render all other sources meaningless. And even if the source is reliably present, one cannot guarantee a constant outpouring of love. Yet it seems better to wait for the love of the important source than to seek a substitute.

Insofar as a single individual in the life of a child provides (a) intense gratification and (b) far more gratification than any other person, the child will at times be able and willing to forego immediate pleasure because of her confidence in the availability of fuller and more complete gratification at a later time. A hurt child, for example, will sometimes shrug off reassuring caresses from other adults and run some distance to receive the same comfort from his own mother. We take this kind of behavior for granted, since mothers are initially at the zenith of most people's pleasure gradient, but there is wide variation in the extent of this peaking. Institutionalized children, for example, have extremely flat gradients—they are of necessity promiscuous in their affections. Middle-class America is at the opposite extreme, with the mother vastly overshadowing all other persons. Simple communities lie in between these two extremes, with many different adults (as well as older siblings) playing a large part in seeing to the child's basic needs and satisfactions. Anthropologists call this pattern "diffusion of nurturance."

Concentration of nurturance in the mother, which tends to occur in the isolated nuclear family of today, engenders oedipal motivation. By this I mean simply that mental connections involving the concept "mother" retain inordinately high priority throughout life. They promise the "greater pleasure" for the sake of which the organism's natural striving for pleasure is suspended. The more extreme this concentration—the steeper the pleasure gradient—the longer gratification will be willingly postponed, in some cases indefinitely.

An old flat-gradient adage says: A bird in the hand is worth two in the bush. But is it worth a hundred? At some point the postponement will begin to seem worthwhile. The adage also stresses the value of tangibility. Flat-gradient individuals are highly earthbound (diffusion-of-nurturance societies, for example, show little inclination to romanticism in love affairs). They are not fascinated with obstacles and memories and fantasies—they want immediate pleasure. The steep-gradient individual, however, may find himself in a situation in which a *symbol* of the mothering one will outweigh the *reality* of some other pleasure-giving person. A person or situation that evokes an echo of the mother will outweigh one that does not. The Freudian idea of transference can be viewed in this light: The romantic lover has invested most of his love in the *symbol*, which can be attached to any real-life person who can trigger it. Eventually, reality may loosen the glue that holds the symbol and the person together, at which point he falls in love with someone else. What remains constant is the steep gradient. There is always One that is valued overwhelmingly over all others.

The process through which the romantic lover learns to invest in this symbol of the mother, rather than in the mother herself, is not complicated. If one person provides most of the child's pleasure it becomes extremely important to please that person— even to anticipate her wishes and preferences. The mother (for in most cases it *is* the mother) is incorporated by the child and becomes an internal force directing his emotional life.

There is nothing mysterious or magical about this. The mind is a complicated piece of circuitry that connects not real objects, but the representations of those objects and the individual's responses to them. If a person loses a limb, the mental pathways associated with that limb do not immediately disappear—in fact the person for a long time tends to hallucinate the limb as still existing, so powerful are these representations. Similarly, when we lose loved ones we may behave in many ways as if they were still alive—our feelings, interests, and behavioral patterns may still be organized around their existence. What survives in ordinary oedipal motivation is not so much a desire for incest with the mother as an internal pattern of emotional responses—a readiness to put all one's emotional eggs in one symbolic basket. Behaviorally, this may display itself as intense monogamous attachment or extreme fickleness or any gradation in between—since the key to oedipal motivation is its lack of attachment to reality one cannot discern it by reference to its objects alone. One may fall in love once in a lifetime or every day; what is symptomatic of oedipal motivation is the intensity of that feeling—its tendency to blot out all other relationships so long as it is attached to a given person. It is also revealed by the ability to invest that love in symbols—mementos of the loved one, memories, fantasies of the future.

But the best index of all is the ability to defer pleasure. This may or may not be apparent in the everyday erotic life of the individual, but it will appear somewhere as a powerful force in the personality. People who show a strong tendency to plan, to strive earnestly toward far-distant and symbolic goals, to hold strong internalized values that are not responsive to context ("inner-directed" people, in Riesman's terms) are oedipally motivated, in the sense of having a steep-gradient mental apparatus.

This leads to many paradoxes. The word "romantic" tends to suggest wispy poets or the Brontë sisters. One would never dream of applying the term to captains of industry or political leaders, many of whom would scoff at overt expressions of romanticism. Yet the man who devotes his existence to fulfilling a maternal wish, renouncing immediate pleasures for ever-receding achievement goals, has romanticism rooted in every fiber. He foregoes everyday pleasures because he is after bigger game. But what *is* that greater pleasure? Power, wealth, fame, success do not produce ecstasy, but only the thin and pallid sensation of ego-satisfaction or pride-of-mastery. The "greater pleasure"—total and unconditional gratification by the mothering one—is illusory and anachronistic. The time is out of joint for oedipal personalities because they are out of joint with the time—still engaged in the mechanical fulfillment of a design programmed into them in infancy. Their interest in the here-and-now is largely limited to those pieces of reality that can be incorporated into the program. Very little arouses interest for its own sake.

In a study of successful Americans—business and government leaders, professionals, and artists—Cuber and Harroff found that for a majority of their subjects sex was "almost non-existent, something to be stifled," or a source of fear and avoidance. Unable to give or receive gratification, sex was merely a matter of tension release. They "performed" it, as a necessary "nuisance," with a "minimum of fanfare"—"like any other body function . . . it needs attention from time to time."

This is well to remember in relation to occasional public figures who are portrayed—publicly or in private rumor—as highly erotic. Sexual "conquests" may feed an ego or enhance one's status. Brief sexual encounters may drain off surplus tension in the manner Cuber and Harroff describe. Some may even manage to carve out a few more extended erotic interludes from their busy lives. But by and large, a successful public career is not compatible with leisurely and gratifying love-making. There are only so many hours in a day, after all, and strong involvement in a love relationship—even a marital one—will ultimately impinge upon career activities ("he's neglecting his work for this affair"). Should the careerist choose love he would cease to be a careerist.

Cuber and Harroff, commenting on the heavy emotional price their careerists have paid for their success, observe that many of them have been "able to inhibit the sexual side of their nature without visibly jeopardizing their mental health." It never occurs to them to question the relation of success itself to mental health —mental health is always defined by the values of the culture and career success is our most cherished virtue. Yet one need only walk down a city street to become aware of the hideous toll of human suffering—emotional, physical, mental, social—that these successful careerists have produced in the course of denying their own humanity. For when a careerist throttles his humanity in the service of achievement, what kind of a world can he build except one in which humanity is throttled?

America was formed on the principle that movement is excruciatingly slow when people move together—maintaining all their intricate and delicate interrelationships at every step of the way, stopping to repair any ruptures that might develop from the jarring motion, and nourishing a sensitivity to their natural surroundings. This snail's pace has been good enough for Nature, but a man, with his brief life span, is preoccupied with changes that are quick and visible and will serve as a monument to his ephemeral ego, so like a shrew or a piranha in its combined puniness and voracity. To get somewhere quickly, the American way is to take nothing and no one.

In the same fashion, oedipal motivation fosters intellectual learning of a narrow mechanical sort, but makes complex or emotional learning more difficult. The commitment to a symbolic goal alerts the individual to any message that can be enlisted in the service of that goal, but blinds him to messages that seem irrelevant to that goal, or call it into question, or place it in a larger balanced context. Our social sickness, like all sickness, is a state of imbalance. Our technological hypertrophy was achieved not in spite of or alongside of, but *because* of our social decay. We traded social integration for mechanical power, casually trashing the most exquisitely complex social organisms—built up slowly over generations. The technological advances of the past two hundred years are fondly imagined to have come free, or to have been paid for. They have not been paid for. Their cost in human unpleasure is incalculable—human beings, and, indeed, all living things, will still be paying the price for hundreds of years. What we have lost cannot simply be plugged in later on when we finally get to some technological Land of Oz and start to look around for the rewards. It is lost forever. Many of our social responses and organic sensitivities are already so blunted that we may become incapable of living in co-operative communities in another generation or so. It is not only that these qualities are disappearing at an accelerative rate, but that the conditions that nourish their emergence are now almost impossible to re-create.

I have argued that wisdom and understanding—the appreciation of totalities and interrelationships—are impeded by the steep-gradient structure. For the less one's emotional interest is invested in the here-and-now, the less fully one can grow from experience. If we wish to enhance the type of intelligence that I.Q. tests measure, then clearly we should design a society like middle-class America, in which oedipal motivation is exaggerated. If, on the other hand, we wish to enhance wisdom and understanding, we should seek precisely the opposite arrangement: diffusion-of-nurturance communities that will produce flat-gradient personalities.

Reality and Guilt

Perhaps this will become clearer if we look at another steep-gradient attribute: guilt. Guilt is highly valued as a mechanism for social control in mobile societies since it does not depend (like shame, punishment, social disapproval, or community constraint) on the presence of a stable social unit. An individual can feel guilty anywhere or anytime. Guilt is usually said to derive from "love-oriented" techniques of child rearing: Since the loss of love is the most terrible threat the child experiences, she internalizes the values and wishes of the parent so as to be able to anticipate and forestall parental displeasure. Guilt is a signal, like anxiety, that continuation on the same course will produce a disaster—in this case, the loss of parental love (and, as the child grows up and makes these wishes and values her own, the loss of self-love, self-respect). But love must be concentrated overwhelmingly in a single source for its loss to constitute such a disaster. Internalized private parental (as opposed to community) values are largely a function of concentrated parenting, and are, hence, a steep-gradient product.

Concentrated parenting allows parental displeasure to supersede all other forms of reality as a potential source of threat. The flat-gradient child will give more heed to a threat to her survival than to the threat of any one individual rejecting her. Not so the steep-gradient child. Just as culture can create substitute realities, so can the family—simply on a more individualistic basis. A steep pleasure gradient seduces the individual into substituting a parent-world for the real one. In this imaginary parent-world, good behavior and benign intent are rewarded, even when no parents are around. In the real world, whoever is so insensitive to the environment as to walk on thin ice will fall through, no matter how well-behaved they may have been. The steep-gradient individual's awareness of this becomes blurred. The whole world becomes a familial stage. Relationships become defined in obligatory terms, so that people imagine that the erotic interest of a partner can be earned through good behavior or coerced through indebtedness. Life is conducted on the principle of accumulating guilt coupons: "If I suffer enough, I will ultimately be rewarded." Or, to give it its more contemporary form: "If I cleave to the right values, am true to myself, the world will reward me." This guilt-based parent-world is obviously important to the development of mechanical insensitivity to feedback—of single-track intelligence rather than wisdom.

Achievement, Specialization, and Power

Achievement is always a specialization—the hypertrophy of some characteristics at the expense of others. It always involves an imbalance in the totality of the individual psyche. There is nothing wrong with this imbalance in itself—it makes for variety and entertainment in human affairs—so long as balancing occurs over time or across the community. In every group people accept narrow and warped self-definitions (clown, cynic, old reliable, sexpot, taskmaster, and so on) as the price of entry, and group members love nothing more than to narrate events about each other that confirm these caricatures. The individuals themselves even derive pleasure from having much of their humanity squeezed out of them at the door—their eccentricity is, after all, what secures their membership. A group of fully human and balanced individuals could change membership every day and never notice the difference. Limitedness serves to dramatize mutual interdependence, reminding everyone that they cannot survive without each one since none is whole. This is a lie, of course, since everyone is potentially whole; and groups do survive membership changes if they are gradual enough for the survivors to adjust and modify their caricatures. But it is a useful and necessary lie, and indeed, if we focus on this issue of proper timing (as we should), it is even a kind of truth.

The real lie begins when people become permanently trapped in their caricatures even outside a group context. In our society, for example, most positions of eminence are filled competitively, and hence require a permanently intense and narrow motivation. Success is achieved by becoming a machine—an engine without a governor, singlemindedly devoted to winning competitions and aggrandizing the ego. But it is important for followers to fantasize that these fragile beings on whom they depend are motivated by something other than pure narcissism. Hence the frequency with which American political leaders profess their humility—the one trait that by definition they cannot possibly possess.

Leaders obviously have a profound need for power, and my emphasis on the pathology of their motivation is tied to this. But power is of two kinds, which we might call positive and negative. Negative power is the ability to control, force, imprison, invade, terrify, and kill others. This is the common meaning assigned to the term, and when I use it without a modifier this is usually what I mean. Those who have a great deal of this kind of power, like the President of the United States and other major heads of state, are able to kill with relative impunity. Oppressed peoples who seek more "power to the people" want at least enough of this kind of power to keep from being killed, to remove the impunity, to create a "balance of power." A balance of negative power is two men with guns pointed at each other's heads. Calling it negative is not to moralize but to emphasize its static quality. When it is in balance nothing can happen—a state of zero is its high point. When out of balance someone sooner or later is killed or brutalized.

Positive power is the ability to influence others, to arouse love and respect, and to get one's needs met—without pressure and in a socially naked and unadorned state, devoid of status, position, or other weaponry. Western peoples rarely use the term in this sense, although it is more common in other cultures. We all know people who possess positive power to a high degree—they are simply people who were truly and unambivalently loved as children. They give and receive with equal facility.

I call this kind of power "positive" because it begins rather than ends at zero, and is dynamic when in balance. That is to say, two people with equal positive power will both gain love and respect, will both succeed in influencing the other, will both get their needs met. They will not be locked in a stand-off but will develop through their interaction.

The need for negative power is expressive of the lack of positive power. The less positive power one has, the more negative power one needs. But negative power does not feed, nor can it create. One cannot obtain love with it, nor respect for oneself (as opposed to one's status or weaponry). Hence the quest is doomed to failure. He who pursues negative power is in a pathological condition.

Some individuals with a modicum of positive power are unaware of the significance of this gift and pursue negative power anyway: We refer to them as charismatic leaders, and they seem the most benighted of all—like someone who shouts into a microphone even though his voice is already being amplified.

Leaders and successful achievers have highly developed wills, which is useful in times of crisis. But for these people every moment of every day is a time of crisis. Hence they tend to *create* crises around them—altering reality in such a way as to lend an air of authenticity to their underlying world view. Their willful behavior tends to drag everyone into the same state of desperation they themselves are energized to overcome.

It is the especially needy person who must *ensure* getting those needs met. The quest for power or eminence is less a forward than a backward search—an effort to re-establish the dominance of the infant, whose wish is his parents' command. As Bateson points out: "A command can closely resemble a cry for help," and Freud was fond of talking about "His Majesty the Baby." Part of the follower role is to prop up the leader and meet his overwhelming needs for attention, recognition, and service. Followers can do this either because their own needs are less urgent and they can get them met without going to all that trouble, or else because they lack the will that would enable them to erect this mammoth insurance system. That is to say, they either had their needs met early by many persons, or never had them met by anyone and lack any faith that such gratification will ever be forthcoming.

This raises a question that may have occurred to many readers: If dominant mothers and inconspicuous fathers produce high achievers, why haven't urban ghettos generated a great flock of black Carnegies, Edisons, and so on? Should not blacks from poor families with absent fathers turn out to be steep-gradient individuals?

The answer to this is complex. First, it is simply not possible, despite their desire, for most mothers in conditions of acute poverty to provide enough gratification for a steep-gradient structure to emerge. Child rearing tends to be a catch-as-catch-can affair —the child now a dearly beloved, now an oppressive burden. Of necessity, furthermore, it must often be shared. This is true of all acutely poor groups. It is, after all, only a very few who manage to rise out of their social class at any one time. Ambitious mothers who can concentrate their attention on a child to the extent that permits high but conditional gratification are in short supply among the grossly poor. Hunger and danger are highly corrosive of such concentration.

Second, some steep-gradient individuals simply become overwhelmed by maternal needs and are unable to function at all. McClelland observes that while fathers are generally trivial in the lives of high achievers, they are usually around during the very earliest years—long enough to provide some sort of balance in the family setting until the child is old enough to absorb the maternal overload. McClelland also notes that most high achievers find some kind of substitute male to serve as model for them. In the absence of some stabilizing force of this kind, steep-gradient males simply develop the kind of impulsive, grandiose, touchy narcissism that characterizes most warrior societies.

Finally, we must recognize that our notions of what constitutes a "high achiever" are highly class-bound. There is no qualitative difference in achievement terms between a robber baron of the nineteenth century and a heroin wholesaler in the twentieth. Some kinds of exploitation are legitimized by the state while others are not. Underworld success often demands greater skill, adroitness, business acumen, and administrative genius than "legitimate" business, and there are many high achievers in the ghetto that will die unknown and unrecognized.

Women, Mobility, and Achievement

Thus far I have talked about mobility and achievement as if they were something that only concerned men. I have talked of mothers and sons, but said nothing of fathers and daughters. What has been said, however, may help explain why women have been so secondary in the cultures of the past three millennia, and why they will be so primary in those to come.

In patriarchal societies women achieve social mobility only through men. They can either use their sexuality to good advantage—marrying someone of a higher class or becoming a successful courtesan—or they can rise through their sons. That is to say, they can prostitute either themselves or their offspring.

There have, of course, been exceptions—women who have overcome massive cultural resistance to achieve fame in some field of endeavor. While systematic data are difficult to come by, my impression is that with women, as with men, a high achievement drive is often associated with a powerful attachment to the parent of the opposite sex.

It is rarely, however, that a father is the first, most intense, or most reliable source of nurturance for a child. This means that, for women, the main source of gratification and the object of oedipal fantasy are not one and the same. This experience creates a profound difference between the psychic structures of men and women—a difference I believe to have far more powerful consequences than differences in anatomy or copulatory role.

Both sexes begin life with the same primary gratifier: the mother. When they reach the "oedipal age" of three to six years, however, the little boy is talking about marrying Mother when he grows up, while the little girl is talking about marrying Father —he is multiplying his attachment while she is dividing hers. A highly oedipal boy, therefore, has a steeper pleasure gradient than a highly oedipal girl. The difficulty that many creative women have in "getting it together"—in translating their abilities into a coherent career—may not be solely a function of the heavy negative cultural conditioning about achievement they have received. It may also owe something to the fact that their flatter pleasure gradient does not permit so heavy an investment in some sort of ultimate symbolic gratifier. Men who are high achievers are unconflicted because there is nothing in the original family picture to arouse conflict: The father is rejected and dismissed, the mother is all. It is much more difficult to reject and dismiss a mother. Since fathers are typically less central in child care, the girl who makes a heavy oedipal investment is taking a huge risk and stands to lose more than she gains. Boys take far less risk when they embark on the oedipal journey.

This is not to say that the difference acts only to make life easier for boys. Their emotional tasks are simply of a different sort. Little girls have to make a difficult leap of faith during this oedipal phase—have to divide their deepest affection and attach some of it to a relatively ephemeral object. Little boys, on the other hand, must divide *themselves*—must somehow relinquish their dependent attachment to the mother while at the same time retaining her as an object of oedipal fantasy. This is perhaps the origin of the masculine tendency to compartmentalize sexuality—to be more willing to divest it of loving and affectionate meaning. Boys are trained very early to reject and suppress the core of their emotional and interpersonal being—initially, their needs for mothering. They thereby become experts at filtering feelings—at allowing one feeling expression while blocking others normally associated with it. They have the difficult task of altering their relation to the mother while retaining their primary attachment to her. They thus lose what little girls are able to retain: a sense of continuity—a capacity to accept and cherish the idyllic memories of infant dependency. The mother-daughter relationship may often be fraught with tension and competition, particularly in adolescence, but in stable patriarchal societies it tends to be the strongest, closest, and the least conflicted, on the average, of the four parent-child pairs.

These different early experiences, then, suggest that while women will tend to be virtuosi in taking emotional and interpersonal risks, men will tend to be virtuosi in exercising emotional and interpersonal control. Men will be less willing to be vulnerable, to risk involvement and commitment in relationships, to get hurt, to let it all hang out. They will make a greater demand for interpersonal safety in their heterosexual relationships—wanting partners who are docile, affectionate, devoted, faithful, and unchallenging. Women, on the other hand, are more willing to live dangerously in their deepest relationships, more able to invest their love in partners who are distant, cold, and inconstant. This ability is learned early: As Ashley Montague points out, fathers provide far fewer gratifying tactile and security-giving experiences to their children than do mothers.

These differences should diminish rapidly over the next fifty years in response to the revolutionary changes gradually being brought about by the women's movement. It is important that the changes are being introduced at every point in the system—a necessary process if real change is to occur. Mothers are encouraged to de-intensify their child rearing activities, fathers to increase theirs, women to assume more sexual freedom and self-assertion, men to become more vulnerable and emotionally uninhibited, and parents to treat children in ways less differentiated by sex.

The greater emphasis on emotional compartmentalization by men contributes mightily to their ability to exclude feelings from direct consideration in task activities, and hence to their tendency to create machinelike and inhumane environments. It also accords with David Bakan's ideas about the relative importance of what he calls "agency" and "communion" in men and women. Bakan uses the term *agency* to describe the tendency of an organism to maintain its separate existence, *communion* to refer to its participation in some larger organism. Separation, self-armoring, aggrandizement, mastery, and repression are aspects of agency: union, openness, co-operation, and expression are aspects of communion. Bakan argues that agency is more pronounced in men, communion in women. Unfortunately, he seems to assume that this difference is biological, on the basis of some embarrassingly simple-minded psychological studies showing that girls prefer dolls while boys prefer trucks, and so on—that sex-role training, in other words, has been successful. Viewing such differences as biological is a little like saying that people who live in the mountains have a gene that makes them good climbers, or that coastal dwellers are biologically drawn to boats, or that civilized peoples are constitutionally attracted to plumbing facilities. The same psychologists who through painstaking research discover that men and women have different interests, are careful to buy different toys for their male and female children, and evince visible anxiety when the "wrong" ones are chosen.

The tendency toward agency in men is a function of a steeper pleasure gradient: Separation and detachment are made possible in men by the ability to invest in symbolic objects rather than real ones. Similarly, the greater "field-dependence" of women reflects their greater immersion in the dance of life, and the need of men to maintain internal consistency in the face of emotional dependency on a single gratification source. Field-independence is usually regarded with implicit admiration, and it certainly has its uses, but it also vastly facilitates mechanical responsivity. The same may be said of the more rigid homeostatic mechanisms found in men—their lower physiological responsiveness to environmental effects. Bakan suggests that "there is more harmony between the body and environment for the female and less necessity for acting on the environment."

Bakan makes much of the greater social responsivity and connectedness of women, and we may recall Toffler's remark that women are more reluctant than men to slough relationships after a move. People with flatter gradients develop their relational networks experientially, by living in the present. Ultimately they find themselves in a balanced system, with a variety of friends, relatives, and lovers each providing somewhat specialized emotional satisfactions. They are rooted in reality. Those with steeper gradients have more of their emotional life bound up in symbols of the Gratifying One. When such a symbol looms into their field of vision they are often willing to slough their entire relational network in favor of this illusion. Emotionally, with all his planning, scheming, striving, and long-range goals, the person with a steeper gradient is less reality-based. He can invest intensely in a relationship only so long as it symbolizes the One to him, or can be exploited in the service of his oedipal goals. When this ceases to be true he can withdraw from it almost as if it never existed.

If it is true that women tend to have flatter pleasure gradients than men, the impact of the women's movement on Western culture will be profound. Women are oppressed to some extent in all civilized societies. But Western culture is *founded* on the oppression of women and of the values associated with them: wholeness, continuity, communion, humanism, feelings, the body, connectedness, harmony. In Eastern cultures, women have often been even more powerless and constrained, but a higher value has been placed on their sphere—they have been viewed as having a more central role in the basic round of life. The women's movement emerged in the West when the social significance of women in the culture had reached its lowest point in history— when women were excluded from valued occupations, isolated from each other, frequently uprooted by their mobile spouses, and even had their domestic tasks reduced to triviality by technology. This process, whereby the intensification of some social form leads directly to its opposite, I call *social eversion*. We will encounter it again in a later chapter.

Two Routes to Status Change

There are two different routes that can be followed in moving from a lower to a higher class. One can move individually, dissociating himself from peers and entering the higher class as an individual, or one can change the status of the entire group or class. The first is variously called social mobility, social climbing, or bettering oneself, depending on the point of view. The second is called class warfare, revolution, or social evolution, depending on the circumstances in which it occurs. The first is an expression of agency, in Bakan's terms, since it increases separation, detachment, and atomization—the parvenu is integrated neither with his old group nor with the new one. The second is an expression of communion, for it seeks the collapse of social barriers. The first seems less violent in its effects, since it does not immediately disturb the social fabric; in the long run, however, the dissolving of connections that it occasions has the effect of producing instability and social chaos. The second method, conversely, is initially more convulsive, but the upheaval it produces yields social stability in the long run. What we call liberal reform has usually resulted in facilitating the first, or individualistic method. I observed earlier that the social critics of the fifties, in their attack on the somewhat deteriorated remnants of social responsivity left in our society, contributed not a little to the dissolution of connectedness and the further development of mechanistic behavior. Their approval of individualistic mobility—of the heroic deviant who rises above her peers is undisguised. What we call radical, on the other hand, usually involves an effort to bring about the second, or collective mode of change.

It is characteristic of those in the higher class, insofar as they are willing to tolerate any movement at all, to talk up the individualistic route. They stress the value of rising above the crowd, usually through education, emotional self-alienation, and aggressive striving. In this they are merely enunciating the oppressor-oppressed dynamic: only the strong and wily are fit to "protect" the oppressed. It is also characteristic of the earliest spokesmen of the oppressed to ape this view—to regard their role merely as one of enlarging the funnel through which their followers pass individually into the ranks of the oppressors. They exhort the oppressed to self-improvement and try to persuade the oppressors that the advantages of new energetic blood outweigh those of comfortable solidarity.

As oppressed groups become more sophisticated politically they increasingly reject this view and the leaders that represent it. They seek to rise as a group rather than individually. Instead of demanding equality—the opportunity to live up to the values of the oppressor class—they begin to assert the validity of their own values. The first feminist groups, for example, stressed voting rights and equal pay, and even today some groups seem largely concerned with making it possible for middle-class women to develop the same kind of careerist mentality that now afflicts middle-class men. The shift from the individual route to the collective one has expressed itself in a re-evaluation of the division of labor by sex and an attack on the masculine emphasis on agency. The difference in practice is a subtle one, since the reduction of agency in men necessitates an increase in agency in women, which the outsider might find difficult to distinguish from the equal-rights emphasis of the past.

The goal, however, is quite different. Women are in a position to bring to any activity a wholeness of which men are largely incapable, since the imposing specializations of men are achieved by severe emotional warping. If they follow the same path as men, women will merely join the ranks of the oppressors. Yet they cannot shun the specialities of men since that will make them dependent upon men and prolong both the oppression and the specialization. This is why such things as karate classes for women are far from the trivial matter they may seem to be: Nothing feeds oppression so well as the deep inner conviction of the oppressed that they are incapable of protecting themselves.

The difference, then, is internal. Women cannot and should not avoid becoming doctors, for example, but there is a danger, in accepting the peculiar initiation rites that men have developed for this profession, that they will thereby become the kind of doctors that most men are, and medicine will continue to be the ghastly deformity that men have made it. This is why consciousness raising is so important to liberation movements—the pathway along which the oppressed must walk is beset with a thousand pitfalls.

One important technique is to assess how oedipal one's motivation is. Since careerism for both sexes tends to hold oedipal meanings, a woman's ambition may be largely an oedipal rejection of her mother—the individualistic route, in other words. The extent to which she concerns herself with the fate of *all* women will indicate the extent to which she has maintained a balanced attachment to both parents. The same, of course, applies to men—it is the isolated achievers who reject the father altogether, and their achievements are correspondingly one-sided and inhumane. Wholeness of person necessitates an acceptance of our identity with all living things—to cast out or depersonalize anyone is to reject a part of ourselves and to dehumanize our environment.

Oedipus vs. Peter Pan

We began this chapter by looking at the family as the proto-typical class system. I would like to end it by looking once again at youth as a subordinate class.

The counterculture in America has been pronounced dead by those who thought they invented it, but once again, we must not be distracted by media fads. Most of the people who discussed the counterculture did so in a manner that made it clear that they thought of it as a counter*society*, which, of course, it never was. The noisy manifestations have died away, but the values they dramatized continue lazily to diffuse through our culture. Oedipal motivation seems to be on the decline in America, despite the fact that many of the conditions that foster it are still present.

Those who still have it sometimes accuse those who lack it of not growing up, and when we look at the family as a class system the truth of this accusation becomes apparent. Not to grow up is a cultural secession. Oedipal culture is dying because people show a decreased interest in joining its dominant class.

This suggests a modification of my statement about the collective route to status change: Oppressed classes do not typically move as a group *into* the dominant class in a revolutionary situation; they create a *new* dominant class, parallel to and re-placing the old one, which atrophies.

The adults in a society are in a position, as a dominant class, to define what it means to be an adult and what it means to be a child. That is why the word "mature" has always been such a bludgeon in the hands of adults. Yet that power to define is conspicuously weaker than it once was, while self-definition by the young as a class has grown stronger. This has certainly not been a matter of political consciousness. It was in fact the growth of the isolated oedipal family that created the conditions leading to its demise—a good example of social eversion.

Both processes began early: as individual families became more autonomous, children became more insulated from the adult community. Philippe Ariès argues that in medieval times children were treated simply as unfinished adults. They were not dressed differently from adults or given any special attention. Beginning with the Renaissance, and increasingly in the sixteenth and seventeenth centuries, interest began to be shown in the special characteristics of childhood life. Children began to be dressed in special garments (the first children's costume was simply what everyone had worn a century previous) and games originally enjoyed by both children and adults began to be defined solely as children's pastimes—as they remain to this day. At the same time the idea that children were innocent and needed to be shielded from sexuality began to gain currency, and special concern about the child's health and moral development began to appear. Schools began to be institutions especially designed for children, who were increasingly segregated from adults and grouped by age. Discipline was gradually extended to embrace the entire life of the child and exclude him from adult liberties.

But while children were being isolated from the corruptions of adult life and becoming immersed in their own, the family was at the same time becoming isolated from the community—becoming an autonomous unit. The idea of privacy evolved in the eighteenth century—one could no longer call on people without warning, and houses evolved rooms with specialized functions, so that society could be more easily kept at bay. "Until the end of the seventeenth century," remarks Ariès, "nobody was ever left alone." People now began to have private rooms, and the family began to narrow to include only parents and children. The eighteenth century was also the era in which children began to be forced to sleep alone, to be weaned and toilet trained early, and otherwise to be subjected to the kind of discipline that was taken for granted by 1900. In summary, children were, as Ariès puts it, "quarantined" from adult life by family and school so that they could be molded by conscious policy.

The miniaturization of the family and the quarantining of children have both gone much further since the eighteenth century. And while children have been increasingly exposed to the overpowering psychic assault of the small oedipal family, they have at the same time been increasingly protected from the realities of adult life, and immersed in narrowly age-graded cultures of their own. This has meant that the oedipal children fostered by the modern middle-class family could increasingly avoid moving into the adult class at all, but could remain instead in a world of their own making. They could be oedipal *children*, relieving them of the necessity of becoming oedipal adults.

Ariès points out several times the social identity between children and the lower social orders. When children began to wear a distinctive costume it was not merely an archaic one, it was also what the lower classes wore. When certain games were relegated to children, they were also relegated to the peasantry. As children were culturally separated from their elders, the rich were culturally separated from the poor. In both cases "class consciousness" has created cultural changes whose effects are only beginning to be felt.

Parable 5

A Japanese soldier named Soichi Yokoi found himself on the island of Guam when it was occupied by American forces. Faithful to the code of the army, which prohibited surrender, he and a group of comrades took to the jungle and hid themselves in caves. Twenty years passed, and his comrades all died or were captured. The emperor had long since surrendered, but Yokoi remained faithful. For eight more years he stayed in hiding, completely alone. Finally, thirty-one years after leaving his native land, he was discovered and returned to Japan to find it completely transformed. He apologized for disgracing the emperor.

DESIGNING THE LEAD
BALLOON
or
THE DESCENT
TO THE FUTURE

> *It is the way of heaven to take from what has in excess in order to make good what is deficient. The way of man is otherwise. It takes from those who are in want in order to offer this to those who already have more than enough.*
>
> **Lao Tzu**

> *The impure and the organic are interchangeable conceptions.*
>
> **C. S. Lewis**

Western peoples are very mixed up about social change. They tend to believe that it only takes place through conscious public policy, when in fact the changes that really matter are occurring by tiny increments every time someone buys something or builds something. They also imagine that major social changes can be achieved simply by deciding to make them. As a result, one simultaneously hears excited pronouncements that change is perpetual and accelerating, and discouraged complaints that nothing really changes at all.

It is my belief that our efforts to solve social problems have generally created more social misery and injustice than the evils against which these efforts were directed. Americans approach social change with the thoughtfulness of a slot machine addict, throwing laws and administrative orders into the political process like quarters. This is not to make the traditional demand for more planning, which usually means making the same insensitive decisions on a more gigantic scale.

What follows is directed not so much at those who are currently making a mess of our world, but at those who want to correct this condition by making a new mess of their own. It has not been sufficiently emphasized that the miseries from which people now suffer in the Western world were largely brought about by people who were convinced they were making the world a better, safer, and happier place. To assume, without the deepest self-examination, that any bold new program now under consideration would fare any differently is not only arrogant but stupid. The men who had the bright idea of wiping out the mosquito by drenching the world with poison should have known better, but we, after all, have the additional advantage of that fatal experience.

This is not an argument against change, but an attempt to generate some degree of thoughtfulness about it. I would like in this chapter to discuss what I feel to be some profound misconceptions about change that are shared by radicals, liberals, and conservatives alike.

Change and Stress

The first misconception is that it is possible to have change without stress. We are constantly told how adaptable human beings are—how culture has freed us from our bodies so that we can swing with anything that scientific tinkering, governmental tyranny, or intellectual fashion might see fit to inflict upon us.

It is true that humans are adaptable, but that adaptability is finite. It is also true that adaptation is stressful. Indeed, one of the consequences of our overtaxed adaptability is that it is even stressful to adapt to a happier condition when some misery to which we have become accustomed has been removed. Toffler points out that the body responds to novelty with massive physiological mobilization—the "orientation response," marked by a heavy adrenalin output. As change becomes chronic so also does the orientation response, with consequent damage to the organism. This is another example of an emergency mechanism becoming chronic, with the usual destructive consequences.

One of the better-kept secrets of medical science (it doesn't sell pills) is that the major cause of disease is change. People who live in stable environments with adequate nutrition have generally good health, while those who, like ourselves, are subject to constantly shifting living contexts tend to be more sickly. Furthermore, as Toffler has now brought to public attention, there is a direct correlation between the number of major changes (residence, spouse, job, etc.) experienced by a person in a given period and the likelihood of his or her falling ill. Most important of all, this effect holds *even if the changes were desired.*

Change, in other words, has been found to be injurious to your health. Flowers and trees often die when they are transplanted, and so, at times, do animals and people. Travelers fall ill with undue frequency, even though they are free from ordinary pressures and presumably having a good time. Old people, for whom adaptation is more effortful, die with such rapidity upon being institutionalized that the geriatric wards of many state hospitals have been characterized as delayed-action gas chambers. It would seem that the blithe assumption of our culture that chronic change is a fit condition for human beings to live in needs re-evaluation.

On the other hand, most people do survive. Doesn't this argue that we can, in fact, adapt successfully? This, of course, is Toffler's position. After amassing evidence to show the grinding impact of change on the human organism he simply shrugs his shoulders and says faster adaptation is necessary if the technological behemoth is to continue to receive its ever-expanding daily quota of human blood. Like some victory-crazed football coach, he would tape us up, shoot us full of Novocain, and hustle us back on the field.

It is with the psychic equivalent of Novocain that we do manage to adapt to change. By numbing ourselves to life, by distancing ourselves from our senses, by losing events in a haze of conceptualization, we escape the trauma of personal disruption. "People are people everywhere" is a valuable palliative for those who have lost the capacity really to know anyone. From a transcontinental jet it looks as if very little is happening down there. The viewpoint is the same for the suburban drunk, the tranquilized housewife, the nodding junkie. Whatever means is used, the principle is the same: Change only affects you if you are *here*. If you can get far enough off to conceptualize prechange and postchange as the same thing, you are free from the burden of adaptation.

But whether we numb ourselves to it or allow ourselves to be ground up in it, whether we initiate it or just experience it, whether we desire it or dread it, massive environmental change—social or technological, popular or authoritarian, radical or plutocratic—is stressful and brutalizing to the human organism.

The Futility of Positive Programs

The second misconception is that the social system in which we live is static and empty—a motionless container that must be filled with plans, programs, and energy. Energy is indeed required to change *direction,* but this is not the same thing as saying there is now an energy vacuum. The American way is always to *add* something, to start something, to create new activities. Yet vast amounts of energy are already being poured into activities and institutions that already exist, and it usually seems burdensome to supplement all this with something new. Seldom does anyone consider the energy relation between what already exists and what is to be added. If the rich are stealing from the poor, we start a program to compensate the poor. If people are rotting in large custodial mental hospitals, we create some small model treatment centers. The word "model" is very big in our action vocabulary—model cities, model schools, model programs. The concept is a sensible one, but somehow the models never seem to catch on—perhaps because no one pays attention to what keeps so much energy bound up in the old ways.

Since we think of social change as adding something, the issue of cost is always raised—how much will a new program cost? But if change is viewed as redirecting energy rather than taking on a new task, the cost issue becomes less relevant. It is said, for example, that we cannot afford better schools, communities, health care, and so on. But what we can afford least of all is to allow some people to become very rich. This is our most expensive social program: To make it possible, we have spent billions upon billions of dollars, allowed our air and water to become polluted, our environment to become ugly, our cities to deteriorate, our health care to become third-rate, created untold poverty, misery, sickness, suffering, chaos, disorder, and mass murder. We nonetheless managed to afford it.

Most of our social problems would be better solved by negative action than positive action; that is to say, they would cease to exist were we to stop rewarding people for creating them. Our national policy has always been to subsidize the rich and ambitious in various ways: Currently, for example, we provide incentives to those who exploit and brutalize the environment—developers, loggers, highway contractors, oil companies, manufacturers. We soften risks, give tax relief, offer inducements to do what is already highly lucrative. We have given oil companies, through depletion allowances and import quotas, for example, billions of dollars to despoil the environment, maintain inefficient practices, engage in expensive and dishonest advertising (what an oil company spends to change its name would meet a fair-sized city's welfare budget for a year), and preserve the archaic view that they are in the oil business rather than the energy business. The fact that a corporation is taking some risks in order to make a huge profit seems an inadequate reason for giving them charity. It is one thing to pay for a needed service, quite another to guarantee excessive wealth to those doing a mediocre job of supplying it. Faltering industries can be put on a non-profit basis if what they provide is really essential. For while the increasing inefficiency of the mails is sometimes attributed to the fact that it is a government agency, this argument founders on the fact that telephone service has deteriorated even more dramatically in the past decade, despite constant rate increases and fat dividends to shareholders. Furthermore, although the U. S. Mail is itself non-profit, it has provided profits to others through the category of third-class mail, the elimination of which, for profit-making corporations, would do much to improve service.

We worry about overpopulation—particularly of Americans, since the deleterious impact of a single American on the environment is many times greater than that of a Third World person. Yet our tax system rewards us for having children. Similarly, we complain that developers are rapidly bulldozing away all the beautiful open spaces, creating ugly tracts of separated houses surrounded by useless strips of cropped grass. Yet we give tax relief to the property owner.

Anyone can multiply examples—I have mentioned only financial ones—but it scarcely needs a bevy of facts to support the notion that people don't commit transparently foolish acts without incentives. Whatever abuses we find around us are encouraged by us in some way or another, and it makes sense to find out why.

We like to think that a social change begins with a blueprint in our head—that we *initiate* a process of change. This is ignorant and megalomaniacal. When we decide on a course of action we are also *responding* to some change that has already occurred. We are saying that it hurts us and we want to avoid that hurt. Mechanical thinking and the Protestant Ethic have blinded us to the fact that we are links in a continuous feedback chain. We imagine that we are always beginning anew with our bold new programs, and that is the principal reason they fail.

Social Judo, or When the Right is Right

The third delusion about social change is that desirable reforms can be brought about when those who oppose them are either outvoted or re-educated as to what their best interests are. The pomposity of the left is so extravagant on this point that it is worth remembering that most of the evils the left now rails against were first attacked by dyed-in-the-wool conservatives. The histories and biographies on which we are raised present Heroes of Progress overcoming obstinate Obstacles to Progress. With each passing year, however, the conservative grumblings of the Obstacles become harder and harder to differentiate from the arguments of contemporary radicals. The reactionary of yesterday is the visionary of tomorrow.

Those who espouse the idea of linear progress cannot tolerate this kind of cyclical manifestation. Confronted with the statements of men and women who tried to halt the ravages of technology fifty years ago, they dismiss them as having a different meaning or as being right for the wrong reasons. But this is just intellectual snobbery—they were exactly the same reasons, at a time when those reasons were not yet fashionable.

Reactionaries have been railing against technological blight for decades. They have consistently opposed centralized governmental power and the hypertrophy of the executive branch of our government. They have attacked bureaucratization, sneered at the naïve belief in progress, complained that the acceleration in the rate of change was destructive of human values. It is only a decade or so since a concern with ecological issues was dismissed by liberals and radicals as a quaint reactionary preoccupation. Early opponents of Pasteur and the germ theory of disease —regarded for a half century or more as men without vision— sound strangely modern now that that theory has outlived its utility.

Or consider an issue more recently passé: fluoridation—a liberal's cause par excellence. A scientific dictum is embodied in chemical form and applied on a mass basis to a population for its own good. Those who opposed this process were derided as archaic and paranoid—dental health and mental health stood side by side against the forces of dark ignorance. Today, numbed by so many more serious intrusions of the bureaucratic mentality, it seems difficult to recall what the hubbub was all about, but the forces of darkness appear in retrospect to have had a somewhat deeper ecological and political consciousness than their heavenly opponents.

But let us not shrink from contemporary debates. Conservatives today are opposed both to gun control and to unilateral disarmament. For taking these positions they are deemed benighted and violent, but it must be admitted that the positions are at least consistent. Taken together they imply that, given the existence of weapons, the more equally distributed they are, the better. Although I would much prefer that all weaponry be abolished, I regard this position as incontestable.

Having guns so widely available in a disturbed population such as ours makes life extremely unsafe. Yet even a violent and crazy populace should not be disarmed while subject to an even crazier overweaponed government over which it has little if any control. Were I not familiar with the peculiar inability of liberals to relate single issues to broader contexts I would be amazed at their readiness to jettison one of the pillars of the Bill of Rights. Note that the demand for gun control only became widespread when guns previously reserved for fratricide began to be turned against public figures. Every state wishes insofar as possible to maintain a monopoly on murder and violence, but by and large the more it succeeds in doing so the worse things are for its people. The liberals are quite correct in feeling that the power of life and death should not be given to every individual—that if it is given at all, it should be to the entire community. But an authoritarian government is not a community, and it is an unfortunate paradox that the very individualism that invariably spawns such governments often seems to be the only protection against them. Such protection is illusory, since individualism means in practice that everyone stands alone against the centralized co-ordinating force that individualism makes necessary. Still, until something better is formed it is all we have. To reserve all weapons to those in uniform is to abandon the penultimate pretense of democracy. A man in uniform has made himself the instrument of another man's personal power—to what ends he cannot know. He and all those who wear that uniform are concentrated extensions of that power, and hence far more dangerous than a single lunatic with a rifle.

Nor can the conservative preoccupation with competitive power positions abroad be lightly dismissed. The history of human societies is one in which humane, happy, and healthy communities have continually been gobbled up or wiped out by competitive, surly, and emotionally deprived ones, and should we ever evolve from the latter to the former we might suffer the same fate unless the rest of the armed world evolves at the same rate. I do not wish to slide over the fact, however, that this preoccupation is a powerful deterrent to *anyone's* evolving in this direction and hence maximizes the chances of species destruction.

Many will feel these observations are frivolous—a high school exercise in tolerance. Any certified intellectual could put together a host of examples to show that conservatives taking these positions are motivated by less lofty considerations than those I have put forth. Nevertheless, when any large number of people espouse an ideological position and defend it with fervor they are championing a human need shared not only by themselves but by their opponents, who are thereby spared the trouble of paying attention to it in themselves. Anyone seeking social change who ignores such needs will probably fail, and anyone who seeks a more humane world will not achieve it by working for the suppression of such needs.

Radicals, for example, tend often to be compulsively counter-phobic about change, denying their own needs for security, dependency, and stability. They adopt the stance of the fearless adventurer into the unknown—unawed by the dangers that lie ahead and contemptuous of those who tremble and hesitate. It is my impression that when their own needs for stability are too strongly repressed they reappear in their ideology in the form of rigidity. In other words, if I am going to challenge and alter all that exists I will seek my security in the perfection and inalterability of my theory. It is perhaps this more than anything that accounts for the splintering that afflicts movements on the left.

These views are influenced by many years spent leading encounter groups, where I have observed that those who push hardest for an "intense" experience in the group are often the most resistant to it when it happens, while those who seem timid and defensive at the outset sometimes achieve the most profound changes. The emotional conservative in a group allows others to talk a braver game than they feel. In my group experience every position taken, however repellent, irrelevant, or obstructive it may seem at the time, is rooted in feelings that are shared, less consciously, by other group members. Such feelings are ignored at great cost. Real movement occurs when the false emotional division of labor is relinquished in favor of a recognition of (1) the legitimacy of all feelings, (2) the conflicts present within each person, and (3) the realistic differences between people in the way these conflicts are internally arranged. Steam-rollering and compromise can then be abandoned in favor of synthesis—for while basic human feelings and needs are few and simple, social arrangements for their expression and fulfillment are many and complex.

One of the human needs given short shrift by radicals is the need for order, routine, and predictability in daily life. So important is this need that many people can live out their lives in an uninteresting, draining, and oppressive daily grind and still retain a modicum of happiness, while others can live in a perpetual holiday, constantly exposed to exciting new experiences, and be miserable. The traditional schoolroom was created by people who paid no attention to human needs—aside from war it has perhaps been the single most brutalizing influence on Western culture—but those who recognize this have often reacted by creating a school milieu that disregards those few human needs the traditional schoolroom, with its ritualism, its predictability, and its utter freedom from responsibility, *does* satisfy.

The importance of order becomes apparent during periods of civil strife. The initial impact of what is loosely called a "revolutionary situation" is a sense of liberation and excitement—resembling the explosiveness with which children exit from an authoritarian school building. Radicals often mistake this festive air for some kind of permanent breakthrough and are discouraged when it evaporates after a few weeks and there is massive popular support for the re-establishment of social order. Yet we are surrounded by evidence that people are willing to sacrifice almost anything for order, despite their immense enjoyment of periods of release. Even though social order serves primarily the rich—protecting their favored position—the poor seem to want it just as badly. Nor are counterculture people immune from this need, although they are often not attuned to it. Civil disorders simply fit *their* routines better than those of the straight world. When these routines are disturbed for any extended period they react in the same way. As Bateson points out, one person's order constitutes a form of disorder for everyone else, since no one likes to arrange the world in precisely the same way.

The need for order is what makes protest actions so powerful —people are often willing to make some concessions to restore routine. To accept the usual polarized version of these events, however, is to miss most of what is happening. Both sides want order, and both sides want liberation from the constraints that oppress them, but each asserts only one side of this ambivalence, leaving it to their opponents to express the other. Each also believes firmly in the simplicity of its public stance. Underneath, however, there are extraordinary paradoxes. Victory for the protestors depends upon their having a higher tolerance for disorder than their opponents, but it often turns out that they lose precisely because a large segment of the psyche of the establishment is covertly on their side. To the extent the authorities secretly enjoy the liberating sense of crisis and chaos, they will be able to sit it out until the protestors themselves feel a need to return to their routine activities, and the protest may thereby fail. This happened at times during some of the campus confrontations of the 1960s. In other words, the secret enjoyment of disorder leads to a heightened ability to oppose disorder as a weapon.

Another paradox arises when the authorities, driven by a mixture of terrified and fascinated feelings about disorder, use disorder in the form of a violent mob of armed and uniformed men to "restore order," which it usually fails to do (not surprisingly, considering the confused motivation). Protestors are often shocked by this violation of their own sense of order. The demand for the removal of police or guardsmen is itself a demand for the restoration of order.

The simplicity of polarized value positions thus masks an intricate knot of covert emotional alliances. The statement, "I want A, not B, they want B, not A", usually means, "I know they want B more than I want it, and I can count so fully on their pushing it that I am unaware of my own less urgent need for it. At the same time, since I cannot see their need for A at all I must emphasize it at all times." This process is called distributing the ambivalence and is most conspicuous in married couples, who find it almost impossible to keep sight of the complexity of their own needs and feelings in the face of the inevitable drift toward emotional specialization.

Most of us are brought up to imagine that our spontaneous physical and emotional reactions are private and unique—not linked to other people. Our individualistic beliefs thus ensure that all such reactions are in fact *not* spontaneous but contaminated with egoism. Since people are born interdependent (William Condon of Boston University has shown with slow-motion film that the body movements of people in conversation are normally in perfect synchrony, although this is not visible to the naked eye) everyone is accustomed to (and depends upon) having some of his or her feelings and needs expressed by others. To look inside for every need or feeling is therefore likely to produce erroneous assumptions. Some of our own basic needs will be most fully expressed by other people.

None of us express our needs and feelings in an uncontaminated way—they are warped by narcissism, ideology, will, guilt, defensiveness, rationalization, and the sheer complexity of the pathways to expression that we have forged through all this resistance. A man may be able to find sexual satisfaction only by strangling old ladies or masturbating on a dandelion: We can identify with his sexual desire but not with the tortuous pathway to which his ego has confined him; and if he seeks to justify his behavior in terms of spontaneity, he can only expect us to laugh in his face. We are all poor judges of our own spontaneity. What feels "natural" may be only habitual, or merely a new pathway only slightly less circuitous than the old one.

None of this has anything do do with tolerance. Tolerance implies a lack of connection between opposing views and a wilful effort to soften that opposition. It is therefore as self-alienated as slavery, and can lead only to institutions that are indifferent to human feeling. Significant change must involve a fusion of opposites—not a compromise between antithetical positions, but a response that meets the human needs underlying both positions, since such needs are—with widely varying intensities—universal. This is by no means simple—anyone who offers to interpret the "real" needs underlying a given position is simply arrogant. Only those who hold the position themselves can profitably engage in such a quest.

Social miseries arise from gross imbalances in the distribution of energy throughout the social organism. We need to develop the social equivalent of acupuncture—a sense of how to stimulate and balance natural forces in society. Most efforts at social change pay very little attention to questions of energy—assuming that if enough money or anger can be brought to bear on the issue, change will occur. Yet change means the rechanneling of energy, and it does no good at all to view the *status quo* as a block of wood to be carved or burned. The *status quo* is an intricate and dynamic process—its points of stasis are *loci* where opposing forces have immobilized each other. Instead of continually trying to mobilize new energy, it would be more useful to unlock or take advantage of what is already present.

One example of an existing energy channel is the media. The media are motivated to expose, interest, and excite. They cannot avoid trying to do this. Radicals with an appreciation of this energy flow have ridden it with considerable success. Another such channel is advertising. Corporations are heavily invested in creating public good will: If there is a virtue anywhere in the popular consciousness, they want to be the first to claim it. This has greatly annoyed traditional radicals who speak of co-optation. Every large corporation, for example, now claims to be socially conscious and ecologically aware. Most of their statements are utterly deceptive, but this is the way it always begins. When a public lie dances on the stage, the truth is waiting in the wings. For such statements carry a double message: "I am ecologically minded" also says "It is important and virtuous to be ecologically minded." Corporations will ultimately impale themselves on these messages, being forced by competitive pressure to make them more and more convincing. At the same time the public is habituated to the importance of the claimed virtues, and an *expectation* is created that corporations should take responsibility for social issues. To fret over the deceptiveness of these early claims overlooks the importance of the chain of events they set in motion.

If energy is bound up in opposing positions, a vast pool of energy will be released when these opposing thrusts are united. Freud once suggested that if one wished to discover the nature of a hidden impulse, one had only to frame the question in negative form ("What does the dream clearly *not* mean?" "What is the *least* likely thing . . ."). The impulse, he said, is striving outward toward expression, while an inhibition, with equal force, is pushing it back inward; by adding the word "not," the energy of the inhibiting force is suddenly united to the force toward expression. Both are pushing in the same direction and the answer pops right out. Similarly, social change often occurs through a kind of political judo, in which the energy locked in opposing viewpoints is released through an acceptance of the emotional validity within each.

Blueprinting

The fourth common illusion about social change is that it occurs through some sort of cognitive process—a problem is isolated and diagnosed, a prescription is written, a course of treatment designed and executed. When a group of people come together to discuss a social crisis they often have in common only the distress they feel about it. Yet this shared feeling is the first thing that is discarded, so that they can "analyze the problem objectively." Since they have omitted the most important piece of data, and the only common ground they have, they tend to come up with solutions that are not only off the mark, but as destructive of human values as the social distress that brought them together in the first place.

The term "problem" itself reflects a faulty epistemology. It implies that the social environment is static, that those who are trying to deal with it are outside and above it—looking down on it like a math student looks down on a piece of paper. It also implies that the "solution" represents a cognitive beginning—an initiated action rather than an emotional reaction to what has already happened. This is all illusion and self-deception—we do not initiate social programs, we react to our experience, which alters as we do so. Furthermore, we are not and cannot be outside our social "problems." We are inside them—they are the medium in which we swim. Yet this self-deception has consequences, because insofar as we attempt to ignore our own feelings our "solutions" are bleached of humanity. The bureaucratized environment of which we so often complain has largely been created by our treating social crises as if we did not participate in them.

When Toffler rails against the "irrationalism" of the newer trends in our culture it is this kind of schizoid self-deception that he is protecting. Any departure from the railroad-track mentality that claims the future must in every respect be more alienated from the past than the present is stigmatized as a "revulsion against intelligence." Toffler apparently identifies intelligence with Newtonian physics, eighteenth-century rationalism and the pigeonhole departmentalism of the academics. He wants education, for example, to have a "consistent direction and a logical starting point," as if learning began anywhere or went in a straight line. He attacks all departures from conventional scientism as "garish," "sick," and "prescientific," and asks questions like, "What kind of cultural life *should* a great city of the future enjoy," as if it were logical for human interests and desires to be programmed out of the head of some planning commission or "utopia factory." Toffler seems to imply that we must all eat Wonder Bread and shop in supermarkets to be freed from any taint of "nostalgia," "irrationality," or "acting out." But we should not be misled into mistaking arithmetical and compartmentalized modes of thought for intelligence. There is nothing more irrational than the notion that ignoring our own feelings and needs will by some convoluted magic create an environment that will gratify us.

Scientists and would-be scientists often speak, with puritanical pride, about "cold, dry, hard facts"—triumphantly asserting their bloodless world view. Since they never look at any soft, wet, warm facts it is hardly surprising that they have failed to produce any theories that deal effectively with living wholes.

Don't Look Back, the Future May Be Gaining on You

The fifth misconception is that social change is linear. The statement that history never repeats itself has a certain validity, but so does the claim that there is nothing new under the sun. The fundamental relationships between parts, between parts and wholes, between organisms, and between organisms and environment fluctuate within a relatively modest range around a more or less constant norm. On the other hand, every specific arrangement of energy is unique, and the history of our planet has seen the continual proliferation of such arrangements. The bulldozer is not a shovel, and a detergent with a "new formula" may indeed be a new combination, however irrelevant or useless. There is no point in trying to maintain that time merely revolves endlessly, but there is also no point in arguing that the universe moves rigidly in one direction on a fixed track. We have gotten ourselves into a lot of trouble by treating the past as so much garbage, to be cast on a junk heap like the torn pages of a calendar with the days crossed off. A viable ecology requires that the past be recycled too.

There is much we can use back there. Every era is in part a corrective for the distortions of the previous one, but it also contains its own distortions. The railroad-track theory is dangerous in that it implies that if we pursue the future frantically enough, we can escape the irreconcilable opposites around which social systems are formed. Somewhere in the future, it is imagined, we will be able simultaneously to maximize security and surprise, community and privacy, variety and constancy, and everyone will be both equal and better than everyone else.

Our past is a part of us. Who is to say we cannot have it? "You can't go back" simply means "you have to stay on these rails." But human beings are not linear—what has been is as deeply us as what will or might be. Technology and intellectual fashion have pushed people into accepting smaller and smaller temporal fragments of themselves until there is not enough left to form a whole human being. The result of this has been another social eversion—the embracing of passionately nostalgic revivals and religions that allow people to reincorporate the entire universe into their temporally shrunken personalities. Our history is a living part of our being—a reservoir from which to draw nourishment and creativity.

Toffler himself grudgingly admits that continuity is "not necessarily 'reactionary,'" but views the need for such continuity as an unfortunate human limitation, like the need for sleep, for which the machinery of industrialism must occasionally make allowance—presumably until humans can be replaced by some more malleable species. It is inconceivable to him (and he is representative of most *status quo* spokesmen in this regard) that the future might contain any element once rejected by the industrial revolution, yet history is full of such revivals. Toffler's future is merely a linear extrapolation of the century that ended in 1960. Any deviation from that course is a "reversion" and a "rejection of the future." Toffler cannot see that the ideas and trends he dismisses as "reversionism" are simply building the foundation for a different future than he imagines. It is a little like someone of the coal-and-steam era attacking the proponents of electrical power as reversionists because they sought to generate electric power from falling water.

The most dangerous idea imaginable for an individual, group, society, or species is that the past contains no worthwhile arrangements—that the direction one is currently taking is the best of all possible directions, now and forever. Even biological evolution contains some major reversals. Our own biological ancestors found that at one time it was useful to take to the trees, while at another time it was useful to come down out of them again.

Toffler is saying we must climb higher and higher in the trees of technocracy because that is the direction we started in, and hence that is where "the future" lies. Others are nevertheless beginning to climb down. If *they* turn out to be the future, they will have been profoundly changed by their arboreal sojourn—in this sense, there is no going back. There is no reason to assume, however, that the year 2100 will resemble 1975 any more than it will resemble 1800. I suspect that it will have a good deal less hardware than today: Hardware already begins to seem a little unsophisticated in the light of the growing emphasis on relational processes in virtually every domain of human endeavor.

Power and Energy

The sixth misconception about social change is that in order to bring it about one must obtain power. This assumes, first, that what I have called negative power is a neutral force, and second, that social change originates in power centers. Both of these assumptions are false.

The worst evils of our political system come from the centralization of power, irrespective of who holds it. It is the most naïve kind of hero-villain thinking to imagine that a new face will change a system. The major organizations in our society have seen dozens of incumbents pass through their top positions without greatly affecting the oppressiveness of their fundamental patterning. The centralization of power is rooted in paranoid motivation—to imagine that anything benign or lovely could flourish in such an environment is as illusory as the perpetual-motion machine.

Consider the power concentrated in the hands of the President of the United States. It is the power, ultimately, to decide the life or death of every living person. To give such power to a single man or group of men is to court catastrophe. Even a paragon of virtue (and what sort of virtue would pursue such evil power?) could scarcely avoid blundering eventually, simply because he would be unable to keep abreast of the enormous volume of information required to act wisely. Concentration of power means that the locus of decision making is farther and farther removed from the locus of its consequences—that decisions are based on less and less information and are more and more cut off from feedback. The President may be well-informed in an absolute sense, but relative to his arena of responsibility, he is the most ill-informed man in the United States. Fortunately, this same concentration of power contains a self-corrective. In a complex social system the power of the power-glutton is limited by the narrowness and simplicity of his own world view—reinforced by the paucity of information available to him. The more dictatorial he is, the more likely he is to lose touch with the dynamic complexity of the world around him and destroy himself. Authoritarianism, as noted above, works well only in stable, homogeneous systems. Furthermore, power is symbolic, like stock market values. The minute anyone begins to doubt the power of a leader it begins to shrink.

The desire for negative power derives, as we have seen, from fear and mistrust of others—from the feeling that the world's gratifications will not be freely given, shared, or even exchanged, but must be coerced. Alexander Lowen suggests that the only people who can "handle power constructively" are those who have been "fulfilled in childhood and know how to enjoy life." But such people would not want or seek negative power. Anyone who would willingly make the kind of sacrifices required to become President of the United States must necessarily be afflicted with the need to coerce in a particularly virulent form. Such a man is precisely the person to whom such power should not be given. The power to blow up the world cannot be entrusted to anyone sick enough to seek it.

In the last analysis negative power rests on the threat of destruction. One cannot gain power by threatening to create. Anyone can create—props are not required, nor any coercion. Nor does one generally expect innovation or creativity to emerge from centers of power, which are fundamentally conservative in nature—concerned with control, with hanging on, with grasping. Those motivated to seek power tend to mistrust spontaneity, flux, creation—to believe only in what can be controlled, ensured, compelled. They are insensitive to the regenerative processes that occur in nature. They trust, in themselves, only their own defensive structure and learned skills; in others they trust only the tendency of most humans to be impressed by the canopy of status and the accouterments of power. Therefore, although they cannot innovate, it is of desperate importance to them that they stay on top of, abreast of, change. They ride the horse but cannot make it go. Government is largely a negative force—it can regulate, it can maintain, it can destroy.

But can a man who would actively seek the power of the Presidency refrain from using it under stress? If he achieves it, is he likely to tolerate restraints on it—either internally, in the form of decentralization, or externally, in the form of disarmament? International politics as it now exists grinds up millions of healthy individuals in order that the sickest ones can play a kind of chess game. Arthur Janov suggests that it is self-alienation that enables political leaders to discuss mass killing without qualms. Death is not a tragedy for those who cannot feel life. Since they themselves are dead internally, the actual death of others is unreal rather than horrifying.

A male bureaucrat once argued that women should not hold positions of responsibility because of the emotional instabilities associated with menopause, but I would rather take my chances with such a woman than with an ordinary power-hungry male. It seems astonishing that we fear menopausal lability more than the icy pathology that allows a man to order massive destruction and the killing and mutilation of hundreds of thousands of people merely to avoid being called weak, or to win points in a game of international chicken. The lust for power is the most dangerous of all sexual perversions, and the compartmentalized rationalism that often accompanies it is no cause for reassurance. The worst horrors in history have been perpetrated by "sensible," "practical" males "taking the necessary steps" to beat some symbolic opponent to a symbolic goal. Consider how much cold intelligence has been expended on a foreign policy that at bottom is founded on a kind of mad-bomber strategy ("Don't come near me or we all go up!"). René Dubos observes that Captain Ahab was a highly practical whaler: "All my means are sane; my motives and objects mad." The same might be said of Henry Kissinger, who was once quoted as saying that "power is the ultimate aphrodisiac."

These symbolic goals are generally disguised as life-or-death survival issues, but the passage of time always reveals their hollowness. In retrospect it seems to make very little difference to the daily lives of most individuals whether one group or another owns a piece of real estate or controls a governmental apparatus.

One would scarcely do better than chance in trying to guess who had "won" or "lost" a war from the subsequent fortunes of the combatants.

History is vastly misleading, in any case, since it is overwhelmingly, even today, a narration of the vicissitudes of, relationships among, and disturbances created by those inflamed with a passion for wealth, power, and fame. Attempts are made to write social history, but the medium itself interferes with this. Just as archaeology cannot altogether transcend the fact that it is based on human garbage, so history, which is a study of records, cannot transcend the fact that it is based on the products of those maddened by dreams of immortality—those who wish to "make their mark on history." Those who have lived for life itself are lost to record; for that which is green and healthy passes, only the detritus of the death avoiders remains. History is a kind of Marat/Sade of the human race—a diary kept by narcissists, about narcissists, and largely for narcissists. As such, it is useful to the man in power, for it lends credibility to his attempts to convince the populace that his frantic pursuit of symbolic, narcissistic goals represents some real effort on behalf of the people.

Since only madmen are attracted to positions of great power, and since such people are too infatuated to diffuse and decentralize that power, how can we keep them from holding it? How can we give power to those capable of detoxifying it? An obvious although patently unpopular solution would be to choose public officials through some sort of lottery system, such as we now use to hire killers who will not volunteer for the task. The Athenians used such a method, and while it had its problems, most of them could be attributed to the prevalence of precisely the kind of egregious vanity that made it a desirable system in the first place. In the long run it is generally more useful for the person who occupies a given role to feel comfortable in it, but this depends upon power being diffused to the point where the poison is present in small enough doses to be absorbed by the average human.

The idealist who seeks high office to implement high-minded goals is thus engaged in a self-defeating effort. He who seeks such power is an enemy of the people, whatever his program. He will explain his motivation in terms of wanting to "have a real impact," but anyone who acts out of this kind of grandiosity thereby becomes part of the problem rather than part of the solution, since his behavior springs from and helps maintain the motivational core of the oppressive system in which we live.

Efforts to increase the power of a heretofore powerless group are another matter altogether, since they involve the diffusion of power, which should be the central goal of all political activity for the foreseeable future. Community organizing and public exposure of official arrogance are two of the key enterprises in this process. Power is built in large part on the concentration and manipulation of information and hence relies heavily on secrecy. "Top secret" or "highly classified" usually means, "exposure will weaken our power." The right of privacy cannot be allowed the government or any other organization in which comparable power is concentrated, since such privacy is always used by those in power to concentrate that power further. "Private" and "public" are supposed, after all, to be antithetical concepts.

The most important reason for eschewing positions of power is that social change rarely originates in power centers. Many people imagine that Washington, D.C., is "where the action is," but this is true only for power addicts. No major cultural or social innovation ever came out of the Washington political community, although many lesser ones were implemented there. Political leaders merely generalize changes that have arisen elsewhere in the society. The ideas on which new programs are based have usually been around for years. People immersed in government often seem a bit archaic—their information is screened by too many people absorbed with protecting their positions and maintaining secrecy. They are low on information pertaining to system changes, high on facts and figures plugged into rigid and antiquated frameworks. Change in America has come from technologists, businessmen, scientists, inventors, artists, musicians, blacks, street people, the media, and from day-to-day decisions made by millions of completely faceless individuals.

The proper metaphor for Washington and other power centers is the feudal castle. The inhabitants of such a castle had a purely negative function—they could sally forth and destroy, but otherwise led a parasitic existence. The castle had no energy of its own—all was drawn from the farmed lands around it. To attack the castle was absurd for anyone not driven by narcissistic motives, for all of its life lay outside. To take it was to take nothing. One could absorb all the external food and water sources and leave the castle to starve itself. The feudal lord could then sit inside and look out over "his" lands, but he would in fact have been rendered irrelevant.

Leaders do not make change, everyone does. We have been engaged for so long in dreaming of ourselves as agents of change that we have failed in the role of reactor. People are the nerve endings of social systems. If they are stupid enough stoically to bear the pain such a system inflicts upon them, the system will go right on inflicting it. Social mechanisms are mindless, undirected. Insofar as they are deprived of information about human needs and responses, they will be inhumane.

Most Western societies are like people with no sense of pain—they blunder into horrible injuries because they have lost access to vital information from their peripheries. We are the numbed and atrophied nerve endings of our societies. We have been trained to smile politely when some social institution tramples upon us, and every time we do so we give it a lesson in inhumanity.

Parable 6

Once upon a time two poor men—one black, one white—
were traveling together, trying to reach a new and beautiful
land of which they had heard. After some time they met a
witch, who said to them, "Give me a piece of your flesh, and
I will make you wealthy. You will travel in style and ease."
The black man was not interested, but the white man agreed.
No sooner had he done as the witch asked than he was
beautifully dressed and mounted on a fine horse. He was vastly
pleased with the bargain and started to ride off. The black
man could not keep up with him on foot and this made the
white man angry. He scorned the black man's poor clothes, and
when he failed to keep pace he beat him with his crop. When
the black man threatened to leave him the white man bound
him and tied him to the horse and dragged him along on the
ground, for he was afraid to travel alone. This went on for
some time and the black man was badly injured and near
death. Then a change began to come over the white man. He
lost interest in the journey, took no pleasure from his surroundings, and seemed to derive his only satisfaction from comparing
himself to his comrade, whom he now treated as a servant.
He stopped in every village to display his wealth and acquire
more, by gambling or by swindling the inhabitants. Finally,
one day, he encountered another like himself, and trying to
cheat each other, they fell into a quarrel. Words led to blows,
blows to weapons, and both men perished in a gunfight. The
black man, scarred, but otherwise in good health, took the
white man's horse and continued his journey to the beautiful
land.

WATERMELON SEEDS
AND THE WAYS OF
CHANGE

> *Conceivably there was no alternative but
> to push further in the same direction, to wait
> for a neglected force, left in the rear, to fly
> forward again and recover ascendancy.*
>
> **Bellow**

> *Between yea and nay
> How much difference is there?*
>
> **Lao Tzu**

Much of what I have said may seem cause for unrelieved gloom.
To fall into this gloom, however, is to exemplify the narcissistic
pathology I have described. For gloom about the future depends
upon making a linear extrapolation from the present. It assumes
that Western culture will continue on its headlong course toward
disaster, with nothing but human intelligence and enlightenment
to slow it down—a pitiful defense at best. Prophets of doom tend
to see themselves as sounding a desperate alarm in an effort to
arouse people to a herculean exercise of will that will stave off
the disaster; but I have argued that human will is the cause of,

not the solution to, this crisis. To engage in linear extrapolation would make the prospect gloomy indeed.

But there is no need to do so. The future will not be a mere exaggeration of the present. A gloomy prognosis depends on the assumption that conscious human will has transcended the balance of nature and thrown it irretrievably out of kilter, so that man with his mechanical psyche can trample our entire ecosystem into oblivion. But what if this notion of the power of human will is simply another expression of our schizoid grandiosity? What if our conscious cerebrations are governed by a feedback loop too extensive for us to perceive? If humans are in fact incapable of transcending the ecological circuitry in which they are embedded, then the cause for gloom vanishes. Since we value ourselves only as thinking, willful actors, never as fleshly, feeling responders, we like to think of ourselves as intelligent voices crying in the wilderness ("If only I could make them all understand!"). This is simply the arrogance of individualism. If a thought occurs to me, at a given time in a given culture, about the defects and limitations of that culture, it is occurring to others as well, since it impinges on all of us in common ways, albeit to different degrees. Authors of books like this one are fond of imagining themselves to be the cause of future change. They dream of having themselves recorded in history books as having fostered some new trend (a fantasy encouraged by the historians' passion for punctuating history). But books are expressions, not causes, of change. Through them we alert each other that our heads are undergoing some alteration in response to the conditions around us and the feelings those conditions have engendered.

What I am suggesting is that nature *still* heals itself—that humans are still embedded in their ecosystem, despite their grandiose fantasies, and subject to its processes—that as our mechanical-mindedness reaches the danger point corrective processes begin to occur that alter our ways of thinking and acting.

I realize that this statement is almost blasphemous in an individualistic society that worships the idea of free will. Americans are extraordinarily fond of engaging in masochistic acts of various kinds to show that they are not governed by anything but their own free choice, which appears to mean that they are not attuned to their environment, other people, or their own bodies. They share the monotonous delusion that the human will does not have a uniform and predictable structure. Be that as it may, I regard the sudden emergence of ecological consciousness in this country—confused as it often is—as a system effect, no more willful than the march of the lemmings into the sea.

For all the suppression of feedback at a lower level, at a higher level the ecosystem is still functioning. God, in this sense, is not yet dead. Phenomena such as social eversion illustrate this functioning, as this chapter will attempt to show.

The Forms of Change

A straight line moving through a resistant medium becomes a sine wave. Rivers meander through flat meadows, a thin rod forms a loop when pushed against a wall. History is often portrayed in sine-wave images: rises and falls; Dark Ages and Renaissances; Classic, Romantic, Neo-Classic and Neo-Romantic eras.

From up close each rise or fall appears merely as a straightish line, but from a middle distance one is terribly aware of the curves. From still farther away the sine wave itself looks like a straight line. The rise of a great civilization then seems merely to be the concentration of culture, and a decline merely its diffusion, while the quantity and complexity of culture is continually increasing. The idea of linear progress is born.

This straight-line model works rather well if we use a quantitative measure of culture, such as the sheer number of artifacts or symbols per person. On the other hand, we have learned from long experience that a straight line often turns out merely to be a curve so flat that we are unable to recognize it as such. The axis of a sine curve may itself be a sine curve, for example. The truth captured by the old rise-and-fall model was that the components of culture do not change, but are merely recombined in an infinite variety of ways.

Yet these rearrangements are genuinely new and unprecedented. An adequate change model must capture both the static-bound-circular and the linear-open-unstable aspects of evolution. Human beings vocalize as do birds, organize as do ants, communicate symbolically as do bees, grasp as do apes, hunt as do cats, and so on; yet they do not merely repeat these traits—they are organized around an entirely new synthesis.

One problem with the linear model is that it obscures the layeredness of change—what Victor Gioscia calls "temporal stratification." The sailing vessel became obsolete before it achieved its technical zenith, as did the locomotive, radio, and film. Catholicism was in decline before it had gained full ascendancy, in the sense that Protestantism and various rationalistic philosophies began to emerge when the Church was finally succeeding in stamping out paganism. In a similar manner, the Protestant Ethic finally began to be internalized by much of the American working class during the post-World War II period, at which time the middle class began to question it. And as René Dubos points out, the middle of the eighteenth century brought not only the industrial revolution and the imposition of a vast armory of restrictive child-rearing techniques, but also an ardent enthusiasm for nature, "natural man," the return to bucolic simplicity, and so on. The belief that science would solve everything coincided with the belief that our departure from adaptive harmony with nature was the cause of all our troubles and diseases.

This layeredness makes one wonder whether any change is really occurring at all—whether the same ambivalences, the same dualities, are not merely being parceled out in different ways, or among different performers. But the fact that change is nothing more than a rearrangement detracts nothing from its significance. If we separate two parts of a whole, they will be different when re-fused, since their relationships with other wholes will have been altered by the separation. If they are changed as parts, they must be recombined differently. This is the principle underlying the prophet dynamic.

According to this perspective, any pattern, value, ideal, or behavioral tendency is always present in a culture at any time, along with its polar opposite. Only the relative emphasis given each pole and the ways of arranging their simultaneous expression tend to change. One pole is usually dominant, given overt expression, and highly valued; the other forced to express itself around the edges. Elaine Cumming discusses this process in terms of values and "anti-values," suggesting that "firmly held values seem always to be accompanied by contrasting, and even inimical, latent values" that are "available for conversion" into dominant ones. Furthermore, "the more loudly we proclaim a value, the more accessible to us must be some contrasting value." She points out, for example, that while we express our devotion to individualism by locating social pathology inside individual people, treating them as deviant cases no matter how many millions of them turn up, we enforce a collective life upon them in the form of prisons, hospitals, and institutional "homes." She also discusses other pairs of contrasting values such as equality vs. big government and openness vs. privacy, both of which we tend to find great difficulty in reconciling.

This rearrangement theory, then, sees change as merely the fluid patterns formed by the incessant variegated collisions between irreconcilable but equally necessary opposites. Its most important advantage over the linear progress theory is that it allows us to realize that a straight line is not necessarily the quickest path between two points—we can often get to a value most quickly by rebounding off its polar opposite. Not recognizing the opposites within us is what leads to our linear errors. For the expression of either of a pair of opposite impulses will unlock an ambivalent stasis, leading to the expression of the remaining one, and the freeing of bound and neutralized energy. This is why the venting of diffuse hostility is so often a preliminary phase of primitive fertility rituals. By the same token, the shortest road to an understanding of the fringes of the universe may be via the microscope rather than the telescope.

It may even have been useful for our civilization to have been on the wrong track all these centuries, although I am mistrustful of such panglossianism, which tends to blunt our responsivity where it is most needed. One could argue that the development of the schizoid male culture—naturally selected as long as there were many cultures in competition—may turn out to have been the fastest route to the emergence of its mutated opposite, essential now that aggression is no longer of any survival value. It has certainly hastened the development of a global culture, although one can imagine less risky routes. By this way of thinking, science might be encouraged to "make it bigger" and blow itself up. Art has followed this route, using art for art's sake as a kind of self-destruct mechanism. Detaching art from its social and cultural roots and making it pure led naturally to the realization that any event can be an art form as much as any other since all definitions of art are culturally derived. As everything becomes art, art becomes nothing, and pure science may follow the same route. Even secrecy has its value from this perspective, since it is an inherent part of the prophet dynamic—insulation allows independent evolution so that when exposure does come what is exposed has meaning and impact. Unrelieved truth is ultimately entropic.

These speculations, however, are a bit removed from our immediate concerns—pertinent examples of the Columbian strategy of going west to reach the East can be found closer at hand. In Chapter 2 I pointed out that although liberation movements tend to begin with demands for equal treatment, the oppressed group eventually transcends this goal and begins to recognize and affirm its unique superiorities. This affirmation is quite in keeping with the rearrangement theory of change. Yet the liberal, consistency phase of liberation, in which equality is stressed, may exert important leverage in this process. Let me use a rather trivial example to stand for a hundred others. Thirty years ago, when middle-class blacks were almost invisible to the dominant culture, most whites experienced the sight of a black man in a suit and tie as something incongruous. They felt that blacks didn't belong in this kind of costume—that there was something inappropriate about clothing a black body in this buttoned-up pomposity. By the time they overcame this racist reaction many blacks themselves began to feel that such constricting garb should be relegated to whites—that free black bodies belonged in free, expressive clothing. The third stage in the process was that many whites—especially young ones—began to experience the armored pomposity of suits and ties as unfit for *any* lively human body. The liberal phase, in other words, may be a necessary transition, since the application of the principle of consistency to pockets of variation serves to highlight absurdities in the dominant culture which are normally invisible because we are so used to them. *We become sensitized to the discomfort of a familiar cultural pattern by applying it to those for whom it seems unfamiliar.*

Thus consistency itself—the fullest expression of man's mechanical-mindedness—is transformed by natural social forces into something creative, new, and revitalizing. The human will fails of its goal, and humanity profits thereby. Our powerlessness to transcend the circuitry of the natural systems in which we participate—be they physical, biological, or cultural—is our greatest hope.

Social Eversion

The idea that social change is simply the rearrangement of polar opposites can lead to misconceptions. Cultures do not simply seesaw back and forth between individualism and collectivism, or centralization and decentralization, or specialization and fusion of roles, or openness and privacy, or equality and hierarchy, or thinking and feeling, or asceticism and hedonism. The multiplicity of such dimensions means that they can be recombined in an infinite variety of ways—and their expression allocated among different times, places, and categories of persons.

Similarly, the process of social eversion, in which a social pattern turns into its opposite by being pushed to an extreme, must be distinguished from the popular idea of the social pendulum, in which a trend begins to revert to a point of moderation when it has "gone too far." Superficial changes—changes in intellectual and artistic fashion, for example—are often accurately characterized by the pendulum metaphor. They represent movement within what a given culture regards as acceptable limits of variation. They provide a modicum of novelty in a fundamentally stable situation. Real social change, however (although it may first appear to be a pendulum effect), usually takes the form of social eversion.

Perhaps the most classic example of social eversion concerns an oft-noted by-product of the space program. Nothing could be more linear than the kind of scientific thinking that produced space exploration. It represents the extreme form of agency, of limitless narcissistic striving. Yet one major consequence of the space program is that it enabled masses of people to look back on our dwindling planet and reconceptualize it as "spaceship earth"—as a small, interdependent totality. Ecological consciousness on a mass scale thus sprang directly from the fullest expression of its precise opposite—a straight line creating its own curving.

Nor should we ignore the importance of narcissistic thinking itself in eliciting ecological consciousness. Many people have been propelled into awareness by frightening stories of the consequences of human pollution. Such stories are often based on an inflated idea of human power in relation to nature, but this conceit may in the end prove timely. Thus human pomposity has led directly to increased humility about planetary interdependence.

A more abstract example concerns our patterns of thought and language. It is precisely our preoccupation with things rather than processes, objects rather than relationships, digital rather than analogic language, that led to the Platonic attitude toward objects discussed in Chapter 2. This attitude, in turn, has made our relationship to objects distant, detached, and unsatisfying. In response to this dissatisfaction, we turn back to relationships with other people—a more bilateral form of interrelation, and hence, one in which the relationship itself is more likely to be the focus of attention. Now the higher the ratio of living to non-living objects in our consciousness, the more our thinking and language will tend to be analogic—the more prominent will be the iconic and kinesic elements in communication. Note once again that it is precisely through pushing the digital, thing-orientation to an extreme that its opposite re-emerges.

The information explosion provides a similar example. As digital knowledge expands, specialization increases and learning becomes compartmentalized. Academics become potato sorters, who know nothing about relationships since these all lie outside their increasingly circumscribed fields. Yet the fields themselves eventually become so elaborated that it is impossible even to keep up with one's own, now so narrow as to have become irrelevant to any significant reality. This leads in turn to increasing withdrawal of interest from digital learning altogether, and a growing concern with relational understanding and wisdom.

The linear, constricted frame of science, furthermore, has not prevented the emergence, within that frame, of two events that threaten to alter it. The first was the psychedelic movement which, it must be remembered, began in the laboratories of chemists engaged in routine work. The second is the current upsurge in psychic research, triggered largely by military interest in telepathy. Both events have created widespread interest in expanding our root definitions of reality (most scientists, alas, are still trudging along with Newton under one arm and John Locke under the other).

Overpopulation provides still another example. Crowding tends to break down the stable, nourishing, and comfortable bonds that gratify people and make them willing to assume responsibility for children. The loss of this gratification leads to pleasure-*seeking*—to a hedonistic life style in which children seem a burden. As this mood spreads, the birth rate tends to taper off.

For one final example of social eversion we might take the isolated nuclear family with its heavy emotional overload—tending to destroy all efforts at maintaining tolerable emotional distances between family members. The implosion of needs—formerly satisfied in the extended family and the larger community—into the nuclear family has created a kind of behavioral sink within it. This is not a matter of spatial closeness: middle-class Americans today are probably less crowded within their homes than any people in history. It is rather the lack of emotional alternatives—the forcing, in other words, of a steep pleasure gradient on the young—that has produced the sense of emotional overload. This results in a longing for privacy and a phobic feeling about society, for society is recreated in fantasy in the image of overpossessive, smothering parents.

At the same time, the defective awareness of our interconnectedness with others in the community generates loneliness and fear. Both of these feelings—loneliness and the need for privacy—are endemic to a steep-gradient population, in which stable relationships are impossible, and yet personal boundaries cannot be maintained. The reverse is true in a flat-gradient system, in which every individual has a large number of stable medium-intensity ties.

As these feelings escalate, two things happen. First, long-term marriage relationships become increasingly difficult to maintain, and the divorce rate climbs. Second, the oedipal family inflates narcissistic, invidious, and competitive motivation in children. At first these trends exaggerate the pathological conditions that created them: With divorce, mothers are thrown back into even more intense relationships with sons, who grow up to be even more compulsive careerists. Eventually, however, the competitive motivation spills over onto women, who seek a larger role in the more prestigious occupational world. This triggers the women's movement which, as noted earlier, attacks the oedipal family on all fronts. Meanwhile, serial monogamy combined with working mothers deintensifies the mother-child relationship and leads to flatter pleasure gradients in the next generation.

All these examples of social eversion suggest that it is virtually impossible, *if the raw materials are at hand,* to avoid creating what is needed to balance a system, so great is the internal pressure for that creation to emerge.

Trunks in the Attic of Culture

Nature is miserly. It rarely discards any process that ever worked. This is equally true of social systems, and is one reason, paradoxically, why rapid social change can sometimes occur. A society does not suddenly change into something different—it merely begins to emphasize what was once deemphasized, to approve what was once devalued.

Social change seldom assumes a direction that is altogether undefined ahead of time. Most Americans, for example, are aware that their society is becoming less preoccupied with achievement, less future-oriented, more hedonistic, and so on. This is hardly astounding, since the signs are all around them. What *is* interesting is that people already have a sense of what it is they are approaching. People who have never lived in a hedonistic culture nevertheless have an idea about what it is and how it works, and whether they would like it or not.

We take this phenomenon for granted, but it has profound implications. It suggests the possibility that the elements of all cultural arrangements are latent in every cultural system, or at least every healthy one.

For maximum flexibility, the subparts of a system will each maintain the potentiality for all the possible behaviors that could flow from any part of the system. Many cultures, for example, have established certain special days (The Feast of Fools, Mardi Gras) during which the customary rules of the society are set aside. Not only are sexual restrictions violated, but also rules governing status and deference. Those in authority are derided, masters wait upon servants, the most lowly are raised to be king or queen for a day—all rules are turned topsy-turvy.

Such customs should not be thought of merely as a vacation from everyday social constraints. Often the conventions surrounding the inverted mores are as elaborate and constricting as the everyday ones. What these festivals do is keep alive the capacity to use social and behavioral muscles that are not ordinarily exercised. The meek try on arrogance, the arrogant meekness, and so on. Knowledge of behavior opposite to one's normal social role is kept alive. Ordinary complementarities and specializations are transcended, facilitating the possibility of rearranging social roles should this ever become necessary. Like mutations, these customs provide a hedge against change, and hence are much less wasteful and frivolous than they seem at first glance. They also serve to reduce what Bateson calls "schismogenesis"—the progressive differentiation of a society into alienated subgroups, with a concomitant narrowing of the personalities of their members.

These feasts are simply one of many mechanisms through which cultures increase their potentiality for variation. Societies seem to hoard their cultural possessions as if knowing that one of them might some day turn out to be useful again. Mythology and folklore, for example, are full of outdated culture patterns kept alive by dramatization. Universities, when the humanities dominated them, also played the role of cultural attic. Young people learned a lot by messing about in them and playing games. Unfortunately, adults tend always to move in on this kind of activity, afraid that the children will learn too much too fast (just as they sometimes did in the family attic). They put up compartments and try to force them to group the available information in familiar and traditional ways. This has become more exaggerated since the natural and social sciences became ascendant and turned the universities into trade schools. Academic departments and professional schools are to education what the Little League is to play.

This tension between the need to limit and funnel information and the need to keep options open is fundamental to all social systems. It is the same tension that produces the prophet dynamic, and arises at the biological level as well, as Bateson points out. In the wild, the population of a given species "functions as a storehouse of genotypic possibilities." Farmers and breeders, however, like professors, seek to limit the number of such possibilities so as to guarantee a uniform and predictable product in their domesticated species. Bateson, following the biologist, Simmonds, argues the need to maintain this storehouse of variability by fostering enclaves of unselected populations. Such enclaves, designed to offset the ultimately debilitating effect of deliberately selective breeding, would serve exactly the same purpose as free learning settings in a university, in which students do not need to march through a preordained mechanical hierarchy of learning stages, from "elementary" to "advanced." The breeders and professors seek to limit the amount of information going into the system—the breeder for fear an animal will appear with a head too big or insufficiently pointed, the professor for fear a student will ingest an idea before she is "ready" for it. This is necessary to ensure control and maximize production along understood lines, but it progressively destroys the possibility of altering those lines. Even Toffler, in his headlong pursuit of yesterday's future, recognizes this, and favors the preservation of "slow-paced communities" as a form of "mental and social insurance," in case the larger society makes some catastrophic error.

Oddly enough, however, free choice itself can be a principle which limits information, as I noted earlier in connection with arranged marriages. Since personal motivation is always present as a variable, the removal of all *other* bases for selection means that the system will be deprived of a great number of serendipitous rearrangements.

Deviance and Containment

The major way societies store information that is out of keeping with their dominant cultural themes is through the handling of what sociologists call "deviant behavior"—behavior that is disapproved, scorned, and usually punished by the community or its representatives. Sociologists worry a lot about deviant behavior and its control, and some of their puzzlement derives from the curious fact that when the entire focus of a community's energies seems to be the complete eradication of some bit of deviant behavior it nevertheless manages to persist. How can we account for society's impotence in such cases? There seems to be some sort of ambivalence in social systems that prevents the attack on deviance from achieving its logical consummation.

Michel Foucault, for example, describes how madmen in the fifteenth century were often given into the hands of sailors who carried them to distant cities, where they collected in large numbers and were often imprisoned. Although these people were considered a menace wherever they were found, considerable trouble was taken to see to their transportation and to house and feed them. We certainly cannot argue that dedication to humane values or merciful sentiments restrained the townspeople from simply doing away with them—men in those times, just as now, were quite willing to slaughter their fellows over a difference of opinion or a few coins. Yet they seemed in this case to be in the grip of some hesitation—some deeply rooted doubt.

It may be objected that madmen have traditionally carried a sacred aura that provided certain immunity from attack. This is true, and exemplifies the thesis advanced here. These madmen, however, were not viewed as pseudo-shamans and allowed to wander freely in the community—they were regarded as dangerous and were subjected to exile or imprisonment. But they were kept alive. It is as if the townspeople doubted whether they might not lose some potential resource if they were to destroy them entirely.

One sees this ambivalence and doubt in many settings. I have often been impressed with the energy that small groups will sometimes expend trying to accommodate troublesome individuals—willing at times to become completely paralyzed rather than lose a single obstreperous member. In one experimental study of groups the researchers found that although the deviant member is usually disliked, "it would be quite unfortunate to assume that he is therefore isolated from the group or repudiated by it: an accurate sociogram would have the deviant individual encircled by the interlocking sociometric preferences, sheltered by the group structure."

At the community level, deviant behavior is often both expressed and counteracted in relative secrecy, as if society's representatives assumed, not that visible deviance would unite the community in outraged solidarity, as some sociologists have suggested, but that it would contaminate and infect them. In such cases, it seems proper to say that societies respond to deviance as if they wanted to insulate it, to minimize it, to quarantine it, but to preserve it—in other words to *contain* it.

This ambivalence, this hesitation altogether to destroy the deviant trend, is at bottom just what it looks like—doubt that the reprehended or scorned behavior may not prove at some future date to embody a hidden but valuable resource of some kind. The "containment" of deviance is another hedge against social change. The contained deviant trend is like a cadre or a museum's archives or a germ culture or a zoo. In it are contained the seeds of a potential future orthodoxy—as few as possible, but a few.

This is not to imply that there is some deep wisdom in social systems, sagely recognizing the ambiguities of the future beneath the spurious certainties of the present. Societies are blind and witless automatons, forever blundering into destruction and decay. The containment mechanism is as crude and inefficient as is mutation at the biological level. In both cases random variation is maintained at great expense in preference to a more perfect system from which there is no escape.

Perfect adaptation produces almost certain obsolescence. Any self-maintaining mechanism must have a certain amount of error built into it. As Lewis Mumford said long ago, only imperfect systems, full of self-contradictions, have the capacity to survive. The reason that societies today tend to contain deviance rather than expunging it is that those societies are the survivors. Social systems that have survived are magpies and pack rats. They have attics full of alternative themes, values, and behavior patterns that no longer play any active role in the society. These are preserved not only in myth and ritual and folklore, but also in subcultural pockets and stylized individual roles. Of what relevance is Jesus Christ or Billy the Kid or Achilles in a modern industrial society like ours? Of what use a hermit in a gregarious community, a transvestite in a warrior tribe? Of what value are the insane? Foucault suggests that the invention of the mental hospital served the function of preserving the fantastic in hidden reservoirs—keeping alive, during the classical age, buried images that could be "transmitted intact from the sixteenth to the nineteenth century."

Madness involves a dissolution of structures and boundaries. The mad live outside the structural frame that society imposes. They are adrift in a turbulent and unbound sea. But that same sea is a reservoir, containing all the elements from which a social system can be constructed. If they are out of touch with the building, they are uniquely *in* touch with its components. They are thus both to be feared and to be treasured. They know both less and more than others.

The torch of culture does not tend to stay in the same hands for very long—those who are committed to the existing patterns tend to be by-passed by the less "cultured" who leapfrog, as it were, into a new golden age. Each torch holder imagines that his rude, uncultured neighbor can achieve grace only by traversing an imitative path, and is always amazed to find himself outdistanced in a direction he had never even considered. How could a nation of burghers ever surpass one of noble warriors, except by becoming noble warriors? How could Africa ever surpass Western nations, except by becoming Westernized? How can black Americans amount to anything except by becoming just like middle-class whites? But the lessons of history suggest that it is by *not* becoming like the dominant group that significant cultural advances occur.

White liberals used to believe that the stereotype of the warm and earthy black—singing and dancing, living in the present, enjoying bodily pleasures to the fullest—either had no behavioral foundation at all or was an unfortunate compensatory adaptation to centuries of slavery and oppression. I would like to suggest that this behavioral configuration—let us call it the watermelon pattern—was not so much an adaptation to oppression (although no doubt it was to some extent) as oppression was an unconscious adaptation to the watermelon pattern. Once the economic basis for the oppression of blacks had disappeared, blacks were oppressed in part to contain the watermelon pattern: to insulate it, quarantine it, disparage it, discourage it, and keep it alive. While blacks are kept from reaping the fruits of the Protestant Ethic, they were also preserved from its infection and internal rot.

The watermelon pattern was a return ticket in case the Protestant Ethic turned out to be a swindle, and now that the industrial era is about to take up its eternal position as a horrible and aberrant moment in human history, the ticket is redeemable. In times of change it is those who are most whole, least warped by elaborate custom and the degradation of impulse, who are in the best position to innovate creatively.

For the past decade blacks, Indians, and women have all been engaged in bringing neglected treasures out of the basement of our culture, trying to revitalize a sclerotic society. Blacks were the first to recognize this mission. They were intellectual pioneers—showing other oppressed groups how oppression worked and how to transcend it. The assertion "black is beautiful" was a profound cultural invention, as evidenced by the speed with which it diffused to other oppressed groups. For to achieve self-respect when one is a member of a despised minority is virtually impossible—like creating something from nothing. A significant foothold appeared during the early civil rights movement when white liberals went south full of condescension and ended by displaying a certain amount of envy and admiration toward black culture. Racism is like a magic spell—it has to be perfectly maintained to have the proper demoralizing effect on the recipient. One leak and the spell is broken. The mirror of reality replaces the enchanted mirror and the sleeper awakes from her dream of self-hatred. No matter how hard one tries, it is impossible to maintain self-respect in the absence of any validation from the outside. But with the tiniest fragment of such validation blacks rapidly built themselves a strong ideology of mutual respect and cultural assertion.

The black experience opened the eyes of other groups who had endured containment: women, Amerindians, Chicanos, prisoners, mental patients, high school students. All but one of these groups experienced containment in a very physical sense—being enclosed in ghettos, reservations, or institutions. This enclosure serves a double function: For the present, the deviant culture cannot infect the prevailing dominant one, but at the same time it cannot be engulfed and destroyed by it. Oppression and isolation keep it weak, isolated, and intact. Hence the moment at which the oppressed group breaks out of its confinement is a matter of very delicate timing—will the cultural seed which has been preserved in isolation flower amid the rot of the old dominant culture, or will the dominant culture (to mix metaphors a bit) smother it with antibodies? Much of the endless political debate that goes on in oppressed groups revolves around this difficult issue. To some extent it can be said that if the dominant culture is not sick, sclerotic, in decay, the question will never come up—the containment will be successful no matter what. Vigorous oppression based on deluded moral conviction is an almost insuperable weapon, especially against a minority. But if oppression begins to falter, if the illusion of superiority and righteousness starts to crumble, the vitality of the contained deviant culture will burst its chains. This does not mean that the argument over timing is meaningless. If cultures are to be blended (which is what always happens ultimately, even in war or revolution), timing will determine the extent to which the deviant culture plays a major or minor role in the new synthesis. This was the essence of the question of black separatism. To follow the integration route would have been to condemn blacks to an infinitesimal role in the synthesized culture. To preserve voluntarily the very containment that had previously been involuntary was to ensure that the new synthesis, whenever it came, would be a lot blacker.

Even in the oppressed condition there are variations in the degree to which a deviant culture can be preserved intact. A reservation allows more than a ghetto, and a ghetto far more than a prison or mental hospital. Institutions of confinement, as Erving Goffman has observed, have their own built-in culture, which is essentially that of the concentration camp—authoritarian, bureaucratic, infantilizing, and sado-masochistic. About all that is preserved in such institutions is whatever cultural variations people took into them individually. In that sense they are less efficient cultural attics, and their use betokens less vigor and elasticity in the society that places heavy reliance on them. A society that effectively contains a deviant culture by oppressing it without attempting to break it up and dissolve it must at least be acknowledged to be healthy and vital, however repulsive. The Nazi regime revealed its brittleness when concentration camps began to be used on a large scale, and the later attempt to annihilate an entire deviant population betrayed its total non-viability and imminent collapse.

Women are the one oppressed group in America that have not been contained geographically. Since women are not a minority, to have confined them together would have been to sound the instantaneous death knell of the dominant white male culture. Patriarchal cultures have always been petrified about large gatherings of women. The containment of women, therefore, has necessitated the construction of millions of individualized psychic prisons, euphemistically called homes. Women were subjugated by placing them under a loose form of house arrest. The phrase, "he can't even keep his woman at home," used to be a customary way of disparaging a man's domestic competence—virility rested on one's skills as a jailer. *Divide et impera.*

Even though kept apart from each other, women have shared a culture derived from certain common experiences: oppression, exclusion from the sources of power in society, and relative non-commitment (usually stigmatized as "feminine intuition") to mechanical modes of thought. Their emergence as a group has been vastly hampered by the illusion that they already participate in the dominant culture. Consciousness-raising among women has stressed unity and the awareness that they share a vital culture alien to masculine compartmentalism and inhibition.

The likelihood of a deviant culture being contained is a function of how sharply it contrasts with the dominant culture. Black culture is diametrically opposed to the Protestant Ethic of inhibition, frigidity, and miserliness. Feminine culture is antithetical to the male culture of feeling-suppression, schizoid rationalism, and mechanical action. Most Amerindian cultures in one way or another oppose the Western emphasis on individualism, parts-over-wholes, and the exploitation of the environment, favoring instead a view of nature as a balanced whole in which humans play an equal rather than stellar role. It is my impression, furthermore, that those Amerindian cultures most antithetical to our own, like the pueblo cultures, have been better preserved than those (like the plains cultures) more similar to ours.

The fact that so many new and contrasting strains are now being fed into our culture is a sign both of its illness and its vitality, just as a high blood count shows both that an organism is sick and that it is responding vigorously. Rome, during its long decline, exhibited the same eager appetite for alien and deviant traditions, and although it never corrected its self-destructive commitment to massive inequality of wealth and other addictions, this receptivity certainly prolonged its existence. The same phenomenon is visible now, especially the fascination with Eastern thought and new religions. If it leads to a fundamental restructuring of the culture, we may fare better than our ancient predecessor.

There is hope in the emergence of ecological thinking in America. Modern ethnography in the West began to flourish in the beginning of the twentieth century, just as pure non-Western cultures were evaporating from the globe. This in itself betrayed a vigorous pack-rat response on the part of a number of Western societies, but the awareness of totally disparate ways of viewing the world was for a long time the privilege of a few anthropologists. Today every civilized bookstore in the country has a section reserved for books about Amerindian cultures and ecology, and recognition of the rich cultural heritage that the white invaders of America destroyed is growing geometrically. Most important of all, it is increasingly recognized that the absorption of this heritage is not an esoteric recreation, but a necessary step to survival.

Before leaving the topic of containment, a word needs to be said about technique. I have mentioned oppression and isolation, but perhaps the most important of all is the technique of negative definition, described by Ronald Laing in connection with family dynamics.

Laing points out that parents often fix a child in a deviant family role by sending two messages: (1) You *should* be X, but (2) you *are* Y. He observes that the second message is inherently more powerful than the first—that a child can be made to feel guilty by being told "you should be more responsible," but that the statement "You are irresponsible" is irresistible—a covert instruction that carries its own justification within it ("You can be no different because this is what you *are*"). The conscious intent of the parent is to change the behavior, but the unconscious intent is to fix it permanently, and this is, in fact, what the behavior achieves. To define a trait as negative, and simultaneously to insist that it is an intrinsic part of someone's character is to ensure the subservience of that person and the persistence of that trait. This is precisely what containment seeks to achieve, and hence this technique is an essential part of the containment dynamic. "You *should* work and strive, but you *are* lazy and shiftless" was the message through which the watermelon pattern was both negated and preserved.

Neither message need be explicitly communicated in words. The containment of feminine culture in our own society is to some extent implicit. Consider, for example, the impact of current attitudes about housewives' time. Whereas men in their occupations are accustomed to placing some sort of value on their time and that of other men, the assumption is usually made that the time of housewives has no value. Many women are willing to spend an entire day rushing from one store to another in an effort to save a few dollars—work that yields them far less than the legal minimum wage. This attitude is inculcated by the masculine occupational world. For while men schedule appointments with each other—a way of showing mutual respect for the value of each other's time—housewives are expected to operate without schedules. Repairmen, telephone installers, deliverymen, and so on, have been successful in refusing to constrict their own convenience by making scheduled appointments with housewives, who are expected to wait at home until the workman arrives. Nothing could convey more powerfully the low esteem in which the role of housewife is held than this disregard of daily scheduling needs. The lowliest flunky in the masculine occupational hierarchy is given temporal superiority over every non-working woman. The twin message, "You *should* be doing something useful, but you *are* useless," has not been lost upon the non-working woman, who is wont to say, "I'm just a housewife." What is preserved by this containment is an antidote to the narrow and ultimately meaningless utilitarianism of the male world, in which only that which is quantitatively measurable is accorded value.

Our discussion of deviant cultures suggests a danger, albeit a rather remote one. Should all oppressed groups achieve liberation and the world arrive at some sort of unified culture, would not vital cultural patterns be forever lost?

The danger is real, however unlikely it may seem at present. Some vague presentiment of this reality probably contributes to the increasing preoccupation with finding new forms of life elsewhere in the universe. But it should be emphasized again that the containment of deviant groups is not the only means through which societies preserve alternatives. Myth, folklore, drama, and literary fantasies also serve this function. The centrality of Charlie Chaplin in the culture of the 20's and 30's in our own society exemplifies this mechanism. Chaplin's tramp personified the antithesis of all the prevailing values of that culture—values such as ambition, striving, courage, stoicism, toughness, directness, postponement of gratification, dignity, and "manliness." He was a monument to responsivity in a culture rapidly expunging every vestige of it in everyday life.

It is by no means clear why or when a social system suddenly becomes vulnerable to these encapsulated antitheses—why the cell walls suddenly give way and allow the deviant trend to flood through the society and transform it. Clearly some hunger, some lack, some fatigue with the artificial absurdities of existing arrangements makes it possible, but the process is rather unclear.

We call such moments crises. We define an event as a crisis when our ordinary routines cease to make sense. Thus the more meaningless our routines seem in the first place the more a crisis is likely to occur. A crisis lasts (that is, is defined as such) until all the various routines begin once again to make sense. It may seem impossible to go to work and absurd to wash the dishes when a loved one has just died, and in a functioning community other people usually move in to fill the gap, breaking their own routines to perform necessary functions for the bereft. But ultimately a sense that "life must go on" returns—the flood waters recede, the family member returns from the hospital, the dead are relinquished—and routines are taken up again.

Often, however, the routines are changed, incorporating the larger context made visible by the crisis. The coronary patient reserves his energies for enriching rather than emotionally depleting experiences, the devastated city rebuilds with an eye to beauty. Crisis often allows the suppressed and despised parts of a system a chance to infuse new life into it—to give it a second chance, like the one the dream of Marley's ghost gave to Ebenezer Scrooge.

Parable 7

Every spring a trader from Ispahan came to town. He was a clever and energetic man and each year brought quantities of useless and defective merchandise which he unloaded at considerable profit. After a few years the townspeople got wise to the trader, and when he reappeared the following year they attacked and beat him and destroyed his merchandise. The canny trader, however, was determined not to lose this lucrative market and came again the next year disguised as a beardless Egyptian. Although the townspeople had generalized their caution to some extent, the trader's visit was a successful one, and he repeated the maneuver the following year. This time his disguise was penetrated, however, and he was again beaten and relieved of his remaining wares.

From that day on, the stubborn trader appeared each spring in a new disguise. Sometimes he took the role of an old man, sometimes that of a woman; sometimes he was a Hindu, sometimes a Turk. He assumed many postures, many accents, and became an increasingly gifted mimic. Each year he devoted more care to planning his visit to the town —designing his costume, perfecting his accent, gait, idiosyncrasies, and so on. Since the town was a favorite of transient and unscrupulous traders, it was easy for him to lose himself in the throng.

The townspeople, meanwhile, kept a sharp eye out for the trader, whom they regarded as a special enemy. As the years went by they involved themselves more and more in anticipating his visits. Each spring they held meetings to discuss ways of penetrating his incognito, which was all the more difficult as no one could any longer remember what he had originally looked like. They tried to find common denominators in his multi-faceted behavior. They chose scouts to observe all incoming traders and take note of any that seemed suspicious. Eventually they began offering prizes to anyone who could detect the trader. This led to wholesale molestation of traders, and the townspeople were forced to make rules for the contest that would protect the innocent. The prize would be offered only to one who could discover the trader without touching him, and there were heavy penalties for selecting the wrong man. With this the situation became stabilized, for while exposing the trader was now the major spring recreation of the town, the rules of the contest made it extremely difficult to bring about.

Thus it went on for many years. Some years the trader was successful, sometimes the townspeople. The trader viewed the situation in terms of his own ingenuity, his perseverance in the face of occasional severe beatings, and his ability often to outwit an entire town devoted to exposing him. While he never became rich, he lived very comfortably, and was able to accumulate a sizeable nest egg on the profits of his more successful excursions to the town.

The townspeople viewed the situation in terms of the excellent organization they had created to forestall the trader. They were pleased with the determination and co-operation they had shown, and were gratified that often they were able to detect the trader's imposture, despite his almost superhuman skill at disguise. The organizational network that they evolved to achieve this goal served them well whenever they were threatened by danger from fire, flood, or war, and the town had a long and modestly prosperous existence.

After several decades, the trader died. By this time, however, the spring ritual of anticipating his visit had become an elaborate and enthusiastic enterprise, and it was necessary to induct townspeople into the vacant role. Each year thereafter some of them would disguise themselves as traders and mingle among the true outsiders. Any who were successful in remaining undetected for the duration of the Fair divided the prize formerly given to successful detectors. After the prize was awarded there was a huge celebration.

Today, a century later, the Festival of the Trader is still the biggest holiday of the town. Amid the delight of the celebration no one remembers the fierce struggle from which it arose.

Chronicles of Noga

THE BROKEN CIRCUIT

> *There'll always be a Carthage.*
>
> **Hannibal**
>
> *I am here because of you, and you are here because of me.*
>
> **Mulla Nasrudin**

It is quite possible that humanity may prove to be a dead end like the dinosaur—too big (with its technological extensions) and too stupid (with its relational insensitivity) to participate felicitously in the dance of life. Apparently this is not the first time that extinction has threatened human beings, however, and they have yet managed to survive and prosper on the strength of a certain flexibility and craftiness, and a profound inability to commit themselves heartily to a specific presence in nature.

Whether survival or extinction is humanity's destiny simply depends upon whether the self-corrective processes described in the last chapter turn out to include or exclude our species. Western culture seems to be engaged in a frantic effort to heal itself, while at the same instant it is hurling itself toward global destruction at an accelerating rate. Let us be levelheaded in our apocalyptic visions, however: "Global destruction," "ecological catastrophe," "nuclear holocaust," and all the other terms of warning connote a degree of finality for which there is no realistic referent. None of the plausible global disasters presently envisioned would extinguish all life on the planet, although most of them would pretty well annihilate mammalian species. By and large, to talk of a dead planet is mere hyperbole. Whatever happens, there will probably be an ecology of some sort—perhaps centered around little slugs that consume and break down hydrocarbons.

Nature, then, will heal itself, either because the species that became so noisily diseased will also heal itself, or because that species will destroy itself and permit alternative forms of life to flower with greater joy and grace. Assuming a godlike, abstract posture, one could advocate with equal reasonableness throwing our energies in the direction of self-cure, or fulfilling our self-destructive destiny with as much verve as possible.

But we are not gods, we are humans, and we do not live in the abstract, although the key representatives of our technocracy seem to *exist* in it, rushing jerkily through their own time in a kind of mechanical stupor, as if they did not recognize it. We are humans, and not to attempt to revive our humanity and heal our own sickness would be as pretentious and silly as all our other efforts to be other than who we are.

Furthermore, self-healing processes are already emerging in Western culture, and everything we do in our lives, however trivial, adds energy either to these processes or to our previous linear course.

With the best will and most sophisticated political consciousness in the world, we might manage to devote about 10 per cent of our waking hours to a deliberate attempt to cure the diseased system in which we live, while unconsciously and automatically spending the other 90 per cent feeding and supporting its pathology. There is no point despairing over this or wasting time in guilty conscience-examining, which seldom leads to anything vibrant or healthful. When awareness of our position among these conflicting forces passes from the cognitive to the emotional level—from concept to bodily sensitivity—we can rely upon our own visceral sensations and those of others to negotiate this difficult terrain more creatively and less effortfully.

Western culture, like the schizoid personality structure, is built upon broken feedback circuitry. Responsivity is blocked and in its place is inserted a programmed instruction from an internal conceptual apparatus. In place of feedback from others the individualistically programmed person inserts self-feedback. In place of increasingly fine mutual tuning each individual mechanically obeys his own program, following his own closed circuitry until he spins himself into oblivion. The program is truly his own in the sense that the culture provides a limited selection of ideological instructions and the individual is free to put together his own unique combination. What he is *not* free to do is to disobey the instruction to respond in a mechanistic fashion, perceive nonmechanical forms of transpersonal linkage, or recognize that he has been instructed to be "free" (i.e., mechanical). This is typical of the mystification techniques discussed by Laing and Bateson in relation to the families of schizophrenics.

But no matter what our culture trains us to believe—no matter what we tell each other—we *are* connected with one another. The only thing that changes is how we are connected: organically, mechanically, symbolically, consciously, unconsciously, bodily, verbally, or whatever. Our culture attempts to break the emotional connections between people and substitute bureaucratic ones. By training us to blind ourselves to our fundamental interdependence—feeding us instead the myth that we are isolated particles trying to find a way to come together—we are led to invest our feelings, needs, and desires in abstract goals and institutions, believing all the while that in so doing we are independent of one another. Our culture is like a con man who persuades us to cheat those close to us of their due, and to invest instead in ourselves. He, of course, shows us how to do this, and lives off the proceeds. We are still connected, but now through the con man. He mocks our conformity to persons and tells us to do our own thing, leaving co-ordination to more and more remote and impersonal mechanisms, understood by fewer and fewer people with more and more concentrated negative power. Knowing that coherence is intrinsic to life itself, and that accommodational responses are a part of our human birthright, he rejoices as increasingly impersonal forces—authorities instead of intimate groups, bureaucracies instead of authorities, machines instead of bureaucracies, ideological symbols instead of machines—wag these accommodating instincts, and tells us this progression is in the direction of perfect freedom.

I have already described the evolution of modern humanity's circuit-breaking proclivities. It might also be useful to examine the way in which circuit-breaking is learned at the individual level. We are born into a symbiotic relationship with another human being. Our heartbeats and body motions are in synchrony with hers. This bond must be loosened if the child is to achieve psychic and physical health, and the capacity for sensitive attunement must be extended to include many other people. But that capacity itself need not atrophy, and in most non-Western societies does not. How is that interpersonal attunement shattered, so that the gap left can be filled with rules, procedures, slogans, force, regulation, and philosophy?

Ashley Montague points out a number of ways. At birth the infant in our society is usually isolated almost immediately from the mother and placed in a roofless cage. Often its tactile sensitivity is further dulled by bottle feeding. This is useful training for mastery and for relating to machines: Since the reactions of the bottle are less complex and far more predictable than those of the breast, the infant learns that fundamental needs are satisfied by manipulating inert and unresponsive objects, rather than by interacting in a mutually adaptive attunement with another organism as complex as itself. In most "primitive" societies, furthermore, the infant is constantly held or carried, thus demanding a complex mutual adjustment of movement and position. In most Western cultures tactile sensitivity is also muted by clothing. Even in the few situations where touching is freely allowed, the development of interpersonal sensitivity is limited: "Margaret Mead has pointed out how the attention of the American baby is directed away from the personal relationship to his mother by toys which are introduced into his tub." (Montague.) This, like the bottle, is good training for life in a hardware society. It helps account for our tendency to put our energies into simple mechanical problems that can be "solved" once and for all, ignoring the complex issues that require constant adaptation and readjustment and reduce all our elegant once-and-for-all solutions to trivial irrelevance. Scientific and social scientific research, social legislation, and the approach of American Presidents to the Vietnam War all seem rooted in this bathtub experience. Inanimate objects are so much easier to "handle" and we are so poorly equipped to relate to organisms as complex as ourselves that it is tempting to confuse one with the other.

In addition to all this obligatory lack of contact there is an ideological conviction that a child must "learn to be by herself." Few non-Western societies have invented such a rule. Why must the child learn to be by herself? To prepare for urban living, or for old age? Perhaps, but also so that she can learn to relate to inanimate objects that are easily controlled, and take her instruction from mass dispensers—doctors, television, educational toys, and so on—instead of learning directly by trial-and-error interaction with other organisms.

One of the most powerful techniques ever designed for circuit-breaking in infancy was scheduled feeding. The unresponsiveness to human need that characterizes our social institutions today probably owes something to the fact that they are designed, maintained, and led by people exposed to this form of training. In scheduled feeding the cycle of hunger-cry-feed-hold-sleep is broken by the mother, who inserts the concept of mechanical time, feeding the child according to machine time instead of biological time. The unfortunate impact of this procedure on the infant's well-being has long been recognized, but it is worth noting that it can also be hard on the mother. Scheduling might be convenient for her in some ways, but she is often forced to listen to increasingly intense screaming until the clock rolls around and to negate her own spontaneous yearning to feed, nourish, and comfort the crying infant.

It is usually assumed that the more contemporary emphasis on demand feeding is a complete negation of the effects of scheduling. But from the mother's viewpoint this is not really the case. Instead of being enslaved to the clock she is enslaved to the infant's cry—either way she is supposed to ignore her own internal responses in deference to a mechanical principle. Under the demand system the child's cry is not a phatic communication triggering an emotional need to respond, but is rather a signal with a fixed symbolic meaning. Instead of cry→desire to soothe, we have cry→interpretation (hunger)→automatic requirement of feeding. Parents will thus be circuit-breakers whichever set of mechanical instructions governs their behavior. Both tend to breed insensitivity in children.

The same pitfall emerges with other child-rearing instructions in the early Spockian tradition, despite Spock's frequent admonitions to "trust one's instincts." In the first place, our "spontaneous" impulses are by now far too numbed and polluted to put much trust in, and even if they were not, a book full of instructions and causal connections would soon overwhelm them. A child-rearing manual may be a necessary evil in a society that lacks stable child-rearing communities, but it is rather difficult to be attuned to a child with a book in one's hand and a head full of goals. The manual is for the mother what the bathtub toys are for the child. If the mother manages to sensitize herself to the child, she usually loses contact with her own feelings and needs, and vice versa. My impression of the products of Spockian child rearing is that as a group they are more tuned in to their own viscera than are their predecessors, but even less sensitive to the needs and demands of others—a sensitivity denied them by parents who stifled their own needs in favor of producing "healthy" offspring. It is not the content of the formula that breaks the circuit, but the instructional form in and of itself.

It would of course be absurd to condemn circuit-breaking as an undiluted evil. There are times when the postponement of gratification, the blocking of feeling, the cutting off of communication, desensitization to one's environment, and so on, are valuable and even necessary to survival. But circuits are more easily broken than reconnected, and all circuit-breaking carries within it the danger of escalation spirals that are difficult to halt. Our civilization has reached a point where many channels of awareness have almost entirely atrophied. The most body-centered and "sensorily awakened" American can never match the level of sensitivity that primitive hunters and gatherers possess all their lives. But one cannot possibly retain such sensitivity in an urban environment and live. We cannot be fully attuned in a hopelessly discordant environment, but it is perilous to remain too long out of touch with that environment, or ourselves, or each other.

Attunement

This is the moment, in books of this kind, where one is supposed to offer concrete suggestions for some sort of action. "Enough diagnosis, time for prescription." I do not know why this is so—why books of social analysis should ape the format of a market research report or an engineer's memorandum. The recommendations that are made always seem fatuous to me— either so vague and general as to be implicit in the analysis itself, or so concrete and trivial that one could have offered them without going through any of the analysis. I want to state here that I intend to violate the traditional form: I have no suggestions to offer. I have described a way of being and its pathological consequences. This implies that some sort of reversal of this way of being—this attitude of mind—would be helpful, but how one arrives at it cannot be prescribed but only discovered. To say otherwise would be to announce that I have only been kidding all along. There can be no mechanical prescription for demechanization—any person, armed with some piece of awareness that I hope has been reinforced by this book, can begin to experiment with his or her own circuitry in whatever sphere—personal, political, or occupational—suggests itself.

Any change based on the kind of thinking that needs words like "blueprint" and "implementation" is not change at all but an extension of the problem. Nothing benign will arise without alterations in mind set, and given a more responsive mind set almost any activity would begin to constitute real change. It is characteristic of Americans to ask, "What shall we do?" but the question is wrong. Humanization will not come from doing any specific thing, but rather from doing whatever we do with a different orientation. "What?" is not a question that ever leads to wisdom.

The question, "What shall we do?" is also a self-alienated one, implying that we are unmotivated, unfeeling objects—suitable only for being manipulated by instruction for task purposes, like robots. The same attitude appears in the oft-heard and rather chilling phrase, "we must find ways of *motivating* them . . ." —as if people didn't have motives of their own, but were empty husks waiting to be filled up with needs and desires by social workers, educators, and other people-processors. We tend to define our actions from the outside, in terms of "problems" divorced from any connection with ourselves: "What shall we do about pollution?" instead of, "I'm sick of having my air spoiled, and I want to confront the people who are doing it and make them stop."

The quest for an action formula also expresses a desire to control the future, and even though no formula has ever delivered such control, the act of seeking it requires us to detach ourselves from our environment. Becoming attuned, on the other hand, means taking the risk that commitment always brings. If you commit yourself to a boat, it may sink; if you do not, you will never sink—but never sail either. Becoming attuned means committing one's fate to nature and allowing the possibility of death—the possibility that an environmental change might dissolve everything. In reality, of course, we take this chance anyway, despite all our bizarre security operations. The only way to avoid death is not to be alive in the first place. The only way to avoid the loss of love is never to love. And the only way to avoid obsolescence is never to finish anything. All of these solutions are rife in our society, where we talk a lot about risk-taking but do everything in our power to avoid it. When we assert the importance of flexibility, it is because we fear that we don't have it. What we *call* flexibility usually turns out to be detachment, noncommitment. Our talk of flexibility is nothing more than timidity: we know things are constantly in flux out there, and we tell each other to keep our options open and never put more than one toe in the water. What we fear is that if we committed ourselves wholly to any fixed course of action and it proved awkward, we would not have within ourselves the flexibility to respond in a way that would save us. In this we are probably correct since what detachment produces is in fact rigidity. One learns to swim by swimming—and to respond to shifting pressures by staying in touch with them. Such attunement means greater risk and pain as well as greater joy.

Despite our cultural training, the need to be in a state of risk —to test one's harmony with nature—runs deep in the human psyche. It surfaces in the love of being frightened and exposed to real or imagined physical dangers—an important feature of amusement parks. It surfaces in the love of active and somewhat risky attunement sports like skiing and surfing, in which enjoyment and skill involve moving in a state of sensitive harmony with and adaptation to natural forces. It surfaces in the love of gambling, in which one tests one's harmoniousness with the abstruse order of the universe. It surfaces in "tempting fate."

Champions and virtuosi in every field define their successful performance in terms of two opposing and compartmentalized theories. One stresses control, mastery, self-discipline, and technique. The other stresses innate gifts, inspiration, being psychologically ready or "together," and being in some sort of mystical harmony with the environment. In our society we tend to lay primary stress on the mastery theory and relegate the other to the realm of superstition.

Victor Gioscia points out, however, that we see and hear because our sense organs are synchronized with certain wave frequencies in the environment. We tend to think of seeing and hearing, with all their amplifications, in mastery terms, but in fact we see and hear because we are in harmony with these tiny parts of the environment. One can view great achievements from the same perspective, for they clearly depend upon being in the right place at the right time with the right experience and the right state of mind—in special synchrony with the surroundings.

When I speak of the content of action being less important than the internal orientation with which it is carried out, I have something like this in mind. The attunement attitude is sensorily and viscerally open, receptive, and responsive—capable of altering direction in response to feedback from within and without.

Attunement assumes a motivated and energetic presence. People who "play it by ear" in our society often have no idea what it is they want, and enter the situation with the same emotional and sensory deadness as those who come in highly programmed. Attunement involves an active, focussed responsivity.

Its opposite, the mastery attitude, reveals itself by its overt or covert goal of ego aggrandizement. People often object to remarks such as I have just made that they fail to provide a means for making a large enough impact on the system. They want to leave their mark. But this impulse to grandiosity is what continually recreates the sickness around us. Social action founded in pomposity is part of the problem, not part of the solution. Middle-class radical action often begins with people sitting around trying to figure out how they can make the biggest killing in social change terms and hence leave a monument to themselves. This is sometimes masked by assuming an earnest attitude of social responsibility and global guilt, but this is just spiritual pride. It is the height of pretension to assume active personal responsibility for a whole class or nation, although one might wish, out of a feeling of internal revulsion, to dissociate oneself from and oppose the acts of that class or nation. Responsibility begins and ends with being a responsive nerve ending for every system to which one belongs.

This does not mean that everyone must abandon hope of meaningful change occurring in their lifetime beyond their immediate environment. Good news travels fast, and the media, for all their faults, are hungry for social novelty and do a fair job of spreading it. Anyone who manages to generate around herself a more benign environment will find others engaging in similar processes before long. If one is concerned about having this known as the Mary or John Doe Plan, and implemented on a mass scale, it will soon become a malignant environment for most other people; but if the knowledge diffuses organically the innovation will be modified in a thousand different ways as it spreads and no one will bother about credit for the idea.

The problem is more complicated for oppressed groups, who may find that creating a more benign local environment arouses hostility from representatives of the diseased system. This will force them at the very least into self-defense and probably into a certain amount of willful mobilization. This was the experience of the Black Panthers, for example. Such mobilization arises spontaneously out of the immediate experience of acute oppression, however, and is not to be compared with the James Bond effusions of middle-class ideologues. Attunement requires something different from each person, but it may at times imply diametrically opposite behavior for people of different classes.

Directions

I am engaged here in a rather ironic enterprise: attempting to encourage people I do not know, through a linear abstract medium, to alter their orientation to the world in a way that should induce them to reject my effort as mechanical and invalid. Bearing this inconsistency in mind, I would like to summarize those of my remarks that have obvious prescriptive implications. These are not "things to do," but directions that seem healthy—not processes to initiate, but trends already under way and available for new energy inputs.

(1) *Decentralization.* The diffusion of power was a central tenet of the new left ("small is beautiful, big is ugly"). The old left, of course, favored the opposite trend and welcomed the increasing concentration of power within a few large corporations on the grounds that this would make them all the riper for nationalization. This is sound enough as a strategy, but the idea that changing the formal ownership of a giant bureaucracy would affect the way it functions exemplifies the infatuation with symbols that afflicts rationalistic thought.

Diffusion of power, however, raises issues of co-ordination. Mass organizations create at least the illusion that they provide a system for co-ordinating the activities of large numbers of people. This is largely a hoax, as we can see by the chaos and incoherence in which we live. The illusion is contrived by leaving out of the process of co-ordination almost everything that matters to people and making a great show of precision about the rest. At the same time it must be acknowledged that co-ordination in a decentralized condition requires a far greater output of energy on the part of each person. In the long run this energy output will not be greater in any real sense, since (a) free and equal communication is far more exhilarating than straining oneself through the coercive funnel of an impersonal bureaucracy, and (b) nothing causes a greater energy drain than feelings of helplessness and powerlessness. But so long as the traditional systems exist to create such drains it will seem effortful to transcend them.

What diffusion of power means, then, is the withdrawal of energy and interest from vertical (mass, bureaucratic, authoritarian) channels of communication and the reinvestment of this energy in lateral channels.

At present, centralization and decentralization are going on simultaneously. In traditional spheres the bases of power and wealth are becoming continually narrower. At the same time local alternative institutions organized in explicit antipathy to their large-scale counterparts are quietly proliferating. This means that while traditional organizations are becoming larger and more powerful, they are beginning to lose their human fuel. It will probably be twenty years or more before this begins to have significant effects, and real change will no doubt be achieved only after some serious confrontations have occurred. These confrontations will at first seem unequal—the powerful, armed, and organized few against the weaponless, dispersed, and unorganized many—but dispersion can be a source of strength as well as weakness (you can't shoot down a cloud), and the power loci will have become ambivalent and subject to infiltration by human beings.

An important example of power diffusion is the development of rank-and-file police organizations. The fact that these groups tend to voice reactionary sentiments has distracted most observers from the system effects of such action. There is a kind of naïveté, fostered by intellectuals and the media, that gives undue weight to ideology, but it really matters very little what beliefs these men espouse. What matters is that they have given up their position of powerlessness and are beginning to question their role as hatchet men for the middle class, a role in which they run all the risks and receive none of the rewards. As they refuse to expose themselves to absurd dangers, other solutions will have to be found by the authorities to whom they have heretofore been unquestioningly obedient. Collective action in one's own behalf is the cause, not the result, of sociological wisdom.

(2) *Deceleration.* Democracy is impossible in America for the simple reason that people move around too much to form the kind of stable community bonds on which democracy is founded. Mobility cuts away every opportunity for people to lean on each other and forces them to depend upon vertical bureaucratic systems for their needs. How can a people frame their wishes in political terms when they don't know each other well enough to talk to each other? Instead, questions are framed, defined, and asked by specialists, and answered individually, if at all, by people who have no way to explore their relational implications. Democracy is only possible with some minimal degree of interpersonal coagulation.

To be in transit, furthermore, is not to be really living, since one is during that period detached from her surroundings, either by being physically walled off in a metal vehicle, or psychically, simply be a matter of notifying the person or persons most capable of dealing with the external event.

In modern communities this is increasingly done. One calls the police or fire department or ambulance or Red Cross and may not even talk to a neighbor about it. In the most extreme case people may even hide away and not respond, but this denotes total social breakdown. Ordinarily, even in urban settings, calling the crisis expert is accompanied by some clustering of people.

The heightened communication that crisis brings in vital communities is for the purpose of exploring the potential relational changes posed by the crisis. But the interrelationships in bureaucracies are mechanically defined and do not change in any case. This is why they are so ponderous and so monumentally ineffectual relative to the number of human hours invested in them. The language of bureaucracies is digital language—they can deal competently with an infinite number of discrete events by sorting and classifying, but almost by definition they have no mechanism whatever for dealing with the relationships among those events, and consequently break down whenever called upon to do this. When finally forced to confront a serious crisis, people in bureaucracies typically suspend the bureaucratic structure altogether and shift to an *ad hoc*, informal mode of organization.

Most people are able to make a threefold distinction between mental alertness, knowledge, and wisdom or understanding. The first concerns the rapidity with which new bits of data can be assimilated, the second the number of bits already assimilated, while the third refers to the capacity to appreciate complex interrelationships. The first has always been the province of the young, while the second and third have been traditionally reserved for the old. The knowledge sphere has now been reassigned to the young in response to the information explosion, and even wisdom is no longer attributed to the old. Since the old know so little about the new bits of data, it is assumed that they cannot very well discuss their interrelationships, although in fact the understanding of relationships transcends the content of those relationships, and hence the old have a fund of untapped wisdom which is wasted.

The old are rightly indignant at the elevation of youth. The young are as ignorant as ever about relational questions, and it must be profoundly irritating to hear accolades offered to people who are continually reinventing the wheel. Yet at the same time the old have only themselves to blame for this, since they have abdicated their proper realm in order to invade mechanical domains in which they have nothing special to contribute. Had they sustained their interest in relational matters they might have preserved their birthright. Now there are "experts" even in relational areas to which those seeking wisdom are referred, to their eternal discontent. For an expert cannot by definition have wisdom, since he only possesses information accumulated within a single compartment. He knows nothing of relationships—of "the larger interactive system . . . which, if disturbed, is likely to generate exponential curves of change" (Bateson)—and can only offer as a substitute the fatuities of his field.

An alternative to village life which would be non-cancerous and yet resistant to external cancerous influences would have to place an emphasis on relational thinking and relational language that is utterly foreign to most Westerners. We would have to start thinking in terms of networks and images rather than numbered boxes. Let me give two examples:

(a) When we become aware that a muscle is tense we try to relax that muscle. Following Western medical thinking, we approach the body one segment at a time, imagining that comfort will be achieved when we have tracked down each and every muscle and relaxed it. Escape from wire-taut rigidity is sought by collapsing into a state of corpselike flaccidity. Forcing ourselves into utter submission to gravity, however, is not necessarily a source of comfort. We feel good not when every muscle is flaccid, but when there is a balanced distribution of energy throughout the organism. Tension is not a matter of one malfunctioning part, but of a bad distribution of energy flow. A tense muscle in one part of the body usually means that others nearby are flabby and immobilized, so that the tense one is doing work for the others. Relief is as likely to come from activating the inert areas as from trying to immobilize the overworked ones.

(b) Political science is the study of various bad substitutes for organic relationships. Of necessity they all take as their premise the lack of adequate interpersonal communication. What could be more meaningless, for example, than a vote—a binary response considered apart from the role of the responder or the responder's relationships to all other responders? It is like asking all the cells in a fingernail to decide individually whether they are for or against red corpuscles. Yet the vote is supposedly the foundation of our own political system—we are indeed fortunate that the reality of politics is as far removed from this sort of thing as it is. One can count and classify cells for an eternity and still not have an organism. It is the relationships among units that determine their meaning, not the units themselves.

A perceptive young secretary in a university department once remarked that 80 per cent of her work was unnecessary and could be eliminated if there was any trust in the academic community. The same is true of the kinds of decisions that committees make and remake. Since no one is very intensely connected with any-one else, issues must be dealt with in terms of policy and precedent. Earnest voices are always raised to caution that prece-dents are being set, but a few months later it is hard for anyone to remember why they had ever wanted what they had legislated with such difficulty. Organizations live for years with procedures that came into being as an adaptation to the eccentricities or skills or incompetencies of a single person, long since departed. The truth is, it would take less time and be far more enjoyable if decisions were frankly treated in terms of personal needs and interpersonal relationships instead of pretending that only ab-stract principles were involved.

Institutions are like trees. The green living part consists of re-lationships between people. As these become habitual they leave a dead deposit in the form of structures and procedures. Like a tree trunk, the dead deposit grows continually larger, while the living matter clings to the outside of it. The dead tissue of the trunk is much easier to understand than the living tissue of the bark, and can be more easily dealt with in quantitative terms. It is easy to lose sight of where the life is because the tree still looks very imposing after it is completely dead.

Reconnection is a matter of remaining part of the bark instead of pretending to be a hunk of cellulose—of remembering that the splendid isolation of the human ego is a schizoid fantasy. Primitive peoples know that we are part of one another and of our environment. The primitive hunter begs pardon from the animals he kills because he recognizes their common immersion in an ecological whole. The hunter may err in behaving as if his act of courtesy would affect the animal population, but he would never make the gross error of behaving as if there were no relationship.

Distinctions

I have spoken about reconnection, about responding to internal sensations, about being a good social nerve ending, about recapturing primitive awareness. Such remarks are subject to heavy misinterpretation, since they call up associations to the familiar and useless categories with which we customarily define our experience. For academics this reflex will be irresistible, no matter how much explanation is given, but for those interested in ideas and difficult modes of perception I would like to offer some words of clarification and differentiation—to state what attunement and responsivity are *not*.

They do not imply passivity or fatalism. An organic response is a *response*. For oppressed groups, for example, it might well be social or political action of the usual kind: community organizing, boycotts, demonstrations, and so on. These may be done with varying degrees of attunement for, to repeat, it is less a matter of *what* than *how*. The more the communication takes place solely among those who already think alike, for example, the less it can be considered a force for health. Activity carried out in a mechanical, non-responsive way can be as numbing as passivity. Confrontation is almost always of value, but the best confrontation is one that is bilateral. Guerrilla theater, for example, is usually as much a one-way communication as a lecture and hence just about as effective. Successful confrontations are usually interactive, sometimes violently so.

Americans often feel a little uneasy if they are not engaged in frenetic activity, preferably of an uncomfortable and toilsome variety that betokens victory over their inner inertia. But everyone feels more active and hopeful at some times than others, and there is no particular virtue in futile struggling—a discouragement that is attended to usually lasts a shorter time than one that is not. On the other hand, nothing breeds a sense of helplessness and hopelessness like anger that finds no mode of expression whatever. To walk this tightrope requires great sensitivity.

They are not synonymous with "spontaneity." This is a particularly difficult distinction to make since I have placed so much emphasis on internal feeling states. I have suggested that one's own emotional state is usually a valid index of the functioning of the system in which one participates. I have further argued that one has an obligation—a duty, even—to express that emotional state in some form or another in order that the system can function in a healthy manner, since no system can operate humanely without adequate feedback. Does this not imply a kind of visceral despotism: that whatever I am feeling is real and valid and important and should be acted upon?

One could make a case for such pure impulsivity from a societal perspective, since it does insure a high level of emotional information for the system. Unfortunately, as we all know, it is ultimately fatal for the individual organism, and hence constitutes a kind of kamikaze approach to ecological well-being. Furthermore, since all social systems are structured to limit feedback to some extent, an unfocussed impulsive response, even if disastrous for the individual, may go unregistered by the system. Even a hurt child has brains enough not to waste her tears on empty space, but runs to find a parent before venting her unhappiness.

A more serious limitation on spontaneity lies in the fact that our own viscera are quite seriously corrupted by cultural learning and cannot be completely relied upon as a valid index even of our own emotional state, much less that of the system. All feelings have been tampered with, and tend to express themselves through roundabout channels. For some, the angry channel is constricted, and they tend to feel tearful when angry. For others, the tears channel is blocked and they tend to feel angry when hurt or sad. Others have headaches or stomach pains, and so on. Distress in general is a valid index that the system is hurting and hurtful, but great specificity is not to be sought. It may be true, as anti-psychoanalytic therapies maintain, that no one knows the truth about another's psyche, but it is also true, as the psychoanalysts maintain, that no one knows the truth about himself, either. It is pure pomposity to imagine that our expressed impulses have any more emotional validity than those of our uptight neighbors. Access to our own feelings is spurious in the absence of access to those of others.

"Spontaneity" in our culture tends still to be imbued with narcissistic goals. There is still much invidiousness in our play, much posing, much seeking after admiration and special status. The ideology of free expression is often used to sanctify recognition-seeking without discipline, which is the worst of both worlds for the audience, who must put up with the artist or performer's narcissism without getting anything back. As a friend put it, in response to the artistic effusions of college students: "They all want to have their shit cast in bronze."

They are not necessarily attained through personal development. Since socialization in Western culture makes it dangerous to trust one's own impulses with too great specificity, it might seem logical to devote one's efforts to self-cure, self-mastery, enlightenment, spiritual development, personal growth, or whatever. This position implies that if one achieves personal harmony, then harmony with nature will automatically follow, which is a little like saying that the best way to cement a friendship with a man is to have a love affair with his wife. It might be, of course, but then again it might not. Being attuned to someone is not the same as total identity with her. My own experience with those who have energetically sought internal harmony, with some sense of success, is that they have simply become detached —whether or not this was an explicit goal. And although they often *feel* in harmony with those around them this is usually illusory and unreciprocated. Their feeling of being attuned is merely that of going stoned to a beautiful movie—one is highly sensitized to, appreciative of, identified with others, but disengaged from them—observing and experiencing but not interacting. This is not to say that such a state cannot lead to attunement, for it sometimes does. But it is not the same thing as attunement, which requires an extra step, an external focus. And since the choice to turn inward is not random, that step is rarely made.

To become internally harmonious is to become disharmonious with one's past and cultural environment, since these are what created disharmony in the first place. There is no way to escape all this—it is all part of our being. One cannot become truly harmonious—inside and out—in a discordant world. One can only seek greater harmony within and without simultaneously.

A frequent delusion in this kind of effort is that the part of oneself that seeks internal harmony is one's own, while all the disharmony was somehow imposed from without. Similarly, middle-class Americans trying to overcome their personality difficulties tend to be deterministic about their problems, seeing them as inculcated by their parents and culture. Yet they imagine that their strengths—that with which they strive to overcome these problems—spring full-blown from their own wills, like Athene from the head of Zeus. But if hang-ups come from parents and society, so does the ability to overcome them. And if it is the self that is integrated and overcoming, it is also the self that is being integrated and overcome. And if the hang-ups are manifestations of society, *so is the self that integrates and cures.* We are part of all we experience, however repulsive it may seem, and without an outward focus all is illusion.

They do not imply conformity. Stressing the importance of reconnection is sometimes interpreted as advocating some kind of conformity or "fitting in," although in fact it demands the precise opposite. Avoiding a cybernetic connectedness with the environment by presenting a false conventional self to the world is a schizoid strategy. "Fitting in," furthermore, is a mechanical concept, appropriate to inanimate blocks of matter. It makes the absurd assumption that a one-way adaptation between two organisms is possible—an idea only an individualistic culture could invent. For at bottom conformity and egoism amount to exactly the same thing—an inability to be fully present and emotionally engaged with another person.

Attunement would require us to abandon our automatic tendency to suppress or ignore our visceral reactions to our surroundings. For to ignore, fail to respond to, or wall oneself off from the existing milieu is to maintain it. "Doing your own thing" usually turns out to be a mechanistic process of responding to observable messages from within and ignoring external feedback. Restoring connectedness means reacting—protesting when injured, expressing pleasure when pleased. The institutions we endure today are oppressive because they suffer from a shortage of feedback. They are not without blame for this, of course, since they insulate themselves from feedback as much as possible. But we need to overcome our learned deference to the inhuman and unresponsive projections of our mechanical egos—bureaucracies, machines, structures, statuses, degrees—and transfer this courtesy and consideration to human beings and other living things.

Sometimes humans act as agents of mechanical systems—presenting themselves as mere extensions of an organization or profession, subordinating themselves to their status, position, or some symbol of achieved mediocrity—an M.D. or Ph.D. To the degree that they act in this way they have renounced their humanity and cannot claim to be treated as human beings. Hence a retaliatory cycle is activated: In their "official capacity" they act in an inhumane way, but if we retaliate they feel that hurt at some level as human beings and become both more official (to protect themselves) and more inhumane (for revenge). This is unfortunate but should not lead us to misdirect our sympathies. We are obligated only to allow such persons a moment to reveal whether they will choose to be human or official—the moment they have chosen the latter their claim to have their human feelings considered must be disallowed, since they have opted out of human circuitry. If one wishes to try a conversion—to attempt to reach their humanity through the screen of their self-obliteration, this is a highly desirable enterprise but an ambitious one, fraught with emotional risk. It is important in such cases to maintain clear awareness that the respect and consideration are directed toward the person, not the structure. The only valid index of the accuracy of the effort is the degree to which it detaches the person *from* the structure.

People defend official behavior in terms of the necessity of "getting their job done." To reveal the emptiness of this statement it is only necessary to ask, in as large a way as possible, just what the "job" is. Is medical arrogance healing? Does academic nitpicking inculcate wisdom? Does police brutality protect the people? Do hospital procedures nurture the sick? Do phone company procedures facilitate communication?

One could easily spend her life in such confrontations, and a joyless life it would be: I certainly do not want to advocate walking about unarmed on a battlefield. Yet it is important to be aware that every act of self-restraint in relation to an inhumane structure constitutes positive feedback for that structure—a vote of confidence. Our definitions of "responsibility" have always placed a heavy emphasis on self-control, but "response-ability" means responsivity or it means nothing at all.

To be focussed only on one's own viscera, of course, is not

attunement. Never to accommodate is as mechanical as to accommodate all the time. I feel the need to accent the importance of disruption and protest in relation to mechanical structures because we are so subservient to them. Educated people have learned to say "sick" in place of "wicked" when confronted with individual life-styles and behavior patterns they dislike, but they routinely accept the most bizarre institutions with complete equanimity. In part this is due to an inability to see pathology in the powerful and successful—the achievement of high status is *ipso facto* regarded by psychiatrists, psychologists, and social workers as a criterion of mental health ("he is functioning well") while lack of interest in self-aggrandizement is "ego-weakness." National leaders in their official capacities at times exhibit behavior that would be considered frankly psychotic in one less eminent, and without arousing a ripple of alarm. But the inability to see institutions as pathological extends far beyond the blind acceptance of their representatives. We not only accept warped and brutal institutions as normal, but think nothing of employing psychiatrists and psychologists to persuade perfectly healthy people to adjust to them. Yet the inculcation of sado-masochistic attitudes in military training camps, of fascistic attitudes in high schools, and of feminine self-hatred in marriage is more crippling psychically for those who succeed in these patterns than for those who fail.

One final caution is necessary. If we stop ingratiating ourselves with our mechanical extensions, this should be an end in itself, not a way of making some comment about ourselves. Americans tend to seize any opportunity to prove their uniqueness and specialness, but if this is the motive, the enterprise becomes worse than useless—it actively nourishes the disease. Since we are all unique to begin with, the effort to *make* oneself unique is suspect. It attempts to deny a truth that Americans find particularly hard to swallow: Our differentness is not a personal achievement but a function of our participation in a larger entity. Diversity is created by groups—individuals would arrive at the same place without some kind of human support system, since they would then be entirely programmed by inner circuitry, which is more or less uniform. Connectedness involves a recognition that uniqueness is a collective product.

Epilogue

We are born into intimate mutual-feedback relationships with
our environments, both human and non-human. Commitments to
fantasy break this circuit. Signals are ignored, and behavior becomes mechanical, insensitive. The environment hurts me, but I
am intent on a remote, fantastic goal, and I do not cry out but
forge ahead. Machine that I have become, I hurt the environment
and it cries out, but I cannot hear it, intent as I am on remote,
fantastic goals. Indeed, there is a certain retributive justice to it:
I torture the environment, it tortures me. A positive-feedback
spiral is launched, for the more I make myself into a machine,
the more I will tend to torture the environment, and the more the
environment tortures me back, the more I need to make myself
into a machine.

We have mocked primitive humans for imagining themselves
to be one with nature. We "know" that we are separate from
the environment. We have mastered it. Indeed, we have declared
war on it, and we have won. We have defeated the air, crushed
the sea, slaughtered the land, and stand alone in glorious victory,
sick and gasping, like an infant who has triumphed over its
mother.

All the errors and follies of magic, religion, and mystical traditions are outweighed by the one great wisdom they contain—
the awareness of humanity's organic embeddedness in a complex
natural system. And all the brilliant, sophisticated insights of
Western rationalism are set at naught by the egregious delusion
on which they rest—that of human autarchy.

The achievements of Western culture are materialized dreams, and since they were only made possible by the strangling of our feelings, they have increasingly materialized the evil in man—perverse brutality, whining arrogance, cruel obsessiveness, and devouring power-hunger. And when all these mangled impulses have been given physical form we will be unable to see the sky or the trees or any living thing, so inundated will we be by the machinery we have vomited up from our ulcerated insides.

To reclaim ourselves and our environment we need to drain energy from the narcissistic tumor that possesses us; to listen, sense, and be here; to retrieve what we have cast off, to repossess what we have projected onto others, to make whole what we have truncated; to move together in a reciprocal dance of integrity and grace. We keep searching for the stargate, but it is not hidden. Hovering delicately in the spaces between things, it has been there all the time.

Notes

page 1. Alexander Lowen, *Betrayal of the Body* (Collier Books, 1969), p. 231.

2., para. 4 Lowen, *Betrayal*, p. 116.

5., para. 2 Gregory Bateson, *Steps to an Ecology of Mind* (Ballantine Books, 1972); Norman O. Brown, *Life Against Death* (Vintage, 1959); David Bakan, *The Duality of Human Existence* (Beacon, 1966); William Irwin Thompson, *At the Edge of History* (Harper, 1972).

7. I am indebted to Bruno Beretta for this parable.

9. Bateson, *Steps*, p. 18.

11. Norman O. Brown, *Love's Body* (Random House, 1966), p. 147.

12., para. 4 Grace Stuart, *Narcissus* (Macmillan, 1955), p. 45.

16., para. 2 Ross V. Speck and Carolyn L. Attneave, *Family Networks* (Pantheon, 1973).

16–17. Kiyo Morimoto, "On Trying to Understand the Frustrations of Students" (Harvard University Bureau of Study Counsel, 1972). I also learned about choice from discussions with Fatima Mernissi.

18. Brown, *Love's Body*, p. 184.

20., para. 2 Norbert Wiener, *The Human Use of Human Beings* (Avon, 1967), pp. 129–41.

para. 3 Alvin Toffler, *Future Shock* (Bantam, 1970), pp. 197–215.

22., para. 2 Weston La Barre, *The Human Animal* (University of Chicago Press, 1954), p. 258.

para. 3 Sigmund Freud, "The 'Uncanny,'" in *Collected Papers*, Vol. IV (Hogarth, 1953), pp. 368–407.

23., para. 2 Henri Bergson, *Laughter, An Essay on the Meaning of the Comic* (Macmillan, 1911), pp. 8 ff., 37 ff.

24–25. From Fatima Mernissi.

page 28., para. 3 Toffler, *Future Shock*, pp. 359–64, 428–31, 449–52.

30., para. 1 Bateson, *Steps*, p. 433. What is said here about medicine applies equally well to our approach to social ailments. For malfunctioning part, simply read "party or parties responsible," and for germs read "outside agitators."

32., para. 2 René Dubos, *Mirage of Health* (Harper, 1959), pp. 1–52, 68–72, 80–108.

———, *Man, Medicine, and Environment* (Mentor, 1969), pp. 88–94, 106 ff.; Toffler, *Future Shock*, pp. 325–42.

para. 4 Irving K. Zola, "Medicine as an Institution of Social Control," *The Sociological Review*, 20 (November 1972), pp. 487–504; K. White, et al., "International Comparisons of Medical Care Utilization," *New England Journal of Medicine*, 277 (1967), pp. 516–22.

35. Sandra Levinson and Carol Brightman, *Venceremos Brigade* (Simon and Schuster, 1971), pp. 166–67.

37. Plato, *Phaedo*, 67; Lowen, *Betrayal*, p. 231; K. Kristofferson and F. Foster, *Me and Bobby McGee*.

38., para. 4 Donella H. Meadows, et al., *The Limits To Growth* (Signet, 1972).

38–39. Most of these growth figures are from Toffler, *Future Shock*, pp. 9–35.

39., para. 1 For animal activity, see Ashley Montague, *Touching* (Columbia University Press, 1971), pp. 15–25.

39., para. 2 Dubos, *Man, Medicine*, p. 97; David Bakan, *Disease, Pain and Sacrifice* (University of Chicago Press, 1968), pp. 19–31.

para. 4 Bakan, *Ibid.*, p. 36.

40., para. 3 Toffler, *Future Shock*, pp. 35, 403, 412, 428–29, 458, 460, 468.

40–41. Leon J. Yarrow, "Separation from Parents During Early Childhood," in Martin L. Hoffman and Lois Wladis Hoffman (eds.) *Review of Child Development Research*, Vol. I (Russell Sage Foundation, 1964), pp. 89–136; Gerald Caplan, *Mental Health Aspects of Social Work in Public Health* (School of Social Welfare, University of California, Berkeley, 1955), pp. 123–33. For schizophrenia, see Bateson, *Steps*, pp. 201–27; R. D. Laing, *The Politics of the Family* (Pantheon, 1971); R. D. Laing and A. Esterson, *Sanity, Madness and the Family: Families of Schizophrenics* (Basic Books, 1970); Theodore Lidz, et al., *Schizophrenia and the Family* (International Universities Press, 1965).

41–42. Some readers will realize that I am discussing, in a brutally oversimplified fashion, the issue of universalism versus particularism. Cf. Talcott Parsons, *The Social System* (Free Press, 1951); Max Weber, *The Protestant Ethic and the Spirit of Capitalism* (Allen and Unwin, 1930). For the limitations of authoritarianism, see Warren Bennis and Philip Slater, *The Temporary Society* (Harper, 1968), Chaps. 1 and 3.

44., para. 3 Marshall McLuhan, *Understanding Media* (McGraw-Hill, 1964).

45., para. 4 R. D. Laing, *The Divided Self* (Pelican, 1965), pp. 80 ff., 139 ff.

46., para. 4 Ibid., p. 162.

47., para. 3 Philip Slater, *The Glory of Hera* (Beacon, 1968), Chap. 2; Bruno Bettelheim, *Symbolic Wounds* (Thames and Hudson, 1955).

48., para. 1 C. S. Lewis, *That Hideous Strength* (Macmillan, 1965), p. 46.

49–50. La Barre, *Human Animal*, pp. 258–59, 268.

50–51. Ibid., pp. 240 ff., 246, 260.

51., para. 1 This statement about social fictions is a paraphrase of W. I. Thomas' famous dictum about situations defined as real being real in their consequences. See W. I. Thomas and D. S. Thomas, *The Child in America* (Knopf, 1928), p. 572.

51., para. 2 La Barre, op. cit., pp. 267–68.

52., para. 1 Bateson, *Steps*, p. 434.

55., para. 3 Erich Fromm, *Man for Himself* (Rinehart, 1947); David Riesman, *The Lonely Crowd* (Anchor, 1950), and *Individualism Reconsidered* (Free Press, 1964); William H. Whyte, Jr., *The Organization Man* (Simon and Schuster, 1956); George Orwell, *1984* (Signet, 1961). For imprinting, see Lorenz, *King Solomon's Ring*, pp. 59–61.

56., para. 2 Fritz Perls, *Gestalt Therapy Verbatim* (Real People Press, 1969), p. 154. The Gestalt prayer (p. 4) involves the same lonely-but-brave scenario that has always been popular in protestant cultures, and can be seen as an updated version of the stiff upper lip. It mimics traditional American WASP independence training, and serves as delayed socialization for people with possessive and overprotective parents.

56–57. Marcia Millman, "Nightmare or Paradise?" *Social Change* (in press); Ray Bradbury, *Fahrenheit 451* (Ballantine, 1966); Aldous Huxley, *Brave New World* (Bantam,

1966); George Orwell, *1984* (Signet, 1961); Eugene Zamiatin, *We* (Dutton, 1952).

page 58., para. 3 Cf., e.g., The Performance Group, *Dionysus in 69*, ed. by Richard Schechner (Farrar, Straus, & Giroux, 1970).

58–59. Bakan, *Duality*, p. 89.

60., para. 1 Lowen, *Betrayal*, pp. 38–42.

para. 2 Ibid., pp. 42–43.

61., para. 2 Freud, *Civilization and Its Discontents* (Norton, 1961), p. 62. Lowen, op. cit., p. 257.

para. 3 Ibid., p. 258.

63., para. 2 Laing, *Divided Self*, p. 80.

para. 3 Ibid., pp. 80, 86, 95.

64., para. 2 Bakan, op. cit., p. 89.

para. 3 Laing, op. cit., p. 151.

para. 4 Ibid., pp. 142–43.

65. Ibid., pp. 144–45, 151, 158.

69. Lao Tzu, *Tao Te Ching*, trans. by D. C. Lau (Penguin, 1963), Book One, XIX; Idries Shah, *Wisdom of the Idiots* (Octagon, 1969), p. 13.

69., para. 1 Wiener, *Human Use*, p. 31.

70., para. 3 My book *Microcosm* (Wiley, 1966) is an elaborate description of this process.

72., para. 3 La Barre, *Human Animal*, p. 246.

74., para. 2 On human roles, see Bennis and Slater, *Temporary Society*, pp. 79–87.

77., para. 1 Toffler, *Future Shock*, p. 99.

77–78. William N. Stephens, *The Family in Cross-Cultural Perspective* (Holt, Rinehart and Winston, 1963), pp. 325–39.

78., para. 2 Bennis and Slater, *Temporary Society*, Chaps. 1–3.

80., para. 2 Sigmund Freud, *Totem and Taboo* (Norton, 1950).

para. 4 Stephens, *Family*, pp. 338–39; G. Rattray Taylor, *Sex in History* (Ballantine, 1954); Philip Slater, "Culture, Sexuality, and Narcissism," *Social Change* (in press).

81., para. 2 Weber, *Protestant Ethic*, pp. 121, 153–54.

para. 3 Philippe Ariès, *Centuries of Childhood* (Knopf, 1962), pp. 71–72.

84., para. 2 Notably Emile Durkheim, *The Division of Labor in Society* (Free Press, 1933).

87., para. 3 Slater, *Glory of Hera*, passim.

para. 5 H. R. Hays, *The Dangerous Sex* (Putnam, 1964), pp. 17–21.

88., para. 2 Bennis and Slater, *Temporary Society*, Chaps. 1 and 2.

90., para. 1 Slater, *Glory of Hera,* Chap. 1.

para. 3 Bateson, *Steps,* pp. 309–37.

91., para. 2 See, for example, Alice Ryerson, "Medical Advice on Child-rearing Practices: 1550–1900." Unpublished doctoral dissertation, Harvard University Graduate School of Education, 1960; Montague, *Touching,* pp. 122–26.

para. 3 Ibid., pp. 131–37.

para. 4 Ibid., pp. 126–31.

94., para. 3 David Riesman, *Individualism Reconsidered,* pp. 99–120.

95., para. 1 Richard Bach, *Jonathan Livingston Seagull* (Avon, 1970). Quotations from pp. 27, 29, 30, 41, 57, 58, 60, 61, 64, 65, 86, 88, 106, 112, 114, 120–21; Gary Shaw, *Meat on the Hoof* (St. Martin's Press, 1972); Philip Roth, *Our Gang* (Bantam, 1971).

96., para. 1 Dori Appel Slater points out that in the counter-culture the quest for internal mastery has largely replaced the worldly variety.

97., para. 3 Wilhelm Reich, *Character-Analysis* (Noonday Press, 1962), pp. 248 ff.

98., para. 2 Montague, Ibid., p. 82.

para. 4 Reich, Ibid.

100., para. 2 Theodore Rosebury, *Life on Man* (Viking, 1969).

para. 3 I am indebted to Jacqueline Larcombe Doyle for this observation.

105. Lao Tzu, *Tao Te Ching,* Book One, XIII; Sophocles, *Oepidus the King,* trans. by David Grene (University of Chicago Press, 1959), 1074–80.

106., para. 3 This discussion of the family as a class system describes a norm. There is of course considerable variation in actual behavior from group to group and family to family. The American middle-class family system is more "democratic" than any European type, just as its social class behavior is less formal. The structures, however, are identical in both cases.

109., para. 4 Apollodorus, III, 5, 8. See also the note on p. 347 of the Loeb Library edition.

110., para. 2 Sophocles, *Oed. Tyr.,* 1460–65.

para. 3 Ibid., 103–32.

111., para. 3 Compare the anti-oedipal Stephen Stills song a generation later: "If you can't be with the one you love, love the one you're with." Contemporary popular music shows a striking decline in oedipal romanticism. Even when relationships between young men and older women are portrayed the people involved are real rather than idealized—replete with wrinkles, hang-ups, and bad jokes, along with their more endearing qualities.

page 113., para. 2 Toffler, *Future Shock*, pp. 117–18.

para. 4 David McClelland, *The Achieving Society* (Van Nostrand, 1961), pp. 342, 345, 404–6. A Russian study, which I have not yet seen, purportedly finds that the fathers of "great men" are older than the average. If this is true, it would obviously fit the interpretation suggested here. Freud's own oedipal conflict was profoundly affected by his father's age.

115., para. 2 Alexander Lowen, *Pleasure* (Lancer, 1970), p. 85. Italics mine.

115–116. For a more extensive discussion of this principle, see "Prolegomena to a Psychoanalytic Theory of Aging and Death," in R. Kastenbaum (ed.), *New Thoughts on Old Age* (Springer, 1964), pp. 19–40.

118., para. 2 Riesman, *Lonely Crowd*, pp. 31 ff.

119., para. 2 John Cuber and Peggy Harroff, *Sex and the Significant Americans* (Pelican, 1965), pp. 172–75, 180.

para. 4 Ibid., p. 180.

124., para. 4 Bateson, *Steps*, p. 300.

125., para. 2 McClelland, Ibid., p. 405; Slater, *Glory of Hera*.

126., para. 4 Vivian Gornick, "The Next Great Moment in History Is Theirs," *The Village Voice*, November 27, 1969; Matina Horner, "Toward an Understanding of Achievement-Related Conflicts in Women," *Journal of Social Issues*, 28, 1972, pp. 157–75.

127., para. 2 Montague, *Touching*, pp. 272–74.

128., para. 2 Bakan, *Duality*, p. 15.

para. 3 Ibid., pp. 113–20, 122–24.

132., para. 3 Edward Devereux has suggested to me that it is the decline in parental role specialization that is responsible for the weakening of oedipal trends in our society.

133., para. 2 Philippe Ariès, *Centuries of Childhood*, pp. 33–34, 38–39, 50 ff.

para. 3 Ibid., pp. 47, 50–53, 57–58, 71, 100 ff., 130–33, 329–36, 369, 375, 398–400; Ryerson, "Medical Advice."

134., para. 3 Ariès, op. cit., pp. 59, 61, 92–93, 99, 314.

135. Adapted from a report in the Boston *Globe*, March 1972, by Crocker Snow, Jr.

137. Lao Tzu, *Tao Te Ching*, Book Two, LXXVII; C. S. Lewis, *Hideous Strength*, p. 173.

138–139. Toffler, *Future Shock*, pp. 334–36.

139., para. 2 See, e.g., Dubos, *Mirage of Health; Man, Medicine and Environment;* Toffler, op. cit., pp. 327–42.

139–140. Cf. Bakan, *Duality*, p. 88. For the most extensive and intelligent discussion of this relationship, see Victor Gioscia, *Time Forms* (Gordon and Breach, in press), from which this paragraph is derived.

143., para. 2 Dubos, *Mirage*, pp. 109–39.

146., para. 2 Bateson, *Steps*, p. 4.

147., para. 3 See Slater, "Social Bases of Personality," in Neil J. Smelser (ed.), *Sociology: An Introduction* (Wiley, 1973), Second Ed., pp. 612–24.

149., para. 2 Sigmund Freud, "Negation," in *Collected Papers*, Vol. V., pp. 181–85.

150–151. Toffler, op. cit., pp. 365, 405, 449–52, 460, 467, 480. Italics mine.

152., para. 3 Toffler, op. cit., pp. 360, 393, 428–31, 450–52, 474.

154., para. 2 Lowen, *Pleasure*, p. 108.

155., para. 2 Arthur Janov, *The Primal Scream* (Putnam, 1970), p. 146.

para. 3 René Dubos, *Mirage*, p. 228; *Time*, December 4, 1972, p. 39.

156., para. 2 Cf. Norman Brown, *Life Against Death*.

157., para. 3 China and Cuba may seem to be exceptions to this statement, but are in fact illustrations of it. Revolutions bring about change only insofar as they represent a *diffusion* of power. The innovations are *brought into* a new power center *collectively* and from outside by a disadvantaged group. The decrees of the revolutionary leader merely certify the diffusion of power. If they fail to do this, no real social change is involved and the leaders are considered to have "betrayed the revolution."

161. Saul Bellow, *Mr. Sammler's Planet* (Fawcett, 1971), p. 53; Lao Tzu, *Tao Te Ching*, Book One, XX.

164., para. 1 Gioscia, *Time Forms;* Dubos, *Mirage*, pp. 5–14.

164–165. Elaine Cumming, "Allocation of Care to the Mentally Ill, American Style," in Mayer N. Zald (ed.), *Organizing for Community Welfare* (Quadrangle, 1967).

168–169. Cf. Joseph Chilton Pearce, *The Crack in the Cosmic Egg* (Pocket, 1973); Sheila Ostrauder and Lynn Schroeder,

Psychic Discoveries Behind the Iron Curtain (Bantam, 1971).

page 169., para. 2 I am indebted to Jacqueline Larcombe Doyle for this example.

169–170. This paragraph is based on conversations with Jacqueline Larcombe Doyle.

171., para. 1 Bateson, *Steps*, p. 69.

171–172. Ibid., pp. 356–57.

172., para. 1 Toffler, op. cit., p. 391.

173., para. 1 Michel Foucault, *Madness and Civilization* (Mentor, 1967), pp. 18–31.

para. 3 Robert A. Dentler and Kai T. Erikson, "The Functions of Deviance in Groups," *Social Problems*, VII (fall, 1959), pp. 98–107, quoted in Lewis A. Coser, "Some Functions of Deviant Behavior and Normative Flexibility," *American Journal of Sociology*, 68, 1962, p. 175.

174., para. 3 Lewis Mumford, "The Fallacy of Systems," *Saturday Review*, October 1949; Foucault, op. cit., p. 170.

177., para. 2 Erving Goffman, *Asylums* (Anchor, 1961).

179., para. 3 R. D. Laing, *The Politics of the Family* (Pantheon, 1971), pp. 77–81.

185. Idries Shah, *The Exploits of the Incomparable Mulla Nasrudin* (Dutton, 1972), p. 16.

187., para. 2 Laing, op. cit., pp. 103–16; Bateson, op. cit., pp. 201–43.

188–189. Montague, *Touching*, pp. 65 ff., 230–55, and *passim*.

190., para. 2 Benjamin Spock, *The Common Sense Book of Baby and Child Care*, Rev. Ed. (Duell, Sloan, & Pearce, 1957), pp. 3–10, 48–49.

193., para. 3 Gioscia, *Time Forms*, p. 75.

195., para. 2 A fund of wisdom about the issues involved in size, collective life, and mass power can be found in a counter-culture pamphlet called *Methods of Organization for Collectives*, which can be obtained from *Anti-mass*, Box 31352, San Francisco, California 94114.

202., para. 1 Bateson, op. cit., p. 433.

INDEX

Abegglen, 113
Academy Award presentations, 93
Accelerative rate of growth, 38
Achievement, 122–29
  specialization, power and, 122–25
  women, mobility and, 125–29
Achilles, 174
Adaptation (to bad environment), 40–41
Address, terms of, 107
Advertising, corporate, 149
Aggression, inhibiting, 23
Alcoholics, 90
Alexandra, Czarina, 80
Alienation
  bodily, 30–31, 48–49
  due to superiority, 92
Alien ideas, attacking, 71–72
Amerindians, 28, 176, 178
Androids, 19–20
Animals, maternal instinct in, 62–63
Anxiety, 15, 30, 64, 121
Arabian Nights, The (motion picture), 111

Ariès, Philippe, 133, 134
Art forms, 165–66
Asceticism, 81
Attunement, 191–94
  clarification and differentiation of, 204–7
  requirements of, 194
Auschwitz, 23
Automata, fear of, 22
Automaton behavior, 22–23
Autarchy, 17–18
  schizoid quest for, 45
Authoritarianism, 41–42, 77–82, 154
  association between patriarchy, sexual repressiveness and, 80–81
  freedom and, 55–56
  government, 144
  most important characteristic of, 81
  shift to democratic modes of organization, 76–78
  as social form, 77–78
  submission to, 54

Autistic children, 22
Automobiles, 11
Autonomy, 49, 56
  physical, 84–85, 86
  of the prophet, 74
Awareness, 186–87

Baby bottle feeding, 188
Bad environment, adaptation to,
  40–41
Bakan, David, 5, 39, 58–59, 64, 128,
  129, 130
Balance and harmony, importance
  of, 37–38
Bateson, Gregory, 5, 9, 30, 46, 52,
  90, 124, 171–72, 187, 202
Bellow, Saul, 161
Bergson, Henri, 23
Billy the Kid, 174
Black Death, 99
"Black is beautiful," 176
Black Panthers, 194
Blacks, 178, 194
  white stereotype of, 175
Bodily pleasure, 60
Boston University, 147
Brave New World (Huxley), 56
Brief sexual encounters, 119
Brodey, Warren, 5
Brontë sisters, 118
Brown, Norman, 5, 11, 18
Bugging devices, 11

Caged feeling in people, 44
Cancer, 38–39, 50
  increase in, 31
Casablanca (motion picture), 111
Castoff role in society, heroizing,
  75–76
Catholicism, 164
Chamberlain, Neville, 20
Change. See Social change
Chaplin, Charlie, 180–81
Chayefsky, Paddy, 17–18

Chicanos, 176
Childbirth process, 47, 90–91
Child rearing, 121, 124–25, 164, 190
Children
  competitive motivation in, 169
  cultural separation of, 133–34
  tax rewards for having, 142
Chronic despair, 3
Cimino, Glenda, 35
Circuit-breaking, 185–209
  attunement and, 191–94
  directions, 194–204
    deceleration, 196–97
    decentralization, 195–96
    depolarization, 197–99
    reconnection, 199–204
    what they are not, 204–7
  distinctions, 204–9
  in infancy, 188–90
Civil rights movement, 176
Classic era, 163
Class warfare, 130
Club of Rome, 38
Columbus, Christopher, 166
Communication, instinct for, 23–24
Communication growth, 200–1
Communications media, 148–49
Community
  emotionality and behavior in, 16
  network system, 15–16
  See also Simple community
Compartmentalization, 15, 83, 127,
  155, 168
  authoritarian, 81
  emotional, 128
Competitiveness, 14, 29, 92, 122–23,
  144, 169
Concentration camps, 177
Concepts, truth or falseness of, 4–5
Conceptual systems, 51–53, 62
Condon, William, 147
Conformity, impersonal channels of,
  54

Conglomerate, the, geographical
boundaries of, 4
Consciousness, 52, 82, 149
ecological, 167–68
political, 133
self-, 101, 155, 191
Containment, deviance and, 172–81
Control, technological, 9–14
choices for, 10–11
purpose of, 10
push-button, 12–13
See also Extension of man; technology and
Co-optation, 72
Counterculture, 132
Courage and perseverance, 23–26
Courageous, being, 23
Crisis, defined, 181
Cuber, John, 119
Culture
among lower animals, 61
arrangement of, 3
beliefs and practices in, 51
childhood, 133–34
heroes, 72
parents as, 106
as schizoid approach to evolution, 50–51
social errors in, 62
technological, 62–66
tyrannical proclivities of ego and, 61–62
Cummings, Elaine, 164–65

Dark Ages, 163
Death, fear of, 18
Deceleration, 196–97
Decentralization, 195–96
Democracy, 196
Depolarization, 197–99
Despair
chronic and suicidal, 3
disillusionment of, 3–4
Despotism, 79, 82

Detachment, 46, 56, 128
of art from social and cultural
roots, 165–66
drama, 57–58
individualistic fantasy, 76
talk of flexibility, 192
Deviant behavior, containment of,
172–81
at the community level, 173
Disease
cause of, 139
drug-produced, 31
environmental change, 32
Disillusionment, despair of, 3–4
Divided Self, The (Laing), 45
Divorce rate, 169
Drama and detachment, 57–58
Dresden, bombing of, 23
Dubos, René, 32, 39, 155, 164
Duckling myth, 92–99, 106
function of, 92
impact of, 94
Jonathan Livingston Seagull, 94–
97
as justification of social inequality,
93
mechanical responsivity, 94
sources of pre-eminence in, 97–
99
Western medicine and, 97–98, 99,
100

Early American films, 111
Ecological consciousness, 167–68
Eddison, E. R., 112
Ego, the, 64, 89, 112, 119, 122, 148,
203
culture and, 61–62
evolution of, 61
Gestalt therapy on, 74
Encounter groups, 15
Energy and power, 153–58
Environmental theater, 57
Eugenics, 98

Exploitation
consequences of, 42
legitimate, 125
Extensions of man, technology and,
9–34
arrogant virtues, 26–27
autarchy, 17–18
automaton behavior, 22–23
boosters of, 33
"cannot be stopped" argument, 34
community network system, 15–16
control, 9–14
courage and perseverance, 23–26
genetic code, 19–21
health (Western medicine), 29–
33
impact on, 14–15
individuality, 18
interpersonal styles, 15, 17
mañana mentality, 27
medical thinking (as a machine),
22–23
personal choice, 16–17
rationalism, 33–34
variety among cultures, 27–29

Fahrenheit 451 (Bradbury), 56
Failure, 61–62
Fairy tales, 76, 92
"Fall" (Adam and Eve myth),
47–48
Familiar stranger, theme of, 111–12
Feedback, 22, 40, 46, 49, 142, 163,
187, 205, 211
ignoring, 23
linearity, 45
negative, 45, 52, 61, 62
Finger-tip control, 12–13
Flouridation, 143
Foster, F., 37
Foucault, Michel, 173, 174
Frankenstein (Shelley), 19
Frantic buying activity, 16
Free choice, 172

Freedom, 46, 48–50, 83
authoritarianism and, 55–56
as inherently illusory, 58
from instinct, 49–50
meaning of, 58
of the mind, 59
schizoid type of, 23
search for, 64
self-mystification of, 48–49
and will, 58–62
Freud, Sigmund, 22, 39, 61, 80,
111, 124, 149
Fromm, Eric, 55
Future, the, history and, 151–53

Garden of Eden myth, 46–48
Gatling, R. J., 9
Genovese, Kitty, 59
Gestalt therapy, 56, 74
Gioscia, Victor, 164, 193
Goffman, Erving, 177
Gotterdammerung fantasies, 65
Greek drama, 57
Group communication, 69–70
Guerrilla theater, 204
Guilt, 121–22
Gun control, 143–44

Hannibal, 185
Harmony, internal, 206–7
Harroff, Peggy, 119
Harvard Bureau of Study Counsel,
17
Hays, H. R., 87
Heaven, idea of, 109
Heimlich sensations, 22
Hermits, 56, 174
Hippocrates, 32
Hiroshima, bombing of, 23
Hitler, Adolf, 76
Household prophets, specialization
and, 83–86
Housewives' time, attitudes about,
179–80

Human, meaning of, 4
Human evolution, tempo of, 38–39

Ideology, 76, 144–45
  of free expression, 206
  of individualism, 55
Idries Shah, 69
Incest taboo, 108
Individualism, 44, 53, 55, 80, 144
  arrogance of, 162
  beginning of, 18
  manufacture of mutations, 75
  as a shell game, 82
  social mobility of, 130–31
Industrialism, 11
  mechanical *weltanschauung*, 19
Infantile omnipotence, fantasy of, 12
Influence, receptivity to, 53–54
Instinct, freedom from, 49–50
Intellectuals, skills taught to, 43–44
I. Q. tests, 120
Interpersonal sensitivity, development of, 188
Interpersonal style, marital selection,
  17
Isolated nuclear family, social eversion, 169. *See also* Nuclear
  family, social climbing and

Jack and the Beanstalk, 114
Janov, Arthur, 155
Jesus Christ, 174
Jonathan Livingston Seagull, 94–97

Karate classes for women, 131
Kingdoms, social forms of, 79–81
Kinship, 78–79
Kissinger, Henry, 155
Kristofferson, K., 37

La Barre, Weston, 22, 49–50, 51, 72
Labor, division of, 83–86, 145
  re-evaluation of, 131
  by sex, 198

value of, 84
Laing, Ronald, 45, 46, 59, 62, 63–
  64, 65, 179, 187
Language, 3–4, 85, 168
Lao Tzu, 69, 105, 137, 161
Laura (motion picture), 111
Lewis, C. S., 48, 112, 137
Liberation movements, demands of,
  166
Libido, 89
Limits to Growth, The (Club of
  Rome), 38
Linearity and principle, 43–45
  feedback, 45
  sense of unimpeded motion in, 44
Living by the clock, 60–61
Locke, John, 169
Lorenz, Konrad, 55
Love, 49, 98, 99, 116
  child's loss of, 121
  romantic, 111
Lowen, Alexander, 1, 2, 37, 60, 61,
  62, 115, 154

McClelland, David, 113, 114, 125
Machines, invention of, 22
Machismo ethics, 88
McLuhan, Marshall, 44
Madmen, attitude toward, 173
Man, meaning of, 4
Mañana mentality, 27
Marital selection, 17
Mass production, 63
Maternal behavior, 91
Matriarchy, 87
Mead, Margaret, 188
Mechanical responsivity, 53–57
  duckling myth, 94
Medicine, Western society, 29–33,
  108, 202
  advancement of, 32
  duckling myth and, 97–98, 99,
  100
  as a machine, 22–23

power factor in, 32–33
treatment of infants, 91
Mental hospitals, 57
Middle of the Night (motion picture), 17–18
Millman, Marcia, 57
Mind-body dualism, 59
Modernism, beginning of, 79
Money, being sensible about, 53
Monster films, theme of, 14
Montague, Ashley, 127, 188
Morality, objectification of, 54
Morimoto, Kiyo, 16–17
Mumford, Lewis, 174
Mutation pattern, 75–76, 92, 171

Nabokov, 112
Napoleon I, 28
Narcissism, 18, 25, 79, 80, 95, 156, 161, 167, 169, 199, 200, 212
and longing for immortality, 47
male commitment to, 89
of the prophet, 73–74
Nasrudin, Mulla, 185
Natural selection, 99–100
Nazi party, 177
Negative power, 123–24, 154–55
Neo-Classic era, 163
Neo-Romantic era, 163
Network system, community, 15–16
Newton, Isaac, 169
Nicholas II, Czar, 80
1984 (Orwell), 56
Nuclear family, social climbing and, 105–9
achievement, 122–29
specialization and power, 122–25
women and mobility, 125–29
behavior pattern, 107–8
castes and classes, 106
oedipal strivings, 109–13
parent prerogatives, 108
priorities of pleasure, 115–21

routes to status change, 130–32
sexual intercourse, 108
stratification by age, 108–9
successful executive (McClelland pattern), 113–14
tension within, 109
youth as subordinate class, 132–34
Nursing homes, 57
Nurturance, diffusion of, 116–17

Objectivity, 52
simple community, 41–42
Objects, utilitarian orientation to, 63
Oedipal strivings, 110–11, 112
careerism, 132
decline of, 132
Oedipus myth, 109–10
Oil depletion allowances, 141
Oppression, adaptation to, 175
Order, importance of, 146–47
Overpopulation, 169

Paranoid process, 10, 11, 49, 51, 59, 143
Part tasks, competence at, 83
Pasteur, Louis, 143
Patriarchal revolution, 86–92
competitiveness, 92
duckling myth and, 92–99
as recent phenomenon, 87
specialization, 87–88, 89, 90
Patriarchy, 4, 87
Peloponnesian War, 48
Perls, Fritz, 56
Personal choice, notion of, 16, 17
Personal involvement, 83
Peter Ibbetson, 112
Pharmacology, 31
Pills, side effects of, 31
Plato, 37
Platonism, 62
Pleasure
behavior based on, 60

in non-stress situations, 115–16
obtaining, 13
priorities, social climbing and, 115–21
sexual, 111
Poison, defined, 37
Police organizations, rank-and-file, 196
Political science, 202–3
Pollution, 141, 168
  industrial, 11
  psychic, 11, 50
  technological, 10, 11
Population, growth of, 39
Portrait of Jenny, A, 112
Positive power, uses of, 123
Possessions, value attached to, 63
Power
  achievement and specialization, 122–25
  to allay anxiety, 51
  balance of, 123
  center of, rewards and, 42
  diffusion of, 195–96
  energy, social change and, 153–58
  negative, 123–24, 154–55
  positive, 123
  presidential, 153–54
Pride, 115
Primal horde, myth of, 80
Prisons, 57
Progress, idea of, 3
Prophet dynamic, 69–101, 106, 161
  autonomy, 74
  division of labor, 83–86
  duckling myth and, 92–99
  individualistic delusion of, 73
  narcissism, 73–74
  parent system and, 71, 73
  patriarchal revolution, 86–92
  personality of, 72
  physical autonomy of, 84, 86
Propaganda, "truth squad" approach to, 72

Protestant ethic, 142, 164, 175, 178, 199
Protestantism, 164
Psychedelic movement, 168
Psychic pollution, 11, 50
Psychic research, 168
Psychopathology, 22
Psychotics, 72
Punishment (for social errors), 62
Push-button control, 12–13

Racism, 176
Radical movements, 43
Rationalism, 33–34, 90, 150–51
  compartmentalized, 155
  schizoid process, 178
Reality, 12, 22, 50, 117, 168–69
  despair and, 2–3
  dictating, 61
  guilt, social climbing and, 121–22
  proving one's, 65
Reappearance theme, 111
Reciprocal gift giving, 12–13
Recycling, requirements of, 11
Referral agencies, 57
Reformation, 81
Reich, Wilhelm, 98
Reincarnation, 109
Rembrandt, 48
Renaissance, 133, 163
Reversionism, 152
Riesman, David, 55, 118
Romanticism, 117, 118, 163
Romantic love, 111, 117
Rome (ancient), 178
Roth, Philip, 95
Rudolph the Red-Nosed Reindeer, 92, 93, 95
Rules of society, feast days putting aside, 170–71

Schismogenesis, 171

Schizoid process, 22, 23, 31, 40,
    45–53, 89, 150, 187, 203
  Adam and Eve myth, 46–48
  conceptual systems, 51–53
  emergence of culture, 50–51
  freedom, 48–50
  living by the clock, 60–61
  susceptibility to response, 59
  use of will power, 60
Science fiction, 11–12, 19–20, 112
  film themes, 14
Scientific medicine. See Medicine
    Western society
Security data banks, 11
Self-consciousness, 101, 155, 191
Selye, 39
Sex roles, women's movement attack
    on, 198
Sexual conquests, 119
Sexual mores, changes in, 89–90
Sexual pleasure, 111
Shaw, Gary, 95
Simmonds, 172
Simple community, 200
  child's needs, 116
  collective behavior of, 77
  family crisis, 57
  kinship categories, 78–79
  leaders of, 77
  mass democracy and, 77, 78
  objectivity in, 41–42
  primeval bliss in, 27–28
  social control, 55
Social change, 3, 137–58
  American approach to, 138
  media-defined, 106
  misconceptions, 138–58
    cognitive process, 149–51
    futility of positive programs,
      140–42
    linear, 151–53
    power and energy, 153–58
    stress and, 138–40
    when right is right, 142–49

  pendulum effect, 167
  real, 105, 167
  ways of, 161–81
    deviance and containment,
      172–81
    and forms of, 163–67
    role of cultural attic, 170–72
    social eversion, 167–70
Social climbing, 71, 105–34
  achievement, specialization, and
    power, 122–25
  nuclear family, 105–9
    behavior pattern, 107–8
    castes and classes, 106
    parent prerogatives, 108
    sexual intercourse, 108
    stratification by age, 108–9
    tension within, 109
    youth as subordinate class, 132–
      34
  oedipal strivings, 109–13
  priorities of pleasure, 115–21
  reality and guilt, 121–22
  routes to status change, 130–32
  successful (McClelland pattern),
    113–14
  women, mobility, and achieve-
    ment, 125–29
Social division, concept of, 107
Social errors, 62
Social eversion, 129, 152–53
  examples of, 167–70
Social justice, search for, 41
Social metastasis, 37–66
  adaptation to bad environment, 40
  authoritarianism, 41–42
  cancer metaphor describing, 39–
    40
  drama and detachment, 57–58
  exploitation and brutality, 41–43
  freedom and will, 58–62
  linearity and principle, 43–45
  mechanical responsibility, 53–57
  population, 39

power factor, 42
schizoid process, 45–53, 59
social justice and, 41
technological culture, 62–66
Sophocles, 105
Soulmates, idea of, 111
South Vietnam, 29
Space exploration, 11–12, 167
Spatial closeness, 169
Speck, Ross, 16
Spock, Dr. Benjamin, 190
Spontaneity, 205–6
Status change, routes to, 130–32
Status quo, the, 56, 148, 152
Stephens, William, 77–78, 80
Stereotypic public personality, 72
Stress, change and, 138–40
Successful executives (McClelland pattern), 113–14
Suicidal despair, 3
Surrender signals, human beings 22–23
Swindlers, trust and, 100–1

Taylor, G. Rattray, 80
Technological culture, 62–66
  developments in, 65
  false-self system in, 64
  relationships within, 80
Technological development, war and, 14
Technological growth, competition and, 14
Technology, extensions of man and, 9–34
  arrogant virtues, 26–27
  autarchy, 17–18
  automaton behavior, 22–23
  boosters of, 33
  "cannot be stopped" argument, 34
  control, 9–14
  courage and perseverance, 23–26
  genetic code, 19–21

health (Western medicine), 29–33
impact on, 14–15
individuality, 18
interpersonal styles, 15, 17
mañana mentality, 27
medical thinking (as a machine), 22–23
network system, 14–15
personal choice, 16–17
rationalism, 33–34
variety among cultures, 27–29
Telepathy, 168
Thompson, William, 5
Time machine fantasy, 112
Toffler, Alvin, 20, 21, 28, 34, 40, 76, 77, 82, 83, 113, 129, 138–39, 150, 152–53, 172
Tolerance, implications of, 148
Transference, Freudian idea of, 117
Trust, swindlers and, 100–1

Ugly duckling. *See* Duckling myth
Unheimlich sensations, 22
Unilateral disarmament, 143
U. S. Mail, 141
Unloved person, recognizing, 98–99

Venceremos Brigade (Cimino), 35
Vietnam War, 23, 28, 95, 189

Wars, 14, 48, 113
  of small tribes, 77
Washington political community, 157
We (Zamiatin), 244
Weber, Max, 81
Whyte, Jr., William H., 55
Wiener, Norbert, 20
Women
  consciousness raising, 177
  containment of, 177–78
  in Eastern cultures, 129

social mobility and achievement, 125–29

Women's movement, depolarization by, 198–99

World War I, 48

World War II, 91

Youth, elevation of, 201–2

O49

MEN
TALK

DR. ALVIN BARAFF

//

MEN TALK

HOW MEN REALLY FEEL
ABOUT WOMEN, SEX, RELATIONSHIPS
AND THEMSELVES

A DUTTON BOOK

DUTTON

Published by the Penguin Group
Penguin Books USA Inc., 375 Hudson Street,
New York, New York 10014, U.S.A.
Penguin Books Ltd, 27 Wrights Lane,
London W8 5TZ, England
Penguin Books Australia Ltd, Ringwood,
Victoria, Australia
Penguin Books Canada Ltd, 10 Alcorn Avenue,
Toronto, Ontario, Canada M4V 3B2
Penguin Books (N.Z.) Ltd, 182-190 Wairau Road,
Auckland 10, New Zealand

Penguin Books Ltd, Registered Offices:
Harmondsworth, Middlesex, England

First published by Dutton, an imprint of New American Library,
a division of Penguin Books USA Inc.
Distributed in Canada by McClelland & Stewart Inc.

First Printing, August, 1991
10 9 8 7 6 5 4 3 2 1

REGISTERED TRADEMARK—MARCA REGISTRADA

LIBRARY OF CONGRESS CATALOGING IN PUBLICATION DATA:

Baraff, Alvin
    Men talk : how men really feel about women, sex, relationships, and themselves / Alvin
Baraff.
      p. cm.
    ISBN 0-525-93328-X
    1. Men—Psychology—Case studies.   2. Group psychotherapy—Case studies.   1. Title.
BF692.5.B37 1991
155.6′ 32—dc20   90-29016
                                                                                   CIP

Printed in the United States of America
Set in Caslon 540

Designed by Steven N. Stathakis

To
the real Mitch, Paul, Gary,
Ed, Burt, and Sean

and the clients of
MenCenter™
they represent

I know your courage.

The information and cases are factual.
All names, places, and other
identifying material have
been changed to protect
the privacy of the
participants.

//

CONTENTS

ACKNOWLEDGMENTS   XI

INTRODUCTION: UNDERSTANDING MEN   1

MEET THE GROUP   9

SESSION 1
MEN'S FEAR OF THERAPY   13
INTERPRETATION   23

SESSION 2
"GO TO THERAPY, OR GO TO HELL!"   29
INTERPRETATION   37

SESSION 3
AVOIDING FEELINGS   41
INTERPRETATION   49

Session 4
SEX: LEARNING THE WOMAN'S SIDE   52
INTERPRETATION   61

Session 5
WHEN MEN CRY   64
INTERPRETATION   70

Session 6
MARRIAGE, COMMITMENT, AND
REMARRIAGE   73
INTERPRETATION   80

Session 7
RESISTING CHANGE   83
INTERPRETATION   90

Session 8
THE MAN'S "BIOLOGICAL CLOCK"   93
INTERPRETATION   98

Session 9
VIOLENCE: A MAN'S ASHAME   101
INTERPRETATION   107

Session 10
IMPOTENCE: A MAN 'S HUMILIATION   110
INTERPRETATION   117

Session 11
YEARNING FOR MISSED FATHERS   121
INTERPRETATION   128

Session 12
COURAGE AND CONFRONTATION   131
INTERPRETATION   138

Session 13
THE VALUE OF ANXIETY   143
INTERPRETATION   150

Session 14
ANGER, AGGRESSION, AND DEPRESSION   152
INTERPRETATION   158

Session 15
THE POWER OF COMBINING THOUGHTS AND
FEELINGS   161
INTERPRETATION   168

Session 16
DREAMS: THE INSIDE STORY   171
INTERPRETATION   178

Session 17
MEN WANT CHILDREN   180
INTERPRETATION   188

Session 18
THE THERAPIST AS FATHER   190
INTERPRETATION   198

Session 19
SECRETS, LIES, AND FAMILY PRESSURE   201
INTERPRETATION   208

Session 20
INDECISION AND PERFECTIONISM   211
INTERPRETATION   217

SESSION 21
LONELINESS IN A RELATIONSHIP   220
INTERPRETATION   226

SESSION 22
"WHAT A RELIEF TO BE UNDERSTOOD!"   230
INTERPRETATION   239

SESSION 23
"SHADOW" MOTHERS AND THEIR SONS   242
INTERPRETATION   249

SESSION 24
FROM FEAR TO CELEBRATION   251
INTERPRETATION   261

EPILOGUE
MEN AFTER THERAPY   265

ACKNOWLEDGMENTS

More than two years have passed since I began work on *Men Talk*, and many good people have touched me in caring and encouraging ways.

A special acknowledgment goes to *Kevin Hendzel*, translator and writer, who assisted me in completing this final version of *Men Talk*. Kevin had a full appreciation of the importance of my work and knew I was impatient to get this information out to the public; having known me for six years, he is aware of my "mission" at MenCenter. I am convinced that his valuable assistance in writing and editing *Men Talk* has enhanced the quality of this book. Kevin is an extremely responsible and sensitive writer: loyal, willing and capable of producing at a level that I like. Thank you, Mr. Hendzel.

My colleagues at MenCenter, *Richard Mallory Starr*, *Dana L. Moore*, and *Mark Gorkin*, have been very gracious

about the necessary delay in our joint projects during the writing of this book. My assistant, *Jayne Keedy*, helped keep MenCenter running, and *Robert F. Williams* extended his faith by including me in his prayers.

A hearty thanks to all of you who have lent an ear, enjoyed an anecdote, and been enthusiastic and excited about the book. It helped me and I appreciate you, including the gang at *Julio's*. I am grateful to my friends: *Joani Powell*, for her love and unique female perspective; *John Truran*, who even enjoyed the first draft; *Lenore Walker*, feminist psychologist, for sharing her writing and media anecdotes; *Mark Crawford*, for his practical assistance and loyalty; and *Doug Abbey*, who saw the original journal as I was writing it and said, " This is it, this is your book!"

Echoing those words were *Carol Randolph*, and *Martha Barnett*, who assisted me in preparing the book proposal. Joining supporters were *Rich Lippman*, author of *Eating In*, for providing technical assistance in editing; and *Audrey Chapman*, who led me to my New York agent.

A special thank-you to *Roslyn Targ*, my literary agent, whose energy connected positively with mine from the beginning. Roz is direct, honest, experienced, and a true original. Her enthusiasm and belief in me and *Men Talk* have never wavered.

My warm thanks to *Arnold Dolin*, Vice-President and Associate Publisher of NAL/Dutton, who is also my editor, for his foresight and courage in recognizing the importance and value of psychotherapy and men's issues. Arnold allowed me to develop my own writing style while constantly pushing me to maintain the highest quality possible.

I was supported every step of the way by special members of the MenCenter Board of Advisors: longtime friend *Jerry Olesh*, who has always believed in me and I hope always will; friend *Richard Morey*, whose advice is always practical and useful; and former colleague *Bonnie R. Strickland*, President-

Emeritus, American Psychological Association, who inspired me to make a visible effort on men's issues.

Supporting family members who maintained curiosity throughout this project are: my daughter, *Ramie Baraff Janis*, who does talk to me and appreciates my determination, along with my son-in-law, *Bruce Janis;* my son, *Todd*, who also talks to me openly about personal issues; my mother, *Betty*, who was ". . . glad that darn book is finished" (she loves me anyway); my father, *Abraham*, who, unfortunately, died before completion of this book, though he was very much alive in my memory as I wrote about fathers and death; and my brother, *Jay*, sister-in-law, *Sandy*, niece, *Laura*, and nephew, *Aaron*, all of whom now know why I was so devoted to writing *Men Talk*.

And finally, thanks to *God*, because I do believe he listens when I talk.

MEN
TALK

INTRODUCTION:

//

UNDERSTANDING MEN

No one understands men. Women don't understand men and men don't understand themselves. Surprisingly few psychologists even understand men, since most men do not seek psychotherapy. In the United States therapy continues to be a woman's domain, with 70 percent of a typical psychologist's practice devoted to women. The gap is even wider when we consider the fact that half the men in that remaining 30 percent are there with their wives or girlfriends. In a typical adult practice, only 15 percent are men who are there for themselves.

Why such a lopsided picture? In our society a man's conditioning strongly discourages him from seeking out therapy. This learning process begins at a very early age and is actually an important part of a man's social and emotional development. Boys and girls are exposed to entirely different

sets of teachings and expectations. Girls are taught to honor and understand their emotions. Conversely, boys are encouraged, even forced, to hold in and suppress their emotions. There is hardly a man in America today who didn't grow up hearing such admonitions as "Big boys don't cry!" or "Be a man!" These commands form the young boy's reality. As he matures into adolescence, he learns that when he talks too much about his feelings, he is shunned by the other boys in the group. This is in stark contrast to the reality of young girls, who are encouraged to whisper, gossip, complain, and share secrets. Throughout their young lives, girls place the highest premium on sharing, while boys are expected to place the highest value on competition. Not surprisingly, as boys mature into men they tend to express their feelings through competitive arenas, progressing from "cowboys and Indians" in the early years, through war games and sports in adolescence, and on to business and politics in adulthood.

The result is that a man in our society grows up feeling innately, internally alone. He has learned independence and self-reliance and considers them to reign supreme among his values. He wants to be in control. He cannot imagine ever needing to go for help and rarely considers it an option.

Puberty provides an excellent example of the difference between the sharing, supportive world of the young girl and the isolated, competitive world of the young boy. A mother typically expends a great deal of time and effort instructing and educating her young daughter about the changes occurring in her body. Moreover, when girls discuss their changing bodies among themselves, the atmosphere is one of support, nurturance, and sharing. As every man knows, this is hardly the atmosphere in the locker room. Boys' talk about the sex organs or their development is all wisecracks or exaggerated bragging. In other words, competition. As a result, girls know more about their bodies and what to expect, while boys remain mostly in the dark about their bodies' development. Un-

fortunately, father-son, or even mother-son, conversations about sexual development remain the exception rather than the norm today.

What a shame! The father-son talk provides an important opportunity for the two to bond. Yet, it's often avoided because both father and son feel so awkward. The father can be reassured that there is no "right way" to discuss sex. But initiating "the talk" is better than no talk at all. Boys also lack a full-time male role model. While girls have a clearer role model in their early years since the mother, *their* role model, is more available and present, the boy's role model, the working father, is still mostly absent. At all levels of society, the mother remains the main influence on the children, both boys and girls, and contributes the bulk of their learning and behavior. The part-time male role model has less of an impact on the young girl, but the boy loses out: He must look to his father for guidance. The young boy learns from this process that being absent is okay. The important element for a father is to be *successful*, to be a good *provider*. This nicely complements the boy's rigorous behavioral training in competition among his peers.

These early years of conditioning produce a man who, when faced with emotional trouble, thinks he should know what to do. If he is strong he shouldn't *need* to ask for help. Though his conclusion is flawed, it's reinforced by society: A young girl in a schoolyard tussle is rescued and protected by either parent; a young boy in the same position is encouraged to "fight it out like a man." In adulthood it is not surprising that women find it acceptable, even sensible, to seek therapy when threatened with an emotional crisis. Yet men generally avoid therapy until they've completely run out of all other options. This means that the typical man begins therapy at a much more advanced stage of emotional or professional crisis. It is in most respects his last resort.

Yet today I have a successful full-time practice that con-

sists of a clientele that is 80 percent male. Clearly the need exists. In the early 1980s, when I had a "typical" adult practice, I began to pay attention to the neglected concerns and issues of men in therapy. Actually, it was the women in my practice who called my attention to the needs of men. I was hearing a recurring complaint from the women I was seeing who were completing a successful therapy: "Where are all the men?" There were no suitable men out there. Simply put, the men had not kept up with them. The women had been changing for more than twenty years while the men only looked on.

So I decided to look around and see what was available in the way of information and support for men in the popular media and the press. I was surprised to find that magazines, newspapers, books, and television were flooded with information and support for women on how to dress, have better sex, advance in business, balance a home and career, and countless other topics. This bounty of information was giving these women an adult version of what had been provided to them as little girls: support, guidance, and the sharing of information. Even more surprising was the virtual absence of anything approximating this level of information for men. Most men's magazines were valuable and thorough in providing information for physical endeavors: sports, cars, and outdoor life. There was a dearth of information for men in the popular media on relationships, coping, personal growth, families, stress, sex, or even careers. Until recently there have been a few exceptions to this, and I've come to appreciate such magazines as *Esquire, Men's Health,* and *Men's Fitness* for providing information on personal growth for men and such authors as Herb Goldberg and Robert Bly for pioneering efforts in encouraging men to understand themselves. But these are isolated islands in a sea of emptiness.

When I began this new direction in my practice, there were only a few other therapists who were willing to work

toward establishing a therapy center for men. Good therapists had fairly full schedules with no need to make any drastic change. But again, female and feminist therapists, specializing in therapy with women, were increasing steadily. I felt there was a crying need to address these issues, and I believe *Men Talk* represents an important step in understanding and satisfying this need.

My investigation into men's issues in the early 1980s coincided with a turning point in my career. I had established a successful practice in Georgetown after many years of effort. During the early years of my practice in Washington I developed a specialty in treating alcoholics and drug addicts, in addition to the more typical problems of adults. This was a challenging area for me, and over this period I functioned in many capacities: therapist, consultant, supervisor, and trainer of other therapists. I was also able to draw on my experience as a faculty member years earlier at Emory University, my first professional appointment after receiving my Ph.D. I gained experience in private practice during a three-year tenure in Atlanta. The return to my native Washington was triggered by a typically painful divorce that presented the opportunity and challenge to start anew. The Georgetown practice was enormously satisfying, yet it left me wondering if I was contributing enough to society by helping only a very limited number of people. Even though I was giving free public lectures, I wanted to play a larger role and contribute to this area of men's issues. A great deal of soul-searching and conversations with good friends and respected colleagues followed.

Although there was little concrete support or enthusiasm, I decided to take a risk that could have easily ended in disaster. I decided to establish a center devoted primarily to men's issues and male-female relationships. From a strictly business viewpoint such a move could have been tantamount to professional suicide (a term actually used by one colleague) given

the largely female clientele of virtually all psychologists' practices. But I firmly believed that there were certain elements of working with men that made this move necessary. Above all, I needed to make therapy more accessible to men if I were to attract the kind of men I wanted to reach: resistant, ambitious, high-achieving, and emotionally blocked men facing relationship crises, emotional frustrations, and feelings of emptiness, and especially those hopeless men experiencing the humiliation of impotence. I decided to relocate my practice from Georgetown to the heart of the Washington business district to eliminate the typical excuses men use to avoid talking to a therapist. I took every measure and went to every length to accommodate these men: accessibility by subway, convenient location, flexible hours, sliding fee scales, and both male and female therapists. Now the decision to actually show up would become their largest hurdle. I furnished the suite as a comfortable office environment that has more in common with a law firm than a doctor's office: It became an inviting, nonclinical setting. I even went so far as to change my own style of dress from a more casual look to the more formal suit and tie, as a way of blending in, knowing it would make it easier for men to connect and relate to someone more familiar. I intended to make every conceivable effort to connect to and accommodate these men. I named, and trademarked, my new practice "MenCenter."

The most surprising outcome of all these efforts wasn't that the practice flourished (especially after the media took a strong interest) but rather that I started hearing, for the first time in twenty years of clinical practice, stories proving that all the myths one hears about men are absolutely true: Men *do* feel they are *not* supposed to cry, they're not supposed to ask for help, they are supposed to *know* what to do, period. Perhaps the most gratifying result was how quickly a man was willing to change once he made the commitment to therapy. Moreover, in the course of my consultations with colleagues,

it soon became evident that I was hearing about the lives of men who, under any other circumstances, would never have begun therapy at all. I remember being struck by the notion that it just didn't seem fair that this information was not getting out, and that I was the only one destined to hear it. I felt this material needed to be shared, discussed, and explored with other men—and *women*. This was the environment that gave rise to the idea that culminated in *Men Talk*.

I gave much consideration to my selection of the particular men in the group whom you are about to meet. All of them began therapy with me on an individual basis and knew for some time that group therapy would be introduced into their treatment plan. I also maintained treatment with the men in individual sessions while they were in group therapy; they knew they were not being deprived of private time with me. Within the group setting, each man knew and trusted me. I was his special ally. I chose six men for this group who were united by common issues, especially problems in their relationships with women. Yet they also had many of the other issues I commonly encounter in my work with men: anxiety, stress, expressing anger, making decisions, and impotence. Regardless of the differences in education and occupation, all these men have difficulty in expressing feelings (even anger), in communicating, and in creating intimate relationships. My work with men has taught me the value they place on achieving concrete goals in a set period of time, so I chose a six-month commitment for the group as an initial, and extendable, period.

The group-therapy process is unique and affords several advantages that cannot be provided in individual treatment. It allows the therapist to observe how a man interacts with others. It allows the man to connect and open up to other people who share similar problems and concerns. It also provides a rare opportunity for him to learn his effect on others. He will hear direct, honest reactions to his behavior from other group

members: anger, boredom, and lack of interest. He will have the benefit of their emotional responses, something that is often denied him in the "real world," where people's first choice is to walk away or avoid saying anything at all. Each of the men who takes the risk of opening up in this group will carry away with him some distinct advantages in life.

The sessions detailed in the following pages and the men's lives outlined in the dialogue are all real. The biographies and life stories have been extensively modified and altered to protect identities. The relevant material and interpretations, however, have been retained in their entirety. Each session as it reads here is the heart of an actual session, but it is not intended as a literal transcript. Such a transcript would fill many volumes and prove exceedingly boring. The discussion following each session is designed to provide an encapsulated "interpretation" of the more significant events that occurred during the session, and to help the reader understand the different levels of communication going on in the world. I believe the material presented in this book will prove to be enlightening, informative, entertaining, and above all, an inspiration for women and men to understand and listen when men talk.

A.S.B.

MEET THE GROUP

//

MITCH, 34, is the spitting image of Kris Kristofferson as a leather-clad biker. Mitch's imposing presence, 6'4" frame, shaggy red hair, and unkempt beard contradict his shy, sensitive demeanor and his profession as an aerodynamics engineer. He's been divorced for three years and is now in love with **Lynda**, a legal secretary with whom he has trouble communicating. Mitch also has difficulty expressing anger and exhibits anxiety over just about everything.

PAUL, 41, is insensitive and abrasive. He's 6'1" with thinning hair, clear plastic glasses, and a nasal whine. A Washington patent attorney in the traditional navy-blue pinstripe suit, white Oxford shirt, and striped tie, he's not centerfold material for *American Lawyer*—stomach paunch, bad posture, worn-out suits, and scuffed brown leather briefcase. He looks like an unkempt Willard Scott. Separated from **Sarah**, his

wife and homemaker of twenty years, Paul is indecisive about getting a divorce. He exists in a small studio apartment—alone for the first time—which he believes accounts for his disheveled appearance. He is the only member of the group with children—**Betty**, 18, who's in college, and **Abe**, 17, who's living with Sarah.

BURT, 45, is a quiet, reserved army lobbyist and colonel at the Pentagon. Solid and muscular, Burt stands 5′10″ tall and is always neatly groomed, with his clothes pressed and his shoes shined. His penetrating Paul Newman eyes add depth to everything he says. Burt is divorced and lives alone in the same house he lived in with his ex-wife. He currently dates **JoAnn**, a graduate student. Burt was able to solve his original problem with impotence in individual therapy and is using group therapy to help him improve his relationship with JoAnn.

SEAN, 23, looks remarkably like Woody Allen, but lacks the sense of humor. He looks fragile and boyish with a wide-eyed innocence. Sean recently moved east from Arizona to attend medical school at George Washington University. He's a slim 5′9″, with big brown eyes, wire-rimmed glasses, and fine blond hair. Sean always wears faded jeans, sports shirts, and soiled running shoes. He rides his ten-speed bike to group no matter how cold it gets. He's single and lives in a group house in Arlington. Sean is devastated from his broken romance with **Sandi**, a medical student from New York City, who left him.

ED, 36, is Mr. Ivy League. He is tweedy, preppy, and pudgy behind horn-rimmed glasses, a cold, quiet intellectual. Ed is a typical bureaucrat working as a research epidemiologist for the federal government. He is single and has been living for a year with **Ellen**, a teacher. They both grew up in the same northern California suburb but did not know each other. Ed is an adult child of alcoholic parents, trying to solve problems with communication, depression, and low self-

esteem. His relationship with Ellen is in turmoil because he can't bring himself to propose marriage.

GARY, 33, is the jokester of the group, cynical and sarcastic, streetwise and insightful. He sees the world through a pair of bad-boy Mickey Rourke eyes. Gary is the only man in the group without a college education, which makes him feel inferior to the others. He is a Washington native and lives alone in a small town house on Capitol Hill, where he's also set up an office for work as an insurance estimator. He's wiry, blond, and neatly groomed, the only son of an abusive and alcoholic father—and a recovering alcoholic himself. Gary is single and feels addicted to sex, which makes his relationship with **Leigh**, a 29-year-old virgin, a painful dilemma for him. Later, Gary starts seeing **Marta**, a foreign housekeeper, for an intensely sexual relationship.

MEN'S FEAR OF THERAPY

"I don't really want to be here," Mitch mumbles as he stares blankly at the floor, avoiding eye contact of any kind.

An awkward silence falls over the room. The six strangers in my new group therapy session look unsettled. One focuses out the window. Another stares at his shoes. The rest glance furtively around at this room full of unfamiliar faces not sure of what they've gotten themselves into.

"Why?" asks Burt, the eldest member of the group, breaking the silence.

Mitch looks up at me. "I tried to cancel this afternoon. My dad's in town, and I have to get together with him. He never gives me advance notice—just shows up and expects me to drop *everything* for him. Generally I *do* drop everything when my father comes to town," Mitch admits glumly. " That's the way it's always been."

As I listen to Mitch I feel pleased and encouraged that he has actually found his way here after calling two hours earlier to cancel. The call was full of anxiety about group therapy and meeting his father afterward. I strongly encouraged him to come, and he agreed, although he threatened to be late. He wasn't. In fact, he was the first to arrive, bursting suddenly into the room before the session even began.

Mitch has a strong, imposing presence. He's an enormous man, with wild shaggy red hair and broad shoulders encased in a shiny leather jacket. Today, as usual, he thudded across the room in motorcycle boots, carrying a big black helmet tucked under his arm. Yet despite his belligerent air I know from my work with Mitch he is at heart very gentle. He's the shyest of my patients. This is no heavy-leather biker but an aerodynamics engineer who spent the better part of his youth alone in his room, building model airplanes. These apparent contradictions come as little surprise to me now, after decades of working with men.

In fact, all these men, whom I see individually, have their contradictions, too.

If there's such a thing as the "male mystique," this is it: the contradiction between a man's outer appearance and his inner feelings.

There's Paul sitting next to me in a deep black leather chair identical to mine. Paul is an older, louder, narcissistic patient who apparently has no awareness of his own personal abrasiveness. He has recently separated from his wife of twenty years, his first and only love, and is having a terribly difficult time living alone for the first time in his life. He doesn't take much care of his appearance; after all, for twenty years he was dressed and tended to by his wife, and now he's making do alone. He will profit from group therapy.

Opposite Paul, in the center of the light gray sectional, sits Burt, my oldest and perhaps wisest patient. He has a solid, saturnine countenance, and his body is remarkably fit

for his forty-five years. He swims long distances every day, partly in an effort to offset the great anxiety and depression that plague him. Burt is a military officer who spends much of his time on Capitol Hill, and he has devoted much of his life to army legal issues. He originally came to me complaining of impotence and stayed for help in establishing assertiveness and self-esteem. Recently, his attention has been focused primarily on his relationship problems with his girlfriend JoAnn.

Almost hiding in Burt's shadow, meanwhile, is Sean, the youngest and most fragile member of our group, a young-looking Woody Allen, delicate, boyish, and perpetually, almost owlishly, wide-eyed. He seems lost and vaguely alarmed. Sean is from Phoenix and his calm Southwestern origins leave him at something of a loss here in the highly focused and competitive world of the East Coast. I happen to think Sean the most privileged man in our group, because as the youngest he'll benefit from the wisdom and experience of the other men, be able to learn from their experiences, and perhaps avoid many of their problems—but he wonders if he really belongs in the room.

Ed, a preppy, slightly pudgy man in his mid-thirties who is confused and troubled by problems with his girlfriend, is seated on the adjacent couch. Ed is an epidemiologist who does mountains of research for the federal government and looks like a bureaucrat from central casting: horn-rimmed glasses, grave countenance, neatly combed hair. He is quiet, reserved, and analytical—a type that is often more difficult to reach in therapy because he tends to intellectualize and speak about issues rather than feelings. As an adult child of alcoholics, he has problems with identity, self-esteem, communication, and commitment; his personal life has also been deeply unhappy. Exposing him to group will draw him out and build up his confidence.

The last to venture into the room for this first session was Gary, the wariest and perhaps most deeply troubled of

my patients. For many years a severe alcoholic, Gary missed out on any higher education and as a result is extremely insecure about others' perceptions of his intelligence and social skills. Tonight Gary is neatly dressed in a long-sleeved striped sports shirt and chino slacks—there is a tense air to his tall, thin frame. Gary has Mel Gibson's boyish smile, good looks, and full head of hair. Very much a loner, he has a house of his own in the northeast section of Capitol Hill, where he works alone as an insurance estimator. When I urged him to join us and close the door behind him just ten minutes ago, he entered reluctantly, and seemed genuinely regretful that we must conduct our sessions behind a closed door. After looking around, he seated himself uneasily on the edge of the sectional next to the door, as if to make a quick getaway if things got too rough.

Things can get rough in group therapy. As a matter of course I encourage my patients to face often frightening and troubling problems in the company of vexing strangers. The resulting group process is a special dynamic that will reveal behaviors, fears, tensions, and anxieties that are almost impossible to reach in any other way. It can be frightening, uncomfortable, intimidating.

As Mitch struggles with his feelings of anxiety in our first session, Burt steps in to offer support.

"Are you looking forward to seeing your father?"

"Actually, no," Mitch says with a sad shake of his head of hair. "It's just going to be another drunken scene. My dad drinks, then picks fights, telling me and my sister everything we're not doing right. My sister fights back with him more than I do. The only time I really speak up is when he picks on her."

"So you're the last priority in this situation," I say.

Mitch nods.

Paul jumps in. "Well, as I see it, you're not exercising all

your options. Did your old man just pop into town all of a sudden?"

"I knew he was coming, but he never gives us much notice."

"But," Paul continues, "you did know, right? So you could have told him you were going to be busy that night, that you had other plans, or that you could meet to take a walk in the park for an hour but you wouldn't be free for dinner."

Mitch smiles. "I see what you mean. He always catches me off guard when he calls, but maybe I could be a little more prepared for next time . . ."

As Mitch trails off, a silence descends upon the group.

After a time, Paul looks up. "I might as well go next here. My situation is that I'm separated, but the wife and I are kind of dating again. To tell you the truth, I'd like to keep it that way. I've never lived alone in my life, and being in an apartment and just watching TV by myself is for the birds. And after twenty years of marriage, I feel funny trying to 'date' all over again. And there are some pretty scary diseases going around out there, you know. At least I know what's what with my wife."

After a pause, he continues: "Sarah—that's my wife—and I were both just twenty-one when we got married. I've got two kids, teenagers, Betty, who just went away to college, and Abe, who's a junior in high school, and lives with Sarah. She's depressed a lot of the time, and I just decided I'd had enough of it. The separation is something I'm working on getting over, but it sure as hell isn't easy, believe me."

Burt, who is sitting forward on the couch facing Paul and me, nods slowly.

After a silence, I come in. "Well, for what it's worth, Paul, I don't think any man ever gets completely over his first love. Your situation is especially difficult: twenty years of history doesn't just vanish overnight. It's part of your personal history, a part of you, and always will be."

"People are probably telling you to 'get over it,' " Mitch interjects.

"Yeah, I hear that a lot, and it bothers me. I just hate it." Paul grimaces.

"There is something you can do, Paul," I offer. "Try to remember that you *will* work through this. Being here in group is a good start. And know that eventually you *can* have another relationship."

"Not if he's still dating his ex-wife, he won't!" Gary exclaims from his corner by the door.

This gets a nervous laugh from Paul, who tries to shake it off by looking away. Burt and Mitch are smiling, too.

I ask Paul how his son Abe is taking the separation.

"Oh, he's all right. Doing pretty well with it."

"Did you ever ask him?"

"No. But we never talk much about that kind of stuff."

"How about if we role-play it now?" I ask. Role playing, a technique where a group member and I act out roles of other individuals in ways we think they might actually feel, is a common and useful group-therapy technique. "I'll be Abe and you be you," I suggest. Paul nods, and I, as Abe, turn to face Paul on my left, and begin.

"Look, Dad, I'm really pissed at you for leaving me here with Mom. She's your wife, but now you've left and dumped her on me. At least before you left there were two of us not getting along with her! Dealing with Mom by myself is just one more hassle I don't need right now."

Paul seems somewhat perplexed but manages some response. "Look at it this way, son: It won't be for much longer. You're going off to school pretty soon. And I'm sorry, I didn't mean to cause problems for you. Your mom and I just couldn't stay under the same roof any longer. But any time you want to talk about it, I'd be glad to, okay?"

"But Dad," I continue, "I don't see why I should believe that. You weren't really around for me to talk with before, so

how will it be any easier when you're not even here? You leave here, you come back home, and then you're gone again. I wish you'd just make up your mind once and for all, so I'd know what I'm dealing with."

This stops Paul, who is struggling for a response.

"Have you had your apartment long?" Gary throws out from his corner seat.

I look past Paul to Gary, catch his gaze, and hold it. I suspect that Gary, like many people in group, has jumped in like this to take the conversation to a safer place for him. I wonder if it is stirring something up inside. "What triggered your question?" I ask.

Gary shrugged lazily. "I guess I connect with Paul's mixed feelings about separating. I'm thirty-three, never been married, and it seems like I should want to. But every time I go out with a woman, I try to find something wrong with her. That way I don't have to decide about marriage. And even if I did get married, what if it just goes nowhere? Then I'd have to decide whether to get a separation, divorce, or whatever. The whole thing's too much!"

"Try to be a bit more specific, Gary."

Gary shifts uneasily and looks around at the rest of the group. "Well, when I broke up with Liz two years ago, I was so . . . God, I don't ever want to go through that again! It was horrible. I felt addicted to her. And she came back to me—just once—to . . . well . . . basically to get laid, and I was practically on my knees begging her to stay after that. I was desperate, totally out of control. That was scary.

"Now whenever I date a woman, I really do think I'm locked in, addicted to her. So I'm with Paul on keeping dating simple—no commitment, no strings attached. I'm just going to let my dick dictate where it wants to be from now on," he states emphatically. "I'm never going to get serious about anybody again."

Gary folds his arms and sits back, looking as though he's confident this problem has been solved.

For a while nobody says anything. Finally Burt looks across to Paul. "So what's your wife—Sarah?—like?"

"Burt," I say, "why not tell us a little about yourself?"

Burt smiles, acknowledging that he's been caught. "Well," he begins, in a careful, detached way, "when I broke up with my wife three years ago, I was devastated. But Rosalind was hiding out and depressed for what seemed like forever. She was always going on and on about how she didn't have her own identity. She was a pretty good writer, but the depression just drove her to distraction. She was a nonwriting writer." He looks up and rolls his eyes. "I really did try to talk, to communicate with her, but I guess I didn't do a very good job. She's the one who finally asked for a divorce. I don't think I would have ever asked for one; I expected that we'd just stay married, you know, through thick or thin. Here I felt it was my duty to stand by her forever, and she walks out on me! *I couldn't believe it.* I should have divorced her myself and saved myself a hell of a lot of grief."

I'm watching Burt carefully. I nod at him to show I understand his pain. I wait for others to come in on this, too.

Suddenly Sean sneezes and startles everyone.

"Maybe that's your opening to tell us something of yourself, Sean," I suggest.

Sean becomes very apprehensive at this suggestion. The youngest of the group, he is clearly intimidated by all that is going on around him. "Well, I guess I don't know what you're all talking about. I'm pretty close to my parents, I talk to them all the time. It feels like they've been married forever."

"So why are you here?" Paul demands from across the room.

"Well, mostly because I just broke up with my girlfriend, Sandi. It's not that we don't care about each other. We're just so different: she's New York, Jewish, Ivy League, top med

school. Me, I'm from out West, so I'm a bit more laid back, I take things as they come. I make decent grades and that's good enough for me. I don't even know what I'm going to do with my life yet! I'm in med school but I'm not sure I even want to be a practicing doctor."

Burt, who is crowding Sean a bit on the couch, is interested. "So what's the deal with Sandi?"

"Well, I guess the things that attracted us in the first place, the differences, are what finally tore us apart. I'd still like to get back together, though. Is that too idealistic? Everybody says it is, I hear it all the time. But it's true. I really miss her." As Sean finishes he looks a little deflated. I decide to come in.

"Sean, can you see any similarities between your situation and Paul's?"

Sean shrugs. He doesn't seem at all up to it.

We all sit silently for a while. Rush-hour traffic noises filter up from the downtown Washington streets. As we sit here quietly, it seems the rest of the city is in a hurry to get home.

I turn to Ed. "I'm wondering how you're fitting in with everything that's being said here."

Ed leans forward and pushes up his glasses carefully. We all sense this is uncharted territory for him. "Oh, it's all very interesting," he assures us.

"Could you say more?"

"All right," he continues, looking a little perturbed at me. "It's true, a lot of what you guys are saying makes sense to me. I've been in the same place, too. The longest relationship I ever had lasted three years, and then we sort of went our separate ways. I'm in another one now, but I have all these doubts about whether this is what I really want."

I know there is more to the story than Ed's letting on, but before I can draw him out of his shell, Mitch shifts a motorcycle boot off his knee, and leans forward.

"Well, that's one thing I can say for my relationship with Lynda right now. I like it, I want it, and I don't want to screw it up. In fact, I think I'm going to ask her to marry me. The thing is I just *hate* being alone. I can't stand it. When I was with my ex-wife"—he stops suddenly and breaks into a wide smile—"Whoa . . . I never called her my ex-wife before! Hmmm." Several of the men are grinning back at him as he continues: "She and I just did not communicate. At all, period. So while we were supposedly together in this marriage, I damn sure didn't feel that way. I felt totally alone. I ended up withdrawing even more. And Lynda, the woman I'm living with, says I'm doing the same thing to her, and it scares me. She thinks I need to be in therapy to figure this whole mess out. I'm here because I'm willing to do that, because I sure as hell don't want a repeat of my last breakup." He looks pained. "I don't ever want to go through that again."

I glance at the clock and am surprised to find that we are nearly out of time. I begin to wrap up, emphasizing that I am very impressed and pleased about how they were able to open up as quickly as they have in this first session. Mitch and Burt seem pleased with themselves, too. Ed looks over at Sean and these two appear to be relieved that they made it through. Gary is happy that this first session, the hardest, is over, too. He stands up with a half grin.

I'm as pleased as they are, excited by this group's potential. These men have been unusually active for a new group, and I'm certain they will learn a great deal about themselves, their relationships, and each other as we progress.

INTERPRETATION ────────────

I have discovered that a short personal break after group therapy in the relative isolation of my office is essential to review what has occurred. I take advantage of this time in many ways: I review the session in my mind, sort out how the men are responding and changing, and jot down a few ideas for review before the next session.

Today I feel optimistic about the progress this group will make. They are a courageous lot. To enter therapy at all takes a degree of bravery. For a man to admit to himself that he has a problem he cannot handle is difficult enough. To acknowledge this helplessness to anyone else, even a skilled therapist, is even rougher. To confess to strangers, however, can be frightening. Such is the magnitude of the hurdle faced by all the group members, and this shared anxiety has already brought them together. With time this tentative bond will evolve into mutual respect, trust, and confidence.

This particular group was organized with a specific theme in mind. Each member has a strong desire to change and improve his relationship with women. I have seen all six of these men in individual therapy first; they all know and trust me. Each feels that I am his special ally. My challenge is to sustain this feeling and to encourage each man to extend trust to the others as they all risk revealing themselves in our sessions. All have entered group therapy at my suggestion, on faith rather than instinct. Group is a more complex form of therapy than is individual, and through the process each man will have the opportunity to learn more about how others respond to him, what feelings and reactions he evokes in those he is closest to, and how to make meaningful and effective changes in these relationships.

By beginning this first group session, Mitch was attempting to test out some lessons about anxiety learned from indi-

vidual therapy. At this point he understands that anxiety often represents fear, and that the way to conquer any fear is to go through the feared experience, so he decided to begin the very first session by talking about one of his most difficult topics: his father. This choice pays off for Mitch, as he does feel less anxious and somewhat relieved afterward. Mitch's pattern of handling anxiety has been to withdraw and become silent. What occurred in group was a particularly gratifying breakthrough for Mitch, since as the child of an alcoholic father, his characteristic way of dealing with problems has always been avoidance or denial.

I feel Mitch has taken a risk in presenting his problem with his father to the group and has gained better perspective as a result. However, his response, or lack of a response, to Paul is indicative of another pattern that holds Mitch back: his tendency to grow silent and withdrawn when angry or anxious.

Paul comes in by telling the group that his loneliness is driving him to date his ex-wife, with whom he has been in considerable conflict over the years. Even this unpleasant relationship is preferable to being alone in Paul's eyes. I know from my individual sessions with Paul that the entire dating situation is very difficult and threatening to him. He is also thoroughly confused by his own inability to make a firm decision on the separation and divorce. In fact, Paul's progress toward such a decision is an extremely important element in his recovery and future progress. Nevertheless, Paul's choice to date Sarah is characteristic of what some men do when faced with the loneliness and uncertainty of a separation: they rush back and embrace that which is generally unfulfilling yet familiar.

Burt, on the other hand, represents those men who finally realize that the decision has already been made and clearly understand that either there was a complete lack of ability to resolve problems within the marriage or simply no

progress was made in this area, and therefore the odds of future success with the partner appear slim. As a result Burt, like most men, will not attempt to rejuvenate the relationship.

Even at this point we already see that Burt and Paul share certain common experiences in their respective marriages to depressed women. Both men felt hopeless and ultimately helpless to draw their forlorn wives out of their severe depressions. This is not their role; they can't play therapists to their wives. They both withdrew, became emotionally detached, and ultimately fled.

Both Burt and Paul echo the feeling of most men in my practice who are going through separation and divorce: that it is a thoroughly devastating experience and one from which they typically emerge feeling like a failure. It is important to emphasize that this sense of failure plagues men more than most people realize. After all, the majority of divorces nationwide are initiated by women who have taken the time to go through their own painful period before asking for the divorce. The divorce is often "sprung" on the man in the way Burt has related. The man is shocked. Many men are similar to Burt in that they feel a sense of responsibility to keep the relationship afloat and moving forward. When the bond dissolves, the man commonly feels as though this represents his own personal failure as a man.

Clearly, divorce is one of the most traumatic events a man will face during his adult life. Regardless of the circumstances, divorce means not just the loss of a wife but often the loss of children, homes, friends, money, and self-esteem as well. These men experience a terrible, multiple loss.

An important part of my work with divorced and separated men is to assure them that the painful grieving process *does* get done, the pain *does* diminish, and their energy and enthusiasm for establishing new relationships *do* grow. In fact,

by the time most men finally come to me, they are depressed and feel nearly hopeless, and these reassurances both have a healing effect and serve to establish the groundwork for a successful therapeutic relationship.

Gary enters the discussion from the corner after recognizing his connection to Paul. This makes it easier for Gary because he feels he now has an ally, in addition to me, who will understand his dilemma. He fears marriage, too—he was so terribly hurt by the breakup of what had been the most intense relationship of his life that he dreads this catastrophe happening all over again. Gary is still carrying around a lot of hurt. He strives to avoid emotional involvement and is simply dating to have sex. Gary's broaching of the intensely personal topic of sex and his choice of the slang term "dick" functions as an "icebreaker" for this group and will in fact enable the other group members to talk about sex more freely and openly. I've discovered that even without such a fast icebreaker, men are quite willing to overcome their general inhibitions about discussing and sharing feelings and anxieties about sex.

When asked to enter the discussion, Sean expresses bewilderment on how there could be so little communication in these men's families. He seems to be especially confused about Paul's relationship with his son. This bewilderment grows out of Sean's view of his own relationship with his family, one that appears to be quite open and supportive, with excellent communication. I do not press Sean on the facts about his family, because he is so uncomfortable in this first session. There's plenty of time ahead.

Ed appears to be "laying low" in this first session, and one cue I pick up immediately is his use of the word "interesting." I find that people who describe something as "interesting" in group are usually avoiding a straightforward admission of how they really feel about what is going on. Ed's

superficial comments on his former and current relationships suggest that Ed is being exceedingly cautious and is self-conscious about what he can safely say at this juncture in group.

By contrast, Mitch reacts to Ed's vagueness by offering some strong testimony about his clear feelings for his current girlfriend, Lynda. Mitch's desire to come back into the discussion is further evidence that his initial anxiety about being in the group has diminished and he is now prepared to open up a bit more. Mitch is certainly not alone in his description of a married life that leaves him feeling all alone. He very much wants a successful relationship with Lynda, and his greatest fear is yet another failed marriage. Unfortunately, many men do remarry within a short period of time as a way of avoiding the pain, loneliness, and depression of divorce, and they commonly carry the very same problems, as well as the "bad" feelings, right into the next marriage. It is my responsibility to help Mitch determine whether he is marrying Lynda without having recognized and resolved the problems of his first marriage.

The feelings expressed in this first session are a good indicator of the conventional traumas men suffer when a woman breaks up with them. Loneliness, hurt, depression, anger, desperation, rejection, loss of control: men experience all these feelings, even when the very worst of their relationships dies. They are rarely prepared for the idea of a breakup because they are taught to resist the idea that their feelings are important. Men are commonly driven by the desire to do the "right" thing and therefore are unable to foresee or prepare for the traumas of separation. Additionally, men feel that the grieving process is not what's expected of them. Society demands that men simply stand up, dust themselves off, and get on with life (people saying, "You'll get over it" did disturb Paul). As these men have demonstrated, however, men do grieve, often in profound ways.

This has been an enlightening and revealing first session. As the six men take increasingly greater risks in group by, say, being brutally honest, by confronting one another, or even by allowing themselves to cry, their learning will continue, more of their life experiences will be revealed, and they will find themselves growing in new and unexpected ways.

SESSION 2

//

"GO TO THERAPY, OR GO TO HELL!"

An earlier cancelation has left me with a little extra time before group today, so I am enjoying looking out of the floor-to-ceiling windows onto Farragut Square. These windows and their expansive view are my favorite features of the office. While MenCenter has a handsome conference room, I prefer holding the group sessions in my room; actually, a combination executive office and comfortable living room.

The idea of seeing a therapist is an intimidating notion for most men, so I've carefully created a setting that is familiar, warm, and nonclinical. It's also my preference to be in pleasant surroundings, as so much of my life is spent in the MenCenter suite.

The office has two deep black leather chairs, two light gray sectionals, a side table, a coffee table, and, of course, my desk, which sits at the far end of the room. The artwork

suggests individuality, nothing typical of an office. My plants are important: they represent life and growth. There are two palms. One covers an entire corner and the other sits in the window. And a blooming peace lily takes up space on another section of the windowsill.

Since men are traditionally resistant to therapy, and there is the temptation to use time as an excuse, I've purposely chosen to locate MenCenter in the heart of the Washington business district. I've also surrounded myself with colleagues who offer early, late, and weekend appointments and flexible fees, all in an effort to encourage and support men in their commitment to therapy and growth.

Suddenly my buzzer rings and brings me back from these thoughts. This is my assistant letting me know that the group has assembled in the waiting area. We're ready for our second session.

I open the door to Paul's thin frame in a slightly worn business suit. He nods at me and plops into the same leather seat as last week right next to mine. Mitch is close behind Paul, and I am struck, for the first time, how closely Mitch resembles a red-headed Kris Kristofferson. Burt and Ed enter the room together, continuing a conversation from the waiting room, and take the same seats as last week on the couch. In the doorway is Sean, who smiles at me in a sheepish sort of way and takes his spot next to Burt on the couch. Sean seems to be relieved that nobody took his spot. Gary brings up the rear again this week and takes the couch seat nearest the door, which is still available to him. I realize this has some significance, and the others are already honoring his wariness and option to escape.

After everybody settles in, I look around and smile. The tension in the air so evident in last week's session seems to have largely evaporated. Still there is an uneasy silence.

Paul's nasal tone breaks the silence. "So how'd it go with your father last week?" he asks, staring straight at Mitch.

Mitch seems startled by the question but quickly recovers. "Um, thanks for asking. Actually, I got off easy. Didn't have to say too much, Dad did most of the talking. He did have his drinks, and my sister and I just didn't say a whole lot."

"Why did you choose not to talk?" I ask.

"Guess it's the one that comes most easily," he shrugged. "I get real quiet when my dad is drinking, it always seemed to make the most sense." Mitch seems to be increasingly glum with this revelation. "When I was a kid, I'd go off by myself so I wouldn't have to hear him hollering at me or my mom."

"Your dad sounds like a carbon copy of mine," Ed offers from Mitch's right. "You know, I did the very same thing as a kid. I used to hide from them, literally run away when they started yelling at me, but . . ." Ed falters for a moment. "I, uh, sort of have trouble talking about my folks like this."

"Try to go on, Ed," I say.

"Well . . ."

"You don't want to make 'em look like alcoholics, right?" Mitch throws out.

"Yeah, I guess so. I don't mind talking about me or even about me and Ellen in here. But this is different."

"This is why I'm having trouble with this, Al," Mitch says as he looks at me. "When I say these things about my dad, it's like he's some gutter bum alcoholic. He *is* my father, and I really shouldn't be talking about him this way."

"What's your feeling while you're talking?" I ask.

"I feel damn guilty," Mitch responds, staring at the carpet.

Burt leans forward from Mitch's other side. "I always backed away from my father too, because he was a real screamer. It was embarrassing. I even saw a used-car salesman give in once because of the screaming." Burt is talking straight to Mitch. "I just wanted to slink away and die, believe me," he adds with a shake of the head.

"At least you guys *had* fathers!" Paul interjects.

My attention has so shifted to the men on the couch that I am not watching for Paul's reaction. I'm surprised by how suddenly he is shaken.

"Mine died when I was fifteen, and I didn't even know he was sick!" he concludes with a quaver in his voice.

Burt looks at Paul, then at me, then back at Paul. He seems worried that he may have started something.

"Paul, can you tell us a bit more about this?" I ask.

"It was like everything in my family had to be a big secret," he intones. Paul seems to have developed an interest in the armrest, where he's staring, and he's poking at it incessantly. "I only found out my father was sick when I happened to see his car parked outside of the doctor's office one day. So I asked my mom if something was wrong. So she just told me, 'Your father's sick,' but she never said how bad. Little by little I noticed him around more, and then he was just bedridden. One day he died." Paul has stopped picking and falls quiet for a moment. He looks up and almost seems startled that the rest of us are there. "I was so angry about it."

"What were you angry about?" Burt asks. He is looking at Paul and seems concerned.

"I was so angry he left me," Paul replies, as he slides back in his seat. "He just *left* me, stuck me there with my mother and sister."

It dawns on me that this is the same thing that Paul is doing to his own son, Abe. Paul's also been holding in a great deal of pain.

"This is the first time you've ever said that you were angry with your father for dying and leaving you alone," I note.

Paul's eyebrows shoot up for a moment, and then he nods in recognition.

"Take a look at whether holding in all this hurt and anger

might be something that happens a lot in your life, whether it might be a pattern," I suggest.

"Well," Paul reflects. "Yeah . . . I guess in a way I did that with my wife. Sarah would start yelling at me about something, and I'd yell back maybe once, but she'd keep on me, and I just wouldn't answer. That's how I figured it: If I don't answer, she has to stop yelling. God, I hated it. After a while it became automatic: I'd pretend I didn't hear; stare at the TV, and tune her right out."

Ed begins to fidget and seems disturbed by the conversation. "What's going on, Ed?" I ask.

"I'm just thinking that Ellen and I never argue."

"Never?" Gary looks to his left and catches Ed's eye. He is skeptical.

"Never," Ed says emphatically. "When anything comes up, we both get quiet. When Ellen's mad, it's hard to discuss anything at all. Usually she takes a book, goes into the other room, and stays there for an hour or so. The only thing I know to do is leave her alone."

"I want to say something about all this, Ed," I come in. "This is for you, too, Paul, and Mitch." Everyone has perked up a bit. "What is happening here is you are all using behaviors you learned as children. Ed and Mitch run away from their alcoholic parents. Now, this was a good choice as a kid: protecting yourself from the 'big, angry, powerful' adults. Now the scene is different. You're the grown-ups. But you're still using your childhood defenses. Getting quiet, hiding, withdrawing. Paul, you get quiet with Sarah just as you were expected to do when your mother was mad at you."

Paul turns to me swiftly. "Look, I don't like this. Are you calling me a child?"

"No, just the opposite," I counter. "I'm saying you're an adult. And now you don't have to defend yourself with other adults in an immature way. It works better if you stop and confront Sarah. Otherwise you're never going to find out what

these conflicts are about." I turn slowly to Ed. "Can you see this too, Ed? Do you understand how difficult it will be for you and Ellen to resolve your problems if you just avoid each other?"

"I understand what you're saying, I really do, but . . ."

"What is the problem between you and Ellen?" Gary asks.

Ed sighs. "Well, the bottom line is that I'm on a fence. I can't make up my mind about whether we should get married. One day Ellen just gave me an ultimatum. Go find out why you can't make up your mind. Either make a commitment or let me move out of here and get on with my life. You know what she said? She said, 'Go to therapy, or go to hell!' "

A ripple of laughter runs through the group.

"How'd you respond?" I ask.

"Oh, I guess I was worried. I didn't want to lose her. And she was dead serious about it. So I came here."

"So how are things now that you're doing this?"

"Well, I can see where Ellen and I are getting closer. But I get frustrated that it's so hard for us to have a decent conversation." Ed starts getting agitated and is toying with his wool sweater. "Like last night we went to see this movie. I wanted to talk about it afterward. But it was like she got real defensive. 'Why do you have to pick it apart? Can't you just enjoy it for what it is?' " he mocks in a falsetto voice. "I told her I wasn't trying to pick it apart. I just wanted to have a conversation about it, maybe understand it a little better!"

"What did Ellen say?" Burt asks.

Ed slaps the armrest. "She wouldn't even discuss it! She said I was being too detailed and analytical, that I should just enjoy the movie. I don't get it. Ellen's not stupid by any means. She's got a master's degree. But I can't talk with her like I used to in my other relationships."

Burt is chuckling and shaking his head. "I have to laugh, Ed. I mean, if you want somebody analytical, JoAnn analyzes anything and everything. No matter what I do or say, she's

analyzing it. If I don't say anything, she analyzes that! I can't even be quiet without being analyzed." He pauses. "You wanna trade girlfriends?"

Ed smiles.

Paul looks across at Ed. "You set a date for that wedding yet?"

"Ellen set a deadline last summer, but it passed and nothing happened. Then she set a new deadline for Christmas." He thinks a moment. "It's about nine weeks away. I don't know what to do."

"Draw up a prenuptial agreement," Paul advises. "It's hell going through a divorce and finding out that Sarah might be able to get half of my salary!"

From the looks being flashed around the group, I sense an impatience with Paul. Ed does, too, apparently, and hesitates to answer. I make it clear by my steady gaze that he should continue.

"I'm not really comfortable with that," Ed continues. "It sounds like I don't trust her, like I'm already thinking about a divorce. It's not like I enjoy being undecided, you know." Ed looks around to make sure everybody has heard this. "I feel kind of guilty, because I encouraged her to move in with me, to leave a job and friends in Texas to move here with me. She said to me then that she didn't want to unless there was a possibility of marriage." Ed trails off and goes silent.

"What did you say?" Burt asks.

"That of course it was a possibility. I'd like to buy a house, start a family. But I never made any promises. I guess we also have to worry about the ol' biological clock; she's thirty-two. But if I'm going to get married, I want to be absolutely sure it's the right thing."

Burt has his head cocked toward Ed and has been nodding through this, listening intently.

"What is it, Burt?" I ask.

"Oh . . ." He looks a bit perplexed but then brightens

with recognition. "I identify with Ellen. Isn't that strange? I'm forty-five myself, I worry about what kind of a father I'm going to be at this age." He frowns and looks back at Ed. "I'm not sure JoAnn is really the one for me either."

I notice the clock and decide to wrap things up.

"It's almost time to stop, but I've been wondering why you've been so silent, Sean."

Sean looks up suddenly and catches my eye. "I've just been listening to everyone." He shrugs.

"What's been your reaction?"

"Well, I was thinking you guys are so . . . critical of your girlfriends." He ponders this for a moment. "Are you looking for somebody perfect?"

"I'm not," Burt answers quickly. "In fact, I get the feeling I'm the one who's supposed to be perfect, judging from the way JoAnn is on my case." His gaze shifts to me. "She criticizes me all the time."

"I understand, Burt. Criticism and blame can be so destructive to a relationship. And they can *kill* sex."

"If criticism is constructive, it could be good," Ed offers.

"Ed, when Ellen criticizes you for not talking with her, she's on target. Do you feel good about this?" I ask calmly.

He frowns. "Definitely not."

"Well, see, I don't believe in 'constructive' criticism in a relationship. It's just a cover for old-fashioned criticism. It also manipulates the other person into accepting the criticism without a hassle."

"So there's no such thing as 'constructive' criticism?" Ed asks with surprise.

"Sure," I reply, "and it plays an integral role in a relationship set up for it. For example, between an athlete and a coach, or a director and an actor. Relationships with clearly outlined teacher-student roles. There's no such agreement in a romantic relationship.

Ed seems satisfied with this. He looks around the room

and catches Sean's eye. "I sort of took things away from you right at the end. Did you want to say something else?"

Sean shrugs. "Not really. I just think you need to accept the other person. I know Sandi isn't perfect." After a moment he adds, "But I still love her."

INTERPRETATION ——————

Shared experience is the catalyst bringing the group together. Three of the six have revealed the pain and fright of childhoods spent largely hiding or avoiding their parents. Paul talks about the trauma of the sudden and unexpected death of his father, and how the anger from this event has still not subsided. In fact, this episode and its consequences play a role in Paul's present life. Some of the difficulties these men have in communicating with their women surface during this second session.

It is not unusual that three of the six men—Ed, Mitch, and Gary—all find themselves on the run from adults out of control and hesitate to discuss any aspect of this trauma today. All three men are adult children of alcoholics. One behavioral characteristic of alcoholic and other dysfunctional families is that the child is forbidden to say anything at all negative about the family to anyone outside the immediate family. The alcoholic parents use the defense mechanism of denial, a way of pretending that problems don't exist, and mold the children into using the same denial. The children are then expected to carry on this posture outside the family. This forces the youngster into a state of internal turmoil, because he's told no problem exists, yet he certainly both sees and feels one. The predominant code of keeping secrets within the family has served to isolate these three men. They

lost the freedom to interact openly with their friends and neighbors throughout their childhoods, and they were made to feel guilty or ashamed if they let slip with anything that their parents might deem "wrong."

This behavioral dynamic has consequences for the men in their lives today. As I point out to Mitch and Ed in the session, the hostility and craziness of their alcoholic families drove them into withdrawal and isolation from the family simply as a means of protection. From the child's viewpoint, this may be the best protection available. Now, however, they are mature adults who interact with other adults as peers rather than as authority figures. Their continuing reliance on childhood defenses, coping mechanisms, and habits is ineffectual in an adult-adult relationship. Mitch, Gary, and Ed must choose to engage in conflict: this will be an important part of their learning. They'll discover that conflict is a means of resolution that allows a relationship to grow rather than stagnate, regress, or even collapse.

In Paul's relationship with his father, the unexpected death was traumatic, since he was surprised and therefore unprepared for it. Paul had been carrying his anger around before this session but felt too guilty to tell anyone, because he never understood that anger is a natural outlet for grief. Paul's experience is shared by many men in my practice who have not yet learned how to express themselves when they feel angry. These men grew up feeling anger and hostility all around them and were upset and threatened by it. Anger then became "bad." This is why they are so successful at suppressing angry feelings entirely in adulthood. In my work with men I emphasize that minor annoyances, irritations, and disappointments need to be discussed or diffused *right as they happen*. This eliminates the need for intense, angry outbursts that result from long-term suppression of minor (and major) traumas and everyday difficulties that they've concealed or held in rather than diffused immediately by discussion.

Certainly such a behavioral change, like any change, is difficult to make. But the process will be easier for these men by virtue of their presence in the group. The entire group therapy process offers a strong medium for change. Tonight we see that Paul risked discussing a very powerful childhood trauma with men who are relative strangers to him. In fact, this risk to Paul has been reduced tonight by Ed, Burt, and Mitch, since all have spoken disparagingly about their fathers, offering support rather than censure. As a child, Paul learned from his family to expect rejection or anger if he revealed his true feeling about his father's death. Here, however, the men do not respond as critically as Paul anticipated. This now creates a much more fertile environment for honesty and change. The men are just beginning to sense this.

Other consequences of these early learned behaviors are playing themselves out in these men's lives as well. Clearly, Burt and Ed are having problems communicating with the women they love. Ed pleads with Ellen to talk to him about the movie they've seen together. While Ed expounds at length about the virtues and drawbacks of the film, he irritates and alienates Ellen, who is content with a more impressionistic experience. Ed approaches the conversation on an intellectual, "expert" plane and wants to do a thorough analysis. Ellen prefers and operates better on an emotional plane. Thus, as Ellen listens to Ed she becomes increasingly inhibited and intimidated, because she doesn't know what answer Ed is looking for. In this sense Ellen is like Burt, who also is intimidated by JoAnn's probing questions and constant analysis of their relationship. The true irony, however, is that trading girlfriends, as Burt has facetiously suggested, would be disastrous. While JoAnn and Ed certainly operate well on the intellectual plane, they are "experts" at different subjects. Ed focuses on analyzing facts and exploring rationality; JoAnn, on the other hand, examines emotions and beliefs. Burt and Ellen as a couple would be equally troubled, because they would

never be able to confront each other and would probably be content to avoid discussing problems in their relationship until they grew to unmanageable proportions.

Ed's dilemma stems from much more than poor communication. His indecision, his confusion, and the resulting guilt about his quasi-commitment to marry Ellen derive from two aspects of his personality. One is that Ed is a perfectionist. He is truly afraid that any specific commitment or decision could be "wrong." Like a perfectionist, Ed procrastinates because he wants to be "right." The other aspect is the residual effects of his own childhood. Ed's parents did not have the kind of marriage that would make him too eager to marry. He wants some assurance that his marriage will be better and more fulfilling than his parents'.

All the men in the group, Ed included, have an excellent chance of achieving their goals. A willingness for self-examination and change through therapy can dramatically increase the odds for a successful relationship or marriage.

SESSION 3

///

AVOIDING
FEELINGS

"So I figure that if I see Sarah once a week, then I could get my rocks off, and have the rest of the week to do all my other stuff, like get work done, see the kids, that kind of thing," Paul says. "I'd like to date around some, but you've got to worry about safe sex these days, and I hate using rubbers . . ."

"Wait a minute." Gary cuts in. "You mean you want to have sex once a week on schedule?"

"Well, to tell you the truth, Gary"—Paul shifts forward and shakes his head at Gary—"you wouldn't *want* it more than once a week with this woman. Don't get me wrong. I don't hate her or anything, but sex with her just isn't that great. It's something I do to get relief."

We all wait quietly for Paul to go on.

He inhales deeply. "We do it, and I come, but she can't have one anywhere near that soon, so I end up trying all sorts

of shit, everything I can think of: oral sex, manual stimulation. It's like I have to work and strain and then *work* even more. By the time she finally has an orgasm, I'm just so happy because now we can *stop!*"

Smiles break out all around, except for Paul, who still looks pained. "I don't think it's my fault, either," he concludes, looking up at Gary.

"What do you mean, Paul?" Mitch asks.

"Well, after I moved out of the house, I went out with this one woman a few times and, my God, that lady would have something like two or three orgasms before I ever even thought about coming! I felt so great about it, like some kind of giant. One other woman"—he pauses for a moment as though he's forgotten her name, and then recovers—"all I had to do was stick my finger in and bingo!"

Gary and Mitch burst out laughing. "Get a patent on that finger, Paul!" Gary throws out. Paul has a huge grin on his face, oblivious to the fact that the men are laughing at him, not with him.

After a pause, Gary recovers and sits up tall in his seat. "I don't have to worry about that these days."

"Oh? . . ."

"Yeah." Suddenly he looks intense. "My girlfriend, Leigh, is—you're not going to believe this—a twenty-nine-year-old virgin!"

Eyebrows shoot up all over the room. Sean seems unfazed. Paul coughs nervously, and we all wait for Gary to continue.

"So you can imagine what it's been like. Sex has become this big issue, a big production because I feel so damn *responsible* now as the guy who is going to take her precious virginity. It's absolutely crazy, and . . ." He pauses. "It's so weird because none of my other girlfriends have been like this. Shit, my last girlfriend just loved sex. It was no big thing. We'd fool around, I'd put it in, she'd come, like two or three

times, then I'd come, then we'd order in Chinese and watch the ball game!" Suddenly Paul is very interested.

"Just by fooling around you got her to come three times?" Paul asks with admiration.

"Anyway, I'm not sure I'm completely buying into Leigh's story," Gary continues, ignoring Paul completely. "I'm not sure she's being entirely straight with me." Gary is scratching the side of his long face, and his careful eyes are avoiding the rest of the men. "I mean, maybe she never went all the way before, but she's . . . well, she's too damn good at other things for me to believe that she's totally inexperienced."

"Have you talked to Leigh about any of this?" I ask.

"I tried some, but what's the use? It's just easier not to bother with the sex."

"You *like* that?" Burt asks.

"Ha! You've got to be kidding. Look, guys, I really think I'm just *obsessed* with sex. I've just got to have it. Leigh doesn't understand this. Every day I feel less in love with her because we can't get it on." His eyes shift to the window and stay there. "I think sex is a real problem for me, because I don't put sex and love together. Lots of times when I'm with a woman I don't think about much of anything else." Gary looks back at Burt. "And I never have to love the woman to have good sex. It's just *sex* for me."

"What I want to know," Paul comes in suddenly, "is what's all this emphasis on the 'right amount of foreplay' anyway? I mean, shit, it only takes five minutes, and then, wooosh! and you're in!"

On the couch Burt and Mitch are laughing and slowly shaking their heads. Sean is turning increasingly dark shades of crimson. Gary just glares at Paul.

"Okay, okay!" Paul throws his hands up, "Okay, maybe ten minutes!"

I turn to Paul. "Is that how long you take for foreplay?"

"Uh, well, five minutes or so usually. I don't time it, you know."

The men are still smiling. "I'd say try fifteen minutes, ten minutes minimum," Gary advises, trying to smooth out the situation. He is deliberately polite.

The rest nod in agreement. Paul looks mortified. Sean is sitting on the edge of his seat and still hasn't lost his blush.

"Where are you with this, Sean?" I ask.

"Oh." Sean clears his throat. "Well, I'm still getting used to this kind of talk." He smiles sheepishly and looks around. "Okay. I . . . uh . . . learned a lot from Sandi. I mean, it was nothing for us to spend most of a weekend in bed. And sex was just part of it. Some of our best talks were in bed, just holding each other. Sometimes that would lead into sex. . . . I know that we cared about each other . . . " His words are coming more slowly now. "And she was the first girlfriend I ever really . . . well, loved."

A long silence. I catch his eye. "Sean?"

"Oh, I was . . . thinking about Sandi." He looks across at Paul and sits up a bit. "And I'm also wondering about you. Do you ever, like, do anything spontaneous when you have sex, like what I just described?"

Paul shakes his head.

"What?" Sean asks with disbelief. He is getting angry, too. "Look, Paul, I mean do you ever have sex just on the spur of the moment?"

Paul looks directly into his eyes. "I got blown by a chick I met at Baskin-Robbins once," he says defiantly.

Sean rolls his eyes, and Gary breaks into a big smile: "Don't tell me: flavor of the month, right?" This gets a big laugh all around, with the exception of Paul, who appears not to have heard it.

"So, Sean," Gary looks across the room, "when was your most spontaneous moment?"

"Oh." Sean slowly smiles. "It was with Sandi. In New

York. We were in this highrise building. We got on the elevator and I pushed the button for the top floor, and she just, well, she just *looked* at me, and I understood instantly. We started hugging and kissing and then her hand went up the panel and pushed the "Stop" button and before I knew it we were getting it on right there in the elevator. All it took was one look."

Everyone sits in silence with this for a while.

"Ed, where are you on what we've been discussing?" I ask. I've noticed that Ed has been listening intently but has yet to say anything. He seems to be hiding in Gary's shadow.

"Oh, I've been listening and really relating to what you two were saying about sex," he offers, nodding to Gary and Paul. "Mostly I'm wondering what it is about the way society views sex that puts this expectation on the man to bring a woman to orgasm?"

"That's a legitimate question, Ed," I say. "But I'm wondering, on a less intellectual level, what you yourself are feeling about it."

"Well," Ed responds, "I guess I'm having sort of the same problem with Ellen. After I have an orgasm, I am totally wasted, just out of it, but it feels like there's this job I've got to finish. I was also thinking about this old relationship I used to have, where we had lots of sex, but it was all . . . well, it was all pretty mechanical." He looks over at Paul. "I was relating to you in this sense because you do seem pretty mechanical about it."

Paul sits straight up. "Now, wait a minute! I don't want you to think that I'm just a *machine* or something. I mean, I'll mess around some, do some petting, and—"

"Paul," I interrupt, "could you just listen for a minute?"

"But they're talking like it's the only way I ever—"

"Paul," I say, "can you listen to what they're saying? From the way you describe your sex life, they're getting the impression that it's very mechanical: They're just responding to

what you're telling them. It's important that you learn that this is the effect you have on them and on others. Try just listening to their responses."

"Okay." He looks skeptical.

"Well, I didn't have much of a sex problem in my first marriage in the early years," Mitch says softly. This is the first we've heard from Mitch today. He has been quiet, but intensely interested. "By the time we got divorced, there was no sex and no communication at all. Sex was only part of it."

"You know, you're right," Ed says, "it really is a matter of communication. Like with Ellen now. She's just trying to force me into marrying her, and she's using sex as a weapon. It's her way of forcing me."

"Wait, I thought you said it was communication," Gary objects.

"Yeah, it is. She's so moody she spends all her time all by herself reading in the bedroom and then she dismisses me by saying she's just not in the mood. But she does say," he pauses for effect, "that if we get married she'd want sex more!"

Gary groans.

"Then I think about Paul's situation with his wife, and I know why he doesn't want to stay with her," Ed continues.

"I stayed with *my* wife too long, that's for sure," Burt observes.

"I agree," Mitch interjects. "I don't think Paul should stick with Sarah just for the convenience of it, either."

Burt nods and looks at Paul. "Look, twenty years of bad sex is too much already." He halts and seems to have another thought. "You don't have to ask our permission to leave her, you know."

Paul nods carefully and shifts his weight in the chair. "You're right. But God, the guilt. You have no idea . . . "

"Well, I'm listening."

"The thing is: It wasn't always bad with Sarah. Sex was all right when we were first married and getting along pretty

well. But then she got depressed, went on medication for it, and it was never good anymore after that." Paul begins to run his hand through his hair. "I was just thinking. Maybe the depression was just her way of leaving me. In some ways we were separated long before I moved out."

Burt smiles. "Paul, remember what I told you about my wife? She just up and divorced me one day. And she was depressed *all* the time. I didn't know what to do about it. Seemed like nothing I did could make her happy. But I'll tell you, her decision to divorce me was the best thing in the world for her. Once she stopped blaming me and took control of her life, she got back on her feet." He adds after a pause: "That's the truth."

"Yeah," Paul says. He seems less than enthusiastic.

Sean isn't finished with Paul yet and has seemed distracted through this whole exchange. "I'm just wondering, Paul, did you and your wife ever hug or just, well, cuddle?"

"Nope." Paul's voice has developed a hard edge. "Never did much of that. And to tell you the truth, one of the nice things about being separated is being able to sleep alone. I mean it. Sarah was always all over me when I tried to sleep. She was always sort of inching closer to me all night long, so I finally bought a king-sized bed so I could get some sleep."

"I'm the same way, you know," Gary offers. He appears to be talking to everybody, not just Paul, now. "I don't like cuddling that much, and I know I tend to jerk in my sleep. If a woman moves over during the night, I practically jump right out of bed!"

This seems to surprise everybody, especially Sean. "Oh God, I loved snuggling with Sandi," Sean exclaims. "That was really one of the best parts."

"You know—" Ed begins, but I hold up a hand.

"Sean?"

Sean is starting to tremble and sink back into the couch. He is on the verge of tears.

"What's going on, Sean?" I say softly.

Sean begins to breathe in short, shallow breaths and is fighting for control. Tears begin streaming down his cheeks as he rests his head back against the couch. He is staring at the ceiling.

We all stay quiet and watch Sean carefully.

Finally, I come in. "Your feelings are okay, Sean, stay with them."

Sean shuts his eyes tight and begins to shake his head. "I . . . I lost my best friend," he whispers. He seems incredulous that he's never realized this before. "Sandi was my best friend. And now she's gone. We'd made all these plans . . ." his voice trails off.

Gary reaches for the tissue box and hands it over to Sean.

As we allow Sean some more time, I realize the session is almost up. I feel it is important to offer some encouragement and support before allowing the session to end.

"Sean," I begin, "what you are going through is similar to grieving the death of a loved one. It's normal, healthy really"— I look around the group—"to let out these deep feelings of loss and hurt." I pause and allow him to absorb this.

"Okay?" I ask.

Sean nods.

"This will continue to hurt for a while, Sean. It just means that you're human. Those feelings are okay. If you can hang in, and keep letting them out, you'll be able to deal with this and get through it."

Sean looks at me. He appears relieved.

INTERPRETATION ─────────────

This session reveals the very different approaches of the men to sex, relationships, commitment, and expectations. It is readily apparent that Paul is the most mechanical in his approach to sex. Some of Gary's resentment and anxiety surrounding his lack of a sexual relationship with his girlfriend also surface. Sean seems almost baffled by Paul and Gary as he relates the tenderness and love of his former relationship with a twinge of idealism. Perhaps the most valuable aspect of this session is how clearly we see the lines drawn between men who seek to establish relationships with feelings, commitment, and attachment and those who struggle to avoid them.

From the very outset it is clear that Paul's view of sex is essentially a mechanical one. We hear that sex with his wife is just to "get his rocks off" and is done "just to get relief." For Paul, the purpose of sex is solely to have an orgasm. Much of Paul's view is due to lack of sexual experience and lack of emotional and physical affection in his early years with his mother and father. Sarah was his one and only sexual partner prior to the separation, and this relationship itself was fraught with early sexual difficulties. In fact, early in their marriage Paul and Sarah were both so unprepared for a sexual relationship that the marriage was not consummated for three months.

Clearly Paul's difficulties in his relationship with women go far beyond his lack of appreciation for foreplay. In large measure, Paul has become focused almost exclusively on his own needs to the exclusion of others'. Paul is effectively "stuck" here and has difficulty appreciating the other emotions evident in the group session. When Gary frets about the health of his relationship, Paul alone is intrigued solely by Gary's sexual prowess. Through the whole session Sean senses that Paul has no appreciation for his pain, and he continues to quiz

Paul about cuddling in an attempt to uncover and identify with any common feelings of vulnerability or pain. Paul insists that he never did much cuddling and in fact is glad to have a bed to himself now. This isolation even shows up in the group, as Paul's lack of empathy for Gary's anxiety, Sean's loss, or Ed's marriage proposal dilemma has served to separate Paul from the group. This isolation comes to the surface when Paul vigorously objects to the idea that in sex he is just a machine. He is hurt that the men don't understand him, but even more important he is beginning to feel increasingly secluded from the group because of his own lack of a sense of sharing with group members. Paul wants to belong.

Gary wants to belong, too, and so we are hearing, for the first time, about a very difficult area for Gary: his anxiety and confusion about what to do in his relationship with Leigh. Her virginity has become a severe burden for him and an obstacle for them both. Gary is both resentful ("I feel so damn responsible") and concerned ("as the guy who's going to take her precious virginity") and obviously confused about the direction things will take. It is encouraging that Gary feels comfortable enough to bring this up: it is a positive sign of his growing trust of the other men.

Sean finds all the talk of sex and intimacy to be a bit unsettling. He does, however, make a good adjustment and goes on to share with the rest of the group a lot of the tenderness and caring he felt for Sandi. It is important that the other men hear this from Sean because it so dominates Sean's outlook in the group. He is still suffering from a difficult loss: the pain and rejection of his first love. As the youngest member of the group, Sean retains some measure of youthful idealism: he believes he came from an ideal family, and he tends to think in ideal terms. The loss of Sandi had a shattering effect not only on Sean's emotional state but also on his entire idealistic view. The men now see this: As the conversation shifts to cuddling, the softer, warmer feelings touch Sean's

sadness and reveal the extent of his loss and his hurt at being jilted. Sean is able to release these feelings in a very healthy way by crying.

The very different reactions of Paul and Sean to cuddling, closeness, and bed-sharing highlight a central and important difference between Paul and Gary, on the one hand, and Sean, Burt, and Mitch, on the other. Both Paul and Gary want to be left alone when they are asleep, or are near sleep, a time when we are all quite vulnerable. They are also the two men who have a great deal of difficulty with feelings, especially negative feelings, and seem to be content to have sex without emotion or commitment. In fact, both Paul and Gary seek relationships that are devoid of feelings because they are less demanding and less threatening. Sean, Burt, and Mitch, on the other hand, relish the warmth of their partners and do not fear the vulnerability of this position. These are the men who have learned from the positive experiences of their early marriages (Burt and Mitch) or relationship (Sean) and are content to seek out and reinforce these feelings. All six men find themselves struggling with issues of commitment and attachment to women as they explore these relationships.

SESSION 4

//

SEX: LEARNING
THE WOMAN'S SIDE

"Paul called in sick today," I announce as soon as everyone has settled in. "He says he caught a flu, so he won't be here today."

After a moment Ed looks over at me. "You know, I think we may have beat up on him too much last week." The others smile with recognition.

"Really, I know I was a little pissed at him," Sean offers. Burt and Mitch exchange an uncomfortable look. It occurs to me that as irritating as Paul can be to the group, he does fire everybody up and keeps things going. We miss him today.

"Anything else?" I ask Sean. He shakes his head and looks out the window.

"Well, I know how I feel," Burt says suddenly. "Frustrated! I've been going with JoAnn for nearly a year. She's real expressive, always says what's on her mind, right then and

there." He looks around to Mitch and then to me. "And lately, it seems like she's always criticizing me."

"About what in particular?" I ask.

"Oh, communication, sex, you name it." He and Mitch exchange a smile. "I feel like I'm doing better at sharing my feelings, but I still get tongue-tied when she jumps on my case."

"How's that?" Gary asks with a frown. He looks as if he's worried he may have missed something.

Burt looks over his crossed legs at Gary. "Well, one reason it's hard to come right back with answers is that a lot of times she's griping about our sex life." He coughs nervously but quickly shakes it off. "Once, before I met JoAnn, I had a problem with impotence. But after some work with Al," he nods at me, "I managed to get over that, and for a long time the sex with JoAnn was just great." He smiles.

"So what's the problem?" Gary persists.

"Once JoAnn got pregnant, and got an abortion. I think it may have been because she felt it was too early in our relationship." Suddenly Burt looks pained. He uncrosses his legs and leans forward. "The whole thing was, God, it was emotionally grueling. I really want to be a father, you know, and I'm already forty-five." He shakes his head and spreads his hands open as though he's pleading with Gary. "I wonder, maybe I'm already too old to be a good father!"

We all wait quietly for Burt to go on.

"So here's the deal. JoAnn is thinking about marriage and a baby." Slowly he begins to shake his head again. He is examining the pattern in the rug. "But she's not sure. She wants to get her career going, she's finishing up her M.A. now, before having kids." He looks up and catches Gary's eye. "The problem is, when she gets hesitant, I start questioning the relationship. Then she gets scared I really want a child more than I want her."

"Is she right?" Ed asks quietly.

"Well, sometimes, like now, when she's criticizing me all the time, I think maybe she's right, that I do want a child more than I want our relationship. And I have to decide that pretty soon, because the lease on her place is running out, and we're talking about her moving in with me."

Gary appears surprised, and after a time he looks away.

Ed nods. "I can understand that constant criticism. It seems that no matter what I say or do lately, Ellen always gives me hell for, well, for being the way I am. Then she stomps off and buries her nose in a book."

A shadow of pain crosses Mitch's face.

"Mitch?" I ask.

"I'm listening," he says reluctantly. "Listening, but not liking it," he says. Mitch's large frame seems to have shrunk a bit. "It reminds me of my own marriage." He pauses. "For six years my wife always told me that she didn't need orgasms to enjoy sex. And you know, at first I'd ask her if she had one just to check it out, and finally she told me to quit bothering her about it. So I did! I believed her." Mitch looks surprised about this now. "So one day," he turns and looks directly at Burt, "we're fighting about something, and all of a sudden she starts bitching about our sex life and how I'm so selfish. I couldn't believe it! So I just stopped trying." He throws his hands up in resignation. "Just stopped completely."

"Did she ever bring up the subject again, Mitch?" I ask.

"No. And it was downhill from there. We never had sex again. That was it. Six months later we were divorced."

Suddenly the room feels very heavy. It's already dark outside in the November evening, and the mood in the room begins to reflect it.

"You know," Burt interjects, trying to brighten up the mood, "it's not easy to talk things out at a time like that, Mitch. I mean, lately JoAnn complains that I always come too soon. She likes lots of foreplay, which is fine with me,

but by the time I get inside her, I've been excited for quite a while, and it's hard for me to hold back."

"Have you tried anything, any methods, to hold back?" Ed asks.

"JoAnn was talking about this 'pinch method': stopping and pinching the tip of your penis to keep yourself from coming." Burt seems pretty skeptical about it.

"I'd say the best thing is to keep things simple, Burt," I say. "The last thing you need is anxiety about some new technique. If it seems like work, something you have to stop and think about, you're going to resent having sex." After a moment I add, "How about if you just stopped the friction for a little while?"

Burt's face is blank.

"You don't have to withdraw," I continue, "just rest a little. I bet she'd be glad to wait."

Burt nods slowly. "But remember, now that we use rubbers, I have to think about practical stuff, like making sure we haven't run out of the damn things, getting the packet open, putting the stupid thing on . . ."

"That makes sense," I agree. "How about using the condoms to your advantage?"

"Are you kidding?"

"Not at all," I respond. "Maybe using the condom could be a part of foreplay. For example, why should it be *your* job to put the rubber on? JoAnn could play with it, flirt with it, use it on you like a feather."

Burt is staring at me like he's yet to hear anything he can use.

"Look, Burt," I continue, "right now you're thinking of the rubber as something that's in the way, but just imagine if it's rolled onto you slowly, sensually, teasingly. . . . A condom doesn't have to be just a tool for . . . uh, your tool."

This gets a smile out of Burt. "Well, I never thought

about it. It does seem like a lot more fun than we're having now, anyway."

This is so important I decide to involve everyone.

"Burt, how about a role-play?"

He nods.

"I'll play JoAnn, and you be you." I pause for a minute, then begin again as JoAnn: "Listen, Burt, I hate to bring this up again, but you keep leaving me so unsatisfied and frustrated. You have the orgasm, you hop out of bed, go to the bathroom, and get rid of the rubber—and I'm lying here waiting, wishing you'd never gotten out of bed to begin with! I want us to work this out so that we can both be satisfied."

"JoAnn," he responds, "you know I want that, too. Don't I always get back in bed and hold you and help you have an orgasm? You're good at making yourself come, which is fine with me. I guess I thought it was okay with you, too."

"Sure, it's okay sometimes, just not every time. If I'm making too much of an issue of it, tell me. But I do want you to hear my side."

"To be honest, JoAnn, lots of times 'telling your side' feels more like putting me down, and then I don't know what to say."

"Well, I don't have all the answers, either. But sometimes I wonder if you come so fast because you're somehow mad at me."

"I don't think I'm mad at you, JoAnn. It's just that sometimes it does seem like you're about to come, your breathing changes, you move differently. So I go ahead, and you don't come! Then I try to keep going, but it's hard as hell to continue, and I don't think I'm any different from most men. But after all that foreplay—"

"Burt, you make it sound like you're just doing the foreplay as some kind of favor to me!"

Burt gives me a hopeless look, but the other men are smiling. They've all heard this at some time in their lives.

I turn to Mitch. "Next?" He shrugs and nods.

I begin as Mitch's first wife, Janet: "You just don't care about me, Mitch. You're so selfish. You have your precious orgasm and that's the end of it. I don't even get a chance to get worked up!"

"Well, Janet," Mitch answers with his hands stretched wide open, "you always told me you didn't *care* if you had one or not!"

"My God! If you're so into yourself that you can't see that I—Oh great, now I look like the bitch. Just don't bother me about it anymore! Just drop it!"

Mitch stops the role-play. "That's all there was, Al. We never talked about it again, never had sex again." He looks away. "I couldn't have gotten it up anyway."

"Mitch, remember that the most common factor in impotence is anger, so this is perfectly normal."

"I know." He still looks a little chagrined.

I turn to Ed. "Ed?"

"Al?" He laughs nervously.

"Your turn. You be you. I'll be Ellen. Ed, you always avoid making love with me whenever you're mad. If I say anything negative at all, you won't come near me."

"I don't think that's true at all, Ellen."

"Well, that's how it feels, so why would any woman try to be open with you the way you want her to?"

"But I still don't get why you won't open up to me!"

"Maybe because it scares me. Maybe because if I let myself be vulnerable, you might leave."

"Well, I'm scared, too, Ellen. I worry that if we don't open up to each other now, we'll have a big blowup later. I think you hold in all your feelings, especially when you're mad, and that sometime after we're married, you'll sneak up and clobber me with all of it! So how do I get you to share feelings with me now?"

"Guarantee me that if I do open up, you won't leave me."

"How am I supposed to do that, Ellen?"

"Marry me!" I answer triumphantly. The men all laugh knowingly. Ed turns scarlet. He has taken it seriously, as it was meant.

I look over at Gary, who is on the edge of his seat. He is eager to go next, so we begin with me as his girlfriend, Leigh.

"I gave myself to you, Gary! I thought you'd understand what it meant for me to let you be the *first*."

Gary answers almost sleepily, as though he's already been through this discussion a hundred times. "So why did you? You're almost thirty, for God's sake! It's not like I forced you! Hey, you don't want to have sex anymore? No problem! We won't have sex!"

"Just like a man!" I say, falsetto.

Gary breaks out of the role-play. "You got her pegged, Al. That's exactly what she'd say."

"Okay, Gary," I say, "how about her side? Tell me what you think she really wanted to hear from *you*."

"Oh boy, okay," Gary says, uncrossing his legs. "Uh . . . how about, 'Oh Leigh, you're the most wonderful lay I ever had. I sure do appreciate that you saved yourself just for me and I just can't *tell* you how privileged I feel.' "

The others are snickering, but Gary's on a roll: "And . . . uh, let's see . . . 'Oh, thank you, thank you, thank you. Let me get down on my knees and tell you how I never thought somebody would save herself for twenty-nine *long* years and then decide that I'm the special one who gets it. If I'd only known, I would have made it really special. I would have sent out for flowers, maybe a little brass band. Oh, please *do* forgive me.'

"That what you mean, Al?" Gary asks, grinning. He's almost out of breath.

"Well, is that really what you think she wanted to hear?"

"Yeah, it is, come to think of it. Maybe a *little* less ex-

aggerated," Gary answers. He's gaining his composure again, and he's slid back on the couch. "But you know, the thing is that I *didn't* feel all that. So what do I do? Go ahead and say all this stuff because she wants to hear it?" He looks around the room. "What are we supposed to be doing in this group, anyway—trying to be open and honest or learning lines to use on women?"

"We're here for honesty," I say. "You've still got to be you. But you'll have an advantage if you understand more about how she feels, regardless of how you choose to react to it."

Gary acknowledges this with a shrug. There are several other nods from the men on the couch.

I look over at Sean in his corner of the sectional, and he returns my gaze. "Ready to give it a shot?"

"Sure."

I begin again, this time as Sandi, his former girlfriend: "Sean, I've learned a lot of nice things with you about sex. But now I hesitate to have anything to do with you, because you're always grasping at every little hint that I might want to be your lover again. I need time to think. I have to consider my career and, well, lots of other things."

"Well, Sandi, at least that's more honest than you've been in a long time."

"You're right. I do wish it could have ended a little more nicely between us."

"But Sandi, if you'd be more up front with me like this, maybe we could still work things out."

"Maybe, Sean. I just need time to think about it, okay?"

"That's fair enough."

We end the role-play here. "Any reactions?" I ask in general, looking around.

"Aside from the fact that you deserve an Academy Award for Best Actress?" Gary quips.

I smile and wait.

"Well, I got a lot out of it," Gary picks up again. "I know that's how Leigh thinks—and I just now realized I can't handle it. I'm going to have to end it with her."

"That's your only choice?"

Gary seems mildly surprised. "I think so."

"What about the possibility of talking with her about how each of you feels about all that 'special stuff?' " I ask. "Maybe by having a talk like that, she'll understand better how your feelings about sex differ from hers." I pause. "You might have a chance to expand the relationship rather than run from it," I add.

"I don't know. I can see what she's saying." He shakes his head, looks disgusted. "Seems I should have learned all this relationship stuff in high school, like everybody else."

Ed looks over at me. "My reaction is that I kept hoping you were going to give me some advice on how to get Ellen to open up. I still haven't figured out how."

"Well, role playing is not really about giving advice," I point out as I look around at the other men. "Something did occur to me as we were doing the role-play, Ed: Are *you* really sharing your feelings with her? It might be a good idea for you to consider setting the tone by volunteering more of your own feelings—and I don't mean talking about intellectual things."

Ed nods slowly. He appears to be giving this some careful consideration.

I notice we only have a few moments left, so I try to wrap things up with Ed.

"This kind of problem isn't one you want to try solving after marriage," I tell him. "You need to learn to start communicating now—it's the only way you'll find out if she's really the woman you want to marry."

"I understand."

INTERPRETATION ————————

The multiple role playing in tonight's lively session has highlighted many of the difficult areas in these men's relationships and lives. As is often the case in role playing, it has been especially useful in helping the men understand their partners' positions, both how and why they feel the way they do. Several different elements of these relationships surfaced during the role playing: criticism and the damage it does to relationships; the confusion, poor communication, and resulting misunderstanding in sex and lovemaking; and the anger, frustration, and pain of failed relationships and marriages.

Tonight's session actually began on a slightly different note, however: Paul's absence. After his experience in the group last week (where Paul felt not only isolated but misunderstood as well), it is likely that the explanation for his absence goes beyond his illness. It has been my experience that there is a strong psychosomatic aspect to many illnesses, particularly those that are easily contracted: colds, flu, and the like. Paul's experience in childhood, where such misunderstanding or anger was punished by isolation because he had been "bad," could have laid the groundwork for feeling sick: here was something that would serve to isolate and protect him from the group. It is indeed regretful that Paul missed the session: he would have benefitted handsomely from it.

In fact, the real issues in this session surfaced as soon as Burt started with his one-word description of his mood: "Frustrated!" Clearly Burt and JoAnn are locked into a difficult position. Burt feels threatened and confused by what he feels is criticism from JoAnn, while JoAnn herself is frustrated and unsatisfied with some of Burt's sexual practices: bounding out of bed soon after his orgasm and occasional premature ejaculation. What really drives this dilemma is the dynamic of their encounters: JoAnn raises an issue by criticizing some-

thing Burt has done; Burt in turn takes this as an attack and immediately goes on the defensive. There is little doubt that the relaxed and comfortable mood needed for sensuality and sexuality vanishes here. The culprit in this case is criticism. I have come to believe that there simply is no such thing as constructive criticism in such cases. In most cases such phrases as "You're not satisfying me," "You only care about yourself," or "You're not good enough" immediately drive the partner to a defensive position. It is much more useful and constructive to use similar phrases to refer back to oneself: "I'm not feeling loved," "I'm frustrated," or "I feel neglected" not only are less threatening statements but they open the door to frank and open discussion as well. Not coincidentally, these are the phrases I've chosen for the women in my role playing. As we have seen, they have had the effect of prompting more open and honest dialogue.

One result of this dialogue is that Burt and JoAnn reveal a lack of understanding of what annoys or upsets the other. Burt does what he and many men feel is the natural thing after orgasm: get the condom off before he loses his erection and it falls off. It hasn't occurred to him that he needs to tell JoAnn this. Likewise, JoAnn has never let Burt know that this little excursion away from the bed leaves her feeling alone and abandoned. Unfortunately, such objections rarely surface until a whole multitude of minor complaints have accumulated and crossed some magic threshold, at which point a whole cascade of grievances spill out at once: "You have an orgasm too fast," "I can't stand it when you get out of bed like that," "I don't like not being able to continue" all come out at a staccato pace, and often leave the man, especially Burt, at a loss for words. It is important that such concerns be aired as soon as possible and not be left to accumulate and fester. This way they can be dealt with immediately and the two people can head off painful confrontations.

An excellent example of failed communications is dem-

onstrated in the role-play with Mitch. Like most men, Mitch wants to bring his partner to orgasm. I know from my work with Mitch that he has asked Janet how he could help her to have an orgasm, and Janet replied that she could enjoy sex without an orgasm. What doesn't surface until later is that Janet took Mitch's question as pressure for her to have an orgasm, and her reply is designed to simply take away this pressure. Mitch proceeds with his own satisfaction believing that Janet really doesn't need an orgasm, and the stage is set for the confrontation we observe in the role-play. A more straightforward reply by Janet in this case could have resulted in a different outcome: experimentation, mutual support, and encouragement.

Of all the men in the group, Gary probably has the best idea of what a woman wants in bed. Yet Gary's problem is an entirely different one. Gary is avoiding a strong connection to Leigh because he fears commitment and above all wants to keep from encouraging her in any way. In fact, Gary fears the feelings associated with commitment because he equates such feelings with addiction. Gary's way of keeping the emotions down is to use humor and stay light about the subject both in the role-play and in the relationship. At one point he even suggests that the solution is to break off the relationship. I immediately encourage Gary to consider options other than escaping or running away from Leigh, as they are likely to serve him better in the long run.

A lot of work in therapy is about considering other options. The realization that these options exist often grows directly from the kind of honest and straightforward dialogue we have had in tonight's role playing.

SESSION 5

///

WHEN MEN CRY

"When do you ever get over breaking up?" Sean asks in a slightly quavering voice.

In his worn jeans and tennis shoes, Sean looks the part of a typical student. Tonight he is sitting back on the couch, staring up at nothing in particular. His young, round face looks troubled. The other men are watching him carefully. Nobody speaks.

"There is no definite time period, Sean," I come in finally. I look around at the others, quite aware that each has a similar story of rejection and pain from some time in his life. "Anybody here have a similar experience?"

"Well, how long were you going together?" Paul asks with sort of a shrug.

Sean looks up at him warily. "A little over a year . . . uh, a year and two months," he says softly.

"What?" Paul exclaims. "A year and two months! Man, that's nothing. Try getting over a twenty-year marriage!"

"Hey, she was my first love!" Sean throws back, glaring straight at Paul. Burt and Gary exchange a smile and shake their heads, clearly in response to Paul's comment. Sean sits up suddenly. "And maybe . . . maybe we had more love in our twelve . . . uh, fourteen months than you had in your twenty-year marriage!"

Sean appears to be gaining some energy from this exchange. He's become a bit wide-eyed and his pale complexion is gaining some color.

"I've had a couple of letters from her, too, you know." Suddenly Sean frowns and seems temporarily lost. "They don't say much, though."

"Is there anything about wanting to get together again?" Burt asks from Sean's right elbow.

Sean shakes his head slowly. The energy has drained out of him by now.

"What do you want them to say, Sean?" I ask.

"I . . ." Sean stops abruptly and looks away. He is fighting tears but is determined to answer. "I want them to say that we'll get . . . get back together again." These last words break his resistance, and he begins to sob quietly.

A lot of uncomfortable glances are exchanged around the room. Sean waves his hand in my general direction: "Go on to someone else."

Now most of the men are sitting quite still as though they want to respect Sean's pain. Gary, however, looks as though he's about to climb the wall.

"Where are you, Gary?"

"What?" He's startled by the question.

I take a moment to shift my look in his direction. "How does seeing Sean's pain, his raw emotion, make you feel?"

"Awful!" Gary shudders. Something in Gary's tone makes this entirely believable. "I know how shitty I felt when I got

dumped a couple of years ago." He takes a deep breath. "It was very bad news. Remember, I told you guys about her. She was my 'addiction.' God, I was down on my knees with my arms around her legs and I just wouldn't let her go!" He ponders this for a long moment, and then looks up at Sean. "It's worse being dumped. Being the 'dumpee.'"

Paul is nodding his head vigorously.

"Actually, I let myself cry," he says straight to Sean. "It helped."

Sean cracks a weak smile but looks away.

"You know"—Gary brightens suddenly—"there's this lady that lives above me, and sometimes she gets into a snarling round with her boyfriend, and afterward I can hear her crying and moaning for half the damn night. *Nobody* hurts like *this* lady, let me tell you!" He looks around, but nobody says anything. "Well, I think, Oh my God, at least I don't feel as bad as she feels!" He slides back on the couch, seemingly satisfied with this explanation.

Ed is frowning at Gary as though he has no idea why he got off on this story in the first place. He looks at me for an instant and then down at his right foot, which is crossed over his left leg, Ed's perpetual pose. "Okay," he begins. "*My* biggest breakup"—he stops and looks at Sean—"it wasn't my first love, was about three years ago." Ed is speaking in a very matter-of-fact voice, almost like a reporter. "As far as I was concerned, this was *it, the* relationship. I was just sure we were going to get married. One night, right out of the blue, she dumped my ass. I was stunned." Ed looks to his right, where Gary is staring at him, listening intently. "I remember, I just felt . . . numb."

"So you're a 'dumpee,' too. Did you cry about it?" Gary asks.

"I don't really cry about anything," Ed replies. This appears to surprise even him. "I do have dreams about crying,

though. I dreamed I cried for my father once. It was a powerful dream: bitter, horrible sorrow."

Burt has cocked his head and looks puzzled. Ed sees him and realizes probably some explanation is called for.

"For most of my life my father, my parents, were in politics." He begins. "They were always away from the house. You know, going to parties, receptions, functions, and being seen. Of course they were both drinking like crazy the whole time, and one day it all just came crashing down: my father lost his job, his career, his whole life, really."

"How would your father feel if you were to cry?" I ask, trying to bring Ed back to his emotions.

Ed looks at me for a moment and then grows quiet. He is thinking. "He wouldn't take me seriously. Actually . . . you know, he'd walk away."

"Why do you think you were crying in the dream?"

"I'm not really sure if it was for myself or my father, his career, the fact that we were never close, whatever. I couldn't say."

"Ed, your deep sadness *is* coming out in your dreams," I point out. "This is how you are dealing with it. Your dreams are very powerful. I would encourage you to let yourself cry when you're feeling it."

Ed nods.

"Ed, let me ask you something," Mitch interjects. This is the first we've heard from Mitch today. "When you broke up"—he looks hesitant for a moment—"uh . . . when the woman broke up with you, did you ever talk about the reasons why, about what went wrong?"

"Nope. I just remember going home after that date in a daze." He looks Mitch straight in the eye. "I never spoke to her again."

"I want to say something," Sean injects. He is leaning forward now and is running his hands through his blond hair. "I really feel . . . dumb. Crying here. Before I came to group,"

he coughs, "really, it's been all week, I've been debating with myself: Should I bring all this mess up or just let it go?"

"What was your debate?" I ask. "Say it out loud."

"Okay." Sean pushes his hair away from his forehead, and I see that his swollen eyes have vanished. He has brightened considerably. "On the one side it was like—how would it sound to talk about the breakup? I mean, everybody here has been married six years, twenty years, or whatever; they've got all this experience." He clears his throat and continues. "But then, on the other side, I realized that I really do need to say something and the stuff in my life is important, too."

"Any reactions?" I look around at the men.

"Actually, I'm glad you did say something, Sean," Burt offers. "I sit here next to you every session, and you always look so preoccupied or . . . distracted, or whatever." He smiles. "Now I know what's been going on."

"Yeah, well, I don't think anybody ever gets over a love completely," Gary shrugs. "I know I think about Liz every day of my life."

Burt catches my eye and smiles. We had been discussing this very issue in individual therapy just yesterday.

"In therapy we imply that you get over it," I now say, "but I'm not so sure, personally. I think you always carry some love for the person you gave your heart to. Still," I add, "it's important to detach our feelings from one love relationship so we can focus that energy on others."

Burt nods, and Mitch smiles at me. He is leaning back on the couch with his arms spread wide.

"So," Paul says, looking at Sean, "do you go to pieces over other things, too?"

Sean looks at me then back at Paul. "Not at all," he assures him. "In fact, I've never fallen apart about anything else at all!"

"Do you cry, Paul?" I ask.

"Nope. Never do."

"What do you do when you're upset, then?"

"I get depressed." Paul is looking at me a bit defiantly.

"The two can go together, you know."

Paul doesn't say anything for several seconds. "My parents never showed any emotion about anything at all." He scratches his face and looks over at Sean. "I went out with a woman for two years in college. After we split, I couldn't do anything. I didn't date anyone for seven months. I just didn't have the energy. Then Sarah came along and I married her right out of college."

"So how are things with Sarah, Paul?" This is Gary, who's been carefully following Paul's relationship with his wife.

"I'm still seeing her—once or twice a week, remember?" Paul replies, looking over at Gary. "But she's the one who wants the sex."

Gary breaks into a broad grin. "So you're *servicing* her, huh?"

The whole couch breaks out laughing at this. Even Paul chuckles.

"Paul, you seem a bit out of it today," I say after things have settled down.

"Just been a bit down. My flu."

"Hey, Paul, if you were home with Sarah, would she be fixing you chicken soup?" Gary is grinning at Paul all over again.

"Are you kidding? She hates it when I'm sick. She pretty much ignores me."

"You know, your flu made you miss a great session last week," Burt points out. In the role-plays, Al played every girlfriend we ever had and didn't have to change his dress once!"

"I sort of like the one he had on," Gary cracks with a smile.

INTERPRETATION ——————————

In tonight's session, the pain and uncertainty of Sean's situation with Sandi laid the groundwork for the other men—specifically Gary, Ed, and Paul—to discuss two issues that are especially powerful for men: loss of love and control, on the one hand, and the ability (or willingness) to cry, on the other.

Sean, too, finds himself struggling with a powerful and profound loss in his broken relationship with Sandi. For the first time Sean finds the courage to speak up and start the group, as he is driven by the pain of this loss and a desire for support from the other men. In many respects, this group is foreign and detached to Sean; late in the session he describes how he feels here: a younger man with little of the experience or wisdom of the older group members. But nonetheless Sean still finds the strength not only to start the session but also to face Paul down when confronted. In this he is eager to defend the intensity of his love for Sandi. As his first relationship, this was the most powerful love experience of Sean's life. The intensity of love, like that of any emotion, depends on the individual, and Sean's ability to love grew from the love of his parents. In fact, Sean did come from a very physical family where a lot of touching and contact was the norm, so this more evident affection, an element missing in the families of the other men, allows Sean to express outwardly the warmer feelings, sadness and hurt, in crying. Sean is alone among the group members in his ability to cry in such a situation. It is much more of a struggle for the others.

The strongest resistance in this area is from Paul. In fact, Paul, unlike the other men, is unwilling even to extend an element of understanding or empathy to Sean—he dismisses the entire episode ("Man, that's nothing") by comparing it with his own dilemma ("try getting over a twenty-year marriage!"). Later in the session we learn that Paul never cries at all but

just gets depressed or withdrawn. This is a natural result of Paul's family setting in childhood, where emotion was simply not expressed: no crying and virtually no displayed emotion of any kind.

The two men also have difficulty connecting on any empathic level: Paul dismisses Sean's pain as a minor nuisance, while Sean himself has little appreciation for the magnitude of Paul's own loss, which extends far beyond just the loss of love and really constitutes the loss of an entire identity: husband, father, provider, and family man. Yet unlike Sean, Paul is extremely hesitant to express these feelings in any way that will make him vulnerable or will involve crying. So although the two men certainly have shared experiences of pain and loss, their different modes of expression prevent them from connecting on any meaningful, supportive level.

Gary, however, has been hurt badly before, and he has found crying, though not in therapy sessions, to be a healing release. The important difference between Gary and Paul here is that Gary is willing to admit to the group that he has felt rejected, unwanted, and unworthy as the "dumpee." This admission is a way of connecting to Sean and providing some support, and a difficult admission for a man to make. Traditionally, men want to see themselves in control. When a woman initiates a breakup, this puts the man in a powerless, vulnerable position. In fact, Gary's story reveals just how far this feeling of helplessness and desperation can go: he found himself begging her not to leave him.

Ed also relates how he was stunned by a woman who dumped him several years ago. The suddenness of the announcement, the fact that it was unexpected, seemed to surprise Ed more than the rejection. He does not react by crying or hurting but rather by abandoning the entire issue: he never speaks to the woman again. This was his way of coping, but it was not a healthy solution. With this choice Ed never learned why the relationship failed—even though in the ses-

sion Mitch thought it important enough to make a special effort to ask about it—nor was he able to learn how to avoid some of the same problems in his future relationships. Perhaps most important, Ed's refusal to experience the pain means that he carries a lot of hurt and sadness around with him. The fear of this happening again is part of Ed's difficulty in committing to Ellen. Yet he *does* have strong feelings, which come out in the dreams. We see these strong emotions in the dreams where he cries bitterly over his father and his early life with him. The fear of this happening again is part of Ed's difficulty in committing to Ellen.

Dreams are a potent medium for the subconscious mind and reveal a great deal about our inner selves and lives. I consider dreams to be valuable sources of material for work in therapy, and generally I will spend a great deal of time with patients in dream analysis and discussion. I have also found that the material in dreams is virtually always about the dreamer. In Ed's dream the pain is coming from inside: Ed was crying for himself and his loss of his relationship with his father and a yearning for a close, strong bond to him.

The repression of crying among men is common. All men learn at a very early age that crying due to pain, fear, or emotional trauma is not the thing to do. As young boys we all want to be "grown up," so we begin to suppress the urge to cry and continue to suppress it well into adulthood. Paul and Ed do so today, as we have seen in the session. Gary, Mitch, and Burt all defend crying as healthy and have cried at various times in their adult lives, yet they would not cry in a group session. Sean has cried in our session tonight and in doing so demonstrated the dilemma a man faces: Sean is very worried about looking "dumb" for crying, even though it is his natural response. It is gratifying that by the end of tonight's session the positive aspects of crying have become apparent: Sean is not only visibly relieved and alert, he is also more responsive and engaging in the group discussions.

///

MARRIAGE, COMMITMENT, AND REMARRIAGE

"I had a good weekend for a change," Paul announces to no one in particular. Paul is encased in one of his conservative blue suits that has gone a bit shiny with time. He appears satisfied with this announcement and looks around the group, but nobody responds.

"Yeah?" Gary says finally.

"Uh-huh." Paul looks vaguely relieved. "I went out with Sarah on Saturday and I had a date with this woman from the office, Annette, on Sunday night." Paul is beaming.

Burt meanwhile has leaned forward and is pulling nervously at his pants leg. I notice that Burt has on a bright blue and yellow wool sweater tonight, unusually colorful for Burt. Something Paul has said has got him going.

"Look, Paul, I don't want you to take this the wrong way, but . . . well, when are you going to make up your mind?"

"You think this is easy?" Paul is looking right at Burt.

"Look, I *know* it's not easy, I just wonder when you're going to move past it all." Burt has his hands spread wide open as though he's pleading with Paul.

"It's *not* easy," Paul continues as though Burt had said nothing. "Just being around Sarah for any time gives me the willies. But I can't bring myself to actually divorce her." Paul stops abruptly and looks over Burt and out the windows. "You know, I kind of like what we've got now: I get to see her on weekends, and I'm still free to do what I want the rest of the time." He looks back at Burt and smiles. "She wanted to know where I was on Sunday."

"So where is this going?" Burt asks. He is growing a bit impatient with Paul.

"Look, I've already stated my position to her. She knows it. Let *her* file for divorce." He shrugs. "Save me all the guilt."

Mitch is shaking his head. "No way. You'll still feel guilty."

Silence.

"Look, what's the deal with sex," Gary interjects, breaking the silence. "Didn't you two agree to just sleep with each other?"

Paul nods. "Yet Sarah must know that if an act of God lands another woman in my bed, I'm going to sleep with her."

Burt looks away and shakes his head. He probably suspects, as the others do, that it will be an act of Paul that lands a woman in his bed.

"Do you *like* sleeping with Sarah?" Gary asks with a grimace. He wants to stay with Paul on this, although his tone reveals he already knows the answer.

"Not really. It's for her, after all."

Gary nods. "Leigh and I ended up having sex again Saturday night." He shuffles forward on the couch and suddenly grows very intense. He looks over in Paul's direction. "I *don't* want to sleep with this woman! I don't even like lying next to a woman in bed. I can't get to sleep with her right there in

my face!" He has both hands open wide about a half inch from his face. "I'm not used to it and . . . it really pisses me off!" Gary is flushed a bit, and now both of his hands are clenched into fists.

"What happens when you do sleep with a woman?" I ask.

"I wake up every time she touches me," he mumbles. "You know, I used to think I was royally fucked-up because of this, but not anymore. I've just sort of accepted it." He shrugs. "The other women do, too."

"Huh?" Burt asks with a frown.

"Well, I should say my *last* girlfriend did. I didn't mind sleeping with her, actually." Gary has calmed down considerably and is actually smiling a bit. "But then, she was sort of small."

"What did *she* say about it," Burt asks, "your not liking to sleep with women, I mean."

"She said she understood. She also broke up with me, so who knows?"

"Yeah, well it bothers me, too, Gary," Ed says with a nod, "especially when it's hot and you get all sweaty." Ed is leaning back on the couch with his body angled roughly in Gary's direction. "One thing about Ellen: During the night she sort of inches over towards me, and at some point I have to wake her up and ask her to move over or she's going to push me right out of bed and out onto the floor!" A wide grin spreads across his face.

"So how *are* things with Ellen?" Mitch asks. "Get her that ring yet?"

Ed smiles. "We had a really nice dinner last night. It was her birthday."

"So what did you get her, Ed?" Mitch and Ed are just grinning at each other now.

"Actually, I bought her some hand-carved jewelry boxes she admired from a trip we took awhile ago."

I shudder with the vision of Ellen excitedly opening the

first small jewelry box in anticipation of a ring and finding it empty.

"Did she like them?" Mitch asks.

"She loved them." Pause. "She wants to move out of my apartment."

Nobody says anything.

"Because of the boxes?" I venture.

"I don't think so."

"How do you feel about her moving?" I ask.

"Well, it *does* bother me," Ed responds as he scratches behind his ear for what seems like an eternity. He looks at me. "I'm not as upset this time, compared to the first time— that is, when I first came in to therapy."

"I don't understand this. What's the problem?" Paul demands.

"Look, Paul, I'm just not sure I want to get married. I can't make a connection to Ellen. She won't talk to me." He's shaking his head. He looks like a young professor disappointed in a student. "I can't discuss anything, art, literature, that sort of stuff, with her at all—"

"Wait a minute," Paul interjects, uncrossing his legs and leaning forward. "You know what I want to do? I just want to reach over there and take you by the shoulders and just shake you silly! Make up your mind! What's the big deal, anyway? You two get along, you have good sex. Marry her already!"

"Were you listening to me at all, Paul?"

"Yeah, sure, you can't talk to her? Okay. Cheat on her by going to some Mensa meetings or something. You like her except for a couple of things, right? I don't like a damn thing about Sarah; well, I *care* about her, that sort of thing but . . ." Paul pauses. "I never really *liked* her." He gestures in Ed's general direction. "At least you *like* Ellen."

"Sure, I like Ellen. I think the two of us have different ideas about relationships, though, Paul," Ed responds, a little cautiously. He looks as if he's afraid to set Paul off again.

"Yeah, okay. But here's another question for you: Do you *know* what you really want from marriage?"

Ed frowns. "I do think about it a lot, in case you couldn't tell."

"No, no, I understand. That's not what I mean. It's just that I think marriages work out if people really believe in the institution of marriage." Paul shifts his weight in his chair and seems lost in thought for a brief moment. "Look at me," he continues. "I got into a marriage without even thinking about any of the stuff you're agonizing over, and even though I'm separated now—and I see Sarah every week—I felt more secure five years ago in a bad marriage than I feel right now!"

"Paul, Ed can't marry Ellen and just expect her to change," Burt protests.

"So marry her the way she is."

"No way," Burt responds. "It would never work."

Ed is watching this exchange go on like a Ping-Pong game.

"Can you say more, Burt?" I prompt.

"Sure," he says, smiling weakly at me. "I just don't think people change much unless there's some big event, like a major catastrophe, that's all."

"So you don't think people can change in ways other than through traumatic events?"

"No, people change, develop, grow, what have you, slowly as well. I just think it starts off with some disaster."

"I think that is true in most cases," I reply. "Usually it takes some crisis to force people to take a look at their lives." I am thinking about Burt's struggle with impotence. "Certainly both you and JoAnn have grown over the past several months at your own pace. You've been doing quite well at it."

Burt nods.

"I may have a crisis of my own at Thanksgiving," Ed says wearily.

Burt looks over at Ed, and we all wait for him to continue.

"The thing is, Ellen wanted to be engaged by Thanksgiving. Then we planned to get together with my folks for Christmas." He looks up at us and shakes his head. "I have a whole calendar of deadlines with this woman."

Burt takes this comment as addressed to him.

"Ed, it might be a good idea if Ellen knew you were trying this hard. Just tell her you are working on this problem of, well . . ." He struggles for a word ". . . hesitation."

"We have talked about it some."

"Yeah, well, this time talk about it after the holidays, okay? There are enough emotions to deal with this time of year without getting into all that, don't you think?"

"That's for sure. I'll keep that in mind." Ed smiles back at Burt but then scans the room nervously.

"What's going on, Ed?" I ask.

"Well, I'm a little worried. I sort of took the whole session today."

"I really wouldn't be too concerned about it," Paul says. "I don't know about you, but *I* certainly got something out of it."

"Such as . . . ?"

"I had no idea people gave so much time and effort just to the idea of getting married. I just jumped into it myself, didn't give it much thought, you know." Paul reflects on this a moment and then adds: "I never knew people went into marriage thinking about the possibility of divorce."

Mitch suddenly looks surprised. "This from the man who pushes prenuptial agreements?"

"Hey, Sarah is going to get half of everything I own. I can't afford dates as it is!"

"You know, I wanted to ask you about that," Sean pipes up from his corner in Burt's shadow. "What do you do . . .

no, well, um, how do you actually go about meeting . . . women?"

"I've tried a few things, but it's still real hard for me." Paul rustles uncomfortably in his chair. "There are dances, parties, that sort of thing advertised for singles in the Weekend section of the *Washington Post*. I've gone to a couple of those." He brightens a bit. "I think I'm going to answer a personal ad from *Washingtonian* magazine."

"What's the difficult part about it, Paul?" I ask.

"Have you tried being single after a twenty-year marriage?" Paul asks incredulously. He then looks away from me, clears his throat, and frowns. "The real hard part is this: I'm at a party and I go up to a woman who looks pleasant enough, and ask her to dance, and she just looks me straight in the eye and says *No.*"

"Yeah, well, I'm not having much better luck than you are, Paul," Sean says. "You know, people think things are just so easy on campus, that it's just a picnic picking up all these available women. But it just isn't true! At least for me it isn't." He shrugs.

Sean seems lost in thought. We only have a few minutes left in the session when Mitch looks over at Paul. "Paul, if you were getting married today, would you insist on a prenuptial agreement?"

"Yep, sure would. You should, too."

"No way would I do it," Gary objects. "Marriage is a big thing. If you're going to go through with it, you might as well go for the pie in the sky." Ed is nodding his assent. "I don't go for prenuptial agreements, contractual marriages, that sort of thing."

"Contractual marriages . . . ?" Sean looks bewildered.

"Sean," Ed explains with an impish smile, "a contractual marriage would be where you are up at the altar and the minister asks you, 'Do you take this woman to be your lawful wedded wife?' and you say, 'I do . . . for five years.'"

INTERPRETATION ─────────────────

One strong and recurrent theme in these group sessions has been the men's struggle with issues of commitment, attachment, devotion, and separation with the women in their lives. Tonight's group discussion has revolved around the two opposite poles of this struggle: Paul's attempt to come to terms with the end of his twenty-year marriage and Ed's inner debate over beginning a marriage of his own. Even Sean and Paul, who have found little common ground in group so far, attempt to make a connection on this issue: their shared contempt for dating and fear of rejection.

Of all the men in the group, Paul certainly has the most ground to cover in overcoming the problems related to the collapse of his marriage. For his entire married life Paul let Sarah define his role in the marriage and yielded to Sarah's decisions on virtually every aspect of their married life. Like Paul's mother, Sarah had the power. Now Paul finds himself in a separation with no guidance on how to behave. On the one hand, he finds himself clinging to Sarah as a means of reducing his separation anxiety and loneliness, a common response of recently divorced men. On the other hand, Paul is desperately pulling away from Sarah. In this session alone we learn that Paul doesn't "like a damn thing about Sarah" and that she just gives him "the willies." In fact, Paul's central dilemma now is that Sarah isn't around to tell him what to do. What Paul is looking for in our sessions, although certainly not consciously, is for someone to give him permission to divorce Sarah and to assure him that nobody will be mad at him if he does. Such a guarantee would also relieve Paul of any guilt. Yet it is exceedingly difficult for Paul to actually make this decision by himself.

Ed, meanwhile, is finding it difficult to make a firm decision to marry Ellen. The issues surrounding this relationship

are much more complex, however, as there really are two independent modes of thought and action going on here. For her part Ellen repeatedly tries to pin Ed down to a specific date—a deadline, in effect—and these dates come and go without even an engagement ring. What these deadlines do succeed in doing is upsetting Ed: He withdraws from Ellen and broods over whether he should actually marry someone like this. It would be more useful for Ed to confront Ellen and assure her that he *is* working on it (as Burt encourages Ed to do in the session) and that her continuing deadlines are doing nothing but making him angry. Some of this anger was spilling out in his choice of gifts. Ed's empty jewelry box was a bit too close to the "real thing" to be entirely innocent. This gift was an unconscious expression of his anger. Yet in response Ellen does not get openly angry as she should: She expresses her anger in an indirect way and once again tries to get even with Ed by threatening to move out, hoping to scare him into a commitment. Here Ellen drew attention to what was *not* included in the box, rather than to the gift itself. Their reluctance to confront each other openly has contributed to this situation where they are simply "stuck." In this respect, Burt's advice to Ed to approach Ellen with an honest, straightforward explanation is right on target.

One aspect of Ed's difficulty with commitment is reflected in his brief exchange with Gary. Both men are exceedingly uncomfortable sleeping in the same bed with a woman. In a previous session Paul, too, claimed that sleeping alone was a major benefit of separation. In this session Gary gets very agitated when he discusses having a woman "right in his face." Not coincidentally, these are the three men who are most reluctant to let women into their inner lives. The reason they are so disturbed and threatened by such a sleeping arrangement is that they feel vulnerable when sleeping. We are *all* vulnerable when we are near sleep. It is difficult for Ed, Gary, or Paul to defend himself, keep a woman at

bay, or run a mental "censor" when he shares a bed with a woman. Simply put, the men feel safer sleeping alone.

When sharing a bed was last discussed, Sean was shocked to learn that some of the other men preferred a bed to themselves. Sean continues to have a very rough time adjusting to Sandi's absence, both from his bed and his life. In tonight's session, Sean recognizes, to his credit, that he and Paul do share some problems and anxieties as the two men who have suddenly found themselves thrust into the dating world all over again. Dating is all the more difficult for these two men, as the relationships they are ending were with their first loves. In fact, neither Sean nor Paul was ever very comfortable with dating. Paul avoided going out altogether for a full seven months because he was rejected by a girlfriend. He later met, and married, Sarah. Sean is beginning to feel pressured by his friends into finding somebody new, and he's uncomfortable with these expectations ("People just think things are so easy on campus, picking up all these available women"). Both men want to avoid possible rejection because it is hard to deal with. I've found that most of the men in my practice who are "suddenly single" are intimidated by this fear. It is difficult for many men to make the transition from the security of a committed relationship to uncertainty and rejection in a new dating situation. For his part, Paul has found a few new avenues for social interaction, and this intrigues Sean, who has yet to really test the waters. Sean's reluctance lies in his silent hope that Sandi will eventually want him back.

SESSION 7

//

RESISTING CHANGE

"You know, Ed, I think I know how you feel," Mitch begins. Tonight his large frame is pitched forward on the couch, and he is speaking softly in careful phrases. "Last week Lynda gave me an ultimatum." Mitch's shaggy red head turns to Ed and he smiles slightly at this word. "She wants to be married by next summer." His gaze slowly moves to the floor.

Ed eyes me for a minute then looks back at Mitch. "Any reason for a deadline in the summer?"

Mitch nods. He is still examining the floor. "We planned to take a trip to Europe, and she thinks she wants to be married by then." His voice has trailed off to almost a whisper.

Ed and Burt exchange glances. We all wait.

"Mitch . . ." Ed says, but he stops himself abruptly and looks momentarily confused. "I thought you *liked* Lynda."

Mitch's head does another bob up and down, and he

takes a deep breath. "It's just I don't know if I'm in favor of . . . if I want . . . this marriage."

"Oh." Ed says nothing more. He seems to be digesting this when Paul begins to shuffle nervously.

"I don't understand this," Paul declares finally, peering right at Mitch. "Why won't you marry her?"

"It's not that I *won't* marry her, I'm just having trouble with the idea of getting married." He frowns and begins to pull nervously at his own fingers. "The whole idea of a fancy church wedding is just really . . . well, I really don't want it, and Lynda does."

"You were married before, right?" Burt asks from Mitch's left.

"Yeah, for six years."

Burt ponders this for a moment. "Well, Mitch, I understand why you want to ditch the church wedding idea. At least I think I do." Burt watches for some response from Mitch, but Mitch is just waiting patiently.

"Okay," Burt says, "a formal church wedding with the same friends, family, ceremony. They might think you're getting pretty good at this!"

"Yeah, plus it's an incredible hassle."

"Mitch," I say, "what else is there?" I've been watching Mitch carefully. His quiet, smooth voice and downcast mood tonight are very much unlike Mitch. "The cold feet you are having must be related to more than just a church wedding."

"Yeah, that's true. I'll tell you what," Mitch says, sitting straight up. "I liked Janet, too! Six years of marriage, everything sailing along fine, and then we hit the skids. I don't even want to *think* about it."

"Could you say more, Mitch?" I ask.

"God, do you know what it was like that last year? Five years of happiness and one year of hell. I was so unbelievably . . . *lonely*, I thought I was going to crack up." Mitch is examining the wall behind Paul and me. "I've just been thinking

about all the things that went wrong. All those things *I* did wrong." Mitch pauses briefly, then looks down from the wall at me. "It could happen all over again this time, you know. I was sure I'd be happy with Janet forever when we first started out."

"Have you discussed any of this with Lynda?"

He shakes his head. "Not yet. The odd thing is, we are communicating better than we have before, but I still haven't said a thing to her about any of this."

We all sit quietly with our thoughts for a while.

"Have you two considered some other arrangement, like living together first?" Burt offers finally.

"Well, yeah, I have, but Lynda would never go for it, and neither would her family, particularly her father." Mitch smiles. "We're talking a very traditional family here. And Lynda has never been married before, so this is all a big deal for her." Mitch shrugs, but he is slightly flushed now and appears to be a bit more self-conscious.

Paul catches his eye. "You know, the way you've been talking today, the way you look—it's sort of what happens to me when I'm depressed, or weak, or low on energy."

Mitch reflects on this. "It's not that, really, Paul. I'm . . . just a little uncomfortable in here today, talking like this." He lets out a breath. "And nervous, too, I suppose."

"What is it you're afraid of, Mitch?" I ask.

"It's just hard to do this in front of a group of men." He anxiously scans the other faces. "I don't know if you all will really understand me . . . or you might think, or say, some- thing about me that might really hurt . . . something negative, you know."

I nod at Mitch. "Speaking in front of people is really one of the hardest things to do, especially in here." I think it's important to give Mitch some encouragement, and he's been very open with the group today. "There aren't many of us

who want to hear negative things about ourselves, Mitch. It seems like a normal concern."

Mitch smiles appreciatively but says nothing further.
Silence.

"I had dinner with Sarah last night," Paul says glumly. He is leaning hard on his right elbow in the chair and seems more disheveled tonight. "I had to see her last night because she refused to see me over the weekend."

Gary frowns. "Weren't you supposed to see her *only* on the weekends?"

"That was our agreement, but all sorts of things have changed in the last couple of weeks. Two of Sarah's girlfriends are mad at her and they have her convinced that *I'm* using *her* for sex, if you can believe that." Paul is shaking his head sadly. "Plus, her mother told her the same thing, so now it's gospel truth!"

"So did you sleep with her or not?" Gary asks.

"Wait! I've been trying to avoid it, remember? Last night after dinner she announced, 'No more sex,' which was just fine with me. I'd be happy to have a brother-sister relationship, actually. So after we've settled all this, I'm happy as pie, and we're driving home, and now *Sarah* decides that 'hands-off' rule is a big turn-on, now *she* wants it!" Gary and Ed exchange smiles. "She came on to me so strong that I got right out of the car and walked off a ways. That stopped her cold."

"So you *didn't* have sex with her?" Gary wants an answer.

"Hell no, I didn't. *She's* using *me* for sex, remember? Not only that, I just felt terrible at dinner anyway. She spent the entire evening just blasting me for ruining the marriage, not giving her enough money, for leaving Abe alone at home with her, just about everything you can imagine." Paul is looking bitter. "So I didn't feel real sensuous."

Mitch looks over in Paul's direction. "What do you want from Sarah, Paul?"

"I want her to say that she likes the separation and wants to be independent. I don't want to be around her." He looks out the window. "The fact is, I'm happier alone than with her."

For a moment we are quiet.

Finally Gary starts to shake his head in recognition. "I know what you mean, Paul." He looks around at the others. "Did any of you see that article on bachelors in America in the *New York Times Magazine?*"

There are a few nods.

"I thought a lot of the bachelors in the article have some of the same problems we discuss in here," he continues, "like the reluctance to commit to a woman." He looks at me. "A lot of the men have just decided to live alone or get a dog. Some have just dropped out of the dating scene altogether." I get the feeling Gary is just reporting the article to me; I'm one of the men who hasn't seen it.

"How does this apply to you, Gary?" I ask.

He eyes me warily. "It makes me feel better about not being married, or living with someone, if that's what you mean." He smiles. "And I'm getting a hell of a lot more work done!"

"Will that be your whole life?"

He shrugs. "I don't know right now. It's just that I don't like the idea of a woman in my apartment. And there just aren't a whole lot of women around worth marrying, as far as I'm concerned." Gary folds his arms and sits back at this comment, confident that it is the last word on the subject.

Burt, however, doesn't leave this alone. "That might be okay for the next ten or twenty years, Gary, but what then? I don't think people want to live and die alone, do you?"

"Look, I don't know. But I'll tell you this: I'd have broken up with Leigh by now if I didn't think it'd disqualify me from group."

Burt frowns. "What in the world are you talking about?"

A flash of anger crosses Gary's face. "All we ever talk

about in here is our relationships with women! I figure if I haven't got one, I don't belong in this special club anymore. So I'm sticking it out with Leigh."

"That's the *only* reason you're still seeing her?" Mitch asks with astonishment.

"Yeah. And I'll tell you what else. This group is breaking into two halves. Me and Paul know how demanding women are. We know they'll just suffocate you if you let 'em." Gary's gaze shifts to Ed and Mitch in the center of the couch. "You two let yourselves be so damn manipulated by women, it's unbelievable! This is the way I see it: Me and Paul are the men. Ed and Mitch are just totally pussy-whipped."

"So where does that leave Sean and Burt?" Ed asks calmly. He has no reaction to being called "pussy-whipped."

"Well, I don't think Burt knows what he wants, but he's still trying to figure it out. Sean, well . . ." He shakes his head sadly. "Sean doesn't even know how much of a sucker he is. Sandi's got him." He cocks his head slightly in Sean's direction. "Sean, look, Sandi's probably not exactly sitting on her hands in Chicago, know what I mean?"

Sean looks away. Ed and Mitch exchange glances, but nobody says anything to Gary. Everyone is trying to absorb this outburst.

I decide to explore this further.

"Gary, try to relate your feelings about women to your family experiences."

Gary shrugs. "I came from a family of women, really. I was the youngest—I had three older sisters. Most of the time my poor mom was trying to defend herself against my father, who was totally out of control!" Gary rubs his mouth slowly and looks around. "I was a pretty normal kid."

"I'm wondering, Gary," Mitch says in careful tones, "do you think it's possible that you got a little spoiled by all this attention from the women in your family? Did you know what they wanted?"

"Sure. I did all the things boys normally do around the house. I took out the trash, washed the cars, raked the leaves, that sort of thing." He returns Mitch's steady gaze. "I don't think I'm much different from other men on this, you know. I think I know what women want."

Before Mitch can respond, Sean clears his throat and looks at me expectantly.

"I have something I need to talk about." He looks flushed and tense. "Look, I hate to butt in like this, but I have to tell you I won't be here next week. I'm flying home to Phoenix and I have a layover in Chicago. Sandi and I are going to meet for a few hours at O'Hare."

I see Gary roll his eyes.

"So are you looking forward to it?" Burt asks.

"Not yet. I'm too nervous—I just don't know what to expect." Sean is breathing slower and more deliberately. We all wait for him to continue.

"I don't even know what we'll talk about, to be honest."

"Are you going to ask if she's seeing anybody?" Gary asks with a hint of sarcasm.

Sean grimaces. "I dread the answer. But maybe it would do me some good to hear it."

"You know what I think you should do?" Paul exclaims with a smile.

"No, what?"

"Sneak up behind her and reach around and grab her tits!"

Sean looks stunned. Ed's face is buried in his hands.

"Okay, okay," Paul concedes. He looks disappointed in these two. "Try the Paul test instead."

"I'll bite." Sean looks less than enthusiastic. "What's the Paul test?"

"If she touches you, she's interested. If not: forget it."

Sean opens his mouth, but nothing comes out. Burt takes

this as an opportunity to move things away from where Paul is taking them.

"Sean, look. It probably is a good idea to find out where Sandi is. It will be better for you in the long run. Frankly, the way I see it, if this thing with Sandi isn't going to work out, you've got to get your heart and soul out of it."

"I'm trying, believe me."

INTERPRETATION

Change and the role it plays in these men's lives is beginning to take center stage at this point in the evolution of the group. Mitch finds himself resisting an enormous change urged on him by Lynda. Paul is still reluctantly accepting the changes in his relationship with Sarah. Gary confronts all the men with an accusation that the group itself has changed. Sean, too, has to deal with his changed relationship with Sandi face to face for the first time since the breakup.

Tonight Mitch's resistance to the idea of marriage was ignited by Lynda's ultimatum: Ed was quite accurate in his observation that until tonight's session, Mitch had spoken glowingly of his relationship with Lynda. Mitch is upset because he feels Lynda is forcing something on him. He resists the idea of being told what to do, even though the ultimatum applies to an event over a year away that once appealed to him. Certainly many other aspects of the marriage are unsettling and strange for Mitch: Lynda's desire for a formal church wedding and her reluctance to agree to a live-in arrangement. Added to this is the reality that Mitch prefers the status quo. He hates change, and marriage is an enormous one. So Lynda and her ultimatum represent a lot of new experiences for Mitch; so many, in fact, that they stir up his fear of failing in

a second marriage. But Mitch's decision to be in group means that he is committed to change. We know as early as the first session that Mitch claimed he entered therapy because he "didn't want to lose Lynda." Mitch simply doesn't want to be forced into a decision.

Tonight Paul feels cornered, too: He is confused, bewildered, and angry with the unpredictable changes in Sarah's behavior. The pressure on Sarah to end the sexual relationship with Paul came from her "support network": her friends and parents. In fact, their insistence put Sarah in a bind: She felt obligated to follow their advice to avoid losing their support. Once Paul has agreed, happily, to Sarah's demand, she reverses her position and urges Paul to have sex with her. It is encouraging that at this point Paul demonstrates some of the progress he has made by being able to refuse to have sex on demand and have more respect for what he feels. This represents a significant step for a man who did everything his wife wanted throughout their twenty-year marriage.

Sex on demand is a dilemma for Paul, as it is for many men. Men commonly feel that they should be able to have sex on demand, and that it is their obligation to provide it: They expect themselves to be ready whenever the woman wants sex. Traditionally it has been considered "unmanly" for a guy to say no. In this respect, Paul has been admirably insistent that Sarah respect his wish to maintain the "brother-sister" relationship.

Gary has been very forthright in tonight's group as well. As the talk of the men's relationships with women continues throughout our sessions, Gary feels increasingly isolated from the other men, because his relationship with Leigh is not going well at all. Gary *does* want to be an integral part of the group and wants to feel connected. His decision to confront the men is based on his view that the men either give in to women (and are therefore "pussy-whipped") or are bewildered and stuck in their relationships. His only real connection is to

Paul, the only other man who says no to a woman. Gary is taking a lot of risks in this confrontation: He calls the men names and takes the chance that he may generate anger and rejection. In fact, Gary is doing the group a favor: Not only has he broken the ice to encourage discussion of new topics, he has also made an opening (by his own example) for the men to confront one another. This will have a positive effect on their efforts to make stronger connections both here in group and in their life outside.

SESSION 8

//

THE MAN'S
BIOLOGICAL CLOCK

"So, how'd it go at the airport?" Ed asks with a hint of a smile. Ed seems more relaxed tonight—he's almost buried in the couch—yet he's eager to find out how things have worked out for Sean.

"Well . . . okay, I guess," Sean replies, looking quickly over at me. He appears to be surprised by the attention.

"So what happened, Sean?" Gary asks impatiently.

"It was pretty good, actually, considering our planes got rescheduled and I had to hike halfway across O'Hare to find her." Sean pauses and smiles with the memory. "She was standing there and I walked up and tapped her on the shoulder. She was so surprised to see me! She gave me a huge hug and . . . she kissed me, too." Sean's voice has gone soft now. His gaze shifts to some blank spot on the wall behind Gary.

"What kind of kiss?" Paul demands. "Sister? Mother? Lover?"

"Huh?" Sean looks startled, then seems to remember the Paul test. "Oh . . . it was good—not real passionate, but it made me feel a whole lot better." He grins back at Paul, who shrugs and looks over at Gary. Gary has the beginnings of a smirk on the corner of his mouth. He looks as though he's about to say something, but he clears his throat instead and looks at the floor.

Sean shrugs. "We only had five minutes, you know. We talked about seeing each other at Christmas—same place— the airport. I'm thinking of going to New York in January, too."

Gary catches my eye, and he looks impatient, but it's Ed who speaks. "What does Sandi think about it?"

"We haven't made plans yet," Sean answers quickly. "I just can't deal with asking her right now. I've got too much going on in the lab and about three weeks before exams—"

"Look," Paul interjects suddenly, "when are you going to make up your mind about this?"

Sean stops abruptly, shocked at the interruption, but Paul is on a roll.

"Can't you see how wishy-washy you're being? Not only that—you're boring me to tears!"

Down the couch, Ed's jaw suddenly hardens, and he glares at Paul, who is looking defiant. Gary is mildly amused.

"Thank you for the encouragement, Paul," Sean replies dryly.

"You know, Paul," Burt says calmly, looking directly in his eyes, "I don't know why you're so impatient with Sean, anyway. It's taken him, what—four weeks?—to open up like this in here, then you just shut him down with all this 'wishy-washy' stuff." Burt is shaking his head. "Not real supportive, in my book."

Sean senses an opening and jumps in.

"I don't see that I'm any more wishy-washy than you are with Sarah, Paul! When are you going to make up your mind on Sarah? You ever going to divorce that woman?"

"Some comparison. I was married to her for twenty years!"

Sean rolls his eyes. "Here we go again."

"It's not some adolescent romance," Paul adds as an afterthought.

Burt and Ed start to chuckle at Paul's notion that it was an "adolescent romance," but Mitch is shaking his head slowly in disgust.

"Mitch?" I ask.

Mitch's gaze meets Paul's. "I'd be really pissed if you ever put me down like that. Reminds me of what my father used to do." He leans forward on the couch and suddenly seems much bigger. "I wouldn't stand for it."

Paul's eyebrows rise in mild surprise. "I didn't mean it as a put-down."

Mitch looks skeptical.

"Paul, does Sean remind you of Abe right now?" I ask.

I notice that Sean is momentarily confused, but he seems to then remember that Abe is Paul's son.

Paul nods. "Yeah, he sort of just goes on pointlessly, too."

"So you get impatient with Abe like this?"

"Actually, I guess I do." This is enough to slow Paul down. He pauses for a while to examine one of the ferns in the corner. "Come to think of it, Abe *is* pretty talkative at first, but after about twenty minutes or so, he quiets down. You know, he doesn't say anything at all. I have to start asking him questions or the conversation would just die." Paul grows silent at this and looks around expectantly.

The room is quiet.

"In fact," Paul comes alive again, "I remember the other day I was taking Abe and Betty to the mall, and out of no-

where Abe interrupts this conversation I'm having with Betty
and tells me to quit yelling at her. I really didn't know I was
yelling at her in the first place!"

"Why *were* you yelling at her, Paul?" Burt asks.

"Oh, I don't know. Some stupid thing she did."

This cracks up half the men on the couch, but Paul looks
momentarily bewildered.

"Look, Paul," Burt offers with a wry smile, "you can't
expect Abe to talk to you for more than that twenty minutes
if you're constantly down on him."

Paul pauses, then leans over toward me. "Do you think
I'm down on Abe all the time?"

Before I can answer, Sean interjects: "I do."

Paul and Sean exchange looks, but neither speaks.

"I think you're treating Sean like you treat your own kids,"
I reply to Paul. I've decided to answer a slightly different
question from the one Paul asked. "You treat your kids as
though what they say is unimportant. You treat Sean as though
what he feels, his relationship with Sandi, is unimportant."

"Oh." Paul looks at me momentarily, then peers at the
floor. He seems to be willing to give this some consideration,
so the group falls silent once again.

Finally Ed smiles, and sits forward. "Good news," he announces. "Ellen gave me a stay of execution."

"So that's why you look so relaxed today," Gary says,
nudging him in the arm.

"Yeah, it's true. We talked things over and decided there
are a few problems we really have to work on before we could
ever be serious about marriage." He shrugs. "I felt a whole lot
better."

"How does Ellen feel about it?" Burt asks.

"Actually, I think she was relieved, too. Things were a
whole lot lighter between us the whole weekend."

Burt nods, but Gary is frowning.

"I don't understand why there was the pressure in the

first place," he says. It's not clear if this is a question or a statement. Ed treats it as a question.

"Ellen talks a lot about the fact that she has only a limited number of eggs left, and each month, there's one more gone, so she's running out of time."

He looks at Gary expectantly, but Gary is silent.

"I'll tell you," he sighs, continuing, "I'm sure glad we worked this out. I dread the idea of losing her, having to date all over again . . . being alone."

"You're really lucky, you know," Paul says, gesturing in Ed's direction. "You're a man who's having his cake and eating it too. Two years of living with a woman, good sex, a relationship—and you don't have to get married."

"We're still discussing it."

"I know. I'm just jealous of you. I'd sure like that kind of deal."

"You're jealous? Paul, I've never heard you talk like that before," Ed says with a faint smile.

"I know. I'm trying to be more understanding." Paul looks uncomfortable. "I don't want everybody to think I'm an asshole."

"Who called you an asshole?" I ask.

"Well, nobody did. You guys . . . I just get the feeling you think I'm really insensitive."

I look around at the men. "Reactions?"

"Yeah, I have a reaction," Sean says suddenly. "Fuck *you*, Paul, I'm twenty-three years old and no adolescent."

Gary, Ed, and Burt are dumfounded. They look from Sean to Paul and back to Sean.

Sean is flushed, but he's not through with Paul yet. "Sandi meant as much to me as Sarah did to you." He looks over at me. "I guess I *do* think he's insensitive!"

The men share a laugh that breaks the tension.

"Okay"—Paul holds up his hands—"I know. But it's true— you *do* remind me of my son, and he *is* an adolescent."

"Okay, Paul, but I'm not. Don't think I'm just going to sit here and take this kind of treatment."

"What kind of treatment? You want me to be softer? I don't want to sit here and try to figure out how to say something more politely, you know. I just want to be myself! I'm tired of being attacked."

"Who do you feel is attacking you?" I ask.

"Burt," he responds. "Every time I get into something with Sean, he jumps in on his side."

I know we won't resolve all these issues tonight, but I hope Burt can at least give Paul something to take with him before the end of the session. I look in Burt's direction, but he's already sitting forward, ready to go.

"I don't intend to attack you, Paul," Burt says, "it's just that I think Sean deserves the time in here. You have plenty, you know. Also,"—he spreads his hands wide in Paul's direction—"I thought *you* got something out of that exchange: Now that you know more about how your children see you, maybe you have an idea of what to do about it."

Paul is frowning, but he looks at Burt and slowly nods.

INTERPRETATION ——————————

This was the first major confrontation between group members. At eight weeks into the group process, the men have not only learned the value of open, honest exchanges, but they have also begun to reap some benefits from the resulting confrontations. This interaction is a valuable component in group therapy, because it allows each member to learn his effect on others and also to apply this learning after practicing in the safety of the group.

Tonight's confrontation between Sean and Paul was set

up by Sean's report on the events with Sandi in the Chicago airport. Sean paints a rosy picture of what was actually a very brief encounter with Sandi in a crowded public place. In the process, Sean reveals his idealistic view of the relationship and his unwillingness to act on either Gary's or Burt's suggestions and encouragement to move beyond this point. Paul grows impatient with Sean because he is waiting for any facts that would indicate the situation has changed. When none are forthcoming, he jumps in with a demand for facts ("When are you going to make up your mind about this?"). We soon learn that Paul treats Sean much like he does his son Abe. Tonight it's almost as though Paul is quizzing his own son by demanding that he get to the point, while Sean/Abe clams up as soon as he feels Paul's critical attitude.

In fact, Sean does not engage Paul until Burt intervenes. Then Sean accuses Paul of being wishy-washy, too, while Paul once again dismisses Sean's "adolescent" relationship. At this point, the other men, particularly Mitch, are becoming agitated at Paul's condescending attitude toward Sean. In truth, Paul's impatience with Sean mirrors his impatience with his son, Abe. Paul's very limited range of emotions and responses to his children resulted from a severely emotionally deprived childhood. He has lacked empathy, patience, and curiosity in his relationship with both Abe and Betty, which is the same treatment Paul received from his parents. Much of Paul's "hardness" is merely a cover for a frightened man who wants to be liked by others.

Paul exposes some of his vulnerability by admitting that he fears the men think he's an "asshole." Paul chooses this term, even though it's never been voiced here. Paul feels attacked by Burt anytime he gets into a confrontation with Sean. Paul's right, in one sense—Burt's clearly responding to Sean in the same way as Paul: as a father. Burt wants to be a father more than anybody in the group. He senses Paul's harsh attitude toward Sean, so he naturally comes to Sean's rescue as

the "good father" he wants to be, something he missed with his own father. Burt had a highly judgmental, critical father, and his strongest desire is to avoid this when he's a father. Sean is the beneficiary of Burt's fatherly kindness in group.

Although Sean's blunt rebuke of Paul seems caustic, it was important for Paul to hear it. It is likely he would shrug off a confrontation of any less intensity. This one has captured his attention. If Paul chooses to follow these suggestions, this encounter could prove to be a valuable catalyst for improving his interaction and connection with his own children.

SESSION 9

//

VIOLENCE:
A MAN'S SHAME

"I don't know what to do about Betty," Paul begins with a slow shake of his head. "She'll be home for the holidays. I've got to take her for three whole weeks." He is rubbing his forehead so intensely I'm suddenly worried he'll leave a bruise.

The room grows quiet. Mitch coughs into a cupped hand but says nothing. We wait for Paul to continue.

"She could do anything, you know, she's got the run of my apartment. Last time she stayed with me she ran up ninety bucks in long-distance calls on my number!" Paul pounds his armrest for emphasis. "I made her pay for those and I'll be damned if I'm going to pay this time either!"

Gary is eyeing Paul cautiously; he's not sure it's safe to come in with a question right now.

"Paul," Gary says finally, "why is she staying with you if you don't want her?"

"It's not that I don't *want* her, I'm just afraid I can't *handle* her." He shrugs. "She's a teenager. She just does whatever she wants." Paul looks right at Gary. "What if I have to go on a business trip?"

"So?"

"So she'll have a couple dozen teenagers over in my apartment in ten seconds flat. What a joy. Plus the place just reeks of smokes when she's around."

"You could just tell her not to smoke in the apartment," Mitch suggests with a shrug.

"I've tried that. It works for about three days, and then she just blazes up in front of me."

The door pops open suddenly, and Burt walks in. He shuffles a bit as he crosses the room and sits in the center of the couch. Paul's eyes follow Burt's progress to his seat. Burt looks up at him apologetically and motions for him to keep going.

"But I do have the last word on what goes on in the apartment," Paul continues. "If she gets totally out of control, I'm still bigger than she is, so I'm sure I can handle it."

"You're *bigger* than she is?" Gary asks.

Paul nods.

"What are you going to do, pound her into submission?"

"Uh . . . well, no. It's just that she's gotten so big she intimidates Sarah, and I'm not letting her do that to me."

I notice Burt is looking terribly uncomfortable during this. He's rubbing his chest slowly and frowns every time Paul speaks. I catch his eye, but he looks away quickly.

Gary is nodding. "I remember one time in my life when I got that way: violent with a woman, I mean. It only happened once. I was living with this woman right after I turned eighteen. I came home drunk one night, and we got into a terrible, violent fight. At one point I just hauled off and smacked her halfway across the room." He's shaking his head in disgust. "It was awful." He looks up at Paul. "I think there's

some basic character defect in me that comes out when I'm drunk. I've been sober for six years, and I've *never* had the urge to do that since."

Paul nods slowly. "I've had to get physical with Sarah. Not hit her, but one time I had to restrain her after she—*she*, mind you—attacked *me*. She wanted to scratch my eyes out! I had to pin her down and wrap her in the bed sheet just to hold her down!"

"Look, I'm not feeling well, you guys," Burt says abruptly. He's slightly flushed, and his right hand continues to massage his upper chest.

"It started at work this morning, this pain in my chest, and up here." He motions to his shoulder. "I don't know, maybe it's the way I have to hold the fiddle during practice."

"What's the feeling, Burt?" I ask.

"I'm a little worried. I've been thinking about my father. He died of a heart attack."

We are silent for a moment.

"I know what that's like," Paul says. "My father died of a heart attack, too." He shifts to face Burt a bit more directly across the glass table. "Last year I had a pain right there"—he indicates his upper chest—"and I went to a walk-in clinic for an EKG. I'm glad I did; it was an incredible relief to know that I was okay."

Burt nods and looks over at me. "Maybe I should head over to G.W. Hospital and get checked out."

"I think it's a good idea," Paul states emphatically.

"Are you scared?" I ask.

"A little."

"Burt, you're free to go, if you want to, but I think you will feel better if you talk about your feelings. Was any of the discussion bothering you?"

Burt shakes his head.

"Then I think he should play it safe. Get a doctor's opinion," Sean interjects. He is worried about Burt.

"I don't know what to do," Burt says.

I sense the eyes focused on Burt and me. I don't want to push Burt out the door and alarm him, yet I don't feel comfortable forcing him to stay in the group.

"It's your choice, Burt," I say.

"I'd better go," he says, rising slowly. He retraces his route back around the table. I meet him halfway and walk him to the door.

"Please call me later and let me know how you are feeling," I say.

He nods and closes the door behind him.

There is a stillness in the room as the men exchange nervous glances.

"Do you think he should have gone?" Gary asks.

"It probably was a good idea," I respond. "He needs the physical check first, then we can talk at our next session." I pause and smile at Gary. "It wouldn't make sense to keep Burt talking if he's really having a heart attack."

Gary laughs and looks over at Ed, who is grinning broadly. Sean and Mitch both look relieved; Mitch's arm is now draped across the back of the couch. The tension in the room has mostly lifted. Everyone seems glad Burt is getting checked out.

I decide to take the conversation back to where we were before Burt's problem.

"So, Gary," I say, shifting my weight in his general direction, "was there any violence in your family when you were young?"

Gary shrugs. "Not really. No smashed heads, no broken bones." He pauses. "I had a few run-ins with my dad, though. He could be a real macho asshole." Gary is shaking his head and gazing out the windows. "He'd butt up against me with his chest and give me the old 'I dare you to hit me' routine. What a jerk."

"So did he actually *hit* you?" Paul asks.

Gary eyes Paul for a moment and then nods.

"Once when I was sixteen, I was six feet tall by then, I was doing the dishes, minding my own business, when he came up from me on my blind side and slapped me hard across the face with the back of his hand." Gary stops and looks over at me. "I told him right there that if he ever hit me again, I was going to hit him back. He knew I meant it."

"Did you ever do it?" Mitch asks. He is sitting forward on the couch, and his leg is bobbing up and down nervously.

"Nope, but I came close." He stops momentarily to reflect. "There was one time at the dinner table." He looks over at me and smiles slyly. "I guess I wasn't practicing my Emily Post manners, so he took his dinner fork and slammed it down through my right hand. Damned near pinned it to the table."

Sean is staring wide-eyed at Gary in disbelief. "He actually *did* that to you?"

"Sure." He holds out his hand to reveal several small dots by his right thumb.

Paul is shaking his head. "Never had any of that with my parents. They were real passive, quiet, reserved."

Mitch clears his throat and manages to stop his bobbing leg. "Well, I've had my share of problems with the old man, but he's never actually whacked me." He looks over at Gary. "Usually he just screams at me until I've had enough and I just clam up."

Gary nods.

"What are you feeling as you're telling this, Gary?" I ask.

"Well, I don't feel very good about it." He eyes me warily, "It wasn't a happy time. It's hard to go over it all again. I guess I'm sorta . . . well, embarrassed."

"Embarrassed suggests shame." I pause. "What are you ashamed of?"

"Maybe I'm the one who goofed. I feel ashamed at blaming my father for something that wasn't his fault. I probably

could have avoided the whole thing by avoiding *him*. I could have moved out."

Mitch is nodding, but Paul leans toward Gary on his left.

"So why didn't you?" Paul asks.

"Well, I tried, when I was sixteen. But . . ." he lets out a long sigh and stops.

"But . . . ?" Paul prompts.

"But my mother threatened to commit suicide if I did," Gary says emphatically, peering straight into Paul's face.

Ed shakes his head in disbelief. Paul breaks away from Gary's gaze and looks at me a little sheepishly.

"So you stayed?" Mitch asks.

Gary nods. "I had to, for Chrissake. For another two years."

"Gary," I say, "you are carrying around a lot of guilt, about *not* being responsible enough."

Gary shrugs. "Probably true."

"You were being burdened, Gary. You parents had a responsibility to help you grow up," I continue. "Instead you were threatened and abused. It doesn't have to be broken bones, a swollen face, or black eyes, you know. Your father drew blood with a sharp fork—that's abuse. Your mother made you responsible for her life—that's abuse."

Gary looks at me and nods. "My old man always ragged on me, too—he was always putting me down. He could really make me feel like shit."

"It's hard to grow up believing those put-downs," I say.

"Yeah, well, it was no picnic. It makes me feel for kids, teenagers trying to figure out their lives on their own." He's got Paul in his intense gaze now.

Paul stares back but remains silent.

"I think you're being narrow-minded about Betty," Gary says at last. "She's just a teenager with a lot of energy, Paul. Try going to a bar in Georgetown and check out how much energy is floating around in there."

"I know. I just don't know how to handle it," Paul says a bit defensively.

"Paul, why not consider some alternatives with Betty," I offer. "You could call her to talk and let her know you're feeling anxious about her visit."

Paul shakes his head. "I'm not sure how I'd even approach it."

"Well, a good start would be appreciating that this visit is an adjustment for both of you—she's probably just as anxious as you are. You'll both feel better talking ahead of time."

"Okay." He nods, looking over at Gary. "I'll think it over."

Gary looks pleased with this outcome. He looks at me, then at Paul, and smiles.

INTERPRETATION

Paul's anxiety over Betty's visit in tonight's session has focused attention on the struggle many men face to be successful, loving, and empathic fathers. Having endured a difficult, emotionally deprived childhood, Paul finds fatherhood trying, demanding, and ultimately vexing. His efforts to connect with his daughter falter, and communication between them becomes even more difficult. Paul's own childhood experiences were limited, so his range of understanding of his daughter is equally limited. Gary helps Paul to see the narrow-mindedness of his approach, and in doing so he reveals in some detail the sad events of his own abuse at the hands of his tyrannical father. In fact, tonight's session becomes a forum for discussing violence (Gary's adolescence) and dominance (Paul's physical struggles with his wife). This conversation becomes so threatening to Burt, whose childhood fears were of his father screaming out of control, that it magnifies his physical discom-

fort. His fear of the rising pain in his chest drives him to seek medical attention. His discomfort grows as the discussion becomes more graphic and threatening.

This discussion is launched by Paul's view of Betty as a "problem." Paul's anxiety toward Betty is natural, since Paul himself was treated like a perpetual problem by his anxious mother. Her children were problems that she needed to control. In fact, on many occasions in his early life Paul was confined to his room, locked in the clothes closet, or placed on the toilet for several hours at a stretch just to relieve his mother of having to deal with him. As an adult, Paul entered a very traditional marriage in which his wife was responsible for the children and in which he adopted the same notion that his children were simply potential problems. Now that Paul is separated, he is having to deal with his children, for the first time in his life, on a one-to-one basis. Rather than considering the possibility that he and Betty may both be anxious about the visit, Paul views the entire situation as threatening: one he must control. Gary and I both help Paul see that Betty is probably equally uneasy and upset at having to stay with Paul at all. It is important for Paul to think of Betty as his daughter: a young woman who is troubled and confused by the separation, and one who needs his guidance and assurance that he won't desert her, too.

Gary's questions to Paul lead to some powerful revelations about Gary's own adolescent life. Tonight for the first time he reveals some of the physical and emotional abuse of his adolescence, although he never recognized this as abuse before. During his early childhood Gary was his father's favorite, and his father was proud of him. As Gary moved into adolescence, his need to establish independence and individuality was perceived as a threat to his father: His father simply did not recognize Gary's need to grow. The abuse and arguments started on this issue, and Gary grew increasingly unhappy and confused by these attacks because he had no idea

what caused his father's severe anger. Gary, like his parents and sister, turned to alcohol as an escape from this treatment. In so doing, Gary was incorporating his father's abuse and dislike of him by now abusing himself with alcohol. When Gary got his father to quit hitting him, he started hitting himself. In tonight's session, I urge Gary to recognize that he was indeed abused. Once he is able to confront this reality, other feelings surface: embarrassment and shame over his father's behavior, and guilt from the belief that he was responsible by not successfully avoiding his father. The latter is another example of Gary beating up on himself—of blaming himself for his parents' insensitivity.

As tonight's discussion focuses on rising levels of parental tension and even physical violence, Burt, who fears violence in any form, becomes increasingly agitated and upset. This topic hits Burt from two directions: It is his worst childhood memory—escaping from his screaming father—and it also touches on his special concern: What kind of a father will he be? Will he repeat his own father's mistakes? In this session, these two worries drive his anxiety way over the threshold. Burt was not having a heart attack—he was having an anxiety attack. It was my decision to give Burt the choice of how to deal with this attack, hoping that he would stay and confront the emotional, yet willing to accept his need to attend to the physical. He chose to leave, thereby avoiding the talk of violence that so intimidated and unsettled him. He will have to confront his fear later.

SESSION 10

//

IMPOTENCE: A MAN'S HUMILIATION

Burt is toying nervously with his wool pants. Several minutes have passed since I closed the door, and nobody has said a word. All eyes are focused on Burt. He is growing increasingly self-conscious as the silence continues.

"Okay, Burt, I'll bite. How are you?" Ed asks from behind his horn-rimmed glasses. Tonight I am struck by how strongly Ed resembles a young, ambitious scientist. Only the lab coat is missing.

"Oh." Burt looks up, startled. "I'm okay." He shrugs. "Well, my heart is okay." He smiles weakly.

"Burt," I ask, "do you remember what we were talking about last week when you left?"

Burt nods. "Sure." He gestures in Gary's direction. "You were telling us about what happened with your girlfriend: the time you hit her when you were drunk."

110

Gary nods back at Burt but says nothing.

Burt looks back at me expectantly.

"What were you feeling then?"

"I was worried about my heart!"

". . . and your feeling?"

"I guess . . . anxious."

"And what feeling do you connect with violence, Burt?"

"Fear. I was afraid." Burt pauses a moment. "And definitely *more* anxious." He smiles. A lot of the tension has gone out of Burt's shoulders; he's a bit more relaxed.

I wait for him to go on.

"Well, you got me going, too," he says, looking back at Gary. "I do remember getting very uptight. But I'm okay tonight." His gaze drifts back to me. "We can talk about something else now."

"Let's stay here for a minute, Burt," I say. "What else is making you nervous?"

He eyes me for a minute then leans slightly forward.

"Okay. I'm worried about this." He taps the ear with the hearing aid. "I've got a sixty percent hearing loss in this ear and I'm going to have an operation on it this week."

Ed winces. I notice Paul nodding with assurance.

"I think I have a hearing loss, too," he says. "Half the time I can't hear Abe even when he's in the same room." He shrugs. "Must be getting old."

Burt frowns. "Getting older really worries me, you know. I feel myself slowing down." He is examining his broad hands from behind. "Cuts, little things. They're taking a lot longer to heal."

"How involved is the operation?" I ask.

He shakes his head. "It's minor surgery. It'll take about an hour and a half. Still . . ." He pauses and looks right at me. "I don't want to go under the knife."

"I can understand that," I say, nodding slowly. I pause for a moment. "You know, it's really a normal feeling. Being

scared. The way I see it, minor surgery is when it's surgery on someone else!"

Burt seems relieved at this, then nods.

"I'd hate to have somebody cutting up *my* ears," Ed says with a shudder.

Burt's eyes shift to Ed then back to me. "Well, maybe that's why I'm so uptight lately. Plus the house is in ruins. Everything is unbelievably hectic." He begins to rub the back of his neck. "JoAnn is moving in and she's redoing things all over the house. Plus the workmen have been in and out all week."

Gary coughs and looks past Burt out the window.

"So what did I miss out of your life from last week?" Burt asks, trying to divert Gary's attention from the window.

"A lot." Gary's gaze shifts down from the window to meet Burt's.

"So . . . ?"

"So that's what you get for having a heart attack, or anxiety attack."

"And you're not going to tell me."

"That's right. You miss things. You've got to be here to play."

Gary is not going to budge. He is engrossed in examining the carpet. Finally he looks up at me.

"You know, the thing is, I don't even know why *I'm* here. When we first started this group, I thought we'd be talking about relationships. My relationship hasn't changed that much, and I'm getting bored with this damned issue. I want to talk about something else."

"Reactions?" I ask, looking around the room.

Burt is rubbing his mouth slowly. I sense he is still a little disturbed by Gary's last response to him.

"Well, I know I'm excited after some sessions and not so turned-on by others," Burt says with a shrug. "The beginning sessions in here were a lot more spontaneous, I think. It seems

people are holding back a lot more now." He says this straight to Gary.

"Hey—I talked more than anyone last week!"

"I think *you're* holding back more now," Ed interjects, looking to Burt on his left.

"What?"

"I don't think you've said much in group, at least compared to the rest of us." Ed has skidded forward on the couch to face Burt more directly. "In fact, when you got all upset last week, I thought you were getting ready to drop out of the group!"

"Oh . . . well, I never really thought about that. I *like* group. I like being able to talk to you guys without having to worry about what people will say."

"Yeah, this is the only place you can really do it, you know," Paul says. "I can get away with saying things in here without having to face any of you at dinner or in a meeting." Paul rolls his eyes.

"What's your reaction about group so far, Ed?" I ask.

"Well, it makes sense to me on two levels."

Suddenly I have this vision of Ed donning a white lab coat and getting ready for a lecture.

"On one level we can work together on a common problem as a group. On another level it's valuable to have a bunch of men together, because, well, let's face it, men rarely open up like this, so . . . maybe it will help us all on the outside." Ed looks surprised that he ended with this statement.

"You're right," I say. "Everything you learn in here is absolutely applicable outside. Still what are the *feelings* that go with that thought, Ed?"

He smiles. "It's helped me. It's true. I can speak up a lot more now when before I'd just stay quiet. I can see it at work. I'm talking to more people and they're coming to me a lot more for my opinions." He pauses to examine the glass table.

"Now that I think about it, I actually can talk about Ellen more, too."

Silence.

"Well, I can't figure out if I'm moving forward or what," Paul says finally. "Now that I'm ready to buy a condo, I just don't know if it's the right move. Maybe I should buy a house instead. I don't even know if I'll get the loan." Paul is shaking his head slowly, then abruptly stiffens. "What if Sarah finds out and tries to take half of it?"

"I wouldn't worry about that," Mitch says suddenly.

"Oh?"

"Paul, I really think all this is a smoke screen for deciding about Sarah. You've got to do something about that, make a commitment to change, go through with the divorce, something, I don't know."

Paul nods. "I just got so used to it. I *liked* being married. But I'm not getting involved with any other women now."

"It might be a little soon for you," Burt says across his folded legs. He shrugs. "I don't know, Paul, you still seem so, well, so *angry* with women still."

Mitch nods in agreement.

Burt uncrosses his legs and leans forward. "I know that after my marriage to Rosalind went poof! I was angry at women for almost two whole years. I stayed away from women. Actually, I couldn't get it up anymore, so I just gave up on dating." He lets out a long, slow breath. "After I met JoAnn, I had to deal with this impotence problem. It's what got me into therapy originally. Once we talked it out, I was amazed at how fast it went away. Anyway it took me almost two years to get into therapy because I was so pissed at women."

Mitch lets a small smile of recognition spread across his face. "You *talked* yourself out of impotence?"

Burt shifts uneasily. "Well. talking to JoAnn, and not try-

ing to have sex if I was mad at her. She was a big help. It never happened to you?"

"Yeah, I had a rough bout with impotence, too. I felt so humiliated. I only survived thanks to my friends."

"You had the same friends after the divorce?" Paul asks. He's incredulous.

"They were *my* friends from before the marriage. Janet never really liked any of my biker friends."

Paul nods. "It seems all our friends are gravitating to Sarah, not me."

"That sounds familiar," Burt says with a wry smile. "I had to start all over after Rosalind."

"Yeah, well I'm miserable," Paul says from the bottom of his chair.

"Look, Paul," Burt says with a surge of energy, "why not buy the condo and fix it up? You'll realize you have a life of your own, something away from Sarah."

Paul's chin barely raises off his chest. "I don't know."

"Well, it's certainly worked for me. Ever since JoAnn decided to move in, she's been redecorating my house like a crazed weasel."

Finally Paul smiles.

"I'd hate to have a woman running around my house screwing things up," Gary says, shaking his head.

"Yeah, but you don't understand," Burt says, a grin slowly spreading across his face. "JoAnn is on a search-and-destroy mission. She's going to track down and obliterate anything that ever belonged to Rosalind. She's throwing out all sorts of my old stuff left over from the marriage. Every time I go upstairs I have to duck all the projectiles headed out the door!" Burt slides back on the couch. "Actually, it's about time. I'd let the house go, really, and I feel terrific about her redecorating."

I come in with an English accent: "As Professor Higgins would say, when a woman comes into your life, your serenity

is gone. She'll redo your whole place, top to bottom." I grin and drop the accent. "I don't remember the exact words."

Paul looks blank, but Burt smiles in recognition. Gary leans over at Paul. "It's *My Fair Lady*, Rex Harrison's line, right, Al?"

I smile.

"Yeah, it's great," Burt continues, "but there is a down side to it all. Now that JoAnn has moved in, she has a real presence. She's on me all the time about what I'm thinking or feeling."

"Ugh," Gary grunts, as his hand runs down the full length of his face. "How can you stand having a woman all over you like that?"

"Well, like I said, it's the tough part. But I'm willing to do, to learn, whatever it takes. I figure communication is what I need to work on. I couldn't make it work in my first marriage, and I'll do *anything* to avoid that living hell, let me tell you."

"How is it different for you now?" I ask.

Burt pauses. "What we do is sit down and talk at least once a day about everything, about what's going on. We've also agreed to separate rooms and some private time apart."

Paul snorts. "Man, I thought you two were just living together! What's the big deal? You sound like Sarah's lawyers splitting up property, *my* property."

"I think it's worth the effort at compromise, communication, Paul," Burt replies. "You of all people should know the cost of screwing up a relationship."

"Yeah, that's for damned sure. But I'd never agree to separate bedrooms."

"We don't have separate bedrooms. Just separate rooms, separate space."

Paul shakes his head but remains silent.

"I'd say that a relationship that allows for some privacy sounds pretty good," I suggest.

Burt smiles, but now Gary is shaking his head.

"I don't understand this. What's the point of living to-gether—is it like some practice run for marriage?"

Mitch and Burt exchange smiles, and I realize that Gary is the only man in the group tonight who doesn't want to live with a woman.

"Ellen thinks it is," Ed says. "I'm a little less sure."

"Yeah, well, if I lived with a woman, I sure wouldn't get married. It just doesn't make sense to go that far."

"Have you thought about living with Leigh?" I ask.

He shrugs and looks past Burt and out the windows. "I don't know. Sometimes I think about it, but . . . well, I sort of hope I will meet someone better." He lets out a long sigh. "That's what I'm holding out for."

INTERPRETATION

As the men relate the more intense emotions of anger, resentment, and anxiety, each member of the group is faced with having to respond to these emotions. In tonight's session Burt recognizes that his attack of the previous week was an anxiety attack, and even goes so far as to recognize Gary's angry, violent story as the source of his fear. In that case, rather than confront his anxiety Burt ran from it, much as he attempts to run from the anxiety of his ear surgery ("We can talk about something else now"). Like many men, Burt expresses anxiety in a physical way, even though the cause of the anxiety (Gary's frightening story) was in no way physical. Certainly Burt's upcoming surgery is a cause for anxiety. But in our session the topic of surgery simply opened the door for

Burt to express some of his other anxieties: aging, his previous anger at women, and his present feeling of being overwhelmed by JoAnn. Burt's task in therapy will be to confront the fear underlying his anxieties by going through the feared experience. He has been successful in this area before: Burt's relationship with JoAnn grew and prospered after he confronted, and experienced, the anger, severe anxiety, and humiliation of impotence. Tonight we learn that he is confronting his feelings of uneasiness with JoAnn by making an intense effort ("I'll do whatever it takes") at communication and compromise. In this way, Burt is making progress. Yet in therapy progress rarely follows a straight, direct path: In the space of one week Burt has gone from fleeing the anxiety generated by Gary's story to proudly announcing his commitment to facing the anxiety of living with JoAnn.

Paul is very confused about whether he is making progress in therapy at all. In fact, Paul's marital situation has changed little since he first entered the group, and he continues to deny himself the opportunity to stand completely on his own. Paul is lonely and "miserable" because he's put himself in a bind: he's not married, not divorced, and not single. This situation has not changed in the last few months because he continues to lack the confidence in himself to break with Sarah. On the other hand, Paul has had some very positive results from therapy so far: His interaction with people at work is improving because of what he has learned from being in group. He has also had, for the first time in his life, limited success with women, even though he is not involved with anyone now. Paul feels much more confident and happy when recounting these aspects of his life. Yet there is much ground for him to cover. As Burt pointed out in the session, Paul is still very angry and apprehensive with women, and these feelings are standing in the way of any new meaningful relationship. Paul feels damaged by women. This is a difficult problem for him since his anger toward women, which has existed

since childhood, continued through his marriage with no outlet. He has only recently begun to release some of this anger
in therapy. As this process of release continues, Paul will find
that a lot of his current feeling of tension around women will
fade.

Gary, too, feels tense and uncomfortable as Burt re-
counts the living arrangements he has agreed to with JoAnn.
Gary's response to Burt's story of new intimacy is to draw the
line ("I'd hate to have a woman running around my house
screwing things up"), maintain control, or withdraw ("How can
you stand having a woman all over you like that?"). Clearly,
at this point in his life Gary is feeling threatened by closeness
and intimacy. In fact, he is afraid of being committed, what
he thinks of as being "trapped." This is an especially frightening outcome for Gary, because he has been trapped by
women repeatedly in his life, with the most disastrous consequences. He was trapped for two years in his family by his
mother's threats of suicide if he left, only to fall into an addicted relationship with another woman where he felt equally
trapped. At this point Gary sees relationships as being too
binding, threatening, and ominous.

One consequence of growth and development in therapy
is that the men begin to question not only their progress but
also the value of the process itself. As high achievers these
men are very goal-oriented and practical: They tend to think
that a certain number of sessions will result in a "cure." This
is especially true of Ed, who is very fact-oriented ("It makes
sense to me on two levels"). While Burt is more effective than
Ed on the emotional level, he still tends to withdraw and
conceal his own emotions unless confronted or questioned by
me in group and by JoAnn at home. Ed's statement that he
thought Burt was about to drop out of the group last week
indicates how far removed Burt appears to Ed. Yet when
questioned, Burt acknowledges the security and safety of the
group and is committed to staying with it. Paul seems much

more comfortable with the group members than with people in the outside world: this is the only place he feels a sense of belonging. Gary, too, is feeling very connected to these men. His desire to speak about other issues indicates that he is feeling secure enough with them to move on to other areas. While Mitch does not say directly what he thinks of the group, we do learn the value he places on his male friendships ("I only survived thanks to my friends"), and his comments in tonight's session to Paul are right on target. He's now mentioned a humiliating experience, his bout with impotence. That's extremely difficult for a man to discuss. So, as the man most reluctant to be in group, Mitch has made fine progress.

SESSION 11

//

YEARNING FOR MISSED FATHERS

"How are you doing, Mitch?"

Mitch smiles weakly back at me and runs a hand slowly through his hair. Tonight he is soaked through, his black leather riding outfit offering little protection from the driving snowstorm. He coughs roughly and sits forward. Mitch is much bigger than any of the other men—he's an imposing presence even when he's drenched.

"I'm okay . . . doing better, really," he mumbles haltingly. He catches Gary's frown out of the corner of his eye and realizes the men need to hear what has happened in his life this week.

He takes a deep breath. "Okay . . . my, uh, my father died last week."

"What?!" Gary exclaims. Paul is startled, too. He's sitting bolt upright in his chair with his eyes fixed solidly on Mitch.

For a moment nobody says a word. Ed is the first to come out with a complete sentence.

"I didn't even know he was sick."

"Well, he wasn't sick, really, it was a sudden, massive heart attack." He pauses to wipe more water from the tangled hair matted on his forehead. "I just got back from the funeral today. It was down in Alabama, and I really didn't think I was going to make it back."

A calm silence descends. The sloshy sounds of rush-hour traffic rise from the street—they are the only sounds in the room.

"How've you been doing?" Ed asks softly.

"It's been rough, let me tell you," Mitch says, almost in a whisper. "We all drove down to Alabama for the funeral: Lynda, my sister, and I. We got stuck in southern Virginia for damn near three days, so I couldn't even be there to make the funeral arrangements." He's shaking his head in disgust. "I called Steve, a friend of mine, from our hotel, and thank God he handled all the details, the arrangements you have to make, you know."

Paul is shaking his head in sympathy. Gary is still stunned and hasn't said a word.

"How'd the funeral go?" Burt asks from Mitch's left.

"Huh?"

Mitch's still at the funeral.

"The funeral. How was it?"

"It went fine, actually." He pauses to examine the glass table. "I was really surprised by all of my father's friends there. I didn't even know half of them." He looks at Burt, who is leaning toward him to catch the words in his whispers. "They had so many really nice things to say about him." He shakes his head. "Things I really never knew anything about."

"Such as . . . ?" I ask.

He sighs. "They were all big buddies. I think two of the guys were in the war with him. He'd helped a few of the locals

out when things got rough down there. One guy said he was the most decent, honorable man he had ever known."

Burt is still leaning in his direction. "What do *you* remember about him?"

"I remember him being drunk, that's what I remember," Mitch mutters miserably. "That, and the fact that he was so goddamned pushy and demanding, and . . . well, overbearing. I was just scared to death of the man when I was a kid." He looks up at me. "I really wish I could remember him like his friends did."

Silence.

"Where are you, Mitch?"

"Pissed. I feel cheated. I'm his son. Why didn't he show *me* his good side? . . . Just doesn't seem fair."

"You're on target, Mitch," I say.

"My father died of a heart attack, too," Burt says. He looks over at me for a moment, then back at Mitch. "I remember being real shaky around that time, even though he was pretty far up there, seventy-four, when he died."

"My father was only fifty-five. Can you believe it?" Mitch says as though he's still trying to convince himself. "I figured he'd live to seventy-five at least. I was even trying to work things out with him, you know?"

Gary and I exchange glances.

"Were you still talking to him when he died?" Gary asks.

"Well, yeah, he was in town a few months back. But that's not what I mean. Two weeks ago I sat down and wrote out this letter to him. It took a while just to get up the courage to do *that*."

"What did the letter say?" I ask.

Mitch is rubbing his mouth nervously. He looks down.

"I didn't really know how to put it. In the letter. I guess the most important thing was—that I . . . well, I told him . . . I wanted him to know I . . . accepted him. As a man and as a father. I also said . . . wrote that I loved him."

Mitch's voice has gotten shaky and he won't look at anybody now. He's staring straight down between his legs at the carpet.

Before I can ask Mitch what he is feeling right now, Gary jumps in.

"Did he ever see the letter?" Gary asks.

Mitch shakes his head. "No, but I did. I found it on his dresser when I was down there. It came in that day's mail."

Silence.

After a time, Paul sighs. "All this talk of death just makes everything else so . . . I don't know, insignificant." He shrugs. "My old man died of a heart attack at forty-nine, so I feel like I have this legacy—will I be next? Will I die of a heart attack in eight years when I hit forty-nine?" Paul shudders suddenly and looks down at his shoe.

"Well, Mitch, I tried the same thing with my father," Gary says, scratching the back of his neck. His head is cocked away from Mitch and the rest of the men and is facing roughly toward the ceiling. His gaze shifts to Mitch for an instant, then moves slowly down to the glass table. "I really wanted to patch things up with him," Gary continues. "He's a pretty hard guy to approach, and God knows we had one hell of a history. So we did actually talk a bit. But as things went on I got really pissed at him. He just wouldn't say anything. I'd kid him a bit, toss him a magazine, ask him what movie he wanted to watch, and he'd just *stare* at me." Gary pauses. When he begins again his voice is more slow and deliberate. "One day my mom calls me and I come to find out he has some nerve disease that rendered him speechless. He couldn't talk. At all."

Mitch is nodding.

"It's sad, really," Gary continues. "He's pretty much given in to the situation and spends all his time watching television. And this is a man who just *loved* to read, and hated TV."

"Were you ever able to connect with him?" Sean asks

from his corner. He's been so quiet we are all a bit surprised by his voice.

Gary shakes his head. "No, but I bought him a brand new television set for Christmas. He seems to like it a lot."

Sean smiles and nods.

Silence again. A lot of heavy emotions in the group tonight. These silences are becoming more frequent.

"I wonder where the rest of you are right now," I say, looking around at the others.

Paul coughs and smiles a thin grin. "I had a great time at the River Club last Sunday. Went to this singles dinner where you change seats with each course and that's how you meet everybody. Driving home I realized I had a lot of fun." He slows to brush off his pant leg, then looks over to me. "It's too bad Sarah can't be out enjoying herself."

"Does that bother you?" I ask.

Paul nods. "It's a shame we never could have fun together. In a relationship for twenty years and no fun. But we *were* close, that's for sure. There were days I could predict her every move . . . finish her sentences for her." He pauses. "I was so close to Sarah, it was almost overwhelming. Suffocating." He looks at me. "There were days I was sure it would kill me."

"Yeah, every woman does that to me!" Gary says with a smirk.

"How do you feel about it now?" I ask Paul.

"I'm one hell of a lot freer now. I'm more alive. Last session helped me. You were right, Burt. I've been stuck." He smiles. "I'm doing things I've never done before in my life."

"You do seem to be getting over Sarah—slowly, but, hell, it's progress." Gary smiles.

Paul shakes his head slowly. "Not enough. It's going to be a long time before I trust a woman again. That's it." His gaze drifts slowly over to Gary. "They're vultures, you know."

"Do you really think that, Paul?" Sean asks. He is totally mystified.

"You bet. For the first time I realize I may be alone for the rest of my life."

Sean shakes his head sadly.

"Paul, you are trying to change now. You're doing the work," I point out. "Your views of women will certainly change, too."

"Yeah, well I'll never be like Burt over there." He eyes Sean, too, but says nothing to him.

Burt smiles. "Do you *want* to be like me, Paul?"

"No way. You're always so *cozy* with JoAnn, trying so hard to get along."

"Sure I am. The fact is, we're getting very serious." Burt glances briefly at me. "We're even in couples therapy together now."

Paul rolls his eyes.

"How's that going?" Ed asks. This is something Ed has been considering, too.

"It's tough. After our session yesterday JoAnn wanted to talk and talk about what went on, but I just wanted to leave it alone and enjoy the drive home." He folds his arms slowly. "She always pushes me like that."

"She's a very expressive woman, Burt," I say, smiling.

"She sure is. And I'm trying to deal with it, be more responsive, that sort of thing. My latest method is this: If she wants me to drop everything to talk to her, I tell her I'll be with her as soon as I finish whatever I'm doing."

Gary frowns. "So? Is that the solution?"

"Yeah. I used to just keep silent and continue working. I think she felt totally ignored." He shrugs. "I wasn't ignoring her, of course. I just didn't want to talk right then."

"Sometimes I really worry about you, you know," Paul says suddenly.

Burt looks surprised. "What do you mean, Paul?"

"I just get this feeling JoAnn wants to capture you. I'm very suspicious of her—of her motives." He looks at me and shrugs. "Maybe I'm just negative on women, I don't know."

I look over at Burt. "How do you feel about Paul wanting to protect you?"

"Well, I'm shocked. It's not something I would have expected from Paul, that's for sure. But it's a nice thought."

"Yeah, well, the woman's got you in her web, look out," Paul warns.

I smile. "Burt, you're surprised because it seems that you and Paul have such different views on things, especially women." I pause for a brief moment. "But consider this: If you met Paul when you were married to Rosalind, who was depressed all the time, at the same time Paul was married to Sarah, who was also depressed, you two might have hit it off right away."

Burt nods. "I don't doubt that. I was a different person back then."

"Yeah, well I'll be around to keep an eye on you now," Paul says with a hint of a grin.

"Do you really think she's trying to trap me?"

"I wouldn't put anything past her, past any woman who wants something."

"Really?" Ed asks, interrupting this exchange. "Okay, Paul, Ellen wants a baby. At least I'm beginning to hear a lot about it lately. So what's she going to do to me to get it?"

"Watch the diaphragm. Check for pinholes."

"You've *got* to be kidding!"

"It's no joke," Burt observes. "JoAnn was born that way."

"What?" Ed exclaims. "Look, I can't believe Ellen would ever try to trick me into marrying her."

"Believe it. It happens *all* the time," Paul concludes, with a shake of the head.

"JoAnn's father didn't want more children," Burt contin-

ues. "So her mother tricked him. And she tells it as a joke in front of him."

"She appears to be very narcissistic," I say.

"Definitely," Burt agrees. "She only thinks of herself. JoAnn had a hard time with her and with her father, because he could never stand up to her."

I smile. "Sounds like she was queen for a day, all the time."

INTERPRETATION —————————

Tonight's session began on a very sad note. The death of Mitch's father set the tone for the gloomy mood this evening, yet it also stimulated discussion of topics that are traditionally very difficult for men to face: aging, illness, and death. Moreover, it once again focused attention on a powerful issue for all of these men: their relationships with their fathers.

I can't emphasize enough the importance of the father-son relationship in these men's lives. All the men, on one level or another, have been struggling to deal with the pain and loneliness of childhoods in which their fathers were often viewed as a remote, unfeeling, dictatorial enforcer. Mitch's confusion at the funeral over others' fond memories of his father is characteristic of men who have to bury their fathers after a stormy relationship. Like Mitch, many men ask themselves, "Why didn't *I* ever see the good side of my father?" In fact, Mitch's father saw himself as the breadwinner of the family, the one whose role it was to maintain order and to discipline the children. So what Mitch observed was the side his father chose to show him. What he recalls is the discipline, the criticism, the alcoholism, and the fights. He remembers a father with exceedingly high expectations of him. This re-

lationship has survived into the present day. Mitch has continued to make every effort to please his father. In therapy, Mitch has been learning how much of his anxiety and withdrawal in his adult life are directly related to his early interactions with his father. When he decided to write the letter, Mitch was at the point where he felt it was time to quit waiting. It was time to establish a dialogue. He wanted his father to know he didn't blame him for all of his troubles and he loved him. This was a significant step for Mitch. He went from avoiding the father, dreading him, to a place where he wanted to approach him and connect with him. He had been moving from anger toward acceptance and, ultimately, forgiveness.

Many of the men in my practice mirror Mitch's experience: They yearn for a close, warm relationship with their fathers, a relationship that has long eluded them. Not surprisingly, even though these men are not close to their fathers, they do see them as role models and sense at an innate level that they will follow in their footsteps. Often this is taken quite literally: Paul fears he will die of heart failure at forty-nine like his father; Burt worries that chest pains signal his own heart attack is just around the corner.

Three men in the group—Mitch, Burt, and Gary—all have worked to the point where they feel comfortable attempting such a reconnection to their fathers. Sadly, Mitch's attempt came too late. Gary initially had some success before the onset of his father's illness. His willingness to keep trying is reflected in his gift of a big television set. He wants his father to be happy even if there is now very little chance they will ever connect in a meaningful way. Before his father's death, Burt was able to reestablish a good relationship with his father, whom he remembers fearing as a child because of all the yelling and screaming, ironically related to the pain and sadness prompted by Burt's divorce from Rosaland. It was during this period that Burt's father came to his assistance

and they were able to interact. Yet even in this relationship, Burt felt his father never really understood him.

In my work with men I feel it is important to stress that the purpose of therapy is not to blame. The purpose of the therapeutic process, especially in the case of difficult father-son relationships, is to understand and experience the anger, pain, and frustration, and eventually to move beyond it to acceptance and, finally, forgiveness. It is also important to recognize that the parents, as human beings, have limits. I assure these men that their work in therapy will not only help them deal with their own anger and pain but will also help them to be better fathers. These men have a chance to change their own personal history. The past has already happened; therapy is designed to influence the present and the future.

SESSION 12

//

COURAGE AND CONFRONTATION

After the men have settled in, I close the door. Burt looks over at me and smiles. Ed coughs and shifts to face me; Gary and Paul have just finished a conversation begun in the waiting room. They are now ready to start.

"Before we begin, I have an announcement," I say. "Sean has dropped out of the group. I spoke with him on the phone today, and encouraged him to come in tonight to discuss it, but he refused. He said he feels that he just doesn't fit in."

At first nobody says a word. I notice Ed throws Paul a hostile look, but he is silent. Gary nods slowly as though he has anticipated this.

"What do you expect?" Paul says finally. "He's such a lightweight. I knew he couldn't handle it."

Ed sighs and looks over at Gary, who is shaking his head.

Gary catches my eye and shrugs. "I never really expected him to come back last session, to tell you the truth."

Burt nods his assent.

Paul turns to me. "Didn't *you* see this coming?"

"Not this way," I reply. "I thought Sean would have made it tonight. That he would have at least talked out *why* he wants to leave. It would be better for him, and for us, if he did."

Meanwhile Mitch's black boot is tapping at a rapid pace. He's remained silent so far, but his eyes have been shifting nervously among the men during this exchange.

"Mitch?" I ask.

"Is . . . it okay if I just start now?"

I nod.

He lets out a quiet sigh. "Last night I had this dream that really upset me. I really don't know what to make of it."

"What was the feeling during the dream?" I ask.

He shrugs and slowly runs a hand across his brow. "I don't remember a single detail. I just remember waking up in the middle of the night, all nervous, breathing real heavy. I just lay there for a while. I was pretty soaked." He smiles a little sheepishly. "I couldn't get back to sleep."

"It sounds like an anxiety dream, Mitch, about a conflict going on inside you. What do you think the conflict is about, Mitch?" I ask. I'm hoping for some material about the dream itself.

Mitch answers without hesitation, "Lynda."

Paul has been listening intently to Mitch's story, and now he's growing annoyed. "What *about* Lynda?"

"I think its about my decision to propose to Lynda. I've been getting really anxious about it lately." Mitch looks to Burt, who is sitting on his left. "I'm mostly worried about another marriage ending in divorce, you know?"

Burt nods. "So did you propose?"

"Well, not yet. I told Lynda I wanted to wait until Friday,

wait until I had a chance to talk it over with Al. So she just blew up and said 'forget it! I don't want to go out Friday at all!' "

I smile. "You know, Mitch, it's a rare woman who likes being told that her boyfriend wants to talk over a marriage proposal with his therapist first!"

"No kidding," Burt says emphatically. "If I told JoAnn I wouldn't propose without talking it over with Al, I'd hate to be around for the explosion!"

Mitch shrugs. "Sure, whatever. But the whole mess has got me spinning around inside."

"Look," Paul says, leaning over on his left elbow to face Mitch directly. "I don't want to throw cold water on all this, but there's something here that's bothering me. Your father just died. I know what that's like . . . how hard it is to go through a loss like that." Paul pauses to examine his forearm. He's taking time to chose his words carefully. "So is it possible that this thing about marrying Lynda is so you won't lose her? If you marry her, you won't lose another person close to you?"

Mitch nods, a little surprised at Paul's insight. "Well, it's a possibility. Actually, I've thought of that."

"Well?"

"I really don't know the answer, Paul."

"How about living together first, as a sort of dry run," Burt suggests. His comment is for Mitch, but he's grinning across the table at Gary.

Mitch hasn't seen this. "I couldn't do that, really. She's real traditional, remember?"

"Real *traditional?*" Paul asks, amazed. "You're sleeping with her, aren't you?"

"Well, of course."

"Some tradition!"

"I just want an old-fashioned proposal, that's all, Paul. It's nicer, she'd appreciate it more. It's a lot more romantic."

"Mitch, I've got a question," Ed says, leaning forward to

see around Burt. "Did Lynda really mean it when she said she wouldn't marry you unless you got into therapy?"

"Yeah, she was dead serious. It really scared me at the time."

"I see Lynda's position now as a compliment to you," I interject.

Mitch is staring right at me with a blank look on his face.

"She wouldn't marry you before, Mitch. And she obviously *does* want to marry you now. So she must be seeing some positive changes in you."

He shrugs and then slowly begins to nod. "That may be. We are communicating a lot more now, but a lot of it is just opinion—'Did you like that movie? What do you want to do tonight?'—that sort of thing."

"Do you ever discuss feelings?" I ask.

Mitch shakes his head. "I can't talk to her about what I'm feeling right now. I don't know how she'd react."

"You're right, Mitch," I reply. "You don't know how she'll react. Her reactions are hers and are not under your control. That may be why Lynda is angry—another reason why she canceled out on you Friday. She senses that you're still holding back."

"I *am* holding back."

"I know. You need to discuss this kind of thing with Lynda."

"Now or when I'm married to her?" He smiles.

"Are you that committed to proposing this Friday?"

He nods.

"In that case, I would at least caution you to take your time in making a life decision, especially when you're changing as much as you are," I say. "Take a little time to consider making a life decision when you are changing so much. Also, we know that you *are* still going through the grieving process over your father's death, whether you're aware of it or not."

Burt comes in before Mitch can answer.

"A proposal isn't the same thing as marriage, you know."

I smile at Burt. This is a good point.

"That's certainly true. But my advice still stands. Especially the part about talking to Lynda about your anxieties."

Mitch is listening carefully, and he nods. This is a lot for him to take in at once.

Silence.

"How about some advice for me?" Gary asks.

"About what?"

Gary collects himself and sits forward on the couch. "I'm in a complete state of confusion with Leigh. We've broken up twice, and she keeps coming back, wanting to get back together."

"Don't you want to?" Ed asks.

"Not really. The truth is, the longer I date someone, the more it becomes like a habit to me. Eventually I have to try and *break* the habit." He stops and begins to slowly rub his open palms together. "The longer I stay with Leigh the harder it will be to break the habit. I don't want to become addicted to Leigh."

"Do you love Leigh?" Paul asks.

Gary flashes a sudden, angry look at Paul and says nothing.

Paul looks over at me and raises his eyebrows.

"For what it's worth, I don't think you sound addicted to Leigh," Burt offers with a shrug.

"What do you mean by being 'addicted,' Gary?" I ask. I'm pushing Gary in a sensitive area.

For a long moment Gary says nothing. When he finally speaks, his voice is tight and angry.

"I don't want to be overwhelmed. Out of control."

"I can understand that."

Gary is sitting quietly, angry and pensive.

"Addictions *can* take over your life," I say finally. "Ordi-

narily, for something to qualify as an addiction, you have to give it priority over the necessities of living."

"Man, you are full of advice today!" Paul says in exasperation.

"It sounds as though you're mad at me, Paul."

"No, I'd just rather get feedback from the rest of the group than sit here and listen to your advice!"

"What's with you today, Paul?" Ed demands.

"I'm really getting disappointed in this group, that's all. I'm not happy about the kind of feedback I'm getting." His gaze drifts to me for a moment, but he quickly looks away. "I've started looking around at support groups to see what's out there. I want everyone to interact in here more and not just nag at me all the time."

"That's funny, I get the feeling you nag at us, Paul," Mitch says dryly. "What do you want from us?"

"I want more support."

"Paul, we *have* been helping you with all kinds of things," Ed says quickly, "your divorce, your relationship with Sarah, new women in your life—"

"Don't forget about Betty," Mitch interjects.

Ed nods. "That's true."

Gary clears his throat and leans forward. He looks ready to join the conversation again.

"I understand a little bit of where Paul is on this," he begins slowly. "Sometimes I feel there are only certain topics that are okay to talk about in here." He looks around the room deliberately, taking in all the reactions. "I guess I don't feel I can completely trust everyone yet."

"What would you be talking about if you could trust everyone?" I ask.

"About being an alcoholic."

"Good! You needed to say that. I'm glad you did."

Gary is surprised by my reaction but remains silent. The

men exchange several nervous glances. Nobody is quite sure what to say.

"If you licked that, you're doing better than my old man did," Mitch says, breaking the silence.

Gary nods and looks at the floor.

Some more time goes by. We are all watching Gary.

"Look, Gary, that's something neither of my parents could do," Ed says suddenly. "I think it's great."

"What's your reaction to Mitch and Ed?" I ask.

"I don't know." He looks over at me suddenly. "I wonder if people just say it's great. I don't know how to react to that."

"Well, I mean it," Mitch says emphatically. "You must be pretty strong if you managed to lick alcoholism . . . and, it's okay if you don't believe me. I have a hard time believing people sometimes, too."

"Are you still drinking, or what?" Paul asks.

"No, I've been dry for five and a half years."

"Hey, that *is* good."

"I'm glad you told us, Gary," Burt says. "I'm glad that you felt you could say it."

Gary acknowledges Burt's comment but lapses into silence again.

Gary's silence indicates he is not yet comfortable discussing his alcoholism. Yet I want to encourage him in some way. "You took a real risk tonight, Gary," I say. "How do you feel about it now?"

He shrugs. "I'm sort of embarrassed really." Finally, he looks up at me. "But I'm glad I got it off my chest."

"I wish you'd got it off your chest earlier!" Paul exclaims. Paul is heating up again. "This is just what I'm talking about. I can't get anything out of you guys!"

"Now wait a minute, Paul." Ed cuts him off. "It sounds to me like you have a few secrets of your own. This is the first time we've heard about you sneaking around on the out-

side looking for some 'support' group. Is that what you mean by 'sharing'?"

Paul shrugs. "Yeah, okay. Don't get me wrong. I'm *glad* to hear about Gary's story. I just want *more* of that, and less criticism."

Gary is shaking his head. "I don't think so, Paul. I think you want something completely different. You want us to jump up every night and say, 'Go, Paul! Down with Sarah!' "

For once Paul is *completely* speechless.

INTERPRETATION ─────────

Sean's unexpected decision to drop out of the group has almost no impact on the men in tonight's session. In my experience it is more common for group members to have a much more powerful, sometimes vehement reaction to the abandonment of the group by an individual they have trusted. Sean's decision did come as a surprise to me, as I anticipated more cooperation from him in discussing any possible separation. It is a rare occurrence, in my experience, for a patient simply to drop out of a group without discussion. It turns out that the reactions of the other men, virtually all of whom expected Sean to simply vanish, were much more on target. This speaks to the value of the group process. Through direct observation of Sean in the group setting, the men had a very accurate sense of how Sean would deal with the confrontation in group and the emotional pain of the separation from Sandi if things got too intense for him to handle. When it came to this, Sean reacted with passive hostility by abandoning the group and refusing to deal any further with his feelings of pain and embarrassment over the breakup.

But Sean's story goes much further. In a turbulent indi-

vidual session after his return from Phoenix, Sean told me
that his father had just been released from the hospital following a near-successful suicide attempt over his failed business.
An outraged Sean related how the family business had, just a
few weeks before, nearly collapsed after his father had gam-
bled away all the assets of the corporation in a binge that
stretched over a year. Not only were these events disastrous
for Sean professionally (his future in medical school depended
on these funds), they also had a catastrophic effect on his
very idealistic view of his father and family. Sean was angry
that his father's gambling problem had been hidden from him,
he was furious at his father for throwing the entire family into
complete chaos, and he felt betrayed by his father's handling
of his own medical school trust fund, which evaporated in the
gambling binge. Sean had never felt this kind of anger toward
anyone, especially in his family. The embarrassment and
shame of these events were really overwhelming for Sean, and
it was unfortunate that his choice to leave the group came at
a time when the group could have helped him cope with these
feelings and adapt more successfully. The group would have
experienced Sean as a more "real" person—and definitely could
have connected easily to his anger at his father.

The simmering anxiety of Sean's departure was amplified
by Mitch's nervous tapping tonight. There is definitely a sense
of tension in the air. I am gratified that Mitch feels comfortable enough with the group to bring in and openly discuss a
dream, and that he was willing to hear the men out on their
reactions. Mitch's dream was an anxiety dream. It was about
loss; certainly about the loss of his father, but also about the
possible loss of Lynda if he can't bring himself to propose in
time. The loss of Sean tonight prompted him to talk about
it, even though he could not remember the content of the
dream. I had learned from Mitch in individual sessions that
the funeral was very revealing to him: Mitch saw Lynda during this period as he'd never really seen her before. He ap-

preciated that she took time off from work to drive down to Alabama for the funeral, and she spent many late nights with him grieving and feeling guilty. It was during this trip that he realized he and Lynda were made for each other—that he was deeply in love with her. Much of his anxiety over a proposal of marriage is based on Mitch's fear of failure in a second marriage, not his fear of his choice of Lynda. The former is a reasonable fear, if the problems that caused the collapse of his first marriage have not yet been resolved. This is an issue we have discussed in the group, because the likelihood of similar problems existing is huge unless they're recognized and resolved before a second marriage. Mitch is actively recognizing and resolving the issues of his first marriage, although he continues to deny himself credit for these changes. He has also considered that his proposal may be a response to fill the void of his father's death, an issue Paul brings up this evening. While Mitch's answer to Paul offers no solution ("I really don't know the answer, Paul"), it is much more likely that his father's death has simply been a catalyst for action by Mitch: It has cleared the way for Mitch to examine his relationship with Lynda and given him the opportunity to fully consider whether his relationship with Lynda is a wholesome one.

Paul's advice to Mitch comes in Paul's unique style: direct, forward, almost confrontational. Later in the session, we learn of Paul's dissatisfaction with the group and his search for a support group as a replacement. Paul has been shaky with this group since the third session, and at various times has felt picked on, insulted, or neglected. The fact is, Paul is very confused. Although he has been in and out of therapy for much of his adult life, he still has no idea of what he really wants from therapy or from the group. He quit his last group because it was too confrontational, yet he's mad at this group because they don't share enough with him. The truth is the

men do share a great deal with Paul, but it is difficult for Paul to make a connection because he's never felt comfortable with interpersonal relationships of any kind—he has so little experience in this area. Paul also withdraws any time anger is expressed in the group, because it is so frightening to him. His search for a support group is a reflection of this. Traditionally, support groups are much more comfortable and non-threatening to men like Paul because, unlike therapy groups, there is less confrontation, little expectation of absolute honesty and vulnerability, and a great deal of unequivocal support. This support is what Paul seeks and what Gary, at the end of the session, parodies ("You want us to jump up every night and say, 'Go, Paul! Down with Sarah!' ").

It is interesting that Gary, who has been Paul's ally in group so far, chooses to engage in this little parody of Paul's behavior. In fact, Gary is very angry at Paul for thinking (silently) of leaving after he has established this connection to him. Gary is very careful about the connections he makes, and his greatest fear is an attachment to a woman that will make him lose all control. In discussing what he believes is a tendency to become "addicted" to women, Gary closes on the subject of his real addiction to alcohol. Toward the end of the session, Gary decides to make the leap by revealing this addiction to the group. He takes a real risk here—a risk of rejection, judgment, censure—but makes the leap nonetheless, for several reasons. First, he has long expressed a desire to talk about other problems in his life, and the fear of "addiction" is very powerful to him. Second, he has wanted to open up more in general as his connection to Paul and the other men has grown stronger. Third, and most important, Gary feels the group slipping away: Sean has left abruptly, Paul is shopping around, Ed has questions about what he is getting out of group, Burt and Mitch are resolving their relationship problems and therefore may not be around much longer—all

of this is very threatening to Gary, who is committed to staying. Tonight Gary opens up as a way of saving the group. He wants to reinforce his connection to the men and guarantee that the group will stay together. The group is very important to him. For the first time in his life, Gary feels he belongs.

SESSION 13

//

THE VALUE OF ANXIETY

" . . . So I want more feedback from all of you. Just tell me what you think. Give me a reaction right away. That's all."

Paul has just finished a tedious, rambling monologue while swinging slowly around in the black leather chair. His eyes have yet to make contact with anyone. He's just floating along.

"Okay!" Mitch says with a sudden rush of energy. He reaches forward and seizes the chair with his hand and stops Paul in mid-turn. "How's this? I was so mad at you last week I could have *killed* you!" His enormous frame is only about nine inches from Paul's limp form, but Paul's face remains impassive. No response at all.

"Well, I'm glad to hear your honesty," Paul says smoothly. "But I don't know why you're so mad at me."

Mitch releases Paul's chair and folds himself back into

the couch. He coughs and slowly crosses his legs. He is waiting to cool down before he answers.

"Mitch, how does it feel for you to hold in anger, hold it in for the whole week since last session?" I ask.

Mitch's eyes shift to me, but he doesn't move. "I don't know."

Silence.

"I think . . . well, he's just been bugging me, you know?" he says finally in exasperation. Mitch is eyeing Paul warily. "He wants us to spill our guts all over the floor, to give him instant feedback, and meanwhile he's out shopping for another group!"

"So what?" Paul shrugs. "I want to keep my options open. At least I'm honest with you guys. I don't like what I'm getting in here."

"Paul, you don't like what you're getting *anywhere,*" Ed cracks. Gary catches Ed's eye. Grins flash all around.

Paul frowns. It's the first response he's shown all evening. His black chair slowly spins to face Gary.

"I'm just trying to be more direct in dealing with everybody, okay?"

"Yeah, you look *real* direct Paul," Gary says sarcastically. There is a twinge of anger to his voice. Gary knows something but he won't tip his hand.

"Since we're all being so direct," Ed says. "I'll go next."

Paul's chair creaks one notch to face Ed. Once Ed has Paul's attention, he comes to life.

"Why in the *hell* did you treat Sean like a kid? He's not your son, you know. You can't just abuse him at will. You drove the poor guy right out of the group!"

"No I didn't," Paul responds coolly. "He just couldn't handle it. Nobody drops out just because they don't like me."

"That may be, Paul, but you treated him like *shit!*"

Paul holds Ed in his gaze for a long moment. "Really?"

Ed's face falls. He looks around at the others in mild exasperation. He can't believe Paul is missing this.

"Nothing seems to satisfy you, that's all, Paul," Gary says softly. "Last week I finally got up the nerve to go into this whole thing about my alcoholism and you yelled at me about *that!*"

Paul looks mildly surprised. "I *liked* the last session."

"What did you like about it?" I ask.

Paul has to swing nearly completely around to face me. "It's the first I've heard about his alcohol problem." He sighs. "I was glad to hear that he faced it down. And I was thinking: He must have had an awful time as a teenager, running to booze as an escape."

Paul is trying to build a bridge back to Gary, but Gary is watching him silently over folded arms.

"Well?" Paul asks.

"I'm not going to dig this all up again. I haven't had a drink in six years. That's it."

"Sounds like you're warning us not to expect too much from you," I tell him.

Gary shakes his head. "I just don't want to talk about it every session, that's all. A lot of it's behind me."

Silence.

"I was on the other side of that whole mess," Ed says softly.

He looks at Gary for a moment, then over to me.

"Both my parents drank like fish," he sighs. "My dad was a hotshot city councilman and was falling-down drunk at speeches and conventions all over town. I spent half my life just trying to find something to do to keep myself occupied, and I was only nine years old! I almost never saw my mom in the house—she was off with my dad schmoozing it up and drinking it down." He runs a hand slowly through his thick blond hair. "I remember making up stories to tell my friends just to cover for them; you know, 'They're both on medica-

tion,' 'They just get weird sometimes,' 'You know parents,' 'They're stressed out,' that sort of stuff.'"

Burt leans forward on the couch to face Ed. "Did it ever get any better?"

"After I got away, it got better," Ed replies with a hint of a grin. "College was an incredible relief. I had a lot of catching up to do with people." Suddenly he looks very intense. "You have no idea how lonely that was before college. I was just so mortified I avoided almost everyone!"

"Do you see your avoiding everyone as continuing even now?" I ask.

"Sure. I've never been the type to talk much to people. And I just can't take the leap and get married. I hesitate, analyze, study, reflect, think. I do a thousand things, but I never propose!" He grins at me.

"Some of your hesitancy makes sense, Ed," I say. "Lets face it. Your parents didn't exactly have the kind of marriage where you'd be champing at the bit to jump in yourself."

"But I *do* want to have a family *sometime*. I just don't know if Ellen's the one."

I nod. "That part of your hesitation is related to your perfectionism. Which helps you at one area, your work: You're a scientist, you're very ambitious, you're used to everything lining up, you want Ellen to be predictable before you'll propose to her. And you're afraid to commit to a decision because you're afraid it will be the 'wrong' decision."

"So is there anything *wrong* with knowing what you want?"

"Not at all. It's just a little unreasonable when you're talking about people. The reality is: People aren't perfect. If Ellen were predictable, you'd be bored."

"But I don't have a whole lot of time left. I may have a shot at a job on the West Coast, and Ellen won't go with me this time unless we are *definitely* getting married."

I pause a moment. "Ed, the most important thing for you right now is to know what you really feel. Take your time

with Ellen. You've both been doing better without the pressure of a deadline."

Ed seems pleased with this advice. He stretches his legs out under the glass table and smiles.

Mitch nudges Ed in the side. "Come to me for advice if you get cold feet next time."

"Why?"

Mitch smiles. "I proposed to Lynda."

"Whoaa!" Gary exclaims, sitting up straight. Ed is so stunned, he's stone silent.

"Yeah, it was great. She wanted a ring, but I hadn't bought one yet, so I raced upstairs and looked around." He's grinning wildly. "It came down to a choice between my college ring and a cigar ring."

"So what'd you choose?" Burt asks. He's smiling back at Mitch.

"I went with the college ring. She said that would do for now."

"So when's the big day?" Gary asks.

"We're thinking about the end of July. That's a slow period at Lynda's law firm. Plus, we'll be able to get married in the church she's gone to her whole life."

Ed has recovered sufficiently to speak. "So what made you finally go through with it?"

Mitch shrugs. "Maybe some of it was my dad's death, I don't know. All I know for sure is I don't want to lose Lynda. She's too important to me."

Ed nods. Meanwhile Paul is just grinning slyly.

"What's your reaction to all this, Paul? You've seemed so subdued all evening. I haven't seen you energized about anything," I say.

Paul freezes up suddenly as though he's been caught.

"Paul?"

He inhales deeply, then slowly lets it out. His chair has

stopped its slow revolutions. "I really should have told all of you."

"Told us what?" Ed asks suspiciously. Gary is already nodding even though Paul hasn't said a thing yet.

"I've started on medication."

"No kidding," Burt says. "What kind?"

"Xanax, right now. It's great."

Burt frowns and Paul notices his confusion.

"It's an anti-anxiety drug my doctor originally gave me for this bladder trouble I was having a long time ago. I stayed away from it at first, but . . . boy, is it great. I just feel terrific. It's so much easier to handle Sarah and the kids, work, even group."

"Are you having bladder trouble now?" I ask.

"Nope."

"But you're taking Xanax anyway?"

He nods, a little sheepishly.

I frown at Paul, and he immediately jumps to his own defense.

"Look, Sarah made me take it, okay? And I don't regret it a bit. Everything is so much more even in my life now. I'm even going to go negotiate buying a new car right after this session."

"If Xanax makes *that* fun, I want a cut, Paul," Ed cracks.

I feel a slow burn rising inside. "Paul, here's a 'should' from me: You should have talked to me before taking anxiety pills. Why do you want to use a mood-altering drug?"

"It's medicine, okay?" Paul says defensively.

"No, it's not okay. Did your doctor know you are in therapy?"

"It's no big deal."

"It is a big deal. We could have consulted to coordinate your treatment. It's better for you in the long run. But you have to understand something, Paul. You're here to resolve anxiety, to *face* it. You need to learn what's causing the anxi-

ety. Otherwise, it'll keep recurring and all you can do then is pop another pill."

"It's a physiological problem with me," Paul protests. He's actually shrunk a bit in his chair.

"Paul, look. I'm not meaning to chew you out. I do want you to see that anxiety is a natural *feeling*. It's just as valid a cue to us as feeling happy or sad. Anxiety means you're afraid—but it can be positive for you by helping you to pay more attention to your fear and get through the fear easier. It's better not to mask it when you're trying to figure it out."

"Xanax works better. I'm going to be on it for two months," Paul says defiantly.

Before I can respond, Gary jumps in. "I knew you were high on something ever since I came in here," he says with a shake of the head. "I could see it in your eyes. My whole life I've been around people zonked out on something. I can spot it in a second."

"Look, it's a doctor's *prescription*, okay?"

"Right. Paul, you can get a doctor to prescribe *anything.*"

"So what? I still like it."

We are almost out of time and I feel it is important to connect to Paul on this issue, at least on some level.

"Paul, will you consider a compromise with me? Will you agree not to take the Xanax on your therapy days?"

Paul looks a little disappointed but sits with this for a moment. He rubs his shoulder slowly and looks off over the heads of the men on the couch. At last he opens his mouth. "Deal."

INTERPRETATION —————

In tonight's session Paul starts out with the truth ("I want more feedback from all of you") but knowingly sits on a lie ("I really should have told all of you"). Gary picks up on Paul's deception almost immediately but doesn't trust his instincts enough to comment out loud. I also notice something about Paul as the evening wears on: he lacks his usual tension and harshness. Ironically, Paul is trying to be present in the group and win the trust of the men. Paul claims a desire for honesty even though he has been dishonest in both of the most recent sessions: in his clandestine search for a "support" group and his hesitancy to admit being on tranquilizers. Gary is both angry and disappointed with Paul. The alliance they've shared in group is being strained by Paul's secretive actions and his decision to use mood-altering drugs—a condition Gary angrily dismisses as being "zonked out."

I, too, was disturbed by Paul's decision to take a tranquilizer. Since Paul knows my position on using any tranquilizers while in therapy, he first hides and then vehemently defends its use ("Sarah made me take it," "Xanax works better"). I take the time to explain to Paul why I believe the drug will only detract from his progress. It is important for him to understand that I can be angry without rejecting him, which is a new experience for Paul. I want him to see that I am concerned that he is standing in the way of his own progress. My therapy focuses on insight, combining *understanding* and *feeling,* and the method is wasted when someone chemically dulls the feeling. Most men have a huge struggle connecting with their feelings in the first place. Dulling them with tranquilizers makes that struggle even harder. Paul's attempt to suppress his feeling of anxiety is a mistake: Anxiety is a normal reaction to something or somebody one fears. The only way for Paul, or anyone, to master the fear is to understand

and face the feared situation or person. At this level, anxiety is a useful cue. It pumps up our adrenaline. It gives us a surge of energy. Anxiety gives us a winning edge in any stressful situation. When the anxiety builds to the point where it interferes with normal day-to-day functioning, then tranquilizers may be prescribed to avoid feeling overwhelmed. But I believe they interfere with a person's ability to gain insight during therapy. Paul and the others are here to face their anxiety, not cover it. That's exactly what the men are doing in here—attempting to gain mastery over their anxiety.

Mitch's proposal to Lynda comes so impulsively that he even finds himself without a ring. Clearly Mitch is moving very fast toward marrying Lynda because she has played a stronger role in his life since his father died. By partially filling the void created by his father's death, Lynda's relative importance to Mitch has grown. He's worried about losing her, too. At this early stage in the grieving process, the urgency of the proposal is related to filling his emotional vacuum. Mitch doesn't announce his engagement at the beginning of the session, because he's worried that the men might disapprove of his sudden decision. However, he is comfortable in making the announcement as a way of supporting Ed. I am encouraged that some of the men are willing to share the news and events of their lives in a way that offers real support.

SESSION 14

//

ANGER, AGGRESSION, AND DEPRESSION

"I would like to start tonight."

Burt looks around the room discreetly after this whispered announcement. He coughs briefly and shuffles on the couch. Burt looks solid and trim tonight in yet another bright new wool sweater. The sun is setting on a cold, brisk Washington day. Maybe Burt feels invigorated by the frigid air. Tonight is the first time he has started group.

"I just don't know what to do about JoAnn."

Silence.

Burt is examining the couch arm as he is picking it. Since Sean left the group, Burt has taken Sean's spot on the far left of the couch. He looks lonely in that corner tonight.

"All I hear about is her career, how she won't marry me until she gets her M.A." Burt pauses and looks right at me. "I

just don't know if I want to continue this relationship if she keeps putting me off!"

Ed has been watching Burt carefully this whole time. "Do you want to get married right away?" he asks.

Burt shrugs. "Hell, I don't know. I'm just so damn sick and tired of *waiting*. I waited too long before ending a relationship the last time, and I don't want to get stuck with that again."

Gary leans out to see Burt across Mitch's body. He's frowning. "Been through what . . . ?" he asks.

"Oh. I went through this whole thing with my wife. We put off having children so we could do the career thing, and we really—both of us—got into that. At the time I thought it was a great choice. So when we were finally ready . . ." Burt pauses to look at Gary, then shakes his head sadly. "Well, she had a Dalkon shield and developed one hell of an infection. So that shot having kids at all!"

"Burt, not wanting to repeat a mistake is on target. How might Rosalind and JoAnn be similar?" I ask.

A puzzled expression spreads across Burt's face. "Hmm. Well, I know they both had terrible times with their fathers—that's the first thing that comes to mind. And towards the end . . . Rosalind was depressed and withdrawn so much it damn near drove me crazy, I just had to get out, get away from her." Burt stops to examine his shoe. He looks up at me. "JoAnn can get that way, too, you know."

"Why do you keep going after the same kind of woman, anyway?" Paul demands irritably from across the table.

Burt looks over at Paul and smiles. "Paul, that's actually a good question. I don't really think they are alike in most ways, but they certainly can get depressed. And come to think of it, they can really piss me off when they go into these depressions."

"Yeah, well, I'm on JoAnn's side on this one, that's for

sure," Paul responds, with a shake of the head. "Don't you understand? Kids just fuck up a relationship."

"Paul, I *want* kids, okay? That's not the issue. I would have married JoAnn in a second when she got pregnant, what was it, eighteen months ago? But she wouldn't do it. She insisted on the abortion." Burt's gaze drifts back to me. "And . . . the fact is she said she *would* get pregnant just as soon as we got married." Burt slinks back into the couch. "I never thought *that* would be the problem."

"My God, Burt, you sound just like Ellen!" Ed exclaims.

"Yeah, so what? I'm forty-five years old. I want to be a father before Social Security."

"No. That's okay, I understand." Ed smiles. "It's just when you were talking I suddenly saw *Ellen* sitting there."

"Maybe you two *should* swap girlfriends," I suggest, lightly.

"Haven't we been through this girlfriend-swapping deal once before?" Gary asks with a grin.

"God, that wasn't the session I missed, was it?" Burt says suddenly, laughing before all the words make it out of his mouth.

Ed shakes his head. He's still grinning. "I don't know, Burt, I just think maybe JoAnn needs to hear some of this directly from you. Maybe she doesn't know how important it is for you to have children. You should go to her with some of this."

Burt nods slowly.

"I think Ed has made some good points, Burt," I say. "I wonder if this delay over the M.A. is an excuse for you to break up with JoAnn. If so, you'd better break up with her before she finishes!"

"I'm not thinking like that right now. I *want* to marry her."

"Then why break up with her because of this one delay?"

He shrugs. "You tell me."

"Burt, let's try a role-play. I'll be JoAnn."

"Ready."

"Burt, my career is important to me. You know that. You know how hard I've worked. I don't want to give it up completely right now. Children are so much responsibility, time, energy. If I had to stay home with a baby, I could kiss my career goodbye right now!"

"I'm not asking you to give up your career, JoAnn. I just want children sometime in the near future."

"Well, it seems that's exactly what you're asking. I have goals just like you. Not only that—I want us to live together for a while before we have kids."

Burt frowns. "Now, *that* I don't understand."

"Look, Burt. I just want to feel more secure with you, with our relationship, our marriage, before we have children."

The frown slowly evaporates from Burt's forehead. He breaks the role-play and looks at me. "I can see her saying that."

I decide to let Burt sit and reflect on this, without further comment.

"Well, *I'm* feeling a lot better today, at least," Paul says with a sudden surge of energy. He uncrosses his long legs and sits forward to face Burt directly. "Got a raise, got a new car, had my lawyer write Sarah and insist that *she* pay some child support since I've got all these damn bills and I'm supporting *her* adultery. She's away weekends on my money! Can you believe it? Anyway, I'm pretty glad with where I'm at now. I had a date with a couple of women and I went out Saturday night on a third date with this one. My parents even sent me a five-thousand-dollar check that I didn't expect as a down payment on my new condo."

Gary snickers. He won't look at Paul directly.

"Where are you, Gary?" I ask.

He looks right past Paul and straight at me. "I'm fine."

"I think you should trust your instincts on this. What's going on?"

Gary's look intensifies. At first it appears he isn't going to say a word, then he explodes.

"Man, I'm *just sick of this!* This dude's high as a kite, he's fucking whacked out on Xanax, and we've got to sit here and listen to him drone on like a fucking imbecile!"

Nobody moves. Burt is frozen stiff. Paul is as calm as ever: the Xanax at work. Mitch is eyeing Gary nervously but after a time starts to nod his assent.

"The truth is, I got bored as soon as Paul started, too."

Paul finally catches Gary's eye. "I'm not high," he says.

"Sure you're not. That's why you've got that half-assed smirk on your face two seconds after I yell at you. Nothing's getting through to you, Paul."

"Oh yes it is. This is exactly the kind of feedback I want!"

"Okay, Paul," Ed interjects, "here's my contribution. Why do you keep popping in when another conversation is going and switch the subject to you? I wanted to hear more about Burt and JoAnn."

"So what? Why don't the rest of you jump in, too? Throw an elbow or two and people will pay attention to you, that's what I always say."

"Maybe Sean caught an elbow or two in the stomach," Ed says with a smirk.

"I don't want to hear about Sean, okay? He's already chickened out. I want to hear about the men in this room! Just interrupt me if you want to say something."

"There's no interrupting you," Mitch says angrily.

Paul stops. He's watching Mitch.

"Al has to practically *beg* you to shut up for ten seconds so you can *listen*, so you can hear what is going on in here!"

Paul's eyes have grown wide. In spite of the Xanax, Mitch has gotten to him. The sheer bulk of the man has intimidated

Paul into complete silence. He looks nervously from Mitch to me and back. He won't move at all.

I look at my watch and realize we've just gone over time, but I don't want to come in quite yet. Too much has gotten stirred up and needs to be addressed. There is no stopping the group tonight.

"Look, I don't like where this is going," Paul croaks. He slowly breaks his visual lock on Mitch and looks over at me. "I can still remember what this was like. When I was in seventh grade I got beat up more than once. I don't need this! I don't even want to ride down the elevators with these guys! Can I stay here and ride down with you?"

I nod. "But, Paul, you know the rules: No physical violence against anyone or anything. So I don't think you have to be concerned about something really happening here. And I understand you are the target of some serious anger. What you do have to learn is how you become insensitive and lose those around you, and then find yourself completely alone and boring. This ends up alienating everyone."

"I still want to ride down the elevator with you," Paul says emphatically.

Mitch is still glaring at Paul.

"Mitch," I say, "you've got to let out some of that anger. You're sitting on so much anger I can feel the tension way over here!"

Finally Mitch's glare focuses on me. "You want me to get mad at you?"

"I'm here to help you figure it out, Mitch, including how you might get mad at me. I don't take what goes on in here personally. So yes, get mad at me."

"Oh come on, Al, what the hell is this?" Gary interjects angrily. "We're supposed to yell at you? What the hell are we doing in here?"

"Do just *that!* Get it *out!* Even the talking is letting it out and this is the value—experience it."

"Awww shit, I don't *believe* you."

"I know. You have to try it to learn how to do it."

Gary is shaking his head, but Mitch and Ed are nodding slowly. As the fever in the room cools, the men realize we've gone ten minutes over. There is a slow shuffle for coats as everyone stands and prepares to leave. Paul waits five minutes after everyone else has left and slowly plods out the door.

INTERPRETATION ———————

The intense feelings of anger and confrontation in tonight's session have been valuable catalysts in demonstrating much of the value and purpose of group therapy. It is only in the group environment that interactive behavior can reach such a fevered pitch. The men are faced with runaway feelings and are so confused they need guidance to understand what is appropriate behavior, what they are supposed to do, and what is considered acceptable. This gives me the opportunity in the aftermath not only to show Paul the consequences of his behavior in group, why there is so much anger directed right at him, but also to connect his behavior with Mitch and Gary and to explain the value of these emotions and the importance of facing and experiencing them, as opposed to ignoring them.

The anger starts with Gary, who has felt cheated and excluded from his alliance with Paul by Paul's choice to take the anti-anxiety drug Xanax during therapy. Mitch's anger at Paul resurfaces from last week and focuses on similar issues: Paul's lack of appreciation for others, last week by secretly looking for a substitute group, this week by droning on and on without regard for others. In fact, in both sessions Paul

has given a mixed message: he says he wants to hear reactions, but he can't deal with them once they come out. The increasing honesty and expression of feelings from all the men tonight made Paul exceedingly anxious. In his childhood, Paul's way of dealing with such anger was to withdraw, to "go away." As an adult, Paul has made the same choice: Xanax. The Xanax is Paul's way of "going away" tonight—of hiding from his anxiety and trying to bolster himself in group. Paul wants the men to think he is doing well. He goes into a rambling discourse on how much success he is enjoying and how his life is free of stress and anxiety. Gary and Ed react with anger, and Mitch first gets bored and then angry, too. Ironically, while Paul is trying to put the best face on his life, the men's reactions are just the opposite of what he anticipates. They sense he is regressing and missing the whole point of therapy: he's losing touch with them and even with his own life. In short, they feel cheated and annoyed, and their anger is a natural reaction to such behavior.

When Ed blames Paul for forcing Sean from the group, he releases an avalanche of anger on Paul. This avalanche is something Paul cannot deal with—it is a place he cannot be. He is used to tuning out Sarah and ignoring his children, but he *can't* tune out the men. He simply does not know what to do. He is frightened by this experience, and I need to assure him that no physical harm will come to him.

Yet something larger is going on here as well. With words like "beat up" and "fear" being tossed around, the men have to stop and question themselves: Could they go out of control? Could things get physically violent? That's when the men turn to me to reestablish control. I move the discussion away from feelings and toward intellect by assuring the men that verbal sharing of feelings is always acceptable, and that violence will *not* be tolerated. This is designed to reassure the men that I have control, and I will use it. I also demonstrate to Mitch and Gary, both of whom are extremely angry with

Paul, the value of their anger and the importance of sharing it and, if necessary, focusing it on me. Gary, Mitch, and Ed—the three men who confronted Paul tonight—all came from families where the parents could not deal effectively with anger and went completely out of control. It is my goal to demonstrate that the same feelings of anger can be handled differently, and responsibly—*in* control—as adults.

///

THE POWER OF COMBINING THOUGHTS AND FEELINGS

"Why are you in my seat?"

Paul is standing directly over Mitch, who has calmly seated himself in the black leather chair right next to mine. This is the chair Paul long ago claimed for his own.

Mitch slowly looks up at Paul but doesn't say a word. Paul tries again.

"Do you have something you want to talk about this week, or what?"

Mitch smiles. "No. I took it just so you couldn't have it."

Paul shrugs and backs into a seat on the couch. "Not to worry. I'm not going to talk about myself tonight anyway."

Ed and Mitch exchange a glance. Mitch is smiling but Ed just shrugs. Neither looks very convinced by Paul's statement.

There is a silence that stretches into several minutes.

Paul is sitting tight and Mitch is enjoying a few swings in the leather chair. Gary and Burt are both very still. Ed looks distracted; it takes some time before his even voice breaks the stillness.

"You know, there's a very good possibility I'm going to lose Ellen."

The silence returns and Ed sits quietly examining his feet. He's waiting for a question or comment, but nobody says a word.

"Okay," Ed continues, shifting to face Mitch with his back angled in Paul's direction. His face is drawn; he looks tired.

"I just don't know what to do! I finally got Ellen to go with me to the National Gallery last Sunday, after harping at her for God knows how long, and she just moped through the gallery like a petulant little zombie. She absolutely wouldn't say a word to me. I couldn't even get an answer out of her at lunch!" He's shaking his head miserably. "It got so bad I sort of edged my way ahead from her and basically spent almost two hours by myself, wandering around. About four-thirty I figured I better dig her up because they were about to close, and I found her—ten feet away from the main entrance on those lounge chairs, just staring into space."

Ed's head continues its slow shaking from side to side.

There is a grunt from Paul's direction. "So'd you guys have a fight or what?"

"No. We didn't." Ed's back is still to Paul—he hasn't moved.

"She just hates you in general, right?" Paul blurts out.

At this Ed slides back on the couch so he can see Paul on the far left end. He's glaring straight at him.

"She hates to talk in general, Paul. You'd know that if you'd heard a single thing I've ever said in this group." Ed stops abruptly and pulls off his glasses in one deliberate motion. He rubs his eyes slowly and continues.

"There is no talking to Ellen about anything. We'll get three sentences into a conversation about something, I don't know, Van Gogh, and I'll challenge her on some point and boom! that's it, she'll stop cold and give me this vicious stare"—Ed glowers at Mitch, mimicking Ellen—"and go dead silent." The glasses go back on. "If you think you'll get anything out of her, boy are you sadly mistaken. Nothing. Nada. Ice-cold dead silence."

"Yeah, well, marry her anyway," Paul persists. "At least you like her, right?"

"The truth is, I'm really worried about this."

"Would you *look* at me?" Paul demands.

Ed swings around suddenly, his eyes in a crazy exaggerated stare. "Okay?!"

"Jesus, I know where Ellen is on this, you know? I can't believe you're still mad at me from last week! Why the hell won't you let me help you?"

Ed rolls his eyes. "It's not like you've done much for me so far, Paul. God knows how long you'll be around anyway. Find any nifty support groups out there?"

"That's not fair: I'm here, right? I'm trying to connect to you and you're on this intellectual binge going on and on about Van Gogh. Then you're mad at Ellen because she can't argue like you, she's just not fucking good enough, huh?" Paul breaks off and looks away, but then has another thought.

"If I were Ellen I'd close you out, too."

"Yeah, well, lucky me."

"Don't you ever have anything nice to say about her?"

Ed grins wickedly. "Oh sure, Paul, like we've heard the sweetest love stories about Sarah. I've got this vision of her as some monstrous vulture, sucking blood out of you by the gallon."

"So what?" Paul shoots back. "I think of Ellen as this quiet, oafish dolt tagging along after you while you give her

failing grades on her answers to your questions. If you got any more intellectual, your head would explode!"

"Jesus Christ, Paul, I've had about enough of this. I didn't come in here for a pissing contest."

"Great! I can't tell you how illuminating this discussion has been. I'm thrilled you let me help you out. It's a pain in the ass trying to deal with you. No wonder Ellen clams up. We're both wasting our time with you." Paul folds his arms and slides back on the couch away from Ed. His bitter stare is locked on the carpet.

Silence.

"Have you two given up on each other?" I ask calmly.

"You bet," Ed mumbles. Paul just glares at me out of the corner of his eye. Eventually, he nods.

I don't want the conversation to end without resolution, so I encourage them.

"This is not exactly the way to go about learning to resolve a conflict."

More silence.

"Look," Ed says suddenly, "I just don't know where to go with this guy!"

I nod. "I understand where you're at, both of you. But there is value in Paul's reaction: He's able to see where Ellen is, and that could be something to learn from."

Ed scowls. Paul finally looks right at me.

"I'm not going to do it. I'm not going to get beaten up by him. That's it!"

I allow some more silence before coming in again.

"I encourage both of you to stick with this. You can learn more from each other by interacting than by smoldering in your corners. You're repeating in here what happens in your relationships outside."

During this entire exchange Burt has grown completely still. Gary has slid so far back in his corner that he's almost hidden by the palm.

I'm about to ask for others' reactions when Ed grunts.

"Look. Here's the deal. I know Paul might be able to help, okay, that's fine. It's just that . . . well, I'm really *scared*. I'm just afraid of losing her."

"What other feelings?" I ask.

Ed has buried himself in the couch now and appears to have actually grown smaller.

"This possibility—it makes me . . . it hurts. It's sad. But if I can learn from Paul, then I'll make myself hang in."

Paul sighs quietly. "You're too demanding of Ellen, and she's afraid she's not going to say the right thing."

"I . . . don't want to lose her." Ed's voice has developed a quiver. "I'm sad to realize that I might be driving her away."

Ed is connecting on a truly emotional level. These are real feelings from Ed and I feel for him.

"I understand that, Ed, I can feel it," I say. "Another thing"—I allow a small smile—"I'm glad you're in touch with 'sad' and 'scared.' It's easier to connect to you when you include feelings in what you say."

Ed scratches the back of his neck and nods back at me slowly. He's growing more relaxed; this has been a burden lifted from his shoulders. Even Paul, who has actually begun to look at the other men again, has sat forward and is listening to my words. As soon as the last phrase is out of my mouth, Paul jumps in.

"Look, I want to ask you guys something. Why is everybody so down on me? I really want to know."

"I think . . ." Burt says, but pauses for a moment to reflect. "Paul, this is the deal. You interrupt quite a bit of the time. You take the conversation to where you want it. Sometimes I think you don't really listen to anyone else!"

"Does that bother you?" Paul asks.

"Well, sure," Burt replies, a little surprised.

"Would you be willing to *tell* me when you get annoyed?"

"I could do that."

"How about you?" Paul asks, looking at Mitch for the first time since the session started.

"Paul, my first reaction to you is negative."

"So tell me when that happens, okay?"

Mitch shakes his head. "Sorry, that's not really part of my personality."

Paul shrugs and moves on to Gary.

"Well?"

"You think I haven't tried? Stopping a freight train is easier than interrupting you, Paul."

Paul nods and grows silent. He has ignored Ed.

Gary is still watching Paul. He looks agitated and coughs nervously.

"Paul, here's an example: I've wanted to talk all evening about something." He looks over at me and shakes his head. "Leigh and I broke up last week." He lets out an almost imperceptible sigh and then seems to remember where he was with Paul.

"Oh . . . so I wanted to talk about this, and as soon as you and Ed have your battle, *you* pick up *again*, and I'm sitting over here wondering how I'm going to be able to edge in."

"Oh. Okay, how do you feel about your breakup?"

Gary smiles weakly. "I feel like a complete failure, that's what. I should've ended it last November, but as usual I just hung in there. Same old pattern. Stick with it no matter what. Now I'm afraid I won't have anything to talk about in here. No woman to complain about."

"We talk about a lot of other things in here. *You* do, too," Burt offers. "I was real interested in that story about your father."

Gary shrugs. "Yeah, but my relationship was the first to go down the tubes, right? Not only that . . . shit, *I'm* the only recovering alcoholic in here." Suddenly Gary looks away from the men and out the window. "I just get the feeling I'm a hell of a lot more fucked up than any of you."

Ed and Burt exchange surprised looks.

"You really think so?" Mitch asks from the leather chair.

Gary nods. "Yeah, and I'm this lowly insurance estimator, just work out of my house. The rest of you are like, what, lawyers and all?"

Burt breaks into a wide grin. "Not on your life. You know I work on Capitol Hill. For the army."

Paul looks at Burt and back at Gary. "I'm the lawyer. Patent attorney, remember?"

Ed raises his hand. "Epidemiologist."

"Okay, I know, so everybody's different, it's just—"

"Gary," I break in, "what's going on?"

Gary frowns at me. "Huh?"

"You're all over the place: down on yourself, down on Leigh, down on the guys—and I'll be next. No one's response can satisfy you. You're very hard to pin down tonight."

Gary stiffens and peers at me for a moment.

"Why are *you* putting me down?"

"I'm describing my sense of you now. No point in anyone putting you down—you're already doing it to yourself! You won't hear any of the support anyone is giving you tonight."

"Yeah, okay." He sighs. "The truth is, I thought I was being more open, more vulnerable, I guess. I just heard it as a put-down."

"You are being more open and vulnerable, but you're stopping there and missing everyone's understanding and acceptance. Their reaction to your openness is support—not a put-down." I pause to watch Gary's reaction. "You're not in your real family right now. We're different."

Gary shrugs. "I never thought of it that way."

"Who in your family would put you down? Who are you expecting me to be like?"

"You want me to say my father?"

"I want you to continue to see the truth and reality."

"Okay. I see what you mean. No matter what I said at

home, he always put me down. I do worry that people are going to put me down, so I shy away from them."

"You're catching on, Gary."

"Well, I've got to give you credit, Al." Gary pauses and smiles at me. "I was a wrestler in high school and I don't like to be pinned down."

INTERPRETATION ─────────

The frustration and anger toward Paul from last week continue to fester in tonight's session. In the closing minutes of last week's session, I restated the guidelines of group therapy: any emotional confrontation is encouraged, no physical confrontation of any kind is acceptable. Mitch is more comfortable with the limits and feels free to simply take Paul's chair. Paul immediately discounts the idea that Mitch may be mad at him, which he clearly is ("I just took it so you couldn't have it") and tells himself it's just because Mitch may be "needy" ("Do you have something you want to talk about this week, or what?"). Paul has, in fact, walked straight into the lion's den this evening. The men are basically ignoring him. This does not sit well with Paul at all: He continually tries to edge in with Ed, who is already upset with Paul from last week.

As their confrontation escalates, Paul does make a very good point about Ed's tendency to remain intellectual: it is annoying him and he realizes that his frustration with Ed is similar to *Ellen's* frustration with Ed. Paul understands Ellen: he'd want to walk off, too! When both Ed and Paul clam up and refuse to engage one another, the cycle is complete. Ed and Paul duplicate in group what Ed and Ellen (and Paul and Sarah) have in life: a recurring standoff. Since this is ordinarily the stopping point between Ed and Ellen, I came in to em-

phasize that both men must go beyond this point in order to make progress. Ed is the first to consider that this suggestion has some validity because he's willing to be pushed, to take a risk because he is genuinely afraid of losing Ellen. Ed is visibly upset. As much as Ed dislikes Paul, he wishes to go the extra mile to keep Ellen. Ed *is* in a hard place. Ellen won't address any of these issues and won't go into therapy. Since Ed is making this effort himself, he stands much to gain from this process, and I only hope Ellen can keep up with him.

Once the situation with Ed is resolved, Paul goes fishing for attention. It is clear to Paul that the men are ignoring him, and he wants to do something about it. Tonight he is trying a new tactic. Whereas last week he chose to be calm and reserved by taking Xanax, tonight he is aggressive and confrontational. He goes around the group asking each member to tell him when they're mad or annoyed at him. Even though this is not really successful, since only Burt agrees to it, it does make sense. Paul wants desperately to make a connection to these men even though he continually alienates them. This is why Paul's most important lesson in the group is to learn his effect on others. It is a difficult lesson for Paul to learn.

Gary, meanwhile, is making another advance. He has taken in a lot of valuable information tonight. Initially he believed a relationship was needed to be "in this special club": he learned tonight that the men are interested in his whole life. He also thought he was more "fucked-up" than the others. Tonight it is clear that this is not the case ("You really think so?" Mitch asks with surprise). Finally, Gary has always felt a nagging inferiority on the professional level. He has always assumed that because the other men were more highly educated that they were also more capable and successful than he was. He doesn't yet know that he actually makes more money than anyone else here. Most men measure their success by the amount of money they earn or by the prestige of

their profession. Gary takes a risk making himself more vulnerable, by admitting feelings of inferiority. In this entire process, Gary is accepted and supported, but he won't accept this support. On every subject when some encouragement comes his way, he interrupts and denies that what he does, what he feels, is worthy of respect. It is difficult for me, or for any of the men, to figure out what Gary actually wants here. This is the origin of my "pin-down" comment: He really is quite slippery, very elusive. I want Gary to hear, to consciously recognize and acknowledge, the support he gets this evening. Gary's defensive reactions are based on his family dynamics, which he has continued to use. Now he recognizes that most of the "real" world is not out to put or pin him down and that he doesn't need to be so defensive. Gary has made a valuable and supportive connection to this group and is finding it difficult to allow the group to actually give to him.

SESSION 16

//

DREAMS:
THE INSIDE STORY

Paul has reclaimed his chair. He is sitting absolutely still, peering at Mitch with his jaw thrust forward. Mitch and Burt plop into their seats on the couch and give Paul a quick look. Mitch is grinning slightly.

Paul looks as though he's about to speak, but he waits until Gary and Ed get settled. They've just finished up a long story from the waiting area and are sharing a quiet laugh.

"So here's the deal," Paul begins. His jaw is relaxed now as he glances around at the men. "I've got a new squeeze. She's great, her name is Patti, and I've been out with her twice, and on Saturday, we slept together for the first time." He lets out an almost imperceptible sigh. "Boy, was it nice to sleep with somebody else for a change. Not only that, she suggested, no, insisted, I use a condom."

Gary smiles wryly. "She's afraid you're going to give her something, Paul?"

Paul snorts. "Hell no, *I'm* the one who's glad. From the way she talks I'll bet she's still hung up on her ex, and she's probably sleeping with the guy. But I still like her. She reminds me of Sarah in some ways. And my mom. She's all right."

Paul's gaze has slowly shifted from Gary to Mitch during this exchange. Paul is checking to see if Mitch is listening. He's not. Mitch is instead examining one of my paintings behind Paul's head.

"So is this woman going to be your new girlfriend?" Gary asks, bringing Paul back.

Paul shrugs. "Who knows." He brightens suddenly. "But I'll tell you what, I'd like it. She's got terrific tits, clear out here"—Paul indicates their fullness with his hands. "New implants she got just three weeks ago."

"Do you *like* her, Paul?" Burt asks quietly.

"Oh, sure. We had a real nice talk right when she got out of the hospital. She really opened up to me and told me all about her life. She even went into this horrible story about how her father raped her when she was twelve. *Twelve years old.*" Paul shudders slightly, then falls silent.

The silence continues.

"Paul, what are you feeling as you're telling us this?" I ask.

At first Paul does not respond. His head is tilted down away from me and he does not move when he finally answers.

"A little tense."

"I can understand that," I say, "considering your confrontation in here last week."

Paul looks up abruptly. "So what do you guys think? Let's hear some feedback."

Mitch rolls his eyes, and Paul catches him doing it.

"So?" Paul demands.

"You're boring me Paul. I lost interest already. Lots of facts and nothing about what's going on inside *you.*"

Paul's foot is tapping rapidly but he remains quiet. His eyes are still locked on Mitch.

Now Ed coughs nervously and pauses. Ed looks distracted tonight. He's much more rumpled in appearance, and he looks dejected. Nonetheless, he decides to jump in.

"Well, there's some truth to that, Paul. You're starting to launch into a long story about Patti's tits, about Patti's life, and we're not hearing anything about you. If Al hadn't stopped you to find out what *you're* feeling, we'd probably all be hearing about how her apartment is decorated and why she hates her job. Isn't this exactly what you said you *didn't* want from us?"

"I just want you guys to be honest," Paul shrugs.

"I can do that," Burt says with a slight smile. "My opinion is this. You're moving too fast with this Patti woman. Take it easy. Take it slow."

"Wait a second," Gary interjects. He's got his hand out like he's hailing a cab. "Just stop a second. Give him a *chance,* okay? How can you judge this woman so fast? I don't even know anything about her." Gary looks at Paul momentarily. "I wanted to hear more about you and her." Everyone is silent.

Paul grins. He is surprised, yet pleased, by Gary's sudden vigorous defense.

"Can I go on now?" Paul looks around and then continues without waiting for an answer. "If you want to know how I feel, I feel good to have sex again."

I nod at Paul. "What are your feelings at the moment?"

This time Paul does look at me. "I'm just glad to be in a relationship. That's all. It's tough out there. Really lonely."

Gary is nodding again and I sense the alliance between these two, shaken in recent weeks, gaining some new strength. I want to pull the discussion together.

"I think you both are in a similar place. Neither one of

you has a woman right now." My gaze wanders over to the rest of the couch. "Everyone else is in a committed relationship—Burt, Ed, and Mitch—and you are all sleeping with your women. So this is something we need to recognize." I pause to watch Paul, but he registers no reaction. "I'm concerned, Paul," I continue, "that you threw away the real heart and meat of the reactions from everyone tonight."

This surprises Paul. He looks over at me and frowns.

"The only strong response you had was to Gary, and his response was just empathy—he gave no feedback, no suggestions, no feeling."

"Hey, wait a minute. It was my honest-to-God reaction!" Gary protests.

"I'm aware of that, Gary. But it was the comment Paul had the *least* to learn from. He needs to hear everybody and be aware of the effect he's having on them." I turn directly to Paul. "Gary's empathy is fine; he's on your side on this. But you have to pay attention to the others' reactions, too. They're just as real and important for you."

"I heard them."

"You may have heard them, but you responded as though it was water off a duck's back." I stop to dig up in my mind an image that will appeal to Paul, something that will make a connection to him.

"Paul, look at it this way. It's like the new tits on Patti. They look great—they get your attention. But they're fake. There's nothing there. If you were to suck on them—try to get some nurturance from them—you'd find out they are dry."

Paul just stares at me, then slowly nods. "Okay. So I should focus on *you* as my new test of reality."

"Not just me. *Everyone* in here is a test of reality. You need to hear every one of them. Try not to tune them out. The fact is, Paul, the group is willing to cooperate with you more than you realize."

Paul smiles and taps Gary's knee with the back of his hand.

"You know, the two of us should hit the bar for a drink sometime."

A ripple of laughter runs through the group. Even Gary is amused. He's shaking his head slowly. But Paul's face is totally blank.

"What? What'd I say? You think I'm a queer or something?"

"Oh, for God's sake," Mitch mutters.

"Here's a good example of where you need to pay attention, Paul," Burt observes wryly.

"What?" Paul is beginning to grow restless.

"Paul, remember?" Gary nudges him on the arm. "I'm a recovering alcoholic. I haven't been in a bar in over six years."

"Oh, sure." He shrugs. "Sorry about that."

Gary smiles. "It's okay. I've been pretty hard on you the past few weeks, so I'll let this one go."

Ed has sat in stony silence throughout this light exchange. I know what has him so preoccupied. He avoids my gaze by looking out the windows and then staring at the side of Mitch's head.

"Ed, you can't avoid saying anything," I murmur.

Ed freezes and takes a deep breath. His head swings over in my direction.

"Look, this is pretty hard. My father died last Wednesday night."

Mitch gasps. Gary suddenly sits up and faces Ed. The light tone in the room vanishes.

Silence.

"God, not another one," Paul mutters finally.

Ed eyes Paul. "Yeah, another one." He shakes his head and looks over Paul's shoulder. "I couldn't believe it myself, you know? My sister called me in the middle of the night, and I'm sitting there thinking, *This can't be happening, there*

must be some kind of mistake. It can't be my father,' and this goddamned thought kept running round and round in my head." Ed now has his whole head buried in his hands. Everyone is very still.

"So I didn't know what to say! I'm sitting there listening to her and suddenly it dawns on me what's happened, and I start sobbing and shaking so hard I drop the phone, and shit, I just lost it. Thank God Ellen was there to talk to my sister."

Ed stops to cough and runs his fingers slowly through his hair.

Silence.

"You need to say more, Ed," I urge.

He looks up. "I didn't even say this to you, Al, but—" Suddenly Ed breaks off; his voice has grown thick, and his breathing is uneven. His glasses come off and he reaches for the Kleenex to wipe his swollen eyes. We sit quietly with him for a while. After a few moments of silence and slow, deliberate breathing, he's ready to go again.

"I hadn't even talked to him in six years! I didn't even know he was sick."

"Sounds like you're feeling a lot of guilt, Ed," I say. "Say a little more."

Ed sighs and shakes his head. "Oh, hell, I don't know. I hate to say it, but I was *ashamed* of him. I just wrote him off years ago. Maybe I could have helped him out of this"—Ed looks over at Mitch on his left—"like you were trying to do with your father."

Mitch nods. "Did you ever try?"

"Wait," I interject, "let's keep it in here."

"I was just curious," Mitch protests.

"Well, I'm not sure of that Mitch. This is a difficult topic for you, too. I think you'd rather not deal with Ed's intense feelings right now; after all, you just went through the same thing. So let's keep it here for a while."

Mitch shrugs. "Never mind, then."

Ed looks at me in anticipation. His hands are beginning to shake slightly and I notice his breathing is a little irregular again.

"Ed?"

He lets out a deep sigh. "I had this horrible dream Friday night. I still remember it, because it won't go away and I had damn near the same one last night, too."

"Let me hear the dream. Try to say it in the present tense, as though it were happening now."

"In the dream I have this revolver and I'm out at a shooting range in the desert somewhere and I'm firing away at this target off in the distance. I'm not even getting near it. All of a sudden my arm starts shaking and a shot goes pow! and ricochets off this rock and slams straight into the target. The target turns into a man. The man explodes. I woke up yelling." He winces.

"What do you make of the dream?" I ask.

"I think the man must be my father. It means I killed my father. I'm responsible in a roundabout way."

"What I hear is that you are feeling a whole lot of guilt over your father's death."

"That's for damned sure! And I can't figure it out. He lived by himself, off in this remote apartment without a telephone, and he wasn't in touch with any of us. He was drinking all the time. It was his choice! I was so sure he died of booze I forgot to ask. It turned out the coroner said the cause of death was a heart attack. I felt much better to know he didn't drink himself to death."

"Because?"

"A heart attack just sounds better. I guess it's the shame again."

INTERPRETATION ─────────────

Paul is connecting to a new love interest in a way that is in itself new for Paul: In contrast to his former interactions with women, he is now, for the first time, making an attempt to learn more about a woman (Patti, in this case) by listening to her ("She really opened up to me") and connecting to her more as a person. Because of Paul's crude, rough manner, he is very lonely, and any hint of acceptance is magnified. Patti is especially attractive to Paul because she is familiar and non-threatening, and she reminds him of both Sarah and his mother, women he understands and is familiar with, even though he is very unhappy with both. Once again familiarity and comfort prove irresistible to Paul. The other men sense this and show some real concern. Burt wants Paul to move more slowly to keep from getting hurt and falling into another bad relationship. The men are sensing some superficiality in this relationship, not only because of Paul's detailed description of Patti's new breasts, but because Paul has given only a surface description of Patti (the complaint voiced by both Mitch and Ed), one that excludes Paul's own feelings about her. Paul's only real connection is to Gary's empathy. Certainly misery loves company, but Paul is drawn far too strongly to the sympathy at the expense of listening to the other reactions. The reason for my breast analogy in the session was to emphasize to Paul, in a way that he would understand, that he will get as much nurturance from sympathy as from Patti's artificial breasts. In this way I continue to stress to Paul the importance of hearing the reactions of every man in the group rather than focusing solely on those that are comfortable or "easy" for him to hear. In fact, Paul's wish for a connection to Gary, the "easy" reaction, is so strong that he ends up losing sight of the whole picture: Gary's alcoholism, certainly a strong and present issue in the group, vanishes from Paul's mind.

Ed's revelation of his father's unexpected death was another intense and sad episode in the group. Ed's initial reaction to the news was denial: his old way of dealing with
negative feelings. As Ed catches himself in active denial, he
moves into the real effect: shock and overwhelming sadness.
Ed is another example of a man who has had great difficulty
in his relationship with his father. Like most men I work with,
Ed has yearned for a deep, close connection to his father, and
he has been repeatedly disappointed by his failure to achieve
it. Like Mitch, Ed had made enough progress in his own
therapy to consider a reconnection. This is the source of Ed's
guilt. He felt that it was his responsibility to do more to rescue
the relationship, but he felt he had failed. This feeling of
responsibility on Ed's part is an overreaction: it was his father's responsibility, as a father, to nurture the relationship. If
there was any failure, it was Ed's father's, not Ed's.

In this session we also see Ed's further growth manifested
in other ways: he's allowed himself to cry on and off all week,
and Ellen has been a strong support for his change. In many
ways, Ed's defensive wall is coming down. He's letting himself
be more vulnerable with Ellen, and he learns that this only
invites her increased love and support. Ed finds this very helpful at an extremely difficult time.

The anxiety and pain of this unexpected death are amplified in recurring dreams for Ed: an indication of the power
and presence of the event in his life. Ed's dream reflects his
guilt and the *shock* of the death. The killing by ricochet is Ed's
way of expressing his anger and hostility indirectly toward his
father. In real life, instead of discussing his hurt and anger,
he simply ignored his father and stopped talking to him altogether. This is a reflection of Ed's old way of expressing his
feelings in general: by indirect, oblique, means. Ed's own interpretation of his dream points up his willingness to deal with
his feelings more directly. I think Ed will now pay more attention to *his* role in relationships, especially with Ellen.

SESSION 17

//

MEN WANT CHILDREN

"How's it going, Ed?"

Burt is lounging comfortably on the couch, legs crossed and right arm extended in Mitch's direction. His brow is slightly furrowed. Concern over Ed.

Ed shrugs. "It's been tough, but things are getting better." Ed pauses to brush some dust off his trousers and look over at me. "I've been able to unload a lot of shit in individual. Last Thursday I spoke with Jan, my older sister, on the phone, and she told me about what's going on throughout the family . . . all the other reactions." Ed looks over at Burt and smiles. "All the kids are feeling guilty as hell. We don't know what we could have done differently. He's the one who moved away, yanked his telephone out of the wall, and just disappeared."

Burt nods and gradually looks over at Mitch. Mitch's

black leather boot has kept up a rapid nervous tap during Ed's story, even as his eyes have been glued right to him.

"Any other feelings, Ed?" I ask.

Ed's gaze rolls in my direction. He nods slowly.

"Yeah. Sadness. God, I wish I could have had a *real* father."

Silence.

"Do you miss talking to your dad?" Mitch asks, breaking his own trance.

"Oh, sure. But the truth is, we never really connected. Ever. Even as a kid I couldn't get to him . . . he was off drinking with my mom, living the politician's high life. So I finally gave up." He looks up at Mitch, and I notice for the first time Ed's tight, solid jaw. "It only got worse in the last few years. The guy just vanished down the bottle when my mother left him. Asshole."

"You're still pissed at him?" Mitch asks, surprised.

"You bet. The guy could be a selfish slob. Look what he did to my mother."

As Ed finishes this sentence I'm struck by how alone, lonely, he looks sitting at the edge of the couch.

"Your anger is an appropriate feeling for what you've been through, Ed," I say softly.

Ed nods in my direction and looks over at Mitch. All of a sudden I notice Mitch glowering at me.

"What's going on, Mitch?"

"I'm still pissed off at you. I don't know if I should continue with therapy at all."

"What?" Burt exclaims. "What's going on?" Gary nearly bolts out of the leather chair he claimed from Paul. Both are watching Mitch carefully.

Mitch, however, remains quiet and still. His eyes wander past me and fix on a blank spot on the wall.

"You are in a difficult point in your work, Mitch," I say. "We've uncovered a lot of things in here, so there is a lot of

emotion, a lot of anger, in you, including anger at me. Your best bet right now is to go intellectual. Take note of how your life is improving."

"I don't know," Gary interjects. "I've been deep into this negative shit, too. It's making me freaky. I don't know where the hell I'm at half the time."

Burt turns straight to him. "What in the world are you talking about?"

"I don't know what to say in here. All this down emotion is pushing me into a corner and I'd rather just bail out. Screw it! I've been going through mental masturbation all my life, and when it comes right down to it, who needs it? Plus this therapy costs a *fortune.*"

Now Gary has hunkered down on the couch and folded his arms in a show of defiance.

I let some time pass before coming in.

"Gary, you and Mitch are in similar places. Like I said to Mitch, go with your intellect. Pay attention to how your life has been improving."

"It hasn't been improving."

I try to suppress a smile. "Listen to me, Gary: Your progress has been very impressive. You've taken several risks in here and made some impressive gains."

He shrugs. "I need more goals. I don't know where I'm going or even where I'm headed!"

"I understand this is hard for you, Gary. Both you and Mitch have tended to withdraw from negative emotion, what's going on right here, right now, and not deal with it. It hasn't helped you in life and it won't help you to run from it now. I would encourage both of you to confront this, confront me! And deal with it."

"Oh that's right, we're supposed to yell at you," Gary says with a hint of a smile.

"If necessary."

"So that's 'getting the feelings out'?"

"Partly. Talking about them is one way of 'getting them out.' You don't have to get enraged or act crazy to let them out."

This gets a nod out of Gary, but Mitch still looks a bit skeptical.

The room grows quiet. We all sit and listen to the downtown traffic for a time.

"Can I get enraged for a moment?" Burt asks suddenly with a sly grin.

I return Burt's smile. Before I can speak, Paul sees an opening and jumps in.

"So what's the deal?"

Burt coughs and pulls some lint off his sweater. "Look, I know this should be good news, JoAnn agreed to an engagement on Thursday, but ever since that night her stress has been sky high! She's jittery and jumpy all the time."

Burt is scratching his palms nervously, his eyes are shifting continuously around the room. "I feel like the only thing she really cares about is finishing her degree. So what's it going to be like if we're married? Kids running around, day care, dog vomiting on the floor, shuttling kids to soccer practice. What's it going to be like when she's into lots of things. Am I going to just be invisible?"

"It'll be craziness. Like it is for all of us!" Paul says with a grin.

Burt is less than amused. "You have no idea what it's like to live with a woman who asks your 'reactions' and 'feelings' every thirty seconds."

"*That's* for damn sure. Sarah doesn't speak to me at all!"

"Paul, *I* don't know." Burt examines the palm plant at the end of the couch. "There are days I wonder if it isn't easier to be with a depressed woman like Rosalind than stick around with JoAnn. JoAnn wants to talk incessantly."

Paul shrugs. "Could be worse. She could hate you."

"Burt," I say, "I have this vision of you when you are with

JoAnn. You end up being barraged with words and feel, well, overwhelmed."

Burt nods emphatically. "Absolutely. It can get intimidating. It can get *humiliating.*"

Mitch frowns. "Humiliating?"

Burt nods. "I mean at work. Everybody there either has kids or is pregnant. Every last person. This is no joke! And they all know how desperately I want to have kids." Burt is shaking his head. "They keep asking me when I'm getting married. When I'm having kids. *That's* humiliating. It's even coming out in my dreams."

"Can you remember the dreams?" I ask.

Burt's eyes dart nervously to Mitch and Gary before he answers me.

"I can remember this one. It wasn't a dream: it was a nightmare."

I nod at Burt and wait for him to begin.

"I'm in my kitchen. It's late at night, and I walk into the doorway and I can see my reflection . . . and I'm dressed as a woman! So as I'm standing there, some guy comes into the kitchen and starts to cross in front of me. Before he can make it out of my range, I haul off and kick him square in the balls."

Gary winces and looks away with a half-smile. Paul has a blank look of shock on his face.

"Burt, this is just my immediate association," I say, "but it's pretty clear it's a castration-anxiety dream. Since you feel you are being treated like something less than a man by JoAnn, you get kicked in the balls yourself."

Burt nods.

"And what's your feeling in the dream?" I ask.

"I'm mad. But I don't know why."

"Take a guess."

He grins. "I didn't like the dress?"

I return his smile.

"What do you make of the guy crossing you?"

"It's your turn to answer."

"Sounds like you're mad at being 'crossed,' having your plans blocked, by JoAnn."

Burt is sitting square on the couch, looking pained. He nods reluctantly.

"It might also be helpful to see things from JoAnn's viewpoint," I add. "You are asking her to deal with her thesis, think about getting married, visit her parents, and get ready to be pregnant pretty soon, all within a very short period! That's quite a plateful."

"I know it is, and I really do want to appreciate her view. I'm just nervous about running out of time."

"It might be best for both of you to back away a bit. Take it easy. You don't *need* the extreme pressure of this deadline."

Burt shrugs. "Okay. We'll talk."

Silence.

Paul clears his voice and looks over at me. "I think we need to change this group. Change the format. Try something different."

"What do you have in mind, Paul?"

"A thirty-minute period. Somebody talks for thirty minutes, then we have a time check. We stop to see if anybody else has something going on. Look at poor Brad, here"—Paul motions toward Ed—"his dad just died and he's hardly said a word."

Mitch buries his head in his hands. Burt and Gary exchange looks and smile.

"Ed. My name is Ed, you dolt."

"Oh. Whatever. It was just a suggestion." Paul sits back suddenly and I notice his hands are beginning to shake.

"What are you feeling, Paul?"

"I don't know why I'm in this group if everybody is just going to pick on me."

"Paul, you can't even remember my *name*, for God's sake!" Ed exclaims.

"So what. I'm not mean."

During this exchange I have a sudden picture in my mind of Paul as a little boy trying desperately, and unsuccessfully, to get the other kids to play with him. It's very sad.

"I just don't need this kind of abuse," Paul continues. "I can't get Sarah or Patti to even speak to me. Sarah has been having this goddamned affair for six months, and my kids just caught her in bed, can you believe this, with her lover last Sunday. In my house! I've been feeling like shit ever since. *Damn*, I'm tired of hurting over this."

"And Patti?" Ed asks.

"Oh shit, I don't know," Paul mumbles miserably. "Her life's all screwed up. I'm just trying to help her get her life on track again. But she keeps neglecting me just the same."

"Paul, do you see what's going on?"

Paul shrugs. "Yeah. I'm miserable. Women hate me."

"Look. The rejection and isolation you're describing from Sarah and Patti aren't just outside this room, Paul, they're happening right here. *In the room*. You are playing an active role in being rejected and isolated from the other men. You need to learn how you do this, Paul, how you isolate yourself, or you're going to continue to be left out. You can learn to do it right here. And it won't take long."

Paul brightens considerably. A slight smile, even. He takes a deep breath and runs a quick hand through his hair.

"I appreciate that, Al. I'm glad to hear there is *something* I can do. It's just so damn depressing. But I know I'm making some progress. I don't have the same doubts as Gary over here. I *know* I'm getting something out of therapy. I'm not the same person I was six months ago. In fact, I wish the guys would appreciate it more!"

"Yeah, Paul, but it's impossible for me to entirely erase

my impression of you at once," Mitch says with a shake of the head.

"I wish we heard more from *you*, Mitch," Gary says softly.

Mitch shifts his large frame to face Gary on the other end of the couch.

"I'll talk when I'm ready."

Gary frowns. "I think it would be better if you talk when you're *not* ready. It's tougher, but you'll get more out of it."

"I do what I do. I don't like change. You all know that."

Silence.

"Look, Mitch, I'm going to be honest with you," Gary says abruptly. "I'm not happy with this. I don't appreciate your sitting over there in silence glowering at everybody, staring me down." Gary's voice has begun to quaver slightly. He pauses to recover before continuing.

"I'll tell you what. I've been trying to figure you out, and here's what I have so far. You're sitting on this huge fucking barrel of anger and you're ready to explode at any time." The quaver in Gary's voice has reappeared.

"Gary, are you all right?" Burt asks.

"Sure. I was just . . . well, I was sort of apprehensive about actually saying that, but I'm glad I did."

"I'm not going to explode, Gary," Mitch says calmly.

"Yeah, well, I can see it in your eyes. There is a slow burn going on deep inside. You have this placid, calm exterior, always in control. But I know better. I can see inside of you."

INTERPRETATION ───────────

Mitch's anger at me in tonight's session is a holdover from last week. When I stopped Mitch from interrupting Ed's pain and loss surrounding his father's death in that last session, Mitch withdrew momentarily and has been angry at me ever since. In Mitch's mind, I am being like his father, and his response is identical: anger and withdrawal. It is still hard for Mitch to express his anger directly, because he continues to fear retaliation from his dad. While Mitch occasionally will let out some anger (often in response to Paul), he almost always suppresses or hides it. Gary, on the other hand, who also has trouble expressing anger, is able to pick up on Mitch's behavior immediately and identify it for what it is. When Gary initially prods Mitch to say more about his life, Mitch shuts down further, making him increasingly anxious and uncomfortable. In fact, Gary is quite on target with his observations of Mitch tonight. His confrontation with Mitch is his own attempt to be more connected to him.

Burt has also been sitting on a lot of anxiety, and his threshold was just breached this last week. For the last several months Burt has been playing nice guy at home to JoAnn and has been sitting on his own feelings (anxieties, feelings of inferiority, embarrassment) in an effort to provide support and nurturance to her. There is also an element of anger in Burt that has been buried and just recently surfaced: Burt has been angry at JoAnn for putting so many things ahead of him and his desire for marriage and children. Burt's tendency to sit on anger gets him into serious trouble in relationships: it was the central element underlying his early impotence in his relationship with JoAnn and has been responsible for his own feeling of failure and uncertainty in his past relationship. There is a reason Burt does this. He is trying to keep *JoAnn's* stress down by not revealing his own feelings, but inside he wants

everything taken care of (he secretly wants JoAnn to embrace the idea of marriage and children over her studies). The dilemma for Burt is that JoAnn is a talker, she verbalizes her stress constantly, while Burt is the silent type: he has been overwhelmed by words ever since childhood, when he was intimidated by his screaming father. Burt also is experiencing much humiliation. At work he feels like an outsider, as his colleagues—all of whom are married and have children—ask when he's getting married and when he's having children, the very area of conflict with JoAnn. In Burt's dream we see a great deal of his anger, something that he has been holding in and just now overflows into his dream. The kick in the balls in this dream reflects both his hostility and his own vulnerability. His clothes (he's dressed as a woman in the dream) show that he doesn't feel like a man. He just doesn't have what all the men at work have: he is an unfulfilled man. The "good-natured" teasing at work is making him more vulnerable. Unfortunately, this is a low blow to Burt.

Once again we witness Paul's isolating behavior in group and some of the hostility it generates. Tonight's session has been a microcosm of what happens in Paul's life: His alienating, abrasive behavior isolates him from people, so he tries in any way he can to win "approval" (in his life, he supports Patti; in the group, he proposes a better group "format"). However, Paul is not getting nurturance from either of these two areas: Patti continues to ignore him and the men in the group reject his idea out of hand. Paul is replaying in his adult life that which he learned as a child. For many years Paul felt entirely unwanted by his mother, so he attempted to compensate by becoming "important": by being supportive, doing work, being responsible. But this has not worked for Paul in his adult life: he is encountering failure with all the women in his life and he continues to struggle with the men in group to establish and maintain a strong bond.

SESSION 18

//

THE THERAPIST
AS FATHER

"I've been thinking a lot about what I'm doing to Ellen."

A long silence follows Ed's statement. He pauses to re-move his glasses and rub his eyes; Gary watches Ed go through these motions. We are all very quiet.

The glasses finally go back on.

"I know what I'm doing; it's what you've been telling me in here," Ed says simply. "I criticize her a lot. She's always gotten completely silent after this happens. She'll ignore me, mope around, vanish for hours with a book. The thing is, I never saw it as criticism. I just knew what I wanted and she wasn't it!"

Ed looks over and smiles at Gary. He shrugs back.

"Are you still on her case?" Paul asks. He looks confident tonight, comfortable again in his leather chair.

Ed nods slowly. "Sure. But I don't want to go on like this

forever. Not only that, Ellen is taking the offensive. She'll bite back now. Before she would just sulk or hide. So we spend a lot of time tearing each other down. The woman is beginning to remind me of my mother." Suddenly Ed's head bobs up and he smiles. "First time *that* ever occurred to me!"

"How are Ellen and your mother alike?" I ask.

Ed's eyebrows are still elevated. He's just heard my question.

"My mom never had much good to say about me, to tell you the truth. She'd pop in half-drunk from some party right before my bedtime and start bitching about my leaving the door open, or the dishes in the sink or the garbage piled up in the dining room."

Burt frowns. "Were you the maid?"

"Yes."

"Oh." Burt shrugs and looks over at me with a bewildered expression.

"So Ellen bitches about everything now, too. 'Why didn't you make the bed?' 'What did you do with my book?' 'Don't you ever wash anything?' That sort of thing. I never know when she'll be on the warpath."

"What do you think's going on with her, Ed?" I ask.

"I don't know. PMS?" He's grinning.

"Ed, my thought is that Ellen's therapy is having an effect. Sounds like she's trying her wings. Seeing how it feels to speak up."

"If that's it, maybe I better think twice before encouraging her to continue if we move." He still has a hint of a smile. As Ed is talking, Paul has begun to fidget, and I realize he is going to take the floor very soon. I want to offer Ed some advice before this happens.

"I think this connection you've made between Ellen and your mother—it's a good insight, Ed," I comment. "But what you're describing is a relationship with a lot of negativity. This has got to be hard." I pause. "You need to find a way to turn

this negativity around if things are going to work out for the two of you."

"You're making too many decisions."

Paul has gotten his comment in even before Ed can respond to me.

"What?"

"You're making too many decisions," Paul repeats impatiently.

"What are you talking about?"

"You shouldn't be thinking about making so many decisions right now. You remind me of Mitch! Your father just died, and you're doing the same thing he did. Running off and getting married!"

"I'm not getting married, Paul."

"Are you going to move to California?"

"I'm still thinking about it. There's a very good chance I will." Ed peers at Paul suspiciously. "It's a great opportunity for a dynamite promotion. Why not?"

"You're moving too fast!" Paul shakes his head sadly. Now *Paul* looks like the disappointed professor, Ed's former role.

Ed swings over to look at me.

"Do you think I'm moving too fast?"

"Stay with Paul, Ed."

Ed looks back at Paul. "Do you have a point to make about this, or what?"

Paul shrugs. "I just wouldn't jump into anything too quick, if you get my drift."

Mitch is getting irritated listening to this dialogue. He looks straight at me. "Can you make any sense of this?"

I smile at Mitch and mentally debate whether to allow Ed and Paul to continue. I decide to come in. Paul has swung away from Ed and is looking out the window.

"Mitch, I think Paul is on to something. Neither you nor Ed have really allowed yourselves very much time to grieve. I know you both had very stormy, rocky relationships with

your fathers, but there still was the knowledge, the feeling, that you had fathers, and now that's gone. There's a void in your lives now."

"I know," Mitch says nodding. "I just hope I get over it soon."

Ed looks back at me. "How long is it going to take before I start to feel better, anyway?"

I recall Ed's mental schedule about therapy and I'm reluctant to give him any encouragement in these terms.

"There is no time period, Ed. It is a very individual process. It's not unusual for someone to grieve for over a year."

"Well, I'm not grieving over Sarah anymore!" Paul exclaims.

"Wha—" Ed begins, but his mouth clamps shut immediately.

"Yep," Paul says. "Having a fine time with Patti. Sex is just great, she even grabs me! You know how long it's been since I've had *that?*"

"Paul, I thought Patti was *ignoring* you," Gary says with a frown.

"Not anymore!" Paul looks very pleased with himself.

"She given up that other guy?" Burt asks.

Paul deflates immediately. "Oh. Not really. She's sleeping with him, too."

"Jesus, she sounds like a slut," Gary mumbles.

Paul winces. "She is *not!*"

"Well, that's my impression of her from what you've said, Paul."

"Hey, I like her! I'm sort of . . . wounded by that. 'Slut'!" Paul is shaking his head.

"Paul, do you understand where Gary is coming from on this?" I ask.

Paul looks up at me with a glum expression. He shakes his head slowly.

I look straight at him. "This has been an issue for Gary

in the last several weeks, Paul. You know we've been talking about how Gary is, well, down on women in general right now. There is a lot of negativity around women with Gary."

Gary smiles. "Bullshit, Al, it doesn't have anything to do with 'negativity.' I just think she's a slut!"

Mitch and Gary burst out laughing. Paul sits still, seething by himself. Burt is trying to suppress a laugh. Ed is grinning.

A minute or two passes as things settle down.

"Paul, maybe there is something else we can explore here," I say finally. "Earlier, when Ed was talking, did you recognize your sudden intrusion?"

Paul looks up, surprised. "What?"

"Did you sense you were interrupting things? That Ed might have more to say?"

"Well, I was waiting for a good place to start. I was just afraid I wouldn't get a chance to tell my story."

"Ed was right in the middle of talking about something important to him."

"He cut me off on purpose," Ed interjects.

I glanced over at Ed. "Why do you think he cut you off, Ed?"

"He just wants to get me. Hurt me. He was probably bored, too!"

"I was," Paul mumbles. "I just wasn't that interested."

"Paul," I say. "This is what I was talking about. Your sensitivity to others' feelings and others' reactions to you. These are the two most important things for you to learn in group. It's basic to your work in therapy."

"Yeah, bullshit. It's a dog-eat-dog world out there. Every guy for himself."

Burt looks over at me and shrugs.

"A cute cliché, but not really accurate in our society, Paul. It is important for you to realize that this insensitivity is going to keep alienating you from a lot of people."

Paul flashes me a look of anger. "I have friends! Lots of them! I'm only alienated in *here*!" He pauses to examine his shoe. "Maybe it's time for me to quit group."

Silence.

"It's ironic for you to say that in a session you could get so much out of—things you say you want: expression of feelings, feedback, knowing your effect, being heard."

Paul sighs. "I don't know."

"Since I'm probably off to California in a month or so, I'll be out of the picture, Paul," Ed says with a twinge of sarcasm.

"See, Paul, you can't quit now!" Gary exclaims, picking up for Ed. "You'll have more time in here when Ed is gone."

Paul peers at Gary. "I just don't think we bond very well."

"What?"

"I would like us to *do* something together. Something symbolic."

Gary smiles. "You want us to dance around the room or go big-game hunting?"

"I think we should do a group yell."

"A what?"

"A yell. Just scream all together for a few seconds. At the top of our lungs! It's a great release. It lets out energy and you feel lighter." Paul has begun to speak faster—he's looking around the room for support.

There isn't any. The others look very suspicious. Ed has a broad smirk on his face, but Mitch is looking worried.

"I think you should check out who is going to yell with you, Paul," I say.

"I hate screaming. I won't do it," Mitch says suddenly.

Paul quickly looks at Gary.

"You've got to be kidding! Most ridiculous thing I've ever heard," Gary says.

Burt and Ed both shake their heads before Paul even gets to ask them. He plops back in his chair.

"Isn't *anybody* going to yell with me?"

I sense that once again Paul is completely alone in group and desperately in need of an ally.

"I'll yell with you, Paul, if you want," I say, trying to provide a modicum of encouragement.

Paul perks up. He's all grins.

"Okay, this is how it works. On the count of three, we let 'er rip, okay?

I nod.

"One . . . two . . . three . . . AAAAUUUUUUUGGG-HHHHHHH!"

Out of nowhere Mitch bolts up and over the glass table, crashing into the centerpiece and tripping over Gary's outstretched legs. He jumps back up off the floor and turns to us, face ablaze. *"I'm never coming back here again!"*

He vanishes, slamming the door.

Complete silence. Every man in the room is stunned.

"Everyone stay here, I want to catch Mitch," I say, moving quickly past the toppled table and out the door. My assistant silently points the way for me.

Mitch has retreated to the conference room. As I enter the room, I find he is off in the far corner, nose pinned to the long glass windows watching the slow drizzling rain.

For several moments I don't say a word. I wait until he senses my presence.

"I'm glad you're here," I say softly.

He shrugs.

"Are you okay?"

He nods.

"Will you wait for me? I'll be right back."

"Okay," he croaks.

I back out and return to my office and the other men.

Paul is pacing nervously back and forth in front of my desk. Burt has stood and half-pulled his sweater over his head. He's ready to go. I ask Paul and Burt to have a seat.

"It's all my fault," Paul mumbles. "I don't belong here."

Burt shrugs. "I'll be away for a couple of weeks, anyway. Maybe this is a good time to quit for me, too."

"You're reacting to the yell, Burt," I say. "Everyone is. It has been upsetting to all of us. Stay with your reactions, but recognize them for what they are."

Burt shrugs and coughs nervously.

"I'm still trying to figure out why the hell you screamed," Gary says. He's glaring at me by now.

"Why do you think I did, Gary?"

"To support *him?* You've got to be kidding!"

"How is Mitch?" Ed asks softly.

"He's okay. Let's end here. We've already gone overtime and I want to spend some time with Mitch before he leaves."

There are a lot of enthusiastic nods.

I return to the conference room. Mitch hasn't moved at all. I make my way around the long center table and take up my own spot in front of the windows at the other end of the room.

"Mitch, I'll leave you alone if you want."

He shakes his head. "No, it's okay."

Silence. The rain has grown into a steady downpour. The room is nearly black.

I edge slowly toward his window panel.

"The scream?"

He nods. "I don't know what happened."

I let out a long sigh. "It touched something, Mitch. Something very powerful for you. We can figure it out later. How do you feel now?"

Mitch shrugs. "I don't know. I feel so weird."

"You're not. Why don't you take a few minutes to be by yourself to calm down before getting on your bike. I'll be in my office if you need me."

Mitch sighs, and turns to me, running a slow hand through his hair.

"Sure. Hell, I can't ride in this rain, anyway."

I leave, thinking he's one of my sons. I've got to raise Mitch much more gently this time around.

INTERPRETATION

A very emotional, intense, powerful session. The conflict between Paul and Mitch over the past several weeks bursts into the open tonight. Mitch feels so threatened by the sudden scream that he panics and flees for survival. He is absolutely terrified by the scream, both because he dislikes screaming in general ("I hate screaming. I won't do it") and, once again, he saw me in the role of his father, screaming at him against his will. Mitch's impulsive, childhood response, running away from the yelling, takes over without warning tonight, as he bolts from the room as a means of escape. Once he is out of the room and taking refuge in the conference room, Mitch returns to reality. He feels quite confused and very embarrassed by his behavior, yet he knows it is essential for us to discuss it at a later date. In many ways, Gary's explanation of my decision to yell with Paul tonight is right on target: I feel Paul is desperately in need of support. He wants to scream, he complies with my request to check out who would scream with him, and he explains the purpose of the yell itself. The complete rejection of Paul's idea by all the men once again isolates Paul, and I feel he needs to know that at least I am on his side. For that reason, I decide to yell with him.

The others' reactions to the yell are no less revealing. Burt is up and ready to go. Not only is he ready to leave this group session, he is ready to walk away altogether. Burt is upset: he sees Mitch's explosion as the end of the group. Like

many men, Burt wants endings to happen as fast as possible. He is much more willing to say, "That's it!" and walk off, rather than deal with the prospect of the group's ending. Paul is initially pleased by my agreement to yell with him but is terribly shaken by Mitch's escape. Ironically, Paul's wish to engage in a symbolic act of "bonding" serves to *further* isolate him from group. Paul is feeling like more of an outsider and is even worried he'll be kicked out of group. Gary is the only man who appropriately expresses his anger at me for agreeing to yell with Paul. This shows how much Gary has changed since the early group sessions: In the first few weeks Gary was much more likely to indulge Paul, to give him the benefit of the doubt, at the expense of the others (once referring to the others as "pussy-whipped" and himself and Paul as the only "real" men), while tonight he berates me for siding with Paul. Gary's connection to the other men, unlike Paul's, has grown much stronger, and he is no longer willing to ally himself with Paul at the expense of his link to the others. Ed has the mildest reaction. He is surprised and curious. But Ed has already begun to disengage from the group mentally as he becomes increasingly committed to moving to California, and therefore he is less threatened by Mitch's sudden and dramatic bolt.

In spite of Paul's struggle to connect to these men, many of his comments in this session are very valuable and reveal genuine sensitivity. Paul has also grown and has been a risk-taker in the group. He is concerned that, like Mitch, Ed is moving toward marriage to fill the void of his father's unexpected death. As I pointed out to Ed, the tenuous nature of his relationship with his father is really irrelevant to the grieving process: He has suffered a real loss, because now the hope or desire of reestablishing this connection is lost forever. Both Mitch and Ed hate the pain they are going through, and they are exhausted by the grieving process. Ed even expects a deadline for grieving. This is a common reaction of men to

grief: They want a time limit—a schedule—so they can mus-
ter their courage and work through it and be done with it. I
do not give Ed any time limit at all; I am concerned that if a
deadline is set, he will hunker down and try to reach it without confronting the feelings as they occur. The grieving process goes as rapidly as the man is willing to experience the
feelings of the loss.

It is also important to at least give Paul credit for *trying*
to "bond" in tonight's session. No matter how it appears, Paul
has made progress. His "dog-eat-dog" view of the world is
based on how he grew up. He learned to be insensitive with
others, particularly his mother, as a way of dealing with her
insensitivity to him. In his adult life, Paul had neglected Sarah
and the kids for many years, yet he has begun to turn this
around, particularly with his children. Paul also treats Patti far
better than he treated Sarah. In the group, his connection to
Gary is his strongest, so he was naturally upset and angry
with Gary for labeling Patti a "slut." He took this accusation
very seriously; he wants to preserve his relationship with Gary,
not have it threatened. Gary's "slut" comment also revealed
much about Gary's own life. Gary is the only man in group
without a permanent relationship, and the last thing he wants
is to lose Paul to a committed relationship: He would then
stand entirely alone as the only "single" in the group.

SECRETS, LIES, AND FAMILY PRESSURE

"No more Paul!"

"Gary, what're you talking about?" Mitch asks, sinking into the couch.

"He's gone, out." Gary jerks his thumb toward the door like an umpire calling Paul out.

Mitch glances over at me and back to Gary. He's getting a little testy.

"Did he *tell* you that?"

Gary nods. "Last week, he caught me in the waiting room before I could leave. He shook my hand and said it was nice knowing me, good having me in the group." Gary shrugs. "He's not coming back."

Mitch peers at me. "Is that true?"

"Yes. He told me in his individual session. I encouraged

him to come tonight and discuss it in person, but he was adamant. I don't think he'll be back."

"Did he give a reason?" Burt asks with a frown.

"He's upset and feels like he doesn't belong here. And he's really afraid of you, Mitch."

Mitch rolls his eyes and slides back on the couch. "What a jerk. I already *told* him I've never hit anybody. What's with this guy? He never listens to a damn thing we say."

"Any other reactions to Paul's leaving?" I ask, scanning the room.

Mitch is still collapsed on the couch. Gary and Burt exchange looks. There is a slight smirk on Gary's face. Ed decides it's up to him to start.

"I don't know about the rest of you, but I'd about had it with Paul, anyway. The guy was really beginning to really piss me off."

This phrase hangs in the air.

Ed is staring at the rug and rubbing his mouth slowly. His gaze has not shifted when he speaks again. "The guy wanted all his precious 'feedback,' and when we *gave* it to him, he never heard a word of it." Ed looks over at Mitch with a shrug. "Last week when he interrupted me, I had this sudden urge to reach over and stuff a sock in his mouth!"

Gary blurts out a laugh that startles us all. Ed frowns. He is not amused.

"I'm serious!"

"Yeah, I know," Gary says.

"I'm with you," Mitch says softly, looking over at Ed. "I like group a lot better without Paul."

Gary looks at his watch. "You mean you like the last ten minutes?"

Mitch eyes Gary for a moment, then smiles. "I almost didn't come here tonight at all."

"But you did."

Mitch shrugs. "Sure. I made up my mind at the last min-

ute. I was in the bookstore downstairs wandering around trying to decide."

"Can you say what your thoughts were, Mitch," I suggest, "what went into your decision?"

Mitch nods slowly and fixes his eyes right on me. "I didn't know if I could trust you anymore." Pause. "I didn't know what was best, come in here, stick with it, or just split and risk screwing things up with Lynda." Mitch exhales slowly. "I didn't know a lot of things."

Burt is nodding. "I'm glad you decided to come on in."

Mitch acknowledges this with a quick nod over at Burt, but he's still stiff and awkward.

"What else, Mitch?" I ask.

"I can't understand it. Why in the hell did you scream your head off with Paul last week when I told you that I hated yelling?"

"I'll answer your question in a moment, Mitch, but first tell me what you are feeling toward me."

Mitch is beginning to steam. "I'm getting angry again. I was angry last week! You really pissed me off with that little screaming stunt."

I nod and scan the room. "Any other reactions to what happened in the last session?"

"He's right, Al," Gary says softly. "None of us wanted to do it. Paul was trying to cram another goofy idea down our throats and we weren't buying it. Now, look, I *know* you wanted him to feel he wasn't completely alone, but *he was!*" Gary slowly looks away. "I think you made a tactical error this time."

I look over at Burt. "You haven't said much. What was your reaction to last week?"

"I got scared. I definitely thought our group had collapsed."

"Because?"

"I just couldn't see how it could go on anymore. I thought everyone would be scared away."

Silence.

"Okay," I begin, "I've given that session a great deal of thought. Gary, your description is pretty accurate. I *did* sense Paul's frustration and alienation. I wanted him to have at least one ally. If I could do it over again, I would tell Paul I would join him in a scream *after* group—and anyone who wanted to join, could."

Gary smiles. "You two would've still been all alone."

"Yeah," Mitch cracks, "now Paul's *completely* alone."

"You know, Mitch," Gary says softly, "Paul really was afraid of you. I think your dash out of here last week scared the living hell out of him."

"I tripped over *you*, not *him.*"

Gary smiles. "I know. I have the marks on my legs to prove it. But that's not what I mean. I think your size intimidated him. Hell, it intimidates *me!*"

Mitch frowns.

"Do you recognize people can be scared of you, Mitch?" I ask.

"Yeah, I've heard that, but I don't really see it myself."

"Oh, come on," Gary protests. "How can that be? You look like Robocop in leather, for Chrissake!"

Mitch blinks a blank look at us all.

Ed gestures in Mitch's direction. "I back off a lot with you, too. There are times I want to push you, find out what's eating you, but, well, it's probably safer just to let you steam on low boil all by yourself."

"Look, Ed," Mitch says in exasperation, "I'm sorry I'm so scary. You don't know how frustrating it is to be stuck like this."

"Well, what *is* bothering you?"

"I don't know where to begin; I'm worried. Am I just getting cold feet with Lynda, am I going to fuck up *another*

marriage, am I going to end up single, on the street, by myself?"

Gary smiles. "You're in a bind either way by that description, Mitch. If you're with Lynda you're 'fucking up the marriage'; if you're without her, you're single: 'on the street.' " Gary pauses and catches me with a look out of the corner of his eye. "Being single isn't all that bad, you know. I used to think it was, but I kind of like it now."

"I wouldn't. I don't want to lose Lynda."

"Join the club," Ed says glumly.

"Ellen?"

"Yeah, and you know what? I've actually been feeling a lot better about Ellen. I can see where there's some hope for us. But" —he sighs—"all I'm getting from her is anger. She's still really pissed about the way I treat her. So I'm hearing a lot of criticism: 'You're too demanding,' 'Why do you want to control me?' 'Can't you just leave me alone?' Ed looks over at Gary with a wry grin. "But at least she's talking to me!"

"Maybe she's another JoAnn in the making after all," Burt observes with a grin.

Gary snorts. "You guys can have it."

"It's a lot better than staring at the back of her head as she storms out of the room," Ed says with a shrug.

"Are you two sleeping together?" Gary asks suddenly.

"We're in the same bed."

Gary pauses. "Okay. Are you getting laid or not?"

"I haven't touched her in six weeks."

Gary's eyes grow wide with surprise. "I'd say the prognosis is baaaaad for that relationship."

"Would *you* want to have sex with somebody after snipping at her heels for an hour? It's a turn-off."

"So what are you going to do about it?" Gary asks.

Ed shrugs. "Ellen and I were at a party last week up on Connecticut Avenue. There's this woman I know from work, Anna, who was there, and she was giving me the serious eye."

Ed pauses to look straight to Gary. "You know, I could *see* something happening right in that living room under the right circumstances, if she came up to me, said the right things, started flirting. I think I'd like it. Who knows what would happen?"

"*Did* anything happen?"

Ed shakes his head. "It's just a thought."

Silence.

"Speaking of thoughts. I've thought about leaving group lately," Gary says straight to the palm in the corner. "We're coming up on my six-month time limit for therapy."

"Say more about it, Gary."

Gary looks from the palm to me. "It's just I've been feeling better, you know. I've set certain goals. I don't want to be around in group therapy for too long."

I nod. "The time limit, though. That's just another pressure."

"Yeah, and that's just therapist talk," Gary shoots back. "I've got other things to spend my money on."

"Gary, I understand that, but look. It's been my experience that when a patient starts using money as a reason for leaving therapy, particularly one whose business has grown as much as yours, it's usually a smoke screen for something else."

"I'm just setting my priorities." Gary's jaw has grown rock hard.

I'm struck by how quickly Gary has been overtaken by anger. It's time for me to move this discussion from the intellect into feelings.

"What's your anger at me, Gary?"

"You're trying to tell me what to do. I'm not going to let you do it."

"I see."

"Don't try to invalidate me, Al. I don't want you pushing me in some direction I don't want." Gary's deep, intense eyes

drift to the door and then find their way back to me. "What do you think about that?" he asks.

"I think you're projecting on me, Gary," I say evenly. "You're reacting to me like somebody else in your life. Who would push you around?"

"I'm not answering you."

"My guess is that you're reacting to me as though I'm your father."

At this Gary grows silent, and looks away. A few minutes pass. I'm conscious of the clock ticking from behind my desk.

"What are you feeling, Gary?"

Gary coughs nervously. "I'm getting embarrassed."

"What is embarrassing you?"

"My father. My family. The whole mess. I'm embarrassed that everybody has to keep hearing about those losers."

"Can you stay with that, Gary?"

Gary shrugs. "I've just spent so much of my life covering for them—lying about the drinking, you know. It's my first reaction. It makes me sick that it still happens. I'm tired of it. Things got so bad in high school, lying so much, that I started drinking *myself.*"

Silence.

"Gary?"

He looks up.

"What's going on inside?"

"I really feel awful. I feel *mortified.*"

"Why mortified?"

"The secret's out."

"Who is mortifying you?"

"You are."

"No, but it seems that way to you . . . I see that . . . It's coming back, Gary. You are feeling what you felt as a teenager. Mortified by your father and his attempts to hold you down—to stop you from growing up. I won't hold you down. I'll help you grow up where you missed."

Gary is absolutely still. There is no sound or motion in the room. The others are watching Gary carefully.

Slowly a calm grin spreads across Gary's face. He looks up at me and I return the smile. Smiles of recognition.

"You know, Al, I figured I'd inch *something* out of this therapy for myself someday, and, well, it looks like we made it."

INTERPRETATION ————————

Paul's decision to abandon the group without discussion or reflection is triggered by his perception that Mitch is totally out of control—he is afraid of a direct physical attack by Mitch. In recent weeks, Paul had become increasingly intimidated by Mitch's quiet, angry undercurrent, and the explosion in last week's session was simply too much for him to bear. The suddenness and finality of Paul's decision (which was, after all, largely made in the waiting room right after group ended) are due to Paul's feelings of fear, rejection, and alienation from the group—his sense that he has not been accepted and is not fitting in. This has always been Paul's supreme struggle both in group and in the outside world: how to get along with people. Unfortunately, Paul is the one who will miss out by this sudden and irrevocable decision to leave group. This action itself is a repeat of his childhood: when upset or confused as a young boy, Paul would automatically escape or withdraw, and therefore never learned how to confront his fears or resolve his conflicts. Nonetheless, Paul *has* grown from being in group. He is now, more than ever, firmly committed to divorce. Also, his relationships with Betty and Abe have literally never been better, and he has had some measure of success with new women, a first in his adult life. Many men

accomplish some goals in therapy and then decide to stop. A few do return to build on these initial successes and continue to grow in new areas.

Mitch's outburst, on the other hand, results in a major breakthrough for him. For the first time, he is able to get angry at me directly. Instead of withdrawing (his old behavior), in tonight's session, Mitch squares off against me with some very harsh words ("You really pissed me off with that little screaming stunt"). Mitch's very decision to return tonight indicates that he values the group and recognizes how it is helping him, particularly in his relationship with Lynda. Much of what Mitch is learning right now is integration of the intellectual (which he always had) and the emotional (which he always buried). This learning process can be very difficult sometimes. Mitch admits outright that he is confused: he doesn't know if he can trust me, and he doesn't fully understand what is happening. Yet he's willing to sit with those mixed feelings and risk trusting that I am on his side. Mitch knows I won't abandon him, so he doesn't abandon the group.

Unlike Paul, Gary and Ed have chosen to deal with their feelings and reactions to Mitch. This is how they will get through their fear (unlike Paul, who will remain afraid of Mitch). In the aftermath of Mitch's explosion, Ed is more open and willing to express both fear and anger. Gary has made progress on this front by openly confronting Mitch on his anger two sessions ago, pointing out that he scared Paul to death last week, and then even getting openly angry at me. This represents significant growth for these two men, both of whom are adult children of alcoholics, who are accustomed to abuse and neglect. It has always been hard for either Gary or Ed to take the risk of trusting other men.

Ed's revelation of his struggle with Ellen indicates that this relationship is at a critical crossroads. Although Ellen has begun to open up, much of this dialogue takes the form of criticism, a terribly destructive force in any relationship. It

has been my experience that such criticism is always damaging to a relationship. It hinders real communication, reduces the desire for intimacy or sex, and in the area of sex, can lead to impotence. In fact, the situation between Ed and Ellen is ripe for some outside influence. If they were married, it would be an ideal setting for an affair. Ed's fantasy of flirting with another woman at a party is an honest recognition of where he is with Ellen at this point. He yearns for more warmth, acceptance, and physical intimacy.

Gary is the group member who has made the greatest strides in recent weeks. His assessment of Paul's departure, Mitch's terrifying effect on Paul, and even my tactical error are all right on target. These are a good indication of Gary's increasing sensitivity. His willingness to say these things up front in group is evidence of his growing confidence and self-esteem. It is still, however, much harder for Gary to express anger directly. His "safe" way out has always been humor. So his anger at me toward the end of the session is initially expressed through money. In this session, he is very wary of me and is worried I am trying to control him. His natural response is to try to take some of that control back by "denying" me the money. As we see in the session, the real issue is simply that Gary is afraid of me—I represent his controlling, domineering. alcoholic father. I engage Gary directly to show him that I am *not* his father and will not *treat* him as his father did. When Gary finally has this insight, he is relieved; he moves from anger and distrust to relief and humor. He has taken another step toward equal relationships with peers and men in authority.

SESSION 20

///

INDECISION AND PERFECTIONISM

A driving rain is pounding at the windows. It seems it's been raining all afternoon; the office has a certain dark pall to it. Ed and Gary amble in drenched from the knees down; Burt's hair is totally soaked. Mitch hasn't even shown up yet. He's probably caught in the middle of the storm on his motorcycle.

While shaking out his trousers, Gary looks over at me.

"Where's Mitch?"

"I haven't heard from him. He's probably out there," I reply, nodding at the windows.

Gary shrugs and collapses into the couch. Burt and Ed settle in and spread out—there's lots of elbow room with only three men in the group.

Ed coughs and takes a quick glance at the other two. "Well, for what it's worth, I've got a new deadline, but this one's self-imposed, I guess." Ed pauses briefly to examine his

shoes, which have blackened from the rain. "Between now and the fifth of next month, I've got to make the decision: marry Ellen or move on."

"So what's the verdict?" Gary asks.

Ed's eyes grow wide as he takes a deep breath. "I don't know. Ellen and I are talking now, of course, and that's great. But there are always those other things . . ."

Ed's eyes shift to the door, which has just swung open to admit the enormous, and sopping wet, Mitch. Mitch smiles and I notice his hands are a bright red. I can imagine how cold it was on the motorcycle.

"Look who's here," Gary cracks, "the Incredible Hulk!"

Mitch glances over at Gary and snorts. He crosses in front of me and parks his gear by my desk and then moves quickly to find a spot between Ed and Burt on the couch.

"So, Mr. Hulk, how can we help you?" Burt asks with a grin.

Mitch frowns. "Did I miss something?"

At first nobody answers.

"Not really, Mitch," I say finally, "but since we're on the topic now, do you have any reaction to it? This is the second week it's come up."

"Reaction to *what?*"

I see Gary smile out of the corner of my eye.

"Your size. You're a big man, Mitch. That motorcycle gear makes you look even more threatening." I look over at Ed and Gary on the couch. "Both of you talked about being afraid of Mitch last week."

"Yeah, you can be pretty intimidating," Ed says calmly, "particularly when you're pissed about something, which has been most of the time lately."

Mitch looks surprised. "I really don't give it much thought, you know. I am what I am."

"Mitch, what I'm saying is this: It's important for you to know the effect your size has on others."

Mitch shrugs. "Okay. It's not that I don't believe you. I just don't realize it most of the time."

Gary smiles. "I remember you scaring the bejesus out of Paul." Gary reflects on this for a moment. "It was pretty funny, actually. He didn't even bother to find out *why* you were so mad!"

"Yeah, well, it took me a while to figure it out *myself*. Look, did I interrupt something?"

"Ed's got another deadline," Gary says with a hint of sarcasm. "The fifth of next month?"

"Yeah, that's right. Marry Ellen or hit the road for California, by myself."

"So which way are we leaning?" Mitch asks.

"We're leaning backwards," Ed says through a grin.

"You know, the way you tiptoe around that woman," Mitch says suddenly, "you'd think there's something seriously wrong with her!"

Ed shrugs. "She's put on a good twenty pounds, and she won't get off her butt to do anything, no gym, no classes, nothing to, I don't know, improve herself, I guess."

"It sounds to me like you're still afraid of making the decision," Gary says in a cool tone.

"Afraid? How's that possible?"

"Consider it for a moment, Ed," I say quickly before he can move on. "Assume Gary is right. There is some fear in you. What are you afraid of?"

Ed sighs. "I'm afraid we won't get along. We won't talk. We'll just have children behind a white picket fence and live this boring miserable quiet life."

"Okay, try the reverse: What's the fear if you decide not to marry her?"

"We'd be alone. We missed an opportunity. I don't want to hurt her." .

All of a sudden Mitch looks very concerned. His voice has developed a serious edge.

"Look, Ed, are you really unhappy with Ellen?"

Ed shakes his head slowly. "No, I'm not *unhappy,* I'm just not *happy.* "

"She won't change, you know," Gary says from Ed's right elbow. "If you think she's going to change in some major way soon, you're wrong."

Ed looks at Gary with some expectation, as though he anticipates Gary will say more.

"It's sort of like what happens with an alcoholic," Gary continues. "You marry one thinking, 'They'll quit drinking when they're married and have a nice, safe happy home'— and, boy, is *that* a mistake."

"I understand that, Gary, I just know what I want."

"Ed, you want perfection," I say.

"What?"

"You have some perfectionist tendencies, Ed. You're trying to be perfect. You're trying to be the opposite of your parents. I know how hard it is for you to make this decision. What if it's the wrong one? What if it doesn't turn out 'right'? Plus, you expect Ellen to be perfect."

Ed grins back at me. "So?"

"Here's an idea, Ed. Give me your ideal. What would you want, *right now,* if you could have everything your way?"

"Okay, let's see."

Ed grows quiet as he reflects on this. His eyes squint slightly behind his rounded frames. A frown slowly begins to form on his forehead.

"I can't really tell you. I don't know." Ed looks up at me quickly. "But I *will* make a decision by the fifth. Count on it."

"I believe you."

"I do, too," Mitch says softly. "I just hope it's the right one. I know how important Lynda is to me, and I have this feeling Ellen is someone special to you, more important than you might think." Mitch glances at Ed and over at me. "I find

I want to spend a lot of time around Lynda now. I think it will be the same when we're married."

"How's that coming?"

"It's coming," Mitch sighs. "We've done everything on her mother's list: announcements addressed, selections for the church organist, rings done, flowers ordered. But still . . . I get the feeling lately that I'm paddling upstream against this powerful current, like a river of events that are already in motion"—Mitch spreads his hands in a helpless gesture—"and I can't do anything to stop them!"

Burt looks over at me. "Aren't these called 'cold feet'?"

Mitch gives Burt a look pleading for sympathy.

"Sorry. I didn't know you were that upset."

Mitch nods. "That's okay. When I get like this, Lynda just pats my knee and says, 'Calm down: take it easy.' "

"So how's Lynda handling it?" Burt asks, trying again.

"Oh, she's doing better than I am. I think Lynda is ready for this, while I'm sort of just gliding along."

"You know, Mitch, I can feel your tension clear over here," Ed interjects. He looks at Mitch for a long moment, then shrugs. "Maybe it's just because I'm going through the same damn thing."

"Yeah, well a lot of my shit isn't about this marriage, it's about my other marriage. I've noticed since the engagement that all this flurry of activity has me freaking out—and I'm starting to retreat: Go off, be by myself, sometimes for quite a while." Mitch stops and shakes his head sadly. "There is *no way*, no way I'm going to fuck up this marriage like I did the last one."

Silence.

"It was *all* your fault?" Gary asks.

Mitch looks up. "What?"

"The marriage. It busted up just because of you?"

"Hell, I don't know. I just don't want to make the same mistakes twice."

"Mitch, some of this pressure you're feeling about getting married is natural," I say. "But your worry about repeating mistakes is an overreaction. It's an extra burden—something you don't need right now."

"*That's* for sure."

"It's a bit ironic, too. You're much more aware of how a relationship works now than you were in your first marriage. You're opening up more and you're talking to Lynda when you are upset. The old problems won't be big issues anymore."

Mitch's eyebrows shoot up. "I haven't been opening up, I've been running away! I've had to escape from Lynda and the wedding deal twice this week."

"No, I mean in here. You're much more open now than I've seen you at any time since your father died. It's been impressive. And it's okay if you need to be alone for short periods of time."

Mitch smiles in appreciation but remains quiet.

The silence continues. The rain has stopped outside and the traffic noises are filtering up from below. We sit listening to the street sounds of the city.

"Does anybody need their windows cleaned?" Gary asks suddenly.

"*Windows?*" Burt asks, astonished.

"Yeah, windows. I'm dating this Armenian woman, and she cleans houses for a living." Gary stops and looks around, ready to tally up the takers. "Well, *nobody* does windows anymore, right?"

"Is that why you're dating her?" Burt asks with a grin.

"Not quite. But not far off. She does my cooking *and* my windows." Gary smiles back at Burt. "Her name's Marta. She's a little firecracker: Cute, petite, five-foot-one, hot as a flame."

"Okay," Ed says. "Since Paul's not here anymore, I guess I'll ask: "Are you sleeping with her?"

"All the time. That is the reason for the relationship. I'm

real clear about it, and so is she. It's so different from what Leigh was like in bed: She was a large, gangly virgin. This woman . . . well, this woman is European, plus she's small, easy to handle."

"Is this going to go someplace?" Burt asks.

"Oh, who knows? I'm not worried about it at all. Listening to you all," Gary's hand flips over at Mitch and Ed, "I'm not sure I *want* it to." Gary stops and lets some time go by. "I just realized sitting here that I'm not even the slightest bit jealous of you. Listening to all this sort of makes me feel, I don't know . . . less guilty about not being married or in something serious."

"You don't want a relationship?" Burt asks in surprise.

"It's not that, Burt, it's just that it sounds so hard for all of you now. Who needs it? I'm relieved to only be dating for right now. I'm in no hurry to have kids."

"Do you think you'll ever have kids?" Mitch asks.

"I'd imagine so, at some point. Actually, right now I'd like to have the *experience* of having kids without the reality of it, if you know what I mean. It's too bad there isn't a 'Rent-a-Kid' place where you could pick up a little critter for a few days to see what the experience is all about."

INTERPRETATION

As Ed approaches his latest deadline with Ellen, he continues to manifest the most significant characteristics of the classic perfectionist facing a tough choice: indecision and procrastination. Ed and I have discussed at great length the connection between his efforts to attain perfection and his indecisiveness with Ellen. This is not an unusual combination. To Ed, avoiding a decision means avoiding the danger of being disapproved

of, rejected, or judged "bad" or any possibility of making the "wrong" decision. Ed continues to carry in his head the "voice" of his overcritical mother. In fact, he has incorporated these attitudes from his family so well that he is now his own biggest critic. A lot of this criticism is dumped on Ellen as well. The hope for Ed lies in his willingness to make changes. His attitude toward Ellen has improved dramatically after his earlier confrontations with Paul. Ed is learning his part in his conflicts with Ellen. In tonight's session, Mitch encourages Ed to consider just how important Ellen is to him. There is a lot of support for Ed in the group tonight, and he continues to make himself more emotionally available.

Meanwhile, Mitch is having a man's normal reaction to a big wedding, especially a second formal wedding. Ironically, Mitch's willingness to face his anxieties, and the fact that he feels more anxious as a result, have led him to believe he is regressing. In fact, a year ago Mitch would have chosen to avoid dealing with any of this. He's always preferred the status quo, so all the changes involved in the engagement and the wedding would have simply scared him away. Mitch continues to make progress so rapidly that he's able to deal with, albeit with some anxiety, Lynda's moving in, redecorating his house, and arranging for the wedding. Lynda revealed, in a very valuable couples session, that she too dislikes change and recognizes that things have been easier since Mitch has been in therapy. Lynda is learning that Mitch will respond more willingly to changes when she presents them as a learning experience.

Gary is much more comfortable in group tonight and is able to enjoy relating the excitement of a new girlfriend. Much of Gary's openness comes from his increasing trust and confidence in me: As Gary realizes that I'm supportive of him, his own self-esteem, both in the group and in general, is strongly enhanced. This is a significant step for Gary, whose feelings of inferiority in the group ("I'm a hell of a lot more

fucked up than any of you") have festered for months. Over the last few weeks Gary has gone from feelings of jealousy (over the others' relationships) and inferiority (professionally) to a sense of equality and acceptance ("I'm not even the slightest bit jealous of you"). Gary is pleased with this new sense of himself. He has a new love interest with whom he has an easy time and no self-imposed pressure to call it a "serious" relationship. Gary mentions for the first time tonight the possibility of having a child, another sign of his growth and his broadening perspective. Some of life's other choices are now becoming visible to him.

//

LONELINESS IN A RELATIONSHIP

Burt is beaming. He's sitting back on the couch with his long arms spread wide, taking in the whole scene. He's sharply dressed in uniform tonight. This is the first time Burt has shown up here in his army uniform. Burt cuts a very solid, impressive figure in a full dress uniform.

Ed, Gary, and Mitch filter through the door and shuffle toward their seats. They've barely settled in when Burt nudges forward and looks straight at Mitch.

"It's official!"

Mitch smiles. "What? Are you a general now?"

"JoAnn and I are engaged!"

"I thought you two were *already* engaged," Mitch says through a frown.

"No, no, we just agreed to do it at some time." Burt is all smiles again. "That time is now!"

Ed coughs and starts to rub his palms together nervously. "Tell me, Burt, how'd you actually *do* it? Propose, I mean."

"I didn't. JoAnn proposed to *me!*"

Ed looks taken aback for a moment and swings around to look at Gary, who's shaking his head.

"It was great," Burt says excitedly. "We were just lying there in bed in the hotel—we were out at an army convention in Denver. She looked me straight in the eyes and said, 'I know how much it means to you. I want to marry you. I want to have your children.'"

Ed flashes a grin at Gary, who is also smiling by now.

"What happened to cause all this?" Mitch asks. He's still vaguely confused. "Did her biological clock go off in the middle of the night, or was it the altitude?"

"I don't think that's it," Burt shrugs. "It was just such a nice, calm, quiet time in Denver. We spent almost a week out there at the Armed Forces Convention. You know, away from the hassles of work and commuting. We got involved with each other again, started listening more, started *touching* more." Burt pauses to rub the back of his neck. "The sex was *terrific.*"

"So that's it. Now it's all beginning to make some sense," Gary says under his breath.

Burt returns his grin. "I met her parents for the first time, too. We stayed at her folks' place for a few days. I got along famously with her father." Burt pauses and looks past me for a moment. Then he's seized by a sudden thought.

"And she wants to get married before she finishes her degree. Isn't that *something?*"

"Amazing what a little good sex can do," Gary cracks.

Burt shakes his head. "No, I think she's really come around, Gary."

Gary sighs. "I think so, too, Burt. And you know what? I'm really happy for you, because it's what you want." Gary is looking over his crossed legs at Burt. "But . . . JoAnn sounds so *powerful* to me. I don't know, I guess I'm afraid she's going

to run your life. I mean just *look* at this woman. She decides to get married, so she proposes!"

Burt shrugs. "She's a powerful woman. She knows what she wants. Right now she wants *me.*"

"How does that make you feel, Burt?" I ask.

The glow returns to Burt's face. "Terrific!"

"You know, it seems so *easy* for you," Ed says in something near a whisper. He's looking down, away from Burt.

"How so?"

Ed coughs again, and looks up, catching Burt's eye. "Burt, you have one good week together, and everything falls into place! JoAnn comes around, *she* proposes to *you*, and you ride happily into the sunset together!"

"That's not really fair, Ed. You know how long I've had to wait for this. How much work it's taken. I've damn near had to plan it step by step!"

Ed nods. "Sure. I'm just bitter. Pissed at myself."

"Why?"

For several moments Ed says nothing at all. Finally he lets out a deep breath and his head falls back onto the couch. He's staring at the ceiling.

"I was out of town last weekend, too. Houston. When I was hanging out at the pool, I thought a lot about Ellen. How I missed her. That weekend I wanted to be married. The feeling was there. So I called her on the phone Saturday night and told her what was going on." Ed's head rises off the couch and he looks over at Gary. "I told her I was *ready.*" Ed's head descends back down. "So on the plane back, wouldn't you know it, the jitters start. I'm thinking, *'What the hell am I doing?'* So that night she met me at the airport. She was really excited, and we rode back into town in complete silence. Ellen didn't know what to think, and after we got to my place, I told her. . . . I said I just wasn't sure about it after all."

Silence.

"What did she say?" Burt asks softly.

"She just broke down crying and ran out of the room. I couldn't talk to her that night at all."

Burt lets out a breath and looks at Mitch. They shrug. Gary is still staring at Ed.

"Did you break up with her?"

Ed's head shakes slowly from side to side. "Not even close." At this Ed sits up and shifts his weight forward on the couch so he can see everybody directly. He looks at me and back at Gary.

"That morning, Sunday, I woke up and she was gone. I freaked out, just lost it. I started crying like a baby. I honest to God thought she had gone looking for an apartment—I figured I'd really blown it and lost her."

"So where was she?"

"Well, she was still around, believe it or not, I just didn't know it. She'd gone out to the backyard to our garden, we planted a flower garden together last month, and she was just sitting out there by herself, toeing the dirt and staring at the scarlet roses."

"What was that like for you, Ed?" I ask.

Ed blinks at me for a moment, then smiles. "I was so relieved she was there. She didn't leave."

I nod back at him and allow some time to go by.

"Ed, when you were riding back on the plane and had your second thoughts, what were your fears about marrying Ellen then?"

Ed shrugs. "Well, you all know these by now. I was afraid we wouldn't be able to talk about anything. Share ideas about plays, movies, art. Comment on life." He looks at me. "I really don't want to be alone in a marriage."

"Can you think back to when you were younger for a moment. How is this a repeat of what went on in your family?"

"I—" Ed cuts himself off before the words leave his

mouth. He sits for a moment to reflect, then looks over at me.

"When I was in fifth and sixth grade—ten or eleven, I guess—I remember padding down the stairs at night to ask my parents for something: help on homework, sometimes water, sometimes just to get them to listen to me. My mom would always take me by the hand and drag me back upstairs and lock me in my room. I could always smell the booze on her breath. I hated being alone in that goddamned bedroom."

The room has grown silent. Gary has been nodding during this story. Burt looks uneasy.

"Ed," I say, "can you see that your fear is of being all alone again? Alone in the marriage like you were in the family. You're afraid Ellen is going to do the same thing your mother did—"

"She *is* like my mother," Ed interjects.

I nod. "Remember, as an adult you have more options than you did as a child. Ellen is not literally your mother. She may have similarities, but there also are some differences—for example, she doesn't drink. You do have some choices with Ellen you didn't have with your mother."

"I know. I'm working on that. We are still talking, which I'm glad about."

"Is it doing any good?" Gary asks.

"Oh, sure. It's a *lot* better than being left alone." Ed eyes me for a moment. "She's not just walking off when she gets mad. Anything's better than the ice treatment."

"How long have you and Ellen been together, anyway?"

"Two years, off and on. One year living together."

Gary waves Ed off. "Awww, you'll stay together. That's a long time. You two are *used* to each other." He's smiling.

"Do you identify with that, Gary?" I ask.

"Not really. I haven't been in that place in years. Right now I'm just enjoying Marta. This woman is one hell of a handful, let me tell you!"

"I thought you said she's a little one, a petite, what, European?" Mitch asks.

"Oh, she is, but she's on fire. Listen to this: She dropped by my house on Saturday and hung around until Sunday afternoon. She came back on Monday while I was trying to get some work done and dragged me into the bedroom and wouldn't let me out!" He's grinning wildly. "She left this morning at six. A.M."

"What? You were fucking the whole time?" Ed asks with a sly grin.

"Yep."

"You're kidding."

"No, I'm weak. And tired, come to think of it. But I'm happy! For the first time I can remember, probably for the first time in my life, I'm enjoying the foreplay as much as the climax. It's sort of, well," Gary grins at me, "anticlimactic."

"Are you falling for this woman at all?" Burt asks.

"I'll tell you this: I think I'm getting infatuated. At first I thought, hey, it's about sex, that's okay. The woman is a sexual dynamo and we don't have to worry at all about birth control: she's had her tubes tied. But we've started talking a lot, and I'm learning about her. She's Armenian but was born in Turkey. She's only in the country temporarily, as a Swiss citizen, believe it or not."

Ed looks mildly surprised. "You don't suppose . . . Gary, this woman's not trying to *marry* you, is she?"

Gary laughs. "No way. I've been real clear about that. She seems to accept it."

Ed flashes a concerned look to Mitch and Burt.

"You know, she could have lied about her tubes as a way of getting pregnant."

"So? I'd just say, 'That's it, you lied. Goodbye.' "

Ed shrugs.

"What's she doing in Washington . . . besides doing everyone's windows?" Burt asks with a smile.

"Right now she lives with her sister and brother-in-law and takes care of their little boy. He'll be five in September. She seems to be happy, but I think she's a little lonely." Gary pauses to brush off his pants leg. "Frankly, I get the impression she's looking to get married so she can settle down. It'll save her from having to go back to Switzerland and start all over—new job, new friends."

"Yeah, it'll also give her permanent residency," Ed cracks.

"Well, that's true, but I'm not going to worry myself sick about it like you all—I'm just not headed towards marriage."

"Gary," I say, "be aware that this kind of thing happens a lot here in town—people marry for green cards, permanent residency, all the time."

"Sure. She could also *love* me and want to marry me."

"That's true. This is just something to keep in mind."

"Maybe I should break it off," Gary says suddenly.

"No, no, that's not what I'm suggesting, Gary. I'm saying just the opposite—enjoy the infatuation. It's a great feeling. Just be aware that there may be something else going on with Marta. I'm most of all . . . I'm in favor of being responsible."

INTERPRETATION ————————

Burt's surprise announcement of his engagement to JoAnn, and the fact that JoAnn did the proposing, demonstrate the extent of Burt's progress in group therapy. Burt's changes and efforts at accommodation have been so apparent to JoAnn that her reservations over marriage have disappeared one by one, culminating in her own proposal to Burt in bed while on vacation. I learned from my work in couples therapy with these two that JoAnn has always felt the need both to retain

her identity and to be in charge. Much of this grows out of JoAnn's determination to prove to her parents that she can, on her own, be a successful professional. In many ways, JoAnn has feared she will lose her individuality in marriage, and only recently has she seen that Burt in fact supports her in her career and her independence. This is a subject that Burt has discussed on several occasions with the group. JoAnn has also come to realize, after the stresses and pressures of daily life melted away in Denver, that Burt loves and accepts her as she is. Burt and JoAnn were treated as a couple at this convention, and Burt's acceptance of JoAnn was complete: She knew there was no need to "prove herself" to him. As many of JoAnn's anxieties and reservations about marriage fell away, the idea of becoming a part-time professional to accommodate children began to appeal to her. For the first time JoAnn knew this is what she has wanted. Burt is happy because this is one less conflict: JoAnn will marry him. He also will be able to have children before he gets too "old." Something Burt has wanted for a long time is now just around the corner. It is an exciting time for both Burt and the group.

Meanwhile Ed's powerful anxiety over making the decision to propose to Ellen is very similar to Mitch's "cold feet" experience. It is quite common for men to grow anxious when they have time to reflect on major decisions. Much of Ed's anxiety results from his unconscious fear that Ellen will put him in precisely the same lonely situation that his mother did when he was a young boy. Ed felt he was unimportant to his mother, and he fears he will end up in the same helpless and lonely position with Ellen. One of Ellen's common complaints about Ed before he entered therapy was that he never shared his feelings with her. Yet on Saturday evening when Ed returns, he does what Ellen has asked: he tells her what he feels. Ed expects Ellen to appreciate his openness but instead she is shocked, and ultimately, very hurt. Ed responds by

going through what is essentially a test of Ellen. When Ellen responds with hurt and pain, he waits. When Ed wakes up Sunday morning, many of his old feelings of rejection and abandonment from childhood resurface, and his first thought is that she's abandoned him, like his parents did many years before. But Ellen passes this test: As upset as she is, she doesn't flee, but rather retreats to the garden they planted together. This is a "safe place" for her, a symbol of their bond. It is at this point that Ed realizes not only his love for her but also that, despite the similarities, she is not his mother. Ellen is not going to abandon him.

Gary's development is progressing on two fronts. His level of ease and comfort in the group continues to grow, as he's able to be much more direct in sharing his doubts about Burt's wedding ("I guess I'm afraid she's going to run your life") and his assurances to Ed ("Awww, you'll stay together"). Gary is also enjoying a very intense sexual relationship. This is the first time Gary has been this comfortable and relaxed with a woman, and the first time foreplay has been a joy—fun, exciting, sensuous, sexual, rather than an obligation to him. It is ironic that many weeks ago Gary labeled the other men "pussy-whipped" when in the span of a couple of weeks Marta virtually moved in. I feel it is important to point out to Gary that he could be trapped by this woman, not only because she is (by Gary's own admission) looking to get married but also because she is so much easier for Gary to get along with. For many years Gary dated women who were like his mother: demanding and controlling. He lived with this during his entire childhood and became accustomed to it. Still, he never learned over this period how to defend himself from these women and how to deal with them. Marta is nothing at all like the former women in his life. She's cooperative, giving, nonthreatening, and very sexual. This is something new to Gary and touches his softer side. Yet despite the excitement

and joy, Gary remains insecure about the relationship. It takes only one comment by me ("People marry for green cards, permanent residency, all the time") for him to reverse position entirely ("Maybe I should break it off"). This is a new area for Gary. He will become more comfortable with it over time.

SESSION 22

///

"WHAT A RELIEF TO BE UNDERSTOOD!"

"Aren't we supposed to *end* this group pretty soon?"

Gary is in a dour mood. He's planted firmly in his corner seat and is looking at me over crossed arms.

"What's going on, Gary?" I ask.

He shakes his head. "I don't know. I'm totally burned out. My work load is terrible, but my business is about to drop in half. I can just feel it."

"What about a vacation?" Ed asks lightly.

Gary eyes him for a moment without a word. "Impossible. I can't leave. I'm the only employee! I wish I could go to California with you."

"With me and Ellen," Ed corrects him.

Silence.

"Does this mean what I think it means?" Burt asks with a hint of a smile.

Ed breaks into a full grin. "Can you believe it?"

Gary sits forward and looks straight at Mitch. His arms are still crossed. "Five dollars says he can't say it," Gary says.

"You're on," Mitch answers.

Ed's face is momentarily blank. He's looking right at Gary, who's nearly touching his right arm. A slow look of recognition spreads across his face.

"Ellen and I are engaged to be married."

"Damn!" Gary mutters.

"You can pay me after group," Mitch advises him.

Gary shrugs and peers out the window.

Mitch turns back to Ed. "Also, congratulations!"

Burt smiles. "From me, too, really, Ed. It's been a long haul, no?"

Ed is all grins.

"So tell us about it!" Burt says impatiently.

"Well, guys, I took the leap last Tuesday," Ed begins, the smile still visible on his face. "I figured after all this tortuous soul-searching I damn well better get the *proposal* right!" Ed pauses to gaze around the group. Burt and Mitch are sitting forward and hanging on his every word. Gary is staring at his shoe.

"So anyway, here's what happened. I decided to set up a real romantic dinner—flowers, limousine, first-class service the whole way." He shrugs. "By now, Ellen deserves it!"

"So you picked her up at work?" Burt asks.

Ed nods. "Yep. I *knew* I was nervous when I couldn't even dial the number of the limousine service on Tuesday afternoon! It took me three tries, but I made it, finally." He rolls his eyes.

"Wait a minute," Mitch interrupts. "I forgot to ask. Was all this a surprise?"

"Sort of. I sent over a dozen red roses to her school in the afternoon. Turns out this huge bouquet of red roses, with a note, was delivered to her classroom when she was in the

middle of a class. The delivery guy walked right into the room and put the arrangement in the back of the classroom where she could see it. She was pretty distracted by the roses sitting there during the last half hour. I'll hand it to her though; she continued right through to the end of class."

"When did you find out about all this?"

"Well, right after the class was over she called to thank me. She wanted me to pick her up after work so she wouldn't have to take the flowers on the metro."

Burt smiles. "So she still doesn't know what's in store."

"That's right. But I was relieved to hear from her, actually—it occurred to me after I hung up the phone that I had never told her anything about this, and she would have just gone home at five and I could have missed her in the limo!"

Mitch frowns. "Are you sure you're a scientist?"

"Yeah. It's just that I'm a total miss when I'm nervous. I'm still amazed I made it through at all, to tell you the truth."

"Okay, so what happened next?" Mitch asks, recrossing his long legs in the other direction.

"Next. Right. So the limo picks me up and I get to the school at about ten of five. The limo driver has this tuxedo with long tails down to here"—Ed indicated the length on the back of his calves. "Plus a top hat and white gloves. No cane. So I'm in the limo and the driver hops out and walks into the school to get Ellen. About this time, a crowd is gathering around the limo. This thing is a Rolls-Royce Corniche, and you know how kids are—anything new or unusual and the whole place converges on you. So I'm sitting in the limo staring at these fourth- and fifth-graders making faces at me, and the driver disappears inside the building. Ellen is sitting inside the main doors holding the roses on her lap, and when the driver walks up to her she just stands there staring at him. She doesn't even stand up. She can't see the limo, and has no idea where this guy came from. So finally the driver says, 'Ed is waiting for you.' She *still* doesn't stand up: She thinks this guy

in the tux is about to break out into a singing telegram song. At this point she grabs the guy by the arm and takes him into her classroom, because she doesn't want him serenading her in front of thirty or forty kids and teachers. Meanwhile, the guy has no idea of *where* she is taking him or *why*. He stops halfway and explains that he's a chauffeur, and *'Ed is waiting for you outside.'* This is the third time he's said it. She rushes to gather her things and follows him outside, where I'm besieged by half the school population. The chauffeur gets past the kids and opens the back door, pulls out some champagne and two glasses, and pops the cork into the crowd, showering a bunch of screaming little girls in the front with champagne spray. He then pours out two glasses of champagne for us inside the Rolls and I look over and see a whole crowd of Japanese tourists walking along the street. By now they've spied us. Of course, they have no idea who we are, but they do see the Rolls, so one of them starts snapping pictures, figuring it must be *some* important Washingtonians. So then they *all* stop and start taking pictures, and we can't move in the Rolls because they're blocking the exit!"

"Did Ellen say anything during all this?" Burt asks.

Ed is about out of breath. He shakes his head. "Not a word. I think she was still in shock and embarrassed. She just smiled a whole lot and tried to keep the champagne off her dress."

"So then what?"

"We headed off to Old Angler's Inn. The limo dropped us off in front, and the driver parked it so everybody walking in or out had to go past the Rolls. We sat outside in the garden area and had a wonderful leisurely dinner. And after we finished the wine, I did it. I asked her to marry me." Ed pauses. "Oh. She said yes."

"Did you give her a ring?" Mitch asks.

"You bet. I was prepared this time! It was a beautiful stone. Ellen just loves it."

"I guess that makes up for the jewelry box fiasco," Burt says.

"Yeah, well, I'm getting better at this sort of thing, you know."

"Look, Ed, I've got a question," Mitch says. "What did the rings run?"

Ed hesitates for a moment. It's not clear if he's embarrassed to even mention this or has momentarily forgotten.

"Hmmm. Let's see. The wedding ring was three hundred fifty and the engagement ring was about twelve hundred. That seems about right."

Mitch nods. "Lynda's engagement ring was seventeen hundred, but her wedding ring was only seventy. Mine was almost three hundred, though."

"Hers was only seventy?" Ed asks with surprise.

"She wanted a really thin, petite wedding band," Mitch explains. He shows an imaginary thin band on his ring finger.

Ed frowns. "I've never liked that kind of wedding ring. You can't even see it!"

"Oh, you can see Lynda's."

Ed is shaking his head. "Why do people wear those? It's like they don't even want you to know they're married!"

"No," Gary says suddenly, joining the conversation, "then they just take it off."

"But you can never *see* it," Ed protests. "I wonder . . ." Ed stops and leaves this thought hanging in the air.

"Wonder what, Ed?" I ask.

"Do you think people with thin wedding bands cheat more?"

"If that's the case," Mitch replies with a grin, "you'll have to wear one like *this*." Mitch holds up his right hand and indicates his enormous college ring with his thumb.

Ed shakes his head but remains silent.

"Are you two going to have kids?" Gary asks. He's finally making an effort to be in the group tonight.

"Ellen would like to get pregnant right away." He shrugs. "I'd like to wait at least a few months."

"I would encourage both of you to hold off for a while," I say. "You've got a lot of changes coming up in your life: new marriage, new jobs, new house, new *state*, for that matter. You two need time to adjust to being married first. Then you can think about having kids."

"Yeah," Mitch nods. "They're major stress factors, no doubt about it. There's no use getting into something that may cause the whole marriage to fall apart."

Ed looks back at Mitch with a frown. "You really think that could happen? You sound pretty down on Ellen and me tonight."

Mitch sighs almost imperceptibly. "It's not either of you, Ed. I think I'm down on marriage in general, as an institution. I haven't been able to even touch Lynda in over a week, and that's really weird for us. Normally . . . well, usually we hug and play around and get real physical all the time." Mitch's eyes have shifted to the blank wall behind me. "I'd sure like to know what the hell is going on, I'm just not turned on. I hope I'm not impotent."

"Don't worry," Burt says, "Al knows how to fix that one."

"I think I'm going to be practical for a moment, Mitch," I say. "No psychological interpretation."

"*That's* a first," Gary cracks.

I know something is going on with Gary but I want to continue with Mitch first.

"Isn't Lynda sick now?" I ask.

"Sure. She's *still* sick, going on two whole weeks. She's got this virulent case of mono that's knocked her out almost completely."

"I wouldn't think she's feeling very sexual now." I pause to consider another thought. "*Can* you two have sex, Mitch?"

Mitch snorts. "If you can call it that. The doctor says no kissing and no oral sex at all. And if we actually *do* anything . . ."

Suddenly Mitch's voice drops and he mutters, "Although I can't imagine it"—he looks up at me again—"we have to use a condom."

"It seems natural not to feel sexual right now, Mitch," I point out. "You're taking a fun, casual act like sex and making it into a chore, needing to remember things to keep from catching mono yourself. That's a real distraction in sex."

Mitch shrugs.

"Another thing. I'm glad you're bringing it up after only four days. Before it would be weeks, if ever, before you'd talk about something like sexual problems in here. You're much more spontaneous and open in group lately. It's good to see this change in you, Mitch—it's very positive."

Mitch smiles. "I just wish I had more *optimistic* things to be open about."

"Can we talk about ending?" Gary blurts out.

"Ending?"

"Yeah, the group. Aren't we through in two weeks? I'd like to know, because I can't afford this anymore. I'm dumping all this money into therapy just so I have someplace to complain. I don't need it! It's a luxury that's got to go."

"You're using money as an excuse. You're making more than you ever have in your life," I say.

"Weren't you listening? I *told* you I'm afraid my business is going to drop off."

Gary is sitting very still, steaming by himself at the end of the couch. He's staring straight at me but won't say a word.

"What's your feeling about group ending, Gary?"

"I'm ready. I knew it was coming. Don't *you* think I'm ready to end?"

"What's your feeling about it?"

"I don't *have* any *feeling* about it! Do *you* think I'm ready to end?"

"You sound full of feeling, especially anger, at me."

"So you tell me, what's it about?!"

"Gary, no games please. Let's figure it out together."

Gary is sitting immobile, arms crossed, eyeing me carefully.

"You've been progressing all along. I suggest that you not end therapy yet. You can still get a lot more for yourself. So if you do stop after the six-month commitment—pay attention, I'm not rejecting you, I'm not abandoning you, I'm not giving up on you—you'll be the one leaving."

Gary's body visibly relaxes, and he scans the room.

"Am I the only one who's not ready to stop?"

"No. Ed has more work to do when he gets to California. Burt and JoAnn are seeing me as a couple, and Mitch may continue with both group and individual."

"But isn't it time for us to stop, Al?" Mitch asks. "You said six months."

"The six months was to assure you a minimum of learning and changing, not to stop you in the process."

"Makes sense," Burt nods. "But I'm ready to stop group as planned."

"That's fine." I turn back to Gary.

"What else besides business is bothering you, Gary?" I ask.

Gary scratches his face and shrugs.

"I don't know, Al. I've got to visit my parents again next week. My dad's practically an invalid, he's got this rare nerve disease, it's something like Parkinson's Disease. So he just sits there staring at the TV. He can't even talk anymore. I don't think he even knows I'm there! Mom spends all her time wandering around the house bitching about having to take care of *him*, so . . ." His gaze shifts to the windows. "It's all so depressing, let me tell you."

"So the family problems are part of your anger and depression?"

"No," he answers quickly.

"Your answer is so fast, Gary, you're not even consider-

ing. It would be helpful to at least think about it. It would
explain most of your feelings: Depressed . . . angry . . . tired
. . . and burned out."

He sits quietly with this for a while.

"I don't think they are related."

"I think they are."

"So what do you suggest I do?"

"I'm not suggesting you do anything right now, Gary,
except say more about your anger."

A flash of hot anger crosses Gary's face.

"Look! I'm paying you all this money and you're not doing a damn thing! I have to pay *all* the money and I have to
do *all* the work!"

"Gary, I'm here to work *with* you," I assure him. "It's true
you have to work at it—it's your life and you have to live it."

"So just tell me where I should go! What should I talk
about?"

"Your mother. We've heard a lot about your father, but
you've avoided talking about your mom."

Gary is eyeing me again. I know he doesn't want to say
anything negative about her. He gives in. Finally, he looks at
the floor and shrugs.

"I'm fed up with her. I wish she would leave me alone.
She is always complaining and acting like the victim. She calls
me on the phone and whines about how Dad's illness is such
a fucking burden on her. She thinks he's doing it to get even
with her. Always the victim. *God*, it's *so* depressing. And when
we get into an argument, she won't fight back—she used to,
all the time. Now she gets this 'poor me' voice and whimpers,
'Why are you mad at me, what did *I* do?' " He gestures in
disgust.

"It sounds like the guilt trip all over again," Mitch says
simply.

"Huh?"

"If you don't take her burden away, she's going to just

curl up and die—like when she used to threaten suicide if you didn't stay with her.

"Yeah, well, I'm just tired of listening to the bitching. The woman complains more than . . . well, more than *I* do."

I stay out and let Gary sit with this discovery.

"Can you say anything more about your bitching, Gary?" I ask.

He lets out a deep breath. "I'm not proud of that. I know I bitch a lot." He looks over at me. "I'll never, ever be as bitter as she is, though. It'll never happen.

"I agree. Because you made the decision to change, and she didn't. Otherwise, you could have ended up the same. And that's your main anger and fear right now."

"Now, *don't* lose me again. You are saying I'm better off than she is, aren't you?"

"Yes, I am. But their recent problems have stirred up your old fear of ending up like them. You 'divorced' your family when you started your alcohol treatment. You've been moving up ever since. You won't end up like them."

INTERPRETATION

Ed's excitement and lightness in telling the entertaining story of his engagement to Ellen are the direct result of his relief at having finally made a decision. Ed is no longer blocked in by his fear and procrastination: the demands of his perfectionism. In tonight's session, Ed looks and behaves like a "freed" man. It is clearly the most fun he's had in group so far. And the other men become playful, too: Mitch and Gary make a wager over whether Ed will actually say out loud that he was engaged to Ellen. Ed's enthusiasm and relief are infectious, and

the mood in the room tonight is initially upbeat. Men's light-hearted humor really raises the energy level of the room.

When Mitch switches the subject to the price of engagement and wedding rings, we see some elements of traditional male competition reappear. This competition goes beyond the elements of economics. Mitch and Ed compare the prices of rings for their women in the same way that adolescent boys in the locker room may compare or joke about their penis size. (This is no coincidence. The ring and the penis are both for women.) Ed's momentary hesitation to answer Mitch reflects his realization that he and Mitch are about to cross from a place of mutual support to one of competition. Once in this mode, Mitch goes further by suggesting Ed will need a broad band, implying he feels Ed is likely to cheat. While the origin of this comment can be traced back to Ed's affair fantasy a few weeks ago, Mitch is still on a competitive footing with Ed from the wedding ring discussion, and this, coupled with his own negativity surrounding the situation with Lynda, prompts him to remain competitive and confrontational. I'm glad he did. He's on target. Mitch feels that Ed and Ellen are not ready for marriage.

In fact, what Mitch is experiencing is regular, ordinary wedding jitters. Like many men, Mitch has surges of anxiety and doubt as the big day approaches. Both Mitch and Lynda find themselves in a situation that is common to engaged couples: the partners enjoy each other less as so much energy, time, and effort goes into planning a formal wedding. In this case, both Lynda and Mitch are experiencing the anxiety and stress, though it manifests itself in different ways: irritability and jitters in Mitch and a physical reaction in Lynda (Lynda's lab tests cast doubt on whether she actually has mononucleosis). The most significant sign of progress in Mitch's discussion is his willingness to bring up the difficult sexual issue of impotence in front of everyone, and not be intimidated. Certainly a long step from the "old" Mitch. This will help him

deal with future sexual problems that may arise naturally in the marriage.

From the beginning of the session Gary's mood is out of sync with the atmosphere in the room. Since this is in such sharp contrast to Gary's attitude of last week, I know something had occurred to cause this shift. Gary's attack on me is almost an exact replay of his mother's treatment of his father and comes on the eve of his worrisome visit to his parents. Gary puts me down with the same complaints his mother uses on his father (he's ineffectual, he won't talk, he doesn't help me). Tonight is the first time Gary is able to criticize (and complain about) his mother openly and see similarities in himself, since he had identified with her as a youngster. He has always been extremely reluctant to say anything negative about his mother. While she used guilt to control Gary, she was, nevertheless, his strongest ally in the family. Gary wants to protect himself when he becomes equally depressed and feels he is the victim. So he falls into the old pattern of denial: "I'm not like her." As Gary is able to identify the similarity between himself and his mother, he is able to move beyond his fear that he will be like her. He is adamantly committed to change. Good for Gary.

Gary's anxiety about group ending is a natural response. He has moved into a trusting relationship with the other men and he's going to miss them. At this point, he can't say that directly: it's not the male thing to do.

//

"SHADOW" MOTHERS AND THEIR SONS

"I'd like to start the group tonight," I say.

Gary glances up at me with a look of mild surprise. Burt and Mitch look puzzled but sit forward. Ed's gaze shifts from the empty black leather chair to me. I wait until I have everyone's attention.

"Since next week is our last session," I begin, "I'd like to extend the time by twenty to thirty minutes. Will that be okay?"

Glances around the room, several nods.

"Will it cost any more?" Gary asks.

I smile. "No, it's on the house."

"One thing, Al," Burt says suddenly. "Let me check with JoAnn and get back to you."

"Don't tell me she's running your life *already*," Gary says, leaning back in his corner seat.

Burt gives Gary an even look.

"Not quite. JoAnn and I are meeting downstairs at the end of group next week, so I'm not sure how much time we'll have. We want to go someplace and celebrate the end of group." Burt looks from Gary over to me. "It should be okay, though."

I nod. "I'm glad to hear it's going to be a celebration for you, Burt. We haven't heard much out of you recently."

Burt coughs nervously and shrugs. "I know. To tell you the truth I was ready to quit after that scene with Paul. I figured it was about over, anyway. But it just didn't seem right." Burt catches Gary's frown out of the corner of his eye. "The commitment, I mean. I figured I was in for the six months and I was going to stick with it."

This seems to satisfy Gary.

"Anything else going on, Burt?" I ask.

"Oh, there's plenty going on," he says running a hand over his blond hair, "but now that JoAnn and I are in couple therapy with you, the importance, urgency, I guess—a lot of it's gone away." He pauses and looks to his right at Mitch. "I mean, JoAnn and I are engaged, after all."

"So you don't miss talking in here?" Mitch asks. He looks relaxed tonight—sitting far back on the sofa with his arms spread wide.

For a moment Burt is lost in thought and doesn't answer.

"I sort of miss it, actually," he says. He looks around at the men scattered along the couch. "I should take advantage of what we've got left. There is a kind of . . . support I get in here I don't have with JoAnn in couples." He smiles over at Mitch. "I'm glad you brought that up."

Mitch is grinning back. "Sure."

Silence.

"I need to take a little time, guys," Ed says in a weary voice. "I've got some bad news, again. I found out last Wednesday that my mother has a tumor near her right hip,

about here," he indicates the spot on his own hip with his palm.

"Cancer?" I ask.

He nods gravely.

More silence.

"So what are the feelings, Ed?"

Once again the glasses come off, and Ed scratches his forehead slowly. His glasses are sitting idly in his lap.

"You know," he says in a labored voice, "I can't feel any sympathy for my mom. Isn't that awful?"

Mitch is peering across the couch at Ed but remains silent.

"Are you pissed off at her?" Gary asks calmly.

Ed shakes his head. "Not really. But when I spoke with her yesterday—I called to check up on her—I could *tell* she was smoking a goddamned cigarette, and *that* pissed me off." Ed's voice has developed a nasty edge.

"What's the prognosis, anyway. Is she going to be all right?" Burt asks with concern.

This brings Ed back. "It's too early to tell." He takes a deep breath. "That's *another* thing." He looks over at Gary with sudden intensity. "Can you believe this woman has no health insurance? I spend ten years on her case, trying to get her to get some coverage." He shakes his head sadly. "It's my *field*, so I should know, right?"

"What did she say," Mitch asks with a frown. "Did she just refuse?"

Ed shakes his head slowly. "Not quite. She just protested she was healthy as a horse. Why did she need insurance? So now she can't get near a policy with anything less than a ten thousand deductible."

A look of disappointment crosses Mitch's face as he looks away.

Ed is watching Mitch and sees his response. He exhales a long, deep breath. "Ellen feels I should help her out."

"Are you going to?" Gary asks over his shoulder.

Ed looks back at Gary to respond, but no words come out of his mouth.

The room is still.

"Ed, is the problem money . . . ?" Burt asks softly.

"No."

"I don't know what the big deal is," Mitch says in a booming voice. Burt is so startled he jumps slightly. "She's your mother! If it were my mom, I'd be right there with the wallet out."

"It's not quite the same thing," Ed says testily.

"How is it different?" Mitch is leaning forward on his right knee.

"Mitch, look," Ed begins, peering straight at Mitch. Their faces are only eighteen inches apart. "My mother is a boozer. Our relationship hasn't been worth two shits since I went to college and escaped from that nut house. I don't feel real charitable towards a woman bent on self-destruction." Ed's face has gone crimson, and he's breathing in short, quick breaths.

"Hey," Mitch says, throwing up his hands, "that's fine. I'm just telling you what *I'd* do, that's all."

Ed wipes his mouth slowly and nods.

"What's your mother like, Mitch?" Burt asks. "We haven't heard much about her."

Mitch grins. "She's okay. She lives by herself in a town house up in Silver Spring." He stops to examine his boot and has another thought. "My mom's in pretty good health, except that she probably drinks a little too much."

Burt smiles back, but Gary and Ed throw each other a troubled look and shake their heads.

"You know, Ed," Gary says in a calm voice, "I know what cancer can be like. Once the diagnosis is made and all the doctors get into the act it can be so incredibly expensive—

and devastating." Gary pauses. "It's like standing in front of this racing freight train about to mow you down."

"Yeah, tell me about it," Ed mumbles.

"Ed, have you spoken with any of your brothers or sisters about this?" I ask.

"Not yet. I suppose that's next."

"It is a family crisis and the whole family should be involved."

"Yeah, I know. I've been avoiding it, to tell you the truth."

"I want you to understand that it's not your sole responsibility, Ed. You have other things to do. Settling in with Ellen and your marriage, for one."

Ed sighs. "There's a lot to do. Oh"—he has another thought and looks at me expectantly—"I think I should announce our wedding agreement."

"That's fine, Ed."

Ed scans the group. "Since I don't have any family members in town for the wedding, Al here"—he glances my way—"is going to come to our wedding." Ed pauses. "I'd invite the rest of you, but you know the rules: no socialization outside of group."

"*That's* a relief," Gary says with a sly grin. "I'd need three new suits to go to all the weddings in *this* group!"

"Any reactions to my going?" I ask.

"I'm glad you have the rule," Mitch says evenly. "It might be hard for us to be together at the wedding."

Ed nods and remains silent for a moment. "How are things with you, Gary?"

"Not great." He shrugs. "I drove straight here from my parents' house, and I'm still edgy. The old man's getting worse, not better, and my mom's being her old charming self."

"Still bitching?" Ed asks.

Gary nods. "That place is depressing. It smells old and damp. My mom wanders around the house mumbling about my dad like he's some rotten sack of potatoes she should

throw out." Gary pauses and looks back at Ed. "You know what? She cornered me in the kitchen Friday night and said *her life had been wasted* caring for my dad. Now ain't that some shit?"

"Have you thought about a nursing home?" Mitch asks.

"We're doing that. In fact, that was *another* argument," Gary shakes his head. "They're going to live in a small cottage in this retirement village, and there are good support services for my dad there. And she tells me she *couldn't decide* if she should spend a lousy ten bucks an hour to have some help taking care of him. *That's* what I'm up against here."

"Was your mom always at home when you were a kid, as a homemaker?" Burt asks.

"Yep. The truth is I always thought taking care of everybody was what she *wanted* to do—I thought it gave her life some meaning."

"Aw, hell, maybe it does," Mitch says with a flick of the hand. "She may just be blowing off steam. It can't be easy. That life."

"Yeah, well *being* there certainly wasn't easy. I wasn't looking forward to it. It was the first time I'd seen my older sister, she's forty-four, in about, what, five years? And she was sipping a drink the whole time. Same old story. A slow, painful suicide."

"Gary, is your dad going to make it?" Mitch asks in a low voice.

"Yeah, his mind's about gone, but he's a fighter. He sits in his chair all day, he can hardly get up, he goes like this," and Gary suddenly bends way over in a crouched position and hunches up his back and tries in one long, slow effort to rise up off the couch. He gets about halfway up, and collapses back with a grunt and a heavy sigh. He looks up. "It's so pathetic, I can't stand to watch him—I just walk over and lift him out of the chair."

The room grows quiet again.

"Gary," I say finally, "it looks like there's some separation between you and your family. I'm glad to see you've been able to do it. You need this distance from the craziness to maintain your own individuality and your sanity. I appreciate that this hasn't been easy for you. Your mother, and Ed's, are like shadows—not really a full mother."

"Yeah, well, you're right, there's not a shred of sanity in that house."

Gary notices that I look at the clock, and he quickly turns to Mitch.

"Are you going to continue with me in another group after these two guys run off and get married?"

"I'm getting married, too, you know."

Gary frowns. "I know, Mitch, who do I look like, Paul? I just want to know if you're going to stick with another group."

"Did I miss something?" Burt says suddenly. "I thought group was ending next week."

"Let me clear this up," I say. "Gary and, possibly, Mitch will have more group therapy in another group."

Burt looks at me and nods.

Mitch picks up with Gary again. "I haven't decided whether I'm going to continue or not."

"Are you concerned about the change that represents, Mitch?" I ask.

Mitch leans back so he can see me as well. "I may just want to continue with individual alone."

"How do you feel about group ending?"

"I'm glad it's ending. We've done a lot of stuff in here. I'm going to miss it, though. I don't know what I'll do with this time, I'll have to go right home. It'll be one less boys' night out."

INTERPRETATION ──────────

Ed's issue with his mother appears quite simple on the surface, as Ed chooses to present his problem to the group as a
straightforward choice: Should he provide financial help to his
mother or not? In reality, this problem has much deeper roots
and is anchored in Ed's difficult and troublesome relationship
with a preoccupied and neglectful mother. Since his alcoholic
parents had a codependent relationship that excluded him for
much of his early life, Ed was left alone to figure out right
from wrong, establish limits, and determine guidelines. Ed
had to do his own parenting. One result of this process is a
strong perfectionistic tendency: Ed still has trouble with
guidelines. Another is his anger at his mother for her exclusive
and destructive relationship with his alcoholic father and her
absence in his life. Ed has a "shadow" mother. He finds himself in the unfortunate position of being without the kind of
strong, supportive mother-son relationship that would make
him want to take care of his mother. He lacks a familial bond.
Like many men, Ed finds himself in a role reversal at this
later stage in his life. Forced to be his own unwilling parent
in childhood, Ed is now expected to assume the same responsibility for his own parents in their advancing age. One
consequence of extended life expectancy in our society is that
men like Ed are finding it necessary to deal once again with
parental conflicts that they avoided, dumped, or abandoned
long ago.

Gary, too, has a shadow mother who provided woefully
inadequate parenting. She focused her love and attention almost entirely on Gary's father, to the exclusion of the children. Once Gary matured into adulthood, the mother engaged
in emotional blackmail ("I'll kill myself") to keep Gary around
to give meaning to her life. Aside from his resentment at this
treatment, Gary has picked up a lot of his mother's negative

behavior, some of which surfaced in tonight's session (complaining, bitterness, feeling like a "victim"). One important lesson Gary has learned well is that he has to stay away from his mother and establish and maintain a certain distance in order to maintain his personal integrity and self-esteem.

Mitch, on the other hand, has a close relationship to his mother and feels a strong urge to protect her. So far in group Mitch has steadfastly refused to say anything even vaguely negative about his alcoholic mother ("She probably drinks a little too much"), because he feels she's the only one who's been continually supportive of him. Mitch is his mother's favorite. As such, Mitch is surprised and disturbed by Ed's confusion about what to do about his mother. This would be a simple and direct choice for Mitch.

Burt contributes the least to this discussion, because among these men his relationship with his mother is the easiest. She is in good health and has been left in a comfortable material position following her husband's death. Although Burt is not close to his mother, she is supportive of him and is relatively easygoing.

Virtually all the men I have worked with over the years in therapy have had difficult, disappointing relationships with their fathers and have struggled to maintain decent relationships with their mothers. One result of this feeling of neglect is that these men—Ed, Burt, and Mitch included—desperately want to be loving, available, involved fathers. These men want to provide their children with the support and nurturance that they missed in their early lives. This bodes well for the future generation: men are needed in the family.

FROM FEAR TO CELEBRATION

"Mitch called to say he'd be late."

Gary frowns and looks up at me from tying his shoe. "Haven't we heard *that* before?"

Burt and Ed exchange a look of confusion and shrug at each other. Gary finishes with his shoe, slides back on the couch, and glances over at Burt.

"The first session, guys. Mitch calls ahead, says he's going to be late. So much for changing in therapy." An impish little grin slowly emerges on Gary's face.

Ed is looking at me and misses the smile.

"I don't know—*I've* gotten something out of the group . . . at least Ellen thinks so. She says I'm a lot easier—more fun—to be around, even at parties." Ed looks to Burt on his left and shrugs. "She says people listen to me. They look up to me. They care what I think."

"Is it true?" Burt asks.

"It's true at work. I've got two major research projects to wrap up before we head out to California, and people are dropping in all day to ask my opinion on their work, to gossip, to just hang out. It's driving me a bit crazy, to tell you the truth."

"You don't *like* the way they're responding to you?"

"Well, some of it. I do feel good there."

"Another group therapy success story," Burt says with a flourish.

"I don't know about that," Ed counters quickly. "I didn't say it *all* came about because I'm in here."

"So Ellen, your coworkers, Burt, me, see the results of your therapy, but you 'can't' decide whether your work here has paid off?" I'm grinning at him. "Give yourself some credit, Ed."

Ed sits with this for a while and then returns my grin.

"Are you going to do group therapy out in California?" Gary asks lazily.

"I don't know yet. I think I get more out of individual." Ed eyes me warily for a moment and then glances back at Gary. "The group's been good. Don't get me wrong. And I'm really going to *miss* you guys." Ed pauses with this thought for a moment, as though it's the first time it's occurred to him. "Anyway, I liked being in here a lot. I've never had anything quite like this before." Ed's voice has trailed off to nothing.

Suddenly the door swings open and Mitch rushes in and grabs a spot next to Gary. He unzips his riding suit down to his waist while seated on the couch.

"Sorry I'm late."

"I don't know, Ed," Gary says looking across Mitch. "It's only been good for me in here in the last few weeks. Since Paul bolted. It's given me a lot more time to talk." He looks around at the men and smiles. "I think I like this size a lot more."

"Yeah"—Ed shrugs—"since Paul and Sean left I can actually get my foot into the conversation once in a while."

"Sean, wow, God . . . that seems like *ages* ago," Gary says, with a shake of the head.

I catch Gary's eye and smile. "You're not giving yourself near enough credit, you know. You started opening up, and challenging Paul, several weeks before he left. It goes way back. Same with you, Ed."

Ed gives me a skeptical look.

"Who jumped all over Paul for scaring Sean half to death?"

"Oh. Yeah, that's true."

"It's come out in other ways, too, Ed. You've been much more willing to stand up for yourself in group and in the world outside. You make people listen to you. *You* listen more to Ellen. The two of you got married. Remember why you came to me?"

"I think so." He grins back at me.

Gary leans forward on the couch to see around Mitch.

"He's right, Ed. I've heard more from you lately than from anyone. The only guy who's clammed up completely about himself is Mitch."

Mitch is completely still.

"I talked last week."

"You asked about our *mothers* last week."

Mitch is right next to Gary on the couch, and at this comment he slides back and away so he can look directly at Gary.

"Are you going to start in on me again?"

For a moment Gary is silent.

"I just don't know where you are, Mitch," he says coolly. "You're just not talking and it seems like you're seething with anger."

Silence.

"What are you feeling right now, Mitch?" I ask.

Mitch gives me an icy look, then peers back at Gary. When he answers, he addresses me.

"I'm trying not to get more upset."

"What is it, Mitch?" I ask.

Mitch still has Gary locked in his gaze. This time he speaks to Gary.

"You're attacking me, and I don't like it."

Gary is silent once again. Eventually, he shrugs.

"You're really too sensitive, Mitch. I'm not *attacking* you, I'm telling you what I *think*. You're just being paranoid."

Mitch tenses for a moment and quickly looks away.

Gary glances over at me expectantly but remains quiet. Burt is sitting motionless except for his right foot, which is tapping up and down nervously.

Silence.

"Mitch," I say softly, "can you try letting us know what's going on inside of you?"

" 'Paranoid' is not one of my favorite words," he mumbles. Mitch is slowly and deliberately rubbing his palms together. "And I'm not 'too sensitive.' "

"What are the feelings?"

"I'm embarrassed by this. I'm not 'too sensitive.' " Mitch looks up at Gary. "What the hell does that *mean*, anyway?"

"You're upset because I called you 'too sensitive'?" Gary asks with surprise.

Mitch is silent.

"Gary," I say, "I think it's more your tone and attitude that sound harsh or attacking—not really your words."

"Oh. Well, shit, I didn't mean to be overbearing. If it seems that way. It's just my style."

"What's your reaction to this, Gary?"

Gary lets out a deep breath. He's still watching Mitch warily.

"I'm a little edgy . . . nervous, too. You know, Mitch, I

never know if one of these times you're going to pop up again and *deliberately* smack me."

"So that's the fear?" I ask.

Gary nods. "I was the one that got run over when Mitch charged out of here."

"Look," Mitch sighs, "I told Paul this once before. I've never hit anybody in my life! I'm just angry right now, I don't understand it, and I'm trying to figure it out!"

"Do you want me to apologize, Mitch?"

"No, it's all right."

"I have trouble believing you on that, Mitch," I say.

Mitch looks over at me and laughs nervously. "I wonder why!"

"There are so many times in life when we wish somebody would apologize or say 'I'm sorry' whether the hurt was intentional or not," I point out.

"Look," Gary says suddenly, "don't worry about it. I won't apologize if you don't want me to. The thing is, Mitch, I don't know any other way of getting to you except by being a little cynical. So if I rile you up, at least you say *something.*"

Mitch shrugs and looks away.

"You know something, Gary?" Ed asks with a frown. "You *do* seem sort of cynical—I got the feeling you've been mad at Mitch the whole time tonight."

"I'm not mad at *Mitch.* I'm mad at myself. *That's* been going on all night. I got a call from my mom on Friday with some bad news. My grandmother, who's ninety-two years old and in a nursing home, has been going downhill fast. My mom said we might only have a couple of days left, so could I make it up on the weekend? I said there was no way. I was going to the beach this weekend, so that's that." Gary pauses to run a slow hand over the back of his neck. "So my sister called first thing Saturday morning before I left and told me my grandmother had died. I said I was just heading out for the beach and she shrieked, 'For the beach!' and it dawned on

me, this awful thing I had done, what the hell's wrong with me? So I called Marta and canceled and went on up for the funeral."

Gary's story just hangs in the air.

"Did you feel guilty at the funeral?" Burt asks finally.

Gary pauses and shakes his head. "Even if I'd left Friday, I wouldn't have made it in time to see her before she died. I'm just glad I came to my senses in time to make the funeral."

Burt nods. "Are you feeling better now?"

"A little. I wasn't that close to my grandmother."

"No, I mean in here."

"What?"

"Both you and Mitch looked upset."

"Burt," I come in quickly, "do you have some feelings about what went on between them?"

"Yeah, I was worried about you two." He glances back and forth between Mitch and Gary. "I don't like having to sit around people who get that steamed up."

"Were you going to charge out of here?" Gary asks.

"Probably not."

"Just give my legs some notice, okay?"

"If it doesn't happen this session, it won't happen at all."

We all sit with this thought for a while.

"What are your plans, Burt?" Gary asks in a concerned tone.

"Oh, JoAnn and I are going to stay in couples therapy. I'm nervous but looking forward to getting married. Things are going well. I'm sorry to see the group end, though." He looks over at me. "I'm really glad I got to be in here."

Gary nods. "I'm not going to California or getting married, so I'm thinking of sticking with it in another group. I just don't want to be in therapy for the rest of my life." He looks over at me. "I'm not sure how long I'm supposed to be in therapy until I'm . . . I don't know, 'finished,' or whatever."

I give Gary a smile. "There is no 'schedule' or set time,

but you already know that. Ordinarily, you stay in as long as you make progress and learn and are happy with that."

"How've I been doing? How about a progress report?"

"Oh, I didn't know you wanted one."

"Yeah. Just a 'report card' and how long I'm going to be at this. Not a date, mind you, just an idea."

Gary is pressing me.

"How do *you* feel you've been progressing?"

Gary rolls his eyes. "You're just answering a question with a question! That's not fair. You're just being a psychologist."

"I'll answer you, Gary, but I want your own view first."

"Why?! Why do I have to answer first?! Why don't *you* answer first?"

"Because I don't want *my* answer to influence *your* answer."

"Bullshit, you're playing games with me. Fine. Drop it."

"Gary, I'm not playing a game. I will answer your question, believe me."

"No. Forget it. I'll get over it. I won't be angry after a while. Go bother Mitch."

"Gary, do you really expect me to pretend to concentrate on Mitch while you're sitting there fuming at me? I'm willing to stick with you. I'm feeling frustrated, too!"

"What are *you* frustrated about?"

"I feel you're asking a question you know I can't really answer, and you're trying to back me into a corner, and right now I feel like I'm in your family!"

"Oh, great psychologist, now you're in the family! So what is this, transference?"

"Yes."

"So is that good?"

"Yes."

"Are you supposed to be my father right now?"

"I don't know *which* parent I am, Gary; both of them were so evasive and frustrating and unavailable to you."

"Well, it must be my goddamned father. The son-of-a-bitch would never answer a question. We'd ask 'why' about things and he'd just say 'because I told you so.' We never knew what was happening next. *God*, he pissed me off!"

I pause for a moment. "I really consider that to be a form of child abuse, too, Gary. Your father had an obligation to answer you, to be there for you, that's how you learn."

Gary stops and looks at me with his powerful, intense eyes and then slowly smiles.

I am smiling, too.

"What are you two smiling about?" Mitch demands.

Gary shrugs. "Just smiling."

"I'm smiling because I feel like a good piece of work just got done," I say. I shift my gaze from Mitch to Gary. "The transference is good, Gary, because it allows you to finish some of the negative feelings you had as a kid . . . you won't need the same level of intensity on such things as not having a question answered." I see Gary is still grinning. "It also means you can establish new relationships, that you are changing."

After a pause, Gary looks to Mitch on his left.

"So did you decide to stick in group with me?"

"I don't want to keep being attacked."

"You mean you're not going to do it, just because of *me?*"

"I'm not blaming anything on you. I just said I don't like you attacking me."

"Well, okay, man, listen, I'm sorry. I didn't mean to upset you like that. And whether you want it or not, I do apologize. Okay?"

"Okay. Thanks. I don't want you to feel bad either. I'll be there. I wouldn't change my mind without notice."

"Look," Ed says, "before we run out of time, I want to ask Al: How did you feel at our wedding?"

Burt, who has been a bit tense through this entire inter-

action between Gary and me, perks up instantly, and looks over at me.

"Oh yeah, how was that?"

"It was wonderful. I'm really glad I could be there."

"It was good to have you there," Ed says. "It felt like I had at least *some* family there for me."

"Was Ellen on his back the whole time?" Gary asks, nudging Ed's foot.

"Gary, Ellen was so warm and pleasant, nothing like I'd seen her when she and Ed were in couples therapy together. We had a nice conversation. She looked radiant and happy."

"Of course she's happy, she got what she wanted!" Gary cracks. The grin returns.

Ed, meanwhile, is puzzled. "I didn't know you had much time to talk to Ellen."

"Oh sure," I say offhandedly. "We figured Dostoyevsky's purpose in writing *Crime and Punishment* and we were right in the middle of analyzing Fellini's *La Dolce Vita* when her father came over to dance with her."

Ed tosses a throw pillow at me.

"What did Ellen look like? Traditional wedding and all?" Mitch asks.

"Well, not formal. But she really looked nice: pink chiffon dress, white bouquet, and her hair up in a way I'd never seen it before. Very pretty."

"Did she look good enough for you, Ed?" Gary asks.

"Yes. She really looked good."

"Ed, you looked good, too. You never took your eyes off her as she walked toward you. I was touched during the ceremony."

"Thanks. It means a lot to me." Ed looks pleased.

"Did you two have your honeymoon already?" Burt asks.

"Yeah, we headed out to Virginia Beach for a sort of 'mini-honeymoon'. We'll have the real one when we get out to California. We had a real nice time, except"—Ed looks over

at me and shakes his head—"except for this guy who keeps popping up *everywhere* he's not supposed to be!"

"What are you talking about?" Gary asks with a puzzled look. Ed's got everyone's full attention now.

"Well, Ellen and I just finish this candlelight dinner, and she goes into the bathroom, and I turn on the TV, and who is on the *Dr. Ruth Show*—in the middle of my honeymoon, mind you—but everyone's favorite therapist!" Ed is glowering at me in mock anger.

"What?"

"Yeah, he was taped for some showing of the *Dr. Ruth Show* on cable. So Ellen comes out of the bathroom in this negligee and climbs into bed, and of course I'm still sitting at the foot of the bed listening to this interview. So I turn to Ellen and say, 'Look, Al's on TV!' and she says, 'Come on, turn it off and come over here.' I keep watching. She's going on and on about how we've only got one night at the hotel, but when Dr. Ruth says the words 'penis size' she suddenly clams up and gets real interested." Ed is grinning from ear to ear. "Not a thing happened until the interview was over."

"And then . . . ?" Gary says, leaning forward.

"After two months of celibacy, we both remembered how—it was the best we ever had."

Mitch looks across the table at me. "I don't believe it. You would be on *Dr. Ruth?*"

"Yes. It was educational, and I have a much better opinion of her now than I had."

"But did it really happen on Ed's honeymoon?"

"It's a fact," Ed assures him.

"Well, we do have to end," I say. "Wouldn't want to keep JoAnn waiting for Burt."

At first nobody moves.

"I want you all to know," I say, "that this group has also been a great experience for me. There were some very exciting and moving moments with you."

Silence.

I look across the table at Ed.

"Ed, good luck in your new life. I'd be delighted to hear from you. I'll see the rest of you again. Now we're going to stop."

Ed stands up slowly and walks over to me and gives me a hug. This breaks the ice—Gary turns to Mitch and puts his arm around him and slaps his knee. Mitch stiffens.

"I think we'll get along in group."

"I wonder."

"Hey—they'll all be the 'new kids on the block.' We'll be the 'old-timers.' "

Burt is smiling and stretching, waiting to give Ed a hug.

I move away to watch them.

. . . grinning . . . hugging . . . kidding . . . good wishes.

I'm touched by their warmth toward each other. They've come such a long way in this short time. Good men.

INTERPRETATION ———————————

The tremendous progress Ed has made in therapy is difficult to measure in any quantitative way, and Ed therefore has doubts that the changes can be attributed to therapy. The evidence for his development, his ability to deal with change with less anxiety and fear of making a "wrong" decision, is irrefutable. Not only has Ed made a marriage commitment to Ellen, he's started moving up in his career, accepted a promotion, decided to move across the country, and signed a contract on a house, all without his characteristic anxiety or perfectionistic procrastination. Ed is only resisting change in the area of entering group therapy in California. This is a typical response for men who have connected with a therapist

as well as Ed has with me. Our group is a symbolic "family" for Ed, so he is wary of establishing and losing yet another group (family) in California.

Burt has the least amount of regret over the end of group. He is the most comfortable with this process; it is very natural and easy for him. Like Ed, Burt has a new marriage and a new life ahead, so the ending of group is a natural transition point. Moreover, Burt is content with his life and is happy with the changes he's made and those he's observing in JoAnn. As Burt's relationship with JoAnn settled down over the last several weeks, Burt's career took off: He's had a number of new and exciting professional challenges that have kept him on Capitol Hill. His recent attendance in group has truly required an extra effort on his part. Both Burt and JoAnn are happy to be in couples therapy with me and are making good progress.

The confrontation between Mitch and Gary and their resolution at the end of the session are representative of their development and their bonding in group. A year ago, Gary would never have apologized for the way he phrased a comment, nor would he have been concerned over how such a comment affected someone else. Gary's desire is to maintain a connection to Mitch, and humor, ribbing, and jabbing are all Gary's usual way. Tonight he examines that usual way and realizes that it could be rejecting and hurtful: Gary honors Mitch's response. In fact, it is so important that he offers to apologize twice to accommodate Mitch, and finally *does* to satisfy them both. So Gary has demonstrated his willingness to change in order to safeguard special relationships, such as the one with Mitch.

Mitch is aware of having been the target of Gary's jabs for several weeks ("Are you going to start in on me again?") but has been holding his anger in, letting it build. This is old behavior for Mitch. Gary's forced confrontation gives Mitch a chance to go beyond his anxiety and express his anger. Mitch

then realizes that confronting Gary openly weeks ago before the anger had a chance to grow and develop would have meant less anger inside him. Mitch almost lost his opportunity to continue in group because of anger, but he knows the release of anger, when he ran out of the room, was positive and therapeutic. The realization of his overreaction made it possible for him to return. Gary's apology is a compliment to Mitch, but Mitch dismisses it, since he has always had difficulty with praise and compliments. Mitch must let these affirmations in; they will enhance his ego and self-esteem.

The response to Mitch's changes is very similar to the reactions Ed reported in tonight's session. Lynda, his friends, and his coworkers have all commented on how much more open, confident, and expressive he is. In less than a year, Mitch has gone from doubt to certainty and is left with the normal pre-wedding jitters. He's also making some career changes that will give him more independence and real financial rewards.

My confrontation with Gary tonight is intense. Once again Gary is testing me to reassure himself that I won't abandon him. He wants to make sure he is not continuing in therapy with somebody like his father. This is the purpose of my assurance that I am not abandoning him as his father did. In this intense interchange I feel like I've actually been drawn into his family. I sense the "craziness" that Gary had to deal with anytime he needed or wanted anything. This explains his frustration and rage at his father for not caring about him and for rejecting him. Though Gary thinks I'm playing a psychological game, I am in fact being therapeutic to determine what is motivating the question. As Gary and I get into the struggle, Gary sees me solely in the role of his father, and it is impossible for him to be reasonable with me at that moment. He wants to dismiss me ("Go bother Mitch") in the same way he would like to have dismissed his father, who *would not have hung in* with him anymore. Unlike his father,

I stay with Gary. It does not bother me to stay with Gary through his anger. My refusal to shift attention from Gary as his anger grows is the pivotal point in the exchange. At this juncture, Gary starts hearing *me* and realizes that he *is* treating me like his father and not like Al Baraff. His smile is the result of tremendous relief over this resolution and the insight he gains from this exchange.

Ed initiates the hugging at the end of group, and the men follow through with a warmth and sincerity that is not typical of men and would have been *impossible* for them just a few months ago. The men feel comfortable expressing themselves more warmly than with the traditional male handshake.

Goodbyes are difficult for all men. Ordinarily men want to leave, to say goodbye, as quickly as possible and be done with it. In his previous relationship, Ed just vanished when the woman said she wanted to break it off. Ed never saw the woman again and never knew why she left. Burt stuck with a bad marriage far too long, avoiding the painful and inevitable goodbye. The catalytic event in Mitch's former marriage caused an immediate and complete break: a quick divorce and no goodbye. Gary's difficulty with goodbye was the most severe: He was convinced of being "addicted" to a woman; he believed he was *incapable* of saying goodbye. All the warm goodbyes observed tonight suggest that these men will enjoy much fuller, more meaningful relationships in their lives.

//

EPILOGUE: MEN
AFTER THERAPY

In the two years since the group ended, the lives of these men evolved in many new directions. Some of the immediate benefits of group therapy are evident to the men as they work during the sessions, while others take a much longer period to emerge. In reviewing these men's lives two years later, we see some of the positive, long-term changes in attitude, communication, self-esteem, and confidence that can be traced directly to work initially done in the group.

MITCH

Mitch and Lynda were married at the end of the summer in a small, quiet, yet formal church ceremony. Mitch continued in the new men's group for three months and offered encouraging support for some of that group's timid members. Mitch

and Gary began to work well together, although they continued to clash over some issues of insensitivity and fear of change as Gary pushed Mitch to open up further. Mitch stopped racing motorcycles soon after the birth of their son, Mark David, one year later, and took charge of the social planning obligations for the family. Mitch and Lynda worked together remodeling the upstairs of their home to create Mark's room. During this period Mitch grew away from his mother's dominating influence and found himself concentrating more on his own new family and his role as husband and father. Mitch has returned sporadically for individual therapy sessions as specific problems occur.

PAUL

Paul, whose divorce from Sarah became final less than a year after he left group, is still single and lives alone in northwest Washington. He dates occasionally. Although he dropped out of group, Paul made progress by continuing in individual and facing some of the conflicts of the divorce. Eventually, Paul succeeded in placing limits on Sarah's demands during the divorce settlement. Over time, Paul learned to reject his domineering mother's attempts to control him through guilt. At the same time, he began to recognize and resist Sarah's attempts to do the same thing. Soon afterward, Sarah got a job and struck out on her own, with the emotional support of her parents. It was a difficult time for her. Paul himself reestablished a strong, supportive tie to his children, especially Betty, who asked to spend the summer with him. Paul and Abe worked together on Abe's college choices. While Paul learned a great deal from therapy about not being controlled by guilt and even to give up some control himself, he still had an issue with anger. Following a life pattern of withdrawing when faced with someone's anger, much as he did in leaving group itself,

Paul eventually left individual therapy prematurely rather than work through issues dealing with anger.

ED

Ed and Ellen moved to California the week after group ended. I lost contact with Ed after he and Ellen left the Washington area. I regret that I'm not able to report on their life or progress, but contact with former patients is more the exception than the rule.

BURT

Burt and JoAnn got married two months after the end of group in her parents' church in Denver. They returned to Washington and made a home of the small rambler they had been redecorating the past year. JoAnn soon received her M.A., and was pregnant two months later. She chose to postpone a career prior to the birth of the baby, Jamie Lee, named in honor of Burt's father, James. JoAnn had a very difficult adjustment period after the birth, and Burt was able to come in as the engaged, involved father by taking time off from a very demanding work schedule to be available for feeding, bathing, and private time with the baby. In fact, Burt was the one who got up in the morning so he could be with Jamie. During this period, Burt also became more confident and assertive in his career, one benefit of which was a special one-year posting to Japan for the whole family.

SEAN

Sean completed medical school and has started a residency in pediatrics at Arizona State University in Tempe. The relationship with Sandi never got going again, and he eventually lost contact with her. Some time later he found out from a

college friend that she was involved with somebody else. Eventually, Sean was able to get over the breakup. During a vacation break visiting his parents in Phoenix, he met Debbie, a junior at Arizona State who is the daughter of family friends. Sean's family did pull together, but Sean was forced to take out student loans to get through medical school. The father's extensive personal problems left Sean feeling angry at his father and guilty over feeling this anger. Eventually, this experience had a leveling effect on Sean. He matured rapidly during a fairly brief period of individual therapy.

GARY

Gary continued therapy in the new men's group and immediately took command. Even though the other men were older and more experienced in life, they came to look to Gary for leadership and guidance in group. He was the "pro." During this period his business grew and he finally decided to move his business outside the home. He also purchased a new condo near the State Department. His new office is just two blocks away. His relationship with Marta continued for a few months, but she eventually decided to return home. This separation was different for Gary: the old feelings of abandonment and addiction were less severe and much more manageable. He's now involved with a divorcée who has a six-year-old son. While Gary did get his "Rent-a-Kid," the son's problems became an issue for him. Fortunately, he was able to resolve this in some short-term individual therapy, since his involvement with the new group had ended.

IN CLOSING . . .

The progress and growth we've witnessed in these men during therapy and in their subsequent lives highlight the profound

value of therapy as a learning process and emotional education.

A commonly held belief is that therapy is first and foremost an intellectual process focusing on childhood, with no practical connection to the real world or everyday life. Nothing could be further from the truth. In fact, regardless of the orientation or approach of the therapist, therapy is a powerful, lively learning experience. The learning is immediately applicable in day-to-day living once the patient is willing to try it. It is "fast-forward" learning. As such, it's intense, with many exciting moments and surprises—not all pain and melodrama. Moreover, what is learned is not some abstract concept like algebra or external discipline like German, but rather specific and internal: it is about you. The focus on childhood, adolescence, and dreams is to learn how they connect to present-day behavior. Cause and effect is the key to seeing that it all makes sense. Once this occurs, it is very liberating.

Here's how I see my role: I guide the patient through the process, in essence serving as the teacher or mentor. I feel fortunate to have had so many highly motivated students. We became partners in the journey. We've been on some great trips.